eating right never tasted so good!

As a *Taste of Home Healthy Cooking* subscriber, you'll look forward to:

- 75+ delicious, good-for-you recipes
- Healthy makeovers of all your favorites
- Nutrition facts & diabetic exchanges
- At-a-glance icons: low-fat, low-sodium, low-carb, meatless
- Expert, live-well advice
- Full-color photos
- Instant on-line access to premium subscriber-only content and over 33,000 recipes at tasteofhome.com!

FROM: _____

_____

_____

PLACE
STAMP
HERE

healthy taste of home
cooking

SUBSCRIPTION FULFILLMENT CENTER
PO BOX 5509
HARLAN IA 51593-1009

|.l|..||l.l.l....||....||||..|l..l.l..l.l.l..l.l.l|

taste of home
comfort
FOOD *diet*
COOKBOOK

CHICKEN MARSALA, PAGE 160

taste of home comfort FOOD diet
COOKBOOK

You have in your hands a friendly, easy-to-follow guide that can help you transform the way you eat...not for the short-term, but for life. You can achieve the health and weight-loss goals you want without giving up all of the delicious foods you love.

291   237

A TASTE OF HOME/READER'S DIGEST BOOK

Senior Vice President, Editor in Chief
CATHERINE CASSIDY

Vice President, Executive Editor/Books
HEIDI REUTER LLOYD

Creative Director
ARDYTH COPE

Food Director
DIANE WERNER RD

Senior Editors
MARK HAGEN, FAITHANN STONER

Editors
PEGGY WOODWARD RD, JULIE BLUME BENEDICT

Art Directors
RUDY KROCHALK, JESSIE SHARON

Content Production Supervisor
JULIE WAGNER

Layout Designer
KATHY CRAWFORD

Proofreaders
AMY GLANDER, LINNE BRUSKEWITZ

Recipe Asset Management System
COLEEN MARTIN, SUE A. JURACK

Premedia Superviros
SCOTT BERGER

Recipe Testing & Editing
TASTE OF HOME TEST KITCHEN

Food Photography
TASTE OF HOME PHOTO STUDIO

Editorial Assistant
BARB CZYSZ

Editorial Intern
DANIELLE CALKINS

Chief Marketing Officer
LISA KARPINSKI

Vice President, Book Marketing
DAN FINK

THE READER'S DIGEST ASSOCIATION, INC.

President and Chief Executive Officer
MARY G. BERNER

President, Food & Entertaining
SUZANNE M. GRIMES

SVP, Chief Marketing Officer
AMY J. RADIN

President, Global Consumer Marketing
DAWN ZIER

President/Publisher Trade Publishing
HAROLD CLARKE

Associate Publisher
ROSANNE MCMANUS

Vice President, Sales & Marketing
STACEY ASHTON

Cover Photography
PHOTOGRAPHER, JIM WIELAND
FOOD STYLIST, SARAH THOMPSON
SET STYLIST, MELISSA HABERMAN

Pictured on Front Cover: **TURKEY FETTUCCINE SKILLET, P. 232**

Material for "Walk Off Weight" (p. 36) excerpted from 30-Minutes
to a Healthy Heart, © 2005 by Reader's Digest Association, Inc.

table of contents

the comfort food diet

Cheesy casseroles, hearty stews and decadent desserts. These are only a few of the items people think they must forgo when trying to lose weight. After all, beefy entrees, creamy soups and chocolate fudge aren't usually considered the anchors of a low-calorie recipe box...until now.

*The **Comfort Food Diet Cookbook** is changing the way people eat and prepare their family's favorites, but most important, it's changing lives from coast to coast.*

As a Registered Dietitian, I've found that most of us resolve at one time or another to cut back on calories. Unfortunately, many of us fall victim to fad diets that don't live up to our expectations, or we buy expensive frozen meals that don't satisfy.

That's why I love the Taste of Home Comfort Food Diet. Unlike other diets, this plan takes a commonsense approach to eating, cooking and living. The plan focuses on simple, economical and family-friendly food options that include light ingredients.

With this cookbook, you'll savor 433 of the classic foods you enjoy most and still lose weight! It's easy—just follow the three basics of the Comfort Food Diet (p. 8) and take advantage of the sensational recipes this book offers. Best of all, an incredible Six-Week Meal Plan (p. 46) jumpstarts your efforts.

Take a look inside the *Comfort Food Diet Cookbook*, and you'll discover that a little planning, the right recipes and reasonable portion sizes will add up to surefire weight-loss success.

Diane Werner

—Diane Werner, RD
   Food Director, Taste of Home

lose weight &
EAT GREAT!

A plan from the people who know comfort food best.

At last! An approach to weight-loss that's simple, affordable and delicious! The focus of the *Taste of Home Comfort Food Diet Cookbook* is commonsense: Enjoy three meals a day plus two snacks for a total of 1,400 calories. It's truly that easy!

All of the luscious dishes in the *Comfort Food Diet Cookbook* are ideal for today's family cook...because each recipe comes from *Taste of Home*, the No. 1 cooking magazine in the world, and its popular sister publications. In addition, the recipes call for everyday ingredients, so there's no need to run to specialty stores or purchase expensive items. Each dish was also reviewed by a Registered Dietitian and tested by a home economist at the Taste of Home Test Kitchen. You'll also find Nutrition Facts with all of the recipes and Diabetic Exchanges where applicable.

Take a look inside and you'll see that we've included all the support you need to lose weight:

- *433 recipes for your all-time favorite dishes—each guaranteed to punch up the flavor you expect while paring down calories.*

- *A meal plan that suggests recipes for meals and snacks every day for six full weeks.*

- *A list of more than 80 FREE FOODS that you can enjoy without guilt.*

Now, making the commitment to eat right is easier than ever. With the *Comfort Food Diet Cookbook*, losing weight never tasted so good!

Peggy Woodward

—Peggy Woodward, RD
Food Editor, Taste of Home

more on the WEB

To make your journey as easy as possible, we also launched the *Comfort Food Diet Cookbook* Website. Available only to those who purchase this book, the site offers free recipes, a body mass index (BMI) calculator and dozens of other healthy-living resources. Simply visit www.ComfortFoodDietCookbook.com, and use MyDiet as your exclusive access code.

eat healthy, lose weight and still enjoy the foods you love!

Unlike other plans that have you eating no carbs or only grapefruit, the Comfort Food Diet is a sensible way to live and eat. It is an easy, family-friendly and economical strategy that requires only a minor shift in the way you shop for, prepare, serve and consume your meals.

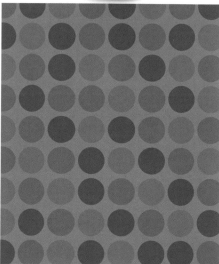

The ideas here are not new: Watch your calories and portions, then burn more calories than you take in...but it's the approach of the *Comfort Food Diet Cookbook* that could be the weight-loss breakthrough you've been looking for. It worked for many *Taste of Home* readers. In fact, we've sprinkled their success stories throughout this book to motivate and inspire you to be the best you can be.

COMFORT FOOD DIET BASICS—
it's really easy!

Do the words "comfort food" and "diet" really go together? Yes! With a little planning, the right recipes and reasonable portions you can drop pounds and still work in some comfort foods over the course of the day so you never feel deprived. Here's how:

1 Eat three meals a day and two snacks that total 1,400 calories.

Most people will achieve safe and reasonable weight loss at 1,400 calories a day for women and 1,500 calories a day for men. So that's what is mapped out for you in the Six-Week Meal Plan on pages 46-67. Check with your doctor before starting this plan to be sure it's right for you and to determine if your caloric needs are different than those suggested here.

Use the following guide to distribute your calories:

- 350 calories for breakfast

- 450 calories for lunch

- 500 calories for dinner

- Two 50-calorie or two 100-calorie snacks, depending on the total calories you're shooting for per day. You can consume more or less calories in a snack or meal than what is suggested here, as long as your daily total is 1,400 or 1,500 calories.

2 Keep track of everything you eat on the Do-It-Yourself Meal-Planning Worksheets (pages 292-295).

Take a look through all the luscious, satisfying recipes included in this book and decide which ones you want to prepare. Plan out all the things you're going to eat for a whole day in advance. Then record what you actually eat.

For each recipe you choose, pay close attention to what measurement is considered a portion.

For example: You can have 450 calories for lunch, so you decide to make a batch of Bean and Pasta Soup (page 126). In this recipe, one 1-1/2 cup serving has 218 calories. So you can savor a serving of this delicious soup for 218 calories and add on a green salad, roll, a banana and beverage and still come in under 450 calories.

Not only do the Meal-Planning Worksheets help you strategize your day, but they also act as a food journal or diary.

A key to the Comfort Food Diet is keeping a food diary of everything you consume in a day. Be honest with your entries because these lists have many benefits. (See Kristen Johnson's success story on page 42 to discover how a food diary helped her lose more than 40 pounds!)

You're less likely to cheat if you know you have to write down that chocolate bar that's tempting you in the afternoon or the extra serving that's calling your name at dinner.

A food diary can also identify eating habits you may not be aware of, and it helps uncover any roadblocks you may face when it comes to preparing and eating healthy foods.

3 Refer to the Free Foods Chart (p. 45), the Smart Snacks List (p. 71) and the calorie lists before each chapter to help you deterimine how many calories are in the foods you want to pair with your main courses.

Free Foods are so low in calories that you can enjoy them without an ounce of guilt. Add them to your meal plans, use them for snacks and pair them with entrees...just be sure to write them down in your food diary or your Meal Planning Worksheet. Similarly, the list of Smart Snacks offers easy ideas to curb hunger while keeping your goals on track. Be sure to record any of these foods in your food diary as well.

The recipe chapters in this book are Snacks, Breakfasts, Lunches, Dinners, Side Dishes and Desserts. Each chapter arranges the recipes in calorie groupings from lower-calorie staples to higher-calorie favorites.

If you've gone over your calorie budgets for breakfast and lunch, for example, and you need to pick a lower-calorie dinner, go right to the first section of the Dinners chapter for lots of tasty lower-calorie ideas.

You might also use the chapter grouping to locate a higher-calorie lunch that would make a wonderful dinner, or to find a low-calorie side dish that's perfect for a snack.

an easy-to-live-with approach

The Comfort Food Diet pairs a no-nonsense approach to smarter eating with plenty of tools to help jumpstart your efforts to live healthier.

You'll find more than 420 recipes, each with complete Nutrition Facts, to help you lighten up meals for yourself and your family. Best of all, the dishes in the *Comfort Food Diet Cookbook* won't ever lead anyone to suspect that they're actually eating healthy, low-calorie food.

The recipes were shared by readers of *Taste of Home* and its sister magazines. These dishes offer the same great home-style flavor our magazines are known for. All the comforting flavor and satisfaction is there…these recipes have just been lightened up a little or use full-fat ingredients sensibly.

Whether you prefer pasta or beef dishes, soups or stir-fries, oven-roasted meals or slow-cooked entrees—you'll find plenty to choose from here.

Company's coming? Now you have recipes to entertain your guests tastefully and still serve foods that help you reach your goals. Need a solution for a scrumptious dessert that won't make you feel guilty later? You'll find that here as well.

You'll also discover strategies to help balance your diet and lighten up your own favorite comfort foods.

There are suggestions on working exercise into your life, consuming more liquids and choosing the best menu items when dining out, in addition to dozens of tips that will educate and inspire you on this remarkable new path.

Here are some tips to keep you motivated when your weight loss is starting to show:

- Give away clothes that are too big. You'll feel better knowing you don't have your oversized items to go back to. And you'll look forward to the day you can buy clothes in the size you really want to be.

- When people start to notice you've lost weight and tell you how great you look, take note of what you're wearing. Those outfits that make you feel skinny are priceless. Wear them more often than your other clothes. They'll help keep you eating well and losing weight!

- Increase your activity level. Now that you've tasted success, push it along by adding an extra walk, exercise class or bike ride once or twice a week. You'll feel better physically, too!

GET STARTED RIGHT AWAY!

You have everything you need to make the ultimate change. Get ready to be amazed by the new you!

BALANCING
your diet

A healthy diet is so much more than calories in versus calories out. You must have balance and variety in order to meet all of your nutritional needs.

FRUITS & VEGETABLES

Fruits and vegetables are an important part of any healthy diet. They are a major source of vitamins and minerals, contribute to daily fiber intake and supply valuable antioxidants and phytonutrients that researchers suggest can help prevent disease. Eating various colored fruits and vegetables will ensure that you are getting a variety of nutrients each day. They are also low in calories, which means a lot of nutritional bang for your caloric buck.

FAT

Generally speaking, healthy adults should limit fat to about 30% of their calories each day. This means at 1,400 or 1,500 calories a day, you should be eating no more than about 50 grams of fat per day. Stick with healthier monounsaturated and polyunsaturated fats like fats found in olive and canola oils, nuts and seeds.

SATURATED FAT

Saturated fat is found mainly in high-fat meats and dairy foods as well as coconut oil, palm kernel oil and some processed foods. Limit saturated fat to 10% of calories or less, which means about 17 grams when following 1,400 or 1,500 calories a day.

TRANS FAT

As it the case with saturated fat, diets high in trans fat can increase LDL ("bad") cholesterol, which increases the risk of coronary artery disease. Trans fat may also decrease HDL (good) cholesterol. Trans fat can be found in vegetable shortening, stick margarine, fried foods, processed foods and store-bought baked goods. Limit trans fat as much as possible and try to stay below 1.5-2.0 grams per day.

CHOLESTEROL

Eating foods high in cholesterol can increase blood cholesterol for some people, which is why it's recommended to limit daily intake to 300 mg even though saturated and trans fats have a more significant effect on blood cholesterol. Cholesterol is found only in foods from animals, such as eggs, meat and dairy products.

SODIUM

High blood pressure is a major risk factor for heart disease, and salt can be a contributor to high blood pressure. High-sodium diets do not cause high blood pressure in everyone, but it is still wise to limit sodium to 2,300 mg per day. One teaspoon of salt contains about 2,300 mg of sodium, but keep in mind that most of the salt we consume comes from processed foods, not the salt shaker. Foods high in sodium include lunch meat, condiments like soy sauce and ketchup, frozen dinners, canned foods, boxed mixes, seasoning packets and foods labeled as "smoked," "cured," "pickled" or "brined."

Simple Substitutions to the Salt Shaker

- Many of us are conditioned to grab for the salt shaker even before tasting our food. Try to get out of this habit. Taste your food first. Savor it. Enjoy several bites without adding extra salt. With time, you likely won't reach for the salt shaker at all.

- Experiment with your recipes by replacing the salt called for with herbs or sodium-free seasoning blends. Try seasoning veggies with a splash of lemon juice.

FIBER

Healthy adults should be eating at least 20-30 grams of fiber each day, although most Americans eat far less than that. Fiber can be categorized as soluble or insoluble fiber. Soluble fiber can help lower cholesterol while insoluble fiber helps maintain a healthy digestive tract. In addition, fiber helps you feel full, which can help prevent overeating. Foods high in soluble fiber include oatmeal, beans and barley, while foods with insoluble fiber include whole wheat and brown rice.

TIPS TO HELP BOOST FIBER

- Leave the skins on fruits and vegetables.

- Add extra veggies into soups and side dishes.

- Sprinkle oat bran or wheat germ over yogurt or stir into casseroles.

- Choose whole grain breads and crackers. Whole wheat or whole grain flour should be listed as the first ingredient on the food label.

- Toss kidney beans or garbanzo beans into salads.

CARBOHYDRATES

Carbohydrates have received a lot of bad press over the years. While it's important to watch the amount of carbohydrates you consume, carbs are an important part of a healthy diet because they fire up and fuel the body's engine.

There are two types of carbohydrates: sugar and starch. Sugars include fructose and lactose. Starches are grains, pasta and potatoes. The body converts all sugars and starches to glucose—a source of energy. Diabetics need to watch how many carbs they consume, however, because their bodies regulate glucose in the bloodstream differently than most.

Choosing whole grains plus eating a variety of fruits and vegetables and reduced-fat dairy products are positive carbohydrate choices…and those choices matter for overall health. The carbs found in packaged cakes, pies and cookies are highly processed and don't contribute to a healthy diet. Cutting them out of your meal plan means eliminating empty calories, which makes sense if you are watching your weight. For instance, 4-1/2 teaspoons of sugar may have about the same calories and carbohydrates as a medium apple, but the medium apple is a far healthier choice.

PROTEIN

Proteins bring oxygen to blood, produce antibodies and help muscles contract. About half of the protein we consume creates enzymes, which help cells carry out necessary chemical reactions. The body needs a constant supply of protein to repair and rebuild cells that are worn or damaged. In general, women should consume 45 grams of protein per day, and men should consume around 55 grams each day.

PORTION SIZE chart

Here are some visual cues for estimating proper portion size.

- **3 oz beef, chicken or fish,** deck of cards

- **1 serving cold cereal,** baseball

- **1 medium potato,** tennis ball

- **3 oz deli meat,** 3 CDs

- **1 serving cheese,** domino

- **1/4 cup grated cheese,** golf ball

- **1 teaspoon butter or jam,** tip of your thumb

- **1 tablespoon peanut butter,** your thumb

- **1 average bagel,** hockey puck

- **1 serving pasta or rice,** cupcake wrapper

a true weight-loss SUCCESS!

I lost 117 pounds and kept it off 5 years!

By Margie Haen

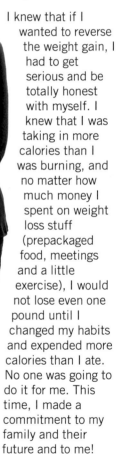
before

after

Like many women, my weight gain came at a time in my life when I was a busy wife and mother who took care of everyone else but had little energy left for me. Once I got serious about my own health and happiness, I lost 117 pounds in 24 months. And, I'm proud to say I've kept it off for five years! How did I do it? The key was watching portion size and exercising.

I'm 5'6", and I weighed 125 pounds when I got married. Within a year, I had gained 10 pounds and was expecting a baby. Since my husband, Curt, traveled a lot, I was home either alone or with a newborn and wasn't interested in cooking for myself, so I ate a lot of junk food. I never lost my "baby fat" and was soon pregnant with my second child.

Now not only was Curt still on the road, but I was also feeding two toddlers. I tried to make sure they had balanced meals, but instead of throwing out their leftovers I just ate them. After I got the babies in bed, I would make myself a huge bowl of popcorn with lots of butter or a large bowl of ice cream with as many toppings as I had on hand. Even though I was running after two kids, I wasn't losing weight—I was gaining it.

When I got pregnant for the third time, I was 198 pounds. After my third child was born, I kept packing on the pounds. I tried all the diets out there. I'd get frustrated because I knew what was needed for real permanent weight loss: a balanced diet, portion control and exercise.

Then one day, as I began to look around, I started to notice how many people my age or just a little older were overweight and battling health problems. At age 47 and 268 pounds, the light finally went on!

I knew that if I wanted to reverse the weight gain, I had to get serious and be totally honest with myself. I knew that I was taking in more calories than I was burning, and no matter how much money I spent on weight loss stuff (prepackaged food, meetings and a little exercise), I would not lose even one pound until I changed my habits and expended more calories than I ate. No one was going to do it for me. This time, I made a commitment to my family and their future and to me!

I started to carefully watch the portions of food I ate, and I began walking.

I woke up at 5:30 every morning and walked for an hour. In the evening I came home from work, got dinner in the oven and walked another hour. I made it part of my daily routine. I figured I brushed my teeth twice a day—I should walk twice a day, too.

When it came to eating, I really didn't cut out anything. I just got smart! One of the hardest things I had to learn, and still have to remember, is to eat until I'm content—not until I'm stuffed. I can still enjoy comfort food in moderation and with the right recipes.

I also wrote down everything I ate. I hated thinking so much about food, but I knew that to succeed, I had to hold myself accountable every day.

Once I lost 35 pounds, I started working out at the YMCA three times a week. I was once too intimidated to use a treadmill, but I soon found that the gym was for people who looked like me, and not necessarily for fitness fanatics.

When I started this journey, I was a size 22. I am now a size 10 and 151 pounds. It took me about 2 years to reach my goal. I've learned that a healthy lifestyle is a choice, and I'm very happy to live my life with that choice in mind. I made a lifestyle change, and I'll never go back to my old ways again.

TRICKS FOR EATING BETTER

- I try to eat slowly and put my fork down after every bite.

- My dinner plates have flowers around the rim, so I make sure the food I put on my plate never touches the flowers. And I never let one food on the plate touch the other foods. Not only is this how I keep an eye on portion sizes, but I found that this is a good way to rein in what I eat at holiday dinners.

- When I'm eating alone, I cut my food into bite-size pieces. Take a bite, then leave the kitchen to go do something, like pull laundry out of the dryer. I come back, take a bite, and then go do something else. It can sometimes take me 30 minutes to eat my breakfast. Since I'm the type of person that isn't normally hungry until 9:30 or 10:00 a.m., I had to figure out something that works for me. Chipping away at a few breakfast foods seems to do the trick. I know that eating a good meal in the morning is very important.

MARGIE'S DAILY ROUTINE

5:15 a.m. Wake up.

5:30 a.m. Out the door walking while eating half of a small banana.

6:30 a.m. Home from the walk, eat the other half of the banana and have a cup of coffee. When I'm getting ready for work, I have either a piece of whole-grain toast with jelly, a half bagel with a little butter on it or a piece of pita bread toasted with jelly. I cut these into bite-size pieces and take a bite, dry my hair, come back into the kitchen, have another bite, put my make up on, take another bite, make my bed, etc. (I live in a ranch house—just imagine the calories I'd burn if I lived in a two-story and I had to climb the steps all those times!)

9:30 a.m. I have a scrambled egg with a sprinkle of cheese, a container of light yogurt or a half-bowl of oatmeal at my desk.

12:00 p.m. For lunch I usually bring leftovers from the previous night. A typical lunch would be 3 ounces of chicken breast or a single serving of tuna, a cup of veggies and a half-cup of cottage cheese. If I go out for lunch, I order a serving of broth-based soup.

3:00 p.m. I nibble an afternoon snack of an apple, raw vegetables, a snack bag with 11 pretzels or a piece of string cheese.

6:00 p.m. (During my weight loss, this is when I'd head out for my evening walk.) For dinner, I eat what my family eats, but watch my portions. I start with the vegetables so I leave less room for the heavier items. I eat brats or burgers without the bun and usually only half or three-quarters of it. Once I'm content, I'm quick to scrape my plate so I'm not tempted to eat more.

9 p.m. Evening snack is a Dixie-size ice cream cup, pudding or Jell-O (I like those store-bought pre-measured cups). If I have popcorn, it's the small individual-size bag.

WATER...
it's simply the best

Looking for a refreshing, no-calorie thirst quencher?

CONSIDER WATER

Water helps you feel full and puts snack attacks on hold. That's why drinking water greatly improves your success on the Comfort Food Diet.

Cell and organ functions require water to keep the body running smoothly. Water prevents the body from overheating, lubricates joints and helps maintain muscle tone...all of which are key with an increase in exercise.

Water also keeps the eyes, nose and throat moist. It helps transport food, vitamins and minerals through the body, aids digestion and helps flush the system of toxic substances.

Some researchers even claim chronic dehydration is linked to heartburn, fatigue, joint and back pain, headaches and other common illnesses, so drinking enough water every day may help prevent those problems—and others.

How much does an individual need? For years the recommendation was eight 8-ounce glasses of water for a daily total of 64 ounces. Today, however, experts disagree on that amount, believing that the body may need more or less, depending on a person's weight, activity level and climate.

However, the liquid we need to replenish our bodies doesn't come from just plain water. Also count liquid from foods such as fruits and vegetables, soups and other beverages. Conventional wisdom says caffeinated beverages that have a diuretic effect shouldn't be tallied in a person's water needs. However, some experts believe there is little to no difference in the hydration levels of people who drink pure water and those who sip beverages with caffeine.

When looking for a no-fuss beverage, water is a no-brainer; but there are plenty of other options. Just consider the following:

LOW-FAT MILK: A glass of low-fat or fat-free milk provides 10 percent or more of the recommended daily intake of protein, potassium and vitamins A and B12. But milk's most notable benefit is the calcium it offers—plus the fact that it's usually fortified with vitamin D.

SOY MILK: Made from soy beans, protein-rich soy milk can reduce the risk of heart disease by reducing cholesterol when incorporated into a healthy diet. Soy milk antioxidants have been found to help increase bone density and strengthen the immune system.

COFFEE: When enjoyed in moderation (about three cups a day) coffee can be a great boost for an early-day workout. Please note that too much caffine can cause anxiety, irritability and restlessness.

TEA: Tea has become a sipper of choice for many because it contains far less caffeine than coffee. Many scientists believe green, black and red teas can lower cholesterol and prevent blood clots.

JUICE: Squeezed from fruits or vegetables, juice is a great source of vitamins and minerals. While 100% juice is a better choice than soda or sweetened drinks with little or no nutritional values, whole fruit or veggies are healthier choices. They have more fiber and are less calorie dense.

The Skinny on Sports Drinks

Commercial sports drinks supply calories for energy and replace the fluids, sodium and potassium the body loses through perspiration. Most athletes do not need a sports drink unless they've exercised vigorously for at least 1 hour.

At that point, however, the body is more than likely simply craving fluid of any sort, and the fluid that best complements most sporting or physical activities is water.

If you're more likely to consume a sports drink instead of water while exercising, then by all means do so. It's important to keep in mind, though, that unlike water, many of these products have high calorie counts.

raise a glass to the
WONDERS of WATER!

All it took was a little determination and a bit of planning.

By Julie Kastello

For several years, I made a New Year's resolution to drink more water. Call me a drip, but each year I'd fail. I knew that the benefits were great, but I just couldn't get myself to drink more water.

To be honest, I was too reluctant to give up my coffee and cola for water…but I knew it was in my best interest to make a change. After resolving (once again) to drink more water, I was determined to stick with it and make water a healthy part of my daily diet. I'm a goal-focused person, so I set a personal goal of drinking eight glasses (64 ounces) of water per day.

I started by looking at my daily routine and being honest with myself. I knew I'd be less likely to drink water if I had to fill a glass several times, so I purchased a six-pack of bottled water. I was daunted by the thought that I'd have to drink all six bottles in one day, until I realized that perception wasn't accurate.

Because the bottles I purchased held 20 ounces each, I didn't need to guzzle them all. If I could drink one bottle in the morning and one in the

> "I knew the benefits were great, but I just couldn't get myself to drink more water."

afternoon, that would total 40 ounces. So I'd get five of the recommended eight glasses this way. Then I'd just have to squeeze in the other three.

Here's how I work even more water into my day. I start by drinking a glass first thing when I awake. If you take vitamins in the morning, that's a perfect opportunity to get your first glass (8 ounces down, 56 to go).

But I'm a coffee drinker, and I didn't want to give it up. So I still drink a few cups, but I sneak sips from my water bottle in between. If I don't empty my first bottle by noon, I finish it with lunch (28 ounces down, 36 to go).

Where I once drank a soda in the afternoon, I now gulp my second 20-ounce bottle of water. It's cool and refreshing and, surprisingly, I don't miss the cola at all. (That's 48 ounces down, and only 16 more to go.)

Since I enjoy a light afternoon snack on most days, I make a point of taking plenty of sips of water between bites. Often times, I don't even realize I'm doing it. This makes it easy to finish another 8 ounces (56 ounces down, 8 to go).

I'm happy to conclude that when I have a glass of ice water with dinner, I've met my personal eight-glass goal without much effort.

H2O TIPS

Here are a few additional tips to help you get into the H2O habit:

- Spend lots of time at home? Keep a pitcher of water in your refrigerator so it's handy, well chilled and inviting.

- When you are at the office, keep a big mug or bottle at your desk. You'll find yourself reaching for it naturally.

- When you drain your mug, don't wait until you finish what you're doing...refill it immediately.

- Drink water with each meal. It's good for your digestion and may help you feel full so you eat less.

- Bored with plain water? Perk it up by squeezing a wedge of lemon or lime into it.

- Eat foods that are high in water content, which includes most fruits and vegetables. A refreshing slice of watermelon is over 90% water.

- Don't pass a water fountain without stopping for a sip or two.

- Try drinking through a straw. Some people believe it's easier to drink more water this way.

making your
FAVORITE comfort foods
fit your healthy lifestyle

Try these strategies for lightening up your favorite recipes:

FOR GENERAL RECIPES:

- Invest in a food scale so that you can weigh foods until you get a feel for what typical serving sizes are.

- Use the leanest cuts of meat: skinless poultry, white-meat poultry, beef with "loin" or "round" in the name and pork with "loin" in the name.

- Consider 4 ounces of uncooked meat to be a serving.

- Cut back on adding high-calorie and fatty ingredients like cheese, olives, avocado and nuts.

- Watch how many high-sodium foods you're including such as anything canned or packaged, boxed mixes, olives, cheese and savory seasoning mixes. Can you find a low-sodium/no-sodium alternative? Perhaps one of the canned products in the recipe can be changed to fresh or frozen (corn, green beans, sliced mushrooms, etc.).

- Watch portion sizes when serving rice and pasta. Pastas are usually 1-1/2 ounces uncooked per serving. Cooked rice is typically 1/2 or 2/3 cup per serving.

- Use 8- or 6-inch flour tortillas instead of 10-inch. The 10-inch tortillas have 213 calories before any fillings are even added.

Replace butter or oil with unsweetened applesauce. Sub egg whites for some whole eggs.

FOR BAKED ITEMS:

- Replace 1/4 or 1/2 of the butter or oil with unsweetened applesauce. Keep in mind that applesauce is a better replacement for oil than it is for butter.

- If you're substituting a substantial amount (1/2 to 1 cup) of applesauce for fat, you can cut down on sugar a bit because of the natural sweetness of the applesauce.

- Substitute egg whites for some of the whole eggs. But don't use all egg whites unless specified in the recipe since that can result in a spongy, tough product.

- Remember that sugar packs on calories. One tablespoon equals 48 calories.

- Sugar can often be decreased slightly without any substitute, especially with recipes that are 40 or more years old since they tend to be disproportionately high in sugar.

- Confectioners' sugar can almost always be decreased in a frosting without missing the sweetness. One tablespoon of confectioners' sugar equals 29 calories.

- If you have trouble with a tough, dense texture in a lightened-up baked good, try substituting cake flour for all-purpose flour the next time you prepare it.

- Decrease the amount of chopped mix-ins such as nuts, chips (use mini chips), raisins, coconut, etc.

- Toast nuts and coconut so smaller amounts have stronger flavor.

- Reduce the amount of frosting. You can usually cut that amount by 1/4 or 1/3 without missing it.

- Reduced-fat cream cheese and reduced-fat butter work well in place of their full-fat varieties in frosting, but since the lighter products tend to be more soft-set, the recipe may need less liquid.

- Keep in mind that it's very difficult to successfully lighten cookie recipes and still keep the original texture and shape. The better option is to prepare cookies as usual and savor a single serving.

making a lifelong ADJUSTMENT!

Without family, I wouldn't have reached my goal.

By Mike Erickson

before

They say your family is a link to your past and a bridge to your future. For me, my family was truly just that—a connection leading to a healthier me.

At 218 pounds, I was overweight. Although I knew the time had come to get serious about losing weight, it took the inspiration of a family member to motivate me to change.

One Christmas, I saw my uncle Dale…29 pounds lighter than the last time I saw him. He looked great, and I could tell he felt terrific. In addition, he had a positive outlook on life I hadn't always seen before. It was refreshing.

At that moment I wanted to feel just as good as he did, I wanted to lose the weight, and I was determined to prove to myself I could be just as successful. Actually seeing someone who already had a great start on their weight-loss plan inspired me. I finally realized no matter what, it could be done. The fact that I wasn't getting any younger made me want to try even harder. Dale's success instantly

squashed all of the rumors and excuses I used as a crutch to starting a weight-loss plan.

In order to begin, I knew I had to set a reasonable goal for myself. I decided I wanted to lose 38 pounds, just enough to set my weight at 180 pounds. In addition, I wanted to be able to go to the beach over summer without having to wear a T-shirt to mask my insecurities.

Although my uncle's success was the initial trigger for my weight-loss goals, all of my accomplishments were made easier with the support of my wife. After I saw Dale, not only did I set

out to change my life, but my wife decided to follow suit. Together, we began reading food labels and counting calories. We changed our bad habits and formed newer, healthier ones.

It wasn't about a temporary change for us. We knew in order to truly be happy and successful we needed to make a lifelong adjustment. The last thing I wanted to do was diet for a short amount of time, not stick with it and gain the weight back. If I was going to commit myself to losing the weight, I wasn't going to take any shortcuts or do it halfway.

In the end, I really wanted all of my efforts to be worth it, and I wanted to be proud of myself for riding out everything and meeting my goal.

I began by giving up my favorite indulgence,

after

fast-food cheeseburgers. By replacing the cheeseburgers with healthier items, I was able to improve my chances of succeeding. I filled myself with salads, fruits and vegetables. My wife and I are creatures of habit, and by tweaking our eating rituals in certain ways, the weight began coming off.

It's amazing how much healthier I felt by simply watching what I ate. By making better food choices every day...every meal...I began to thrive on the extra energy I had. I no longer ate until I was full; I just ate the necessary amount to satisfy my hunger.

Although I had always found it difficult and bothersome to work out, I knew this was the second piece to my weight-loss puzzle. Instead of feeling guilty for taking time out of my already-busy day to exercise, I embraced the time to myself and started out slow.

Initially I began walking about a 15-20 minute mile on the treadmill. Eventually I increased the speed, and currently I walk about 3 miles at a steady pace, burning around 400 calories.

Although working out has become part of my daily routine, I don't panic if I skip a day; I just make up for it the next time. I realize the importance of staying active, yet I don't allow myself to obsess over it. As long as I am staying on track with my plan, I don't have a problem with tweaking it every so often. Once I became used to working out and eating healthy, it no longer felt like a chore...it just became part of my life.

In about six months I reached my goal. Now that I feel good, it's easy for me to stay on track. I won't let myself fall back into my past habits of eating late and eating too much food, because I know I have my wife and family to support me. And after all, my family is the backbone that holds me together.

EASY ADVICE

Here are a few tricks that helped me lose 38 pounds!

- I no longer eat until I am full, and I definitely don't eat until I am uncomfortable. I try to eat foods that are high in fiber and low in calories because I know they will fill me up quickly.

- Keep in mind that there is nothing wrong with treating yourself to your favorite meal, snack or dessert once in a while. Just remember, it's a treat and no longer a habit. Better yet, look through the recipes in this book for lightened-up versions of your favorite standbys. Make these dishes commonplace on your table and you won't feel like you're missing out on your best-loved foods.

- Find someone to support you, or even join you, on your weight-loss journey. The fact that I had my wife to share my experiences with kept me motivated. This isn't to say you can't be successful on your own, but a strong support system greatly helps during the times you struggle the most.

- Eat breakfast every day. I know you've heard it before, but it truly starts your day out right! I feel so much better when I have a small bowl of cereal in the morning and a banana. Take advantage of the fact that the Comfort Food Diet lets you enjoy 350 calories for breakfast!

- Stay active. Don't push yourself in the beginning, but try to maintain a schedule so your body can become accustomed to the change. Even if you start off with a slow mile, the important thing is that you started.

avoiding the pitfalls of
EATING OUT

Just because you're out of your kitchen doesn't mean you're not in control of what you eat.

EATING OUT WITHOUT FILLING OUT

It's tough to resist the allure of restaurant dining. After all, eating out means enjoying good food without doing the cooking yourself. The good news is that every sit-down restaurant offers two sources to help keep you on a lighter course: The menu and the waitstaff.

Oftentimes, a menu explains how dishes are prepared and what they include. Your server can fill in the blanks, answering any additional questions.

Don't be afraid to ask questions. What may seem like an obvious menu choice might not be right for you. For example, restaurants often label meals as "healthy" or "light," when actually they serve small portions that are high in calories.

Begin by reading the entire menu, noting which dishes fit best with your daily calorie plan. Items that are baked, roasted, poached, broiled or steamed are not only flavorful, but they tend to be healthier than those that are fried.

Other light options include vegetable stir-fries, lean-meat shish kabobs and spicy chicken burritos. Still don't know what to order? Fish is a wonderful source of protein and is usually lower in calories. Order a blackened tuna steak or herbed poached salmon.

Have an appetizer for your entree and you can really cut calories. Choose low-fat starters such as a plate of grilled veggies, boiled shrimp with cocktail sauce or a dinner salad.

If something is not prepared the way you'd like, ask if the chef can make an exception. Remember you're in charge. Know what foods to discern, what's "light" on the menu and ask the right questions...and eating out won't mean eating out of control.

WORKING SOLUTIONS

Lots of people find it tough to keep healthy-eating goals when at work. Being away from home, it's easy to stray from meal plans, and all too often the workplace is filled with tempting treats. When you get hungry at work, here's a few ways to stay on track.

At meetings, pass up doughnuts, jumbo muffins and cookies. Instead, choose mini muffins, bagels or fruit. Enjoy a cup of coffee, hot tea or fat-free milk.

At the vending machine, don't spend your cash on Danishes, chocolate bars and snack chips. Instead, try pretzels, baked chips or licorice. At the cafeteria, look for plain sandwiches, broth-based soups and low-fat yogurt. Of course a salad bar can be a lifesaver when the lunch bell rings.

Remember that your best option is planning ahead and bringing food from home. Not only will your brown-bag creations suit your taste buds, but they'll lead to a healthy body as well.

DON'T PASS UP THE PARTY

Just because you're counting calories, doesn't mean you have to be a party-pooper. Just eat a little something healthy before you leave the house. If you go hungry, you're sure to beeline to the buffet table. You might want to bring along a nutritious dish—a variety of vegetables and fat-free dip, for example. Your hostess will appreciate the thought and you'll know there's something lighter to munch on.

Before you start filling your plate, scan the entire table first, identifying the healthiest options. Avoid deep-fried appetizers. They may look bite-size but are sure to pack a calorie-laden punch. Partake in the veggie and fruit platters instead.

Other good choices are shrimp, smoked salmon, wheat or rye crackers and baked tortilla chips with salsa. When it comes to cold cuts, skip the cheese and sausage and go for the healthier turkey option.

Another trick may be to use a cocktail napkin instead of a plate. You'll be less likely to pile on the snacks if you don't have a convenient place to hold them.

Here's a great strategy that works in any situation: Take your time and eat slowly. It takes your system 20 minutes to realize you're full. You can easily overdo it if you're eating too quickly.

For a low-calorie beverage that's still bubbly and refreshing, ask for a sparkling water or tonic on ice with a wedge of lemon or lime.

When going to parties bring along a nutritious dish—such as a variety of vegetables and fat-free dip.

Mini or bite-size desserts are becoming popular. Satiate your sweet tooth with one or two servings.

THE DESSERT DILEMMA

One of the toughest challenges of eating right is turning away decadent desserts. Whether at a restaurant or party, the call of a sweet nibble is one temptation that many folks find hard to resist. The good news is that you can enjoy a treat as long as you do so in moderation and make smart choices.

When dining out, for instance, consider an angel food cake or meringue dessert. Choose a gingersnap or sugar cookie over chocolate mousse or heavy pumpkin pie. You can also opt to cut the calories in half—literally. Just ask the server for a smaller slice or serving or offer to split a dessert with your guest.

When faced with a dessert buffet, decide which foods hold special meaning for you and which you can do without. Forget about eating the least favorite, and sample a small portion of one or two of the things you know will make your celebration complete.

If it's the shopping mall's food court that's calling your sweet tooth, bypass the cookies and cinnamon rolls and look for a cool, refreshing fruit smoothie. Some stands also feature low-fat, frozen yogurt which also makes a great snacking option when on the go.

It's easiest to bypass the dessert temptation, though, by making fat-free frozen yogurt or light ice cream a staple in your freezer. You'll know there's something at home to satisfy your craving, and you can put the money you save back in your wallet without putting extra inches on your waistline.

ENJOYING
the little things

It was time to step up and start taking care of myself.

By Claudia Couchene

before

You cannot imagine how easy life becomes when you no longer have to worry about whether or not you will fit into the theater seat at your favorite show. Trust me, it's one of the best feelings one could ever hope for.

For almost five years now, I have been steadily climbing the weight-loss Totem pole, and with each dropped pound, my life becomes oh-so much easier. With nearly 100 pounds shed, I now take the stairs instead of the elevator. When I want to cut the grass, I don't dread it. Not only is shopping for new clothes a thrill, but I don't get upset if I can't find a parking spot close enough to the mall door. I actually enjoy the walk.

All the small tasks that most people wouldn't think twice about, yet used to torture me, are no longer added obstacles. Now, I can just live like everyone else. What a joy!

My weight-loss has also given me a greater appreciation for life overall. You see, a couple months before I started on my healthy journey, my dear sister passed away from complications associated with being morbidly obese and living with type-two diabetes. Unfortunately I knew I was following in her footsteps, and I needed to desperately change the direction of my own life before I would be in the same situation.

There wasn't anyone to take care of my physical well-being, and I knew it was time I step up and start taking care of myself. When my scale no longer went high enough to read my increasing weight, I knew it was time for a major life change.

I lost the first 30 pounds by solely cutting back on snacks and

after

desserts. I was absolutely thrilled, but once that initial weight came off, I wasn't sure what else to do. I had reached a standstill and didn't know where to turn.

Thankfully, a co-worker of mine asked if I wanted to learn how to lose weight by counting calories and evaluating Nutrition Facts. This was key to increasing progress toward my goal. I began paying attention to portion sizes and limited the amount of food I put on my plate. I also started writing down every single thing I ate every day.

I must admit that the largest obstacle standing in my way was realizing when I was full. A former fan of seconds and thirds, I

began to stop eating after my first plate was empty. Once I practiced portion control, kept a food journal and decreased the number of servings I consumed, the rest of my weight came off without much of a hitch. It is these decisions that keep me feeling healthy, and that feeling alone motivates me to continue on my weight-loss path today.

KEEPING IT OFF

Today, I maintain my weight-loss by making smart choices when it comes to cooking. If a recipe calls for a can of tomatoes, I'm sure to use organic canned tomatoes. Similarly, I rethink how I season my foods. As an alternative to salt, for instance, I use herbs or sea salt to add flavor. These small but helpful choices keep me healthier and successful.

I have also adopted the habit of walking to stay in shape. When I started exercising, my poodle, Fleeka, would help pull me up the hills on our regular walks. It wasn't long before I was no longer dragging behind her, and the two of us now walk in perfect unison...no matter what sort of terrain we're facing.

Every day when I get home from work, Fleeka is so excited for our walk that I find it impossible to disappoint her. Her excitement has been a terrific motivator for me. Today, we walk about 50 minutes, 5 days a week.

To those of you who want to lose weight, only you know when the time is right to begin your journey to a healthier and more fulfilling life, but I truly believe when that day comes you won't ever look back.

CLAUDIA'S HELPFUL HINTS

Starting your own weight-loss journey? Consider these tips that helped Claudia lose 100 pounds!

EARLY MORNING EATS. I've always been a breakfast eater, and thanks to a bevy of light recipes, I can have something different every day of the week. On days when time is tight, I enjoy simple things like oatmeal with mashed bananas and a few walnuts. Eating breakfast gives me energy and keeps me away from the doughnuts.

SHAKE IT UP. Smoothies and shakes made with low-fat ingredients hit the spot without robbing the calorie bank. These refreshing beverages also help me get more fruit and milk into my day. My most recent discovery is a smoothie that combines Greek nonfat plain yogurt, fat-free milk, a banana, orange juice and a touch of vanilla.

PERFECT PLANNING. For many, this is a life change, and I found that menu planning is key to making that change happen. When you know what you're making for dinner and you're all prepared to make it, you're less likely to stop at the fast food drive-thru on your way home from work. I always plan my weekly menu prior to going to the grocery story.

JOT IT IN A JOURNAL. My suggestion for anyone who wants to lose weight is to write down everything consumed and when. This way you don't forget about that handful of chips or mini candy bar or two you ate during the day. The thought of having to write everything down also helps you make healthy choices about snacks and portion sizes.

choose to MOVE

Melting away excess pounds is as easy as putting a little spring in your step.

It's nothing you haven't heard a millions times, and deep down inside, you know it's true. You've got to move to lose weight.

The good news is that you don't need to go to an expensive (and sometimes, intimidating) health club. You don't need to buy special equipment or sign up for classes. All you need is a pair of walking shoes and the desire to succeed, and exercise will become a wonderfully rewarding part of your daily life.

The Comfort Food Diet recommends fitness for surefire success, but suggests activities that are realistic, simple and fun. When thinking about what sort of exercise you might like best, consider something easy that you can do every day…no matter where you are and no matter what your schedule might look like.

It should be aerobic without being burdensome. Working on a stair stepper, for instance, is an outstanding cardiovascular workout. For some, however, finding the time to go to a gym and get on a machine is not particularly convenient.

The hardest part of any workout routine is getting started. Create your workout plan and stick with it. Ask yourself how badly you want to lose the weight, then set your clock an hour early each day and make it happen.

Exercise needs to be fun in order for folks to stick with it. Over the next few pages, you'll find some easy ways to work out that keep things interesting. Choose one or more and get moving! Combined with the recipes in the *Comfort Food Diet Cookbook*, it won't be long before you feel energetic and the fat is simply melting away.

AN OUNCE OF PLANNING...

If exercise hasn't been a big part of your life recently, a bit of planning may help you make the change. Consider the following when embarking on your workout routine:

• Discuss your exercise plans with your doctor. Your physician may even have some advice to help you on your journey.

• Create realistic, specific short-term goals. Don't plan on running a marathon if you can't remember the last time you walked around the block. Set detailed goals that you truly believe you can reach within a week or a month. Once you reach the goal, establish a new, more challenging target.

• Schedule exercise into your day. Pick a time you know will fit your schedule, and stick to it. Many find there's no room for excuses by exercising first thing in the morning. Start your day with a brisk walk or invigorating yoga routine. You'll jumpstart your day as well as your body's fat-burning engine—your metabolism.

• Keep an exercise log. Track what sort of activity you did and for how long. (You'll be surprised at how quickly little bursts of movement add up.) Jot down how you felt during each workout, any new exercises you tried and the pounds and repetitions of any weightlifting that may become part of your regime. Use the log to record your weekly weight or measurements if you'd like.

walk off WEIGHT

Here's a "step-by-step" guide to dropping pounds and feeling great.

It's so simple, convenient and economical, walking couldn't possibly qualify as real exercise, right? Wrong. Study after study shows regular moderate walking can help you reduce your risk of heart disease and lose weight (such as the 117 pounds lost by Margie Haen, featured on page 18).

That's good news, because walking is the most popular fitness activity in the country. In fact, according to surveys, four out of five women who start a walking program stick with it.

In addition, walking is easy on the joints and won't likely cause injury even if it's done on a daily basis. Best of all, you already know how to do it, it can be done anywhere and it's completely free!

Read on to learn how to get the most out of every step you take.

KNOW THE BASICS

Start with a specific goal, such as walking five days a week for 30 minutes at a time. Walk for as long as you're comfortable the first week, and then increase your time by 10% each subsequent week.

Begin each walk with 5 minutes at an easy pace...the pace with which you'd shop for groceries for instance. Gradually increase your speed. Remember, you're walking to burn calories, you're not out for a simple stroll. Walk at a pace where you're breathing heavily but still able to talk. Five minutes before the end of your walk, decrease your speed, and thus your heart rate, to the pace at which you started.

A study published in the European Journal of Applied Physiology found that exercisers felt less fatigue when they added some fast walking bursts early in their workouts. This elevates the heart rate early on and increases the amount of fat you burn.

To get the most out of your walk, pay close attention to your posture. Keep your back straight and your shoulders aligned with your hips. Look up and out, not down. Try to keep your arms bent at a 90-degree angle and swing them as you walk.

When you reach your goal (30 minutes a day, five days a week), set a new target. Consider increasing your walking time or adding another form of exercise.

Walking is now the most popular fitness activity in the U.S. According to surveys, four out of five women who start a walking program continue it.

SHOOT FOR 10,000 STEPS

Don't let that amount intimidate you. You're already closer to this goal than you think. Researchers at Arizona State University found that most people cover 7,499 steps a day, even without a formal sports or exercise program.

Here's even more good news. When it comes to exercise, small investments can yield big payoffs. The key is finding additional opportunities to walk. Pacing while talking on the phone, parking in the back of your office parking lot or walking around the block after dinner can be just as good for you as more vigorous exercise and will help you reach your goal of 10,000 steps per day.

Using a pedometer, find out how many steps you normally take in a day. Then increase that amount by at least 200 steps daily until you reach 10,000.

BREATHE DEEPLY

Many people tend to hold their breath more than they should while exercising. The truth of the matter is that you can't burn fat without oxygen. Muscles need oxygen for energy, so inhale deeply into your lungs by expanding your ribs outward and your stomach forward. Inhale for a count of three. Then exhale fully through your nose for another three counts.

TURN UP THE VOLUME

In a study published in the medical journal *Chest*, people with severe respiratory disease who listened to music while walking covered 4 more miles during an 8-week study than a similar group that didn't listen to music.

Researchers speculate that music helped to distract participants from boredom and fatigue, so the next time you lace up your sneakers, grab your headphones, too!

Use a pedometer

These are small, inexpensive gadgets that measure how far you've walked in steps and miles. They provide motivation by spurring you to meet a particular goal.

STEP it up

Burn more calories, faster with a jog.

Many people reach their health goals by lowering their caloric intake and walking on a regular basis. Some, however, like to kick things up a notch, and eventually replace walking with jogging.

Not only is jogging easy and free, but it almost always results in speedy weight-loss and an improved cardiovascular system. In addition, many joggers claim to feel more optimistic and confident during the day and sleep better at night.

START OUT SLOWLY

If you've just begun adding cardiovascular exercise to your day, start by walking and work your way up to jogging once you feel completely at ease with your walking routine. If you are not used to walking on a regular basis, do not start jogging. Only after you are able to walk several miles comfortably are you ready for jogging.

When you're ready to begin jogging, simply walk the first third of your route to warm up your muscles. Once you feel warmed up, walk faster or start a slow jog. When you feel that you are too breathless to hold a conversation, slow down and revert back to walking.

Once your heart rate has slowed and you feel you've recovered, you can jog again, reverting back to walking when you need to. As you reach the last third of your route, slow down and walk for a proper cool down.

Over time, you'll find that you're more comfortable jogging further and faster. Gradually, you'll begin to jog more and walk less, but always begin and end with walking for proper warm-up and cool-down periods.

It's important to note that jogging places much more stress on muscles and joints than walking. If you are very overweight or you have a history of ankle, hip or knee problems, walking may be a better exercise for you. Similarly, if you suffer from asthma or a heart condition, please talk to your doctor about your desire to start jogging.

If you become lightheaded, lose your balance or experience any discomfort in your chest while jogging, stop jogging immediately. Explain your symptoms to your doctor.

different STROKES for different folks

Have access to a swimming pool? Dive in for a low-impact workout.

Granted, not everyone has a pool in their backyard that's open year-round, but with a little planning most can find a public pool that offers free swim time. And a little splishing and splashing goes a long way...particularly when you want to work several muscle groups at once.

Swimming strengthens your cardiovascular system and works muscles throughout your body. And because water supports your body's weight, swimming is ideal for anyone dealing with joint pain or arthritis or recovering from an injury.

Water also has naturally calming qualities, such as its sound and ability to provide the feeling of weightlessness, making it a great tension reliever. Recent studies also indicate that swimming can help alleviate the effects of depression, and many people believe they sleep better after a workout in the water.

Although swimming laps offers fantastic health benefits, doing a monotonous breast stoke up and down the length of a pool isn't necessarily required. A walk or even a jog through the water, bouncing on the surface of the pool, diving for toys or even playing catch can burn several calories as well. Many organizations and community pools also organize water volleyball teams and offer water aerobics or even aqua kick boxing classes. Plus, swimming is an activity you can enjoy with the whole family...so it doesn't feel like a workout in the least.

CALM WATERS

If you haven't done much swimming in the past, ease into it. Spend some time walking to build up strength and endurance, then hit the water. Remember to stretch and do a few warm-up laps first.

Don't tire yourself out by jerking your head or thrashing your arms in the water as you swim. Make sure you're performing each stroke smoothly and correctly, paying attention to your form and muscle control. Alternate strokes to prevent boredom and to work varying muscles.

You can make your swim more challenging by wearing webbed gloves, which add resistance, or fins, which force your legs to work in both directions, strengthening your thighs, calves and stomach muscles.

YOGA & PILATES pose
easy approaches to exercise

Open your mind to a world of possibilities with these relaxing forms of fitness.

From professional athletes to stay-at-home moms, people from coast to coast have discovered forms of fitness that get impressive results without taxing the body. What's their secret? Yoga and Pilates!

Those who practice yoga and Pilates (pronounced puh-LAH-tees) are often perfectly happy with the benefits of a toned body. But these exercises offer much more; they create a sense of overall well-being in the mind and spirit.

STRIKE A POSE

Yoga focuses on holding postures and poses and mastering breathing techniques. When performed regularly, yoga improves muscle tone and sustains a healthy metabolism, which helps regulate weight. Yoga also improves stamina and balance.

Like yoga, Pilates strengthens the body through a series of gentle, precise and systematic movements that concentrate on the abdominal muscles, lower back and hips. Unlike yoga, however, Pilates doesn't hold poses for long periods of time. Instead, the practice focuses on a smooth flow between the movements.

GETTING STARTED

The great thing about yoga and Pilates is that everyone can reap the benefits they offer. Yoga poses and Pilates exercises can be modified to anyone's fitness level. If you want to try yoga or Pilates, search the Internet to locate a studio in your area, or contact your local YMCA, library or public school system, and ask about the availability of beginner classes. Once you find a class, discuss your fitness goals one-on-one with the instructor.

Many Pilates exercises rely on Pilates machines, but most introductory classes consist of basic mat routines. As such, following a Pilates or yoga DVD (made for beginners) is also an option when getting started.

While yoga and Pilates help turn fat into muscle, most experts recommend combining the routines with a healthy diet and a cardiovascular activity. This shouldn't be a problem! Many of those who practice yoga or Pilates find it easier to participate in other forms of exercise due to increased flexibility.

PUMP it up!

Give your exercise routines a boost with these simple strategies.

Looking for some fun ways to perk up work and play? Look no further. We've got 10 great tips to intensify everyday activities from the book *30 Minutes a Day to a Healthy Heart*, by Frederic J. Vagnini, M.D., and Selene Yeager. Just remember: Start out nice and easy, and slowly work up the intensity.

1 Sneak in surges. Next time you're out walking, pick up the pace! You'll burn more calories and condition your body to walk faster each time.

2 Power-clean. Bet you never guessed you could burn major calories at home! Spin some CDs, grab the cleaning supplies and get moving.

3 Head for the hills. Tackle some inclines once or twice a week. Walking or riding a bike uphill is an added challenge for your heart, muscles and lungs.

4 Dance, dance, dance! Did you know that you can burn almost 500 calories an hour dancing? Some cardiologists say that their dancing patients are their healthiest, so head out to that nightclub and boogie the night away!

5 Find fast friends. Plan walks with someone who's just a hair fitter and faster than you. You'll push beyond your comfort zone to get fitter, faster. You're also more likely to stick to your routine by making a date with someone.

6 Preprogram it. If you're using a treadmill or other aerobic equipment, challenge yourself by using the "interval" program to automatically add inclines, increased resistance and higher-speed bursts to your workout.

7 Seek tougher terrain. Hiking trails, soft sand and grassy fields make you use more muscles and burn more calories, so get off the beaten path every once in a while.

8 Get in the game. Sporting hobbies such as tennis, cycling and even golf (minus the cart) include short bursts of heart-pumping effort. And they're fun, so the time flies!

BURN CALORIES EVERY DAY!

Activity	Calories Burned (per hour*)
Bicycling	544
Gardening	340
Golfing (walking with clubs)	374
Hiking	408
Kayaking/canoeing	340
Swimming	544
Tennis	476
Volleyball (casual)	204

* Based on a 150-pound person. Lighter people burn less; heavier people burn more.

it's all about the WORKOUT!

I started slow but consistent, working out 3 times a week.

By Kristen Johnson

before

Although working out sometimes seems like one of the most dreaded activities to put yourself through, you can't imagine how easy it gets once you actually commit to it. Trust me, I learned this valuable lesson first-hand.

Just like most people trying to lose weight, I knew that exercise and watching what I ate were things I had to get used to if I really wanted to be successful. Although it sounds easy enough, it takes a great deal of commitment to actually get started on your workout plan. But I promise, in the end it's more than worth it.

I started slow but consistent, working out at the gym three times a week. Most days I used the elliptical machine for 30 minutes before a round of strength training on the weight machines. In total, I was at the gym about 90 minutes each day.

On the days I wasn't at the gym, I still kept myself active. Two days a week, I performed an hour of Pilates at home. The combination of cardio and strength training was key to my total weight loss. I was burning calories through my cardio workouts and from the muscle I gained from weight training and Pilates. Not only was this duo helping me feel better, it gave me the variety I needed to stay focused and interested in exercising.

On top of working out, I counted calories and kept track of what I ate to make sure I was staying consistent in all aspects of my weight-loss plan. I kept my goal weight in mind and continued to push myself. I stuck to 1,400 calories a day, which was made easier by keeping a food diary. It was a key component to my weight loss because it kept me honest with myself—in turn, keeping me on the right track.

I followed this routine until I decided I needed some kind of a change. I made the decision to switch from working out at the gym to running. Even though I felt both cardio workouts benefited my weight-loss equally, running gave me a lower resting heart rate and increased my cardio strength. I was also better able to judge how many calories I was burning by keeping track of the miles I ran. I knew that running one mile burned about 100 calories, making losing weight a simple calculation!

It was also easy enough to keep track of what I was eating in my food diary because I made a change to the meals I prepared for myself. I used to thrive on pasta, rice and pizza…basically anything that was loaded with empty carbohydrates. Silly me, I never truly realized I wasn't maintaining a healthy diet.

I now eat a variety of lean meats, fruits and vegetables. I've also

after

become a fan of salmon, hummus and anything whole grain or whole wheat. Although it's a change from the food I was used to, I found ways to give nearly everything I prepare a comforting flair.

I do have to admit, however, that I'm a chips-and-dip kind of girl, but I knew in order to see the progress I wanted, I needed to trade in my bad habits for those my body would be more comfortable with sustaining.

I now eat whole wheat pita bread and hummus for a snack, not quite the same but tasty nonetheless. With these simple substitutions and my regular physical activity, I have lost a total of 40 pounds.

Don't get me wrong; I still eat some of my favorite foods…but in moderation. I now know that I can still enjoy pepperoni, onion and mushroom pizza, as long as I make a few adjustments to the recipe. Now that I've reached my goal weight, I realize that I can enjoy a couple traditional slices every once in a while, too.

I hope you experience the same success I've had with exercise and eating right. Losing weight is a give-and-take process; the more you give up to succeed, the more your body and future will benefit.

DEAR DIARY

Looking back at my journey, the most important decision I made was keeping a food diary. My weight has fluctuated a small bit, but by keeping track of everything I eat, things stay rather even. The diary is my daily reminder; its blank pages seem to call my name every time I eat. This is how I do it:

WHAT?
I record what I eat for breakfast, lunch, dinner and snacks. I also keep track of portion sizes and calories. This way I can add it all up at the end of the day. (See page 292-295 for blank Meal-Planning Worksheets you can use.)

WHERE?
I keep a little notebook in my kitchen where I write down the exact amount of everything I eat. I'm sure to include snacks and even what I nibble on as I prepare meals. If I'm going out to eat, and I'm familiar with the restaurant's menu, I'll either plan ahead and write down what I'm going to order, or I'll write it down as soon as I get home.

WHY?
The diary helps me stay truthful with myself. It keeps track of my daily calorie intake, making sure I don't cheat!

MY SAMPLE ENTRY:

Lunch:

2 slices bread: 80 calories

2 oz. turkey: 60 calories

1 tablespoon light mayo: 45 calories

Lettuce: FREE FOOD

1 apple: 90 calories

1/2 cup cottage cheese: 90 calories

Total: 365 calories

FREE FOODS chart

Eat as much of these foods as you want!

The foods on the opposite page are considered "free foods" because they are basically non-starchy vegetables that won't add up to much as far as calories go. Typically, a "free food" is a food or beverage that has less than 20 calories and 5 or less grams of carbohydrate per serving.

See the chart at right. These foods are perfect for rounding out (or starting) a meal to help fill you up. In addition, they're mostly vegetables, which have lots of nutritional value and a satisfying crunch. Make a big salad, put lots of veggies on your sandwiches or fill up your dinner plate with a large side of cooked vegetables.

The last column on the chart offers items that are also considered free foods but are listed with a specific portion size. That's because you could have a serving of these foods and not count the calories, but if you ate an unlimited quantity, the calories would rack up quickly.

EAT ALL YOU WANT

- Artichoke
- Artichoke hearts
- Asparagus
- Baby corn
- Bamboo shoots
- Bean sprouts
- Beans (green, wax, Italian)
- Broccoli
- Broth or bouillon
- Cabbage
- Cauliflower
- Celery
- Cucumber
- Eggplant
- Garlic
- Green onions or scallions
- Greens (collard, kale, mustard, turnip)
- Hearts of palm
- Herbs (fresh or dried)
- Horseradish
- Hot pepper sauce
- Jicama
- Kohlrabi
- Leeks
- Lemon juice
- Mixed vegetables (without corn, peas or pasta)
- Mushrooms (fresh)
- Mustard
- Okra
- Onions
- Pea pods
- Pickles
- Pimento
- Bell peppers
- Radishes
- Rutabaga
- Salad greens (lettuce, romaine, chicory, endive, escarole, arugula, radicchio, watercress)
- Spices
- Spinach
- Squash (summer, crookneck, zucchini)
- Sugar snap peas
- Swiss chard
- Tomato (fresh or canned)
- Turnips
- Vinegar
- Water chestnuts
- Wine (used in cooking)
- Worcestershire sauce

FREE FOOD AND BEVERAGES— DRINK AS MUCH AS YOU WANT

- Carbonated or mineral water
- Club soda
- Coffee (unsweetened or with sugar substitute)
- Diet soft drinks
- Drink mixes (sugar-free)
- Flavored water (20 calories or less)
- Tea (unsweetened or with sugar substitute)
- Tonic water (diet)
- Water

FREE FOODS WITH RESTRICTED PORTIONS

- Barbecue sauce, *1 tablespoon*
- Cream cheese (fat-free), *1 tablespoon (1/2 ounce)*
- Creamer:
  Nondairy, liquid, *1 tablespoon*
  Nondairy, powdered, *2 teaspoons*
- Honey mustard, *1 tablespoon*
- Jam or jelly (light or no-sugar added), *1 tablespoon*
- Ketchup, *1 tablespoon*
- Margarine spread:
  Fat-free, *1 tablespoon*
  Reduced-fat, *1 teaspoon*
- Mayonnaise:
  Fat-free, *1 tablespoon*
  Reduced-fat, *1 teaspoon*
- Parmesan cheese (freshly grated), *1 tablespoon*
- Pickle relish, *1 tablespoon*
- Salad dressing:
  Fat-free or low-fat, *1 tablespoon*
  Fat-free Italian, *2 tablespoons*
- Salsa, *1/4 cup*
- Sour cream:
  Fat-free, *2 tablespoons*
  Reduced-fat, *1 tablespoon*
- Sweet and sour sauce, *2 teaspoons*
- Sweet chili sauce, *1 tablespoon*
- Syrup (sugar-free), *2 tablespoons*
- Taco sauce, *1 tablespoon*
- Whipped topping:
  Light or fat-free, *2 tablespoons*
  Regular, *1 tablespoon*

six-week MEAL PLAN

Here is a suggested meal plan to take you six full weeks with three meals a day plus snacks. This will keep you right around 1,400 calories a day and help you learn the amount and types of foods that keep you healthy and trim. You can substitute different foods, but be sure you're paying attention to calories. To plan future weeks and record what you're eating, use the blank Do-It-Yourself Meal-Planning Worksheets on pages 292-295.

Points to Remember:

- Focus on enjoying your meals. Eat slowly and really taste and savor the foods you've prepared.

- Take advantage of "Free Foods" to keep you filled up. You can add them to meals or nibble on them throughout the day. Check out the chart on page 45.

- Try freezing leftovers in proper portion sizes for busy days.

- Make healthy choices by keeping the big picture in mind. When choosing packaged foods at the grocery store, consider more than just the calories. Compare the Nutrition Facts to find the brand with the highest fiber and the lowest fat, saturated fat, cholesterol and sodium. If you are concerned about additives and preservatives, choose the brand with the shortest ingredient list.

- Get maximum nutrition for your calories. For example: You could eat three chocolate-covered pretzel twists for about the same number of calories in a 1/2 cup of fresh blueberries. The blueberries offer many great health benefits for your body; however, if the chocolate-covered pretzel twists satisfy your sweet tooth and keep you in your daily calorie allotment, then go for the pretzels.

meal plan | **THE COMFORT FOOD DIET**

day 1

BREAKFAST:

- 1 Berry Yogurt Cup (p. 88)
  98 CALORIES

- 1 large scrambled egg
  101 CALORIES

- 1 slice whole wheat bread, toasted
  69 CALORIES

- spread with 1 teaspoon reduced-fat margarine
  FREE FOOD

- 1/2 cup orange juice
  55 CALORIES

- 1 cup of coffee (with sugar substitute and 1 tablespoon liquid nondairy creamer, if desired)
  FREE FOOD

BREAKFAST TOTAL: **323 CALORIES**

LUNCH:

- 1-1/2 cups Bean and Pasta Soup (p. 126)
  218 CALORIES

- 1 whole wheat dinner roll
  76 CALORIES

- spread with 1 teaspoon reduced-fat margarine
  FREE FOOD

- 1 medium banana
  100 CALORIES

- 1 can mineral water
  FREE FOOD

LUNCH TOTAL: **394 CALORIES**

DINNER & DESSERT:

- 1 cup Three-Meat Spaghetti Sauce (p. 172)
  242 CALORIES

- 1 cup cooked spaghetti
  100 CALORIES

- 1 big green salad (see the Free Foods Chart on p. 45) with 1 tablespoon reduced-fat salad dressing
  FREE FOOD

- 1 cup fat-free milk
  86 CALORIES

- 1 Chewy Chocolate Brownie (p. 276)
  124 CALORIES

DINNER TOTAL: **552 CALORIES**

SNACKS:

- 1 cup Sweet 'n' Salty Popcorn (p. 75)
  76 CALORIES

- 1 cup whole strawberries
  45 CALORIES

WEEK 1, DAY 1, TOTAL: 1,390 CALORIES

day 2

BREAKFAST:

- 4 Asparagus Ham Roll-Ups (p. 88)
  276 CALORIES

- 1 slice whole wheat bread, toasted
  69 CALORIES

- spread with 1 tablespoon no-sugar-added jam
  FREE FOOD

- 1 cup hot tea (with sugar substitute if desired)
  FREE FOOD

BREAKFAST TOTAL: **323 CALORIES**

LUNCH:

- 1 cup Anytime Turkey Chili (p. 127)
  241 CALORIES

- 4 saltine crackers
  52 CALORIES

- 1 big green salad (see Free Foods Chart on p. 45) with 1 tablespoon reduced-fat salad dressing
  FREE FOOD

- 1/3 cup red grapes
  43 CALORIES

- 1 cup fat-free milk
  86 CALORIES

LUNCH TOTAL: **422 CALORIES**

DINNER & DESSERT:

- 1 fillet Dijon-Crusted Fish (p. 176)
  214 CALORIES

- 1 whole wheat dinner roll
  76 CALORIES

- spread with 1 teaspoon reduced-fat margarine
  FREE FOOD

- Shredded cabbage topped with 1 tablespoon reduced-fat salad dressing
  FREE FOOD

- 1 glass ice water
  FREE FOOD

- 1 serving Mocha Pudding Cake (p. 285)
  227 CALORIES

DINNER TOTAL: **517 CALORIES**

SNACKS:

- 1 piece of string cheese
  80 CALORIES

- 1 medium peach or plum
  40 CALORIES

WEEK 1, DAY 2, TOTAL: 1,390 CALORIES

meal plan | THE COMFORT FOOD DIET

day 3

BREAKFAST:

- 1 Broccoli Bacon Quiche (p. 101)
  192 CALORIES
- 2/3 cup red grapes
  86 CALORIES
- 1 cup of coffee (with sugar substitute and 1 tablespoon liquid nondairy creamer, if desired)
  FREE FOOD

BREAKFAST TOTAL: 278 CALORIES

LUNCH:

- 3/4 cup Honey-Dijon Potato Salad (p. 125)
  147 CALORIES
- 1 beef hot dog with a bun
  231 CALORIES
- served with 1 tablespoon each ketchup and mustard
  FREE FOOD
- 1 medium apple
  72 CALORIES
- 1 can diet soft drink
  FREE FOOD

LUNCH TOTAL: 450 CALORIES

DINNER & DESSERT:

- 1 serving Lemon Thyme Chicken (p.182)
  213 CALORIES
- 3/4 cup prepared long-grain white rice
  154 CALORIES
- Steamed fresh or frozen green beans topped with 1 teaspoon reduced-fat margarine spread
  FREE FOOD
- 1 cup fat-free milk
  86 CALORIES
- 1 Chunky Pecan Bar (p. 275)
  88 CALORIES

DINNER TOTAL: 541 CALORIES

SNACKS:

- 1/2 cup sugar-free chocolate pudding (prepared with fat-free milk) topped with a crushed chocolate wafer
  99 CALORIES
- 1/2 cup fresh blueberries
  41 CALORIES

WEEK 1, DAY 3, TOTAL: 1,409 CALORIES

day 4

BREAKFAST:

- 2 wedges Egg White Frittata (p. 106)
  184 CALORIES
- 1 slice whole wheat bread, toasted
  69 CALORIES
- spread with 1 teaspoon reduced-fat margarine
  FREE FOOD
- 1/2 cup orange juice
  55 CALORIES

BREAKFAST TOTAL: 308 CALORIES

LUNCH:

- 1 cup Creamy Pasta Salad (p. 127)
  233 CALORIES
- 1 half-sandwich made with 1 piece whole wheat bread and 2 slices deli smoked fat-free turkey breast spread with 1 teaspoon fat-free mayonnaise
  89 CALORIES
- 1 medium banana
  100 CALORIES
- 1 bottle flavored water
  FREE FOOD

LUNCH TOTAL: 422 CALORIES

DINNER & DESSERT:

- 1 serving Stovetop Meat Loaves (p. 186)
  259 CALORIES
- 1 small baked russet potato
  138 CALORIES
- topped with 1 teaspoon reduced-fat margarine
  FREE FOOD
- Steamed fresh broccoli florets topped with 1 teaspoon reduced-fat margarine
  FREE FOOD
- 1 cup fat-free milk
  86 CALORIES
- 1 Cappuccino Truffle (p. 273)
  43 CALORIES
- 1 cup of coffee (with sugar substitute and 1 tablespoon liquid nondairy creamer, if desired)
  FREE FOOD

DINNER TOTAL: 526 CALORIES

SNACKS:

- 3/4 cup baby carrots
  60 CALORIES
- 1/3 cup 1% cottage cheese with 1/4 cup unsweetened pineapple tidbits
  81 CALORIES

WEEK 1, DAY 4, TOTAL: 1,397 CALORIES

day 5

BREAKFAST:

- 5 Silver Dollar Oat Pancakes (p. 116)
  211 CALORIES
- served with 5 tablespoons Apple Syrup (p. 89)
  50 CALORIES
- 1/4 cup cubed fresh pineapple
  37 CALORIES
- 1/2 cup fat-free milk
  43 CALORIES

BREAKFAST TOTAL: 341 CALORIES

LUNCH:

- 1 sandwich Crab Salad Pockets (p. 128)
  239 CALORIES
- 1 piece of string cheese
  80 CALORIES
- 1 medium pear
  96 CALORIES
- 1 can mineral water
  FREE FOOD

LUNCH TOTAL: 415 CALORIES

DINNER & DESSERT:

- 1 piece Weekday Lasagna (p. 187)
  280 CALORIES
- 1 big green salad (see Free Foods Chart on p. 45) with 1 tablespoon reduced-fat salad dressing
  FREE FOOD
- 2 sesame breadsticks (5g each)
  40 CALORIES
- 3/4 cup Garlic Green Beans (p. 247)
  61 CALORIES
- 1 can diet soft drink
  FREE FOOD
- 1 Chunky Pecan Bar (p. 275)
  88 CALORIES

DINNER TOTAL: 469 CALORIES

SNACKS:

- 2/3 cup Cheerios with 1/4 cup fat-free milk
  93 CALORIES
- 1/2 cup sliced strawberries with 2 tablespoons reduced-fat frozen whipped topping
  47 CALORIES
- 1-1/2 cups air-popped popcorn
  47 CALORIES

WEEK 1, DAY 5, TOTAL: 1,412 CALORIES

day 6

BREAKFAST:

- 1 cup Warm 'n' Fruity Breakfast Cereal (p. 100)
  185 CALORIES
- 1 cup Frappe Mocha (p. 100)
  114 CALORIES
- 1 cup of coffee (with sugar substitute and 1 tablespoon liquid nondairy creamer, if desired)
  FREE FOOD

BREAKFAST TOTAL: 299 CALORIES

LUNCH:

- 6 pieces Antipasto-Stuffed Baguettes (p. 129)
  312 CALORIES
- 1/3 cup red grapes
  43 CALORIES
- 1 cup fat-free milk
  86 CALORIES

LUNCH TOTAL: 441 CALORIES

DINNER & DESSERT:

- 1 serving Spinach and Mushroom Smothered Chicken (p. 171)
  203 CALORIES
- 1/2 cup cooked long-grain white rice
  103 CALORIES
- topped with 1 teaspoon reduced-fat margarine
  FREE FOOD
- 2/3 cup Special Cauliflower (p. 251)
  88 CALORIES
- 1 glass ice water
  FREE FOOD
- 2 Banana-Chip Mini Cupcakes (p. 271)
  130 CALORIES

DINNER TOTAL: 524 CALORIES

SNACKS:

- 1/2 (22g size) crisp rice cereal bar
  45 CALORIES
- 1/2 small apple with 2 tablespoons fat-free caramel ice cream topping
  93 CALORIES

WEEK 1, DAY 6, TOTAL: 1,402 CALORIES

Keep fresh fruit and veggies on hand for a quick and satisfying snack that won't derail your diet. To keep things interesting, try a new piece of produce every week.

day 7

BREAKFAST:

- **2 slices Blueberry French Toast (p. 117)**
  285 CALORIES
- **1/2 cup orange juice**
  55 CALORIES

BREAKFAST TOTAL: **340 CALORIES**

LUNCH:

- **1 Zesty Sloppy Joe (p. 131)**
  249 CALORIES
- **3/4 cup baby carrots**
  60 CALORIES
- **1 piece of string cheese**
  80 CALORIES
- **1 dill pickle spear**
  FREE FOOD
- **1 can diet soft drink**
  FREE FOOD

LUNCH TOTAL: **389 CALORIES**

DINNER & DESSERT:

- **1-1/2 cups Tasty Tuna Casserole (p. 199)**
  334 CALORIES
- **3/4 cup Vegetable Slaw (p. 251)**
  84 CALORIES
- **1 cup fat-free milk**
  86 CALORIES
- **1 Cappuccino Truffle (p. 273)**
  43 CALORIES

DINNER TOTAL: **547 CALORIES**

SNACKS:

- **1 cup Fresh Strawberry Smoothie (p. 75)**
  82 CALORIES
- **1 cup prepared sugar-free gelatin**
  8 CALORIES
- **served with 2 tablespoons fat-free frozen whipped topping**
  FREE FOOD
- **1 chocolate kiss**
  25 CALORIES

WEEK 1, DAY 7, TOTAL: 1,391 CALORIES

> About 75% of the sodium Americans consume comes from processed foods, not from their salt shakers. To keep your sodium intake within reason, use fresh, natural foods whenever possible.

day 1

BREAKFAST:

- **2 Ham and Apricot Crepes (p. 117)**
  258 CALORIES
- **1 small orange**
  45 CALORIES
- **1/2 cup fat-free milk**
  43 CALORIES
- **1 cup of coffee (with sugar substitute and 1 tablespoon liquid nondairy creamer, if desired)**
  FREE FOOD

BREAKFAST TOTAL: **346 CALORIES**

LUNCH:

- **1 serving Vegetable Soup with Dumplings (p.143)**
  258 CALORIES
- **1 medium banana**
  100 CALORIES
- **1 cup fat-free milk**
  86 CALORIES

LUNCH TOTAL: **444 CALORIES**

DINNER & DESSERT:

- **1 serving German-Style Short Ribs (p. 198)**
  302 CALORIES
- **served with 2/3 cup prepared egg noodles**
  147 CALORIES
- **1 big green salad (see Free Foods Chart on p. 45) with 1 tablespoon reduced-fat salad dressing**
  FREE FOOD
- **1 glass ice water**
  FREE FOOD
- **1 Banana-Chip Mini Cupcake (p. 271)**
  65 CALORIES
- **1 cup brewed iced tea (with sugar substitute if desired)**
  FREE FOOD

DINNER TOTAL: **514 CALORIES**

SNACKS:

- **9 tiny twist fat-free pretzels**
  50 CALORIES
- **served with 1 tablespoon honey mustard for dipping**
  FREE FOOD
- **1 medium peach or plum**
  40 CALORIES

WEEK 2, DAY 1, TOTAL: 1,390 CALORIES

day 2

BREAKFAST:

- 1 cup prepared Spiced Oatmeal Mix (p. 107)
  210 CALORIES
- 1/2 a small grapefruit with 1 teaspoon sugar
  48 CALORIES
- 1 slice whole wheat bread, toasted
  69 CALORIES
- spread with 1 tablespoon no-sugar-added jam
  FREE FOOD
- 1 cup hot tea (with sugar substitute if desired)
  FREE FOOD

BREAKFAST TOTAL: 327 CALORIES

LUNCH:

- 1 Ranch Chicken Salad Sandwich (p. 142)
  257 CALORIES
- 1 serving Grape Tomato Mozzarella Salad (p. 129)
  85 CALORIES
- 1/4 cup cubed fresh pineapple
  37 CALORIES
- 1 bottle flavored water
  FREE FOOD

LUNCH TOTAL: 379 CALORIES

DINNER & DESSERT:

- 1-1/4 cups Mushroom Pepper Steak (p. 175)
  241 CALORIES
- 1/2 cup prepared long-grain white rice
  103 CALORIES
- 1 big green salad (see Free Foods Chart on p. 45)
  with 1 tablespoon reduced-fat salad dressing
  FREE FOOD
- 1 cup fat-free milk
  86 CALORIES
- 1 Mother Lode Pretzel (p. 279)
  114 CALORIES

DINNER TOTAL: 544 CALORIES

SNACKS:

- 1 slice Sangria Gelatin Ring (p. 74)
  80 CALORIES
- 1 mini bagel with 1 tablespoon reduced-fat chive
  and onion cream cheese
  63 CALORIES

WEEK 2, DAY 2, TOTAL: 1,393 CALORIES

day 3

BREAKFAST:

- 1 Sage Breakfast Patty (p. 89)
  78 CALORIES
- 1 large scrambled egg
  101 CALORIES
- 1 slice whole wheat bread, toasted
  69 calories
- spread with 1 teaspoon reduced-fat margarine
  FREE FOOD
- 1 cup orange juice
  110 CALORIES

BREAKFAST TOTAL: 358 CALORIES

LUNCH:

- 1-1/2 cups Ham 'n' Chickpea Soup (p. 142)
  312 CALORIES
- 1 piece string cheese
  80 CALORIES
- 1/3 cup red grapes
  43 CALORIES
- 1 glass ice water
  FREE FOOD

LUNCH TOTAL: 435 CALORIES

DINNER & DESSERT:

- 1-1/2 cups Chicken Rice Dish (p. 177)
  296 CALORIES
- 1 big green salad (see Free Foods Chart on p. 45)
  with 1 tablespoon reduced-fat salad dressing
  FREE FOOD
- 1 cup fat-free milk
  86 CALORIES
- 2 Chocolate Gingersnaps (p. 272)
  138 CALORIES
- 1 cup hot tea (with sugar substitute if desired)
  FREE FOOD

DINNER TOTAL: 520 CALORIES

SNACKS:

- 1/2 cup cubed fresh pineapple
  37 CALORIES
- 1 cup prepared sugar-free gelatin
  8 CALORIES
- served with 2 tablespoons fat-free frozen
  whipped topping
  FREE FOOD
- 1 chocolate kiss
  25 CALORIES

WEEK 2, DAY 3, TOTAL: 1,383 CALORIES

day 4

BREAKFAST:

- 1 serving Cheese Tomato Egg Bake (p. 103)
  110 CALORIES
- 1 mini bagel (2-1/2-inch diameter)
  72 CALORIES
- spread with 1 tablespoon whipped cream cheese
  35 CALORIES
- 1/2 cup cubed fresh pineapple
  37 CALORIES
- 1 cup fat-free milk
  86 CALORIES

BREAKFAST TOTAL: 340 CALORIES

LUNCH:

- 1-1/2 cups Shrimp Pasta Salad (p. 151)
  391 CALORIES
- 3/4 cup baby carrots
  60 CALORIES
- 1 medium plum
  40 CALORIES
- 1 bottle flavored water
  FREE FOOD

LUNCH TOTAL: 491 CALORIES

DINNER & DESSERT:

- 1 serving Rosemary Turkey Breast (p. 179)
  166 CALORIES
- Steamed fresh or frozen green beans topped with 1 teaspoon reduced-fat margarine
  FREE FOOD
- 2/3 cup Cranberry Cornmeal Dressing (p. 265)
  205 CALORIES
- 1 cup brewed iced tea (with sugar substitute if desired)
  FREE FOOD
- 1 Chunky Pecan Bar (p. 275)
  88 CALORIES
- 1 cup of coffee (with sugar substitute and 1 tablespoon liquid nondairy creamer, if desired)
  FREE FOOD

DINNER TOTAL: 459 CALORIES

SNACKS:

- 1 piece of string cheese
  80 CALORIES
- 1/4 cup fresh blueberries
  21 CALORIES

WEEK 2, DAY 4, TOTAL: 1,391 CALORIES

day 5

BREAKFAST:

- 2 cups Strawberry Tofu Smoothie (p. 103)
  272 CALORIES
- 1 slice whole wheat bread, toasted
  69 CALORIES
- spread with 1 teaspoon reduced-fat margarine
  FREE FOOD

BREAKFAST TOTAL: 341 CALORIES

LUNCH:

- 1 Veggie Cheese Sandwich (p. 126)
  168 CALORIES
- 1-1/3 cups Broccoli Chowder (p. 130)
  233 CALORIES
- 1 can diet soft drink
  FREE FOOD

LUNCH TOTAL: 401 CALORIES

DINNER & DESSERT:

- 1 cup Mushroom Turkey Tetrazzini (p. 238)
  362 CALORIES
- Steamed fresh or frozen pea pods topped with 1 teaspoon reduced-fat margarine
  FREE FOOD
- 1 big green salad (see Free Foods Chart on p. 45) with 1 tablespoon reduced-fat salad dressing
  FREE FOOD
- 1 cup fat-free milk
  86 CALORIES
- 1 Mother Lode Pretzel (p. 279)
  114 CALORIES

DINNER TOTAL: 562 CALORIES

SNACKS:

- 1 medium peach or plum
  40 CALORIES
- 9 tiny twist fat-free pretzels
  50 CALORIES

WEEK 2, DAY 5, TOTAL: 1,402 CALORIES

Taking time for breakfast has lots of benefits. You get energy, raise your metabolism and are less likely to overeat later. If preparing breakfast is too difficult on busy weekday mornings, a little planning can do wonders. Smoothies can be made a day early and many breakfast bakes can be prepared the night before.

day 6

BREAKFAST:

- 1 wedge Fajita Frittata (p. 104)
  137 CALORIES

- served with 1/4 cup salsa
  FREE FOOD

- 1 cup Mint Berry Blast (p. 89)
  65 CALORIES

- 1 slice whole wheat bread, toasted
  69 CALORIES

- spread with 1 tablespoon no-sugar-added jam
  FREE FOOD

- 1 cup hot tea (with sugar substitute if desired)
  FREE FOOD

BREAKFAST TOTAL: 271 CALORIES

LUNCH:

- 1 Tangy Tuna Bunwich (p. 143)
  336 CALORIES

- 1 cup baby carrots
  80 CALORIES

- 1/2 cup fresh blueberries
  41 CALORIES

- 1 dill pickle spear
  FREE FOOD

- 1 glass ice water
  FREE FOOD

LUNCH TOTAL: 457 CALORIES

DINNER & DESSERT:

- 1 serving Corny Chicken Wrap (p. 238)
  363 CALORIES

- 1 big green salad (see Free Foods Chart on p. 45)
  with 1 tablespoon reduced-fat salad dressing
  FREE FOOD

- 2 sesame breadsticks (5g each)
  40 CALORIES

- 1 cup fat-free milk
  86 CALORIES

- 2 Chocolate Gingersnaps (p. 272)
  138 CALORIES

- 1 cup hot tea (with sugar substitute if desired)
  FREE FOOD

DINNER TOTAL: 541 CALORIES

SNACKS:

- 1 medium apple
  72 CALORIES

- 1-1/2 cups air-popped popcorn
  47 CALORIES

WEEK 2, DAY 6, TOTAL: 1,388 CALORIES

day 7

BREAKFAST:

- 1/4 cup Paradise Granola (p. 105)
  132 CALORIES

- sprinkled onto 1 container yogurt
  (6-ounce nonfat fruit variety)
  160 CALORIES

- 1/2 cup orange juice
  55 CALORIES

- 1 cup of coffee (with sugar substitute and
  1 tablespoon liquid nondairy creamer, if desired)
  FREE FOOD

BREAKFAST TOTAL: 347 CALORIES

LUNCH:

- 1-3/4 cups Chicken Spaghetti Salad (p. 141)
  329 CALORIES

- 1/3 cup red grapes
  43 CALORIES

- 1 cup brewed iced tea
  (with sugar substitute if desired)
  FREE FOOD

LUNCH TOTAL: 372 CALORIES

DINNER & DESSERT:

- 1 Braised Pork Chop (p. 183)
  180 CALORIES

- 2/3 cup Spanish Rice (p. 253)
  156 CALORIES

- Steamed fresh or frozen green beans topped with
  1 teaspoon reduced-fat margarine
  FREE FOOD

- 1 big green salad (see Free Foods Chart on p. 45)
  with 1 tablespoon reduced-fat salad dressing
  FREE FOOD

- 1 cup fat-free milk
  86 CALORIES

- 1 Dark Chocolate Butterscotch Brownie (p. 279)
  110 CALORIES

DINNER TOTAL: 532 CALORIES

SNACKS:

- 1 cup fresh raspberries
  60 CALORIES

- 3 pieces snack rye bread topped with 1
  tablespoon reduced-fat garden vegetable cream
  cheese and 6 cucumber slices
  89 CALORIES

WEEK 2, DAY 7, TOTAL: 1,400 CALORIES

day 1

BREAKFAST:

- 3 slices Sweet Berry Bruschetta (p. 85)
276 CALORIES

- 1/2 cup orange juice
55 CALORIES

- 1 cup of coffee (with sugar substitute and 1 tablespoon liquid nondairy creamer if desired)
FREE FOOD

BREAKFAST TOTAL: 331 CALORIES

LUNCH:

- 2 Tuna Artichoke Melts (2 open-faced sandwiches) (p. 135)
335 CALORIES

- 1/3 cup red grapes
43 CALORIES

- 1 cup brewed iced tea (with sugar substitute if desired)
FREE FOOD

LUNCH TOTAL: 378 CALORIES

DINNER & DESSERT:

- 1 serving Balsamic-Seasoned Steak (p. 159)
188 CALORIES

- 3/4 cup Colorful Roasted Veggies (p. 243)
88 CALORIES

- 1/2 small baked russet potato
69 CALORIES

- with 1 teaspoon reduced-fat margarine
FREE FOOD

- 1 Double Chocolate Cupcake (p. 281)
139 CALORIES

- 1/2 cup fat-free milk
48 CALORIES

DINNER TOTAL: 532 CALORIES

SNACKS:

- 3/4 cup baby carrots
60 CALORIES

- 1-1/2 cups air-popped popcorn
47 CALORIES

- 2 chocolate kisses
49 CALORIES

WEEK 3, DAY 1 TOTAL: 1,397 CALORIES

day 2

BREAKFAST:

- 2 Overnight Yeast Waffles (p. 90)
148 CALORIES

- drizzled with 4 tablespoons of Orange Sauce (p. 87)
68 CALORIES

- 2 Breakfast Patties (p. 85)
85 CALORIES

- 1 cup hot tea (with sugar substitute if desired)
FREE FOOD

BREAKFAST TOTAL: 301 CALORIES

LUNCH:

- 1-1/2 cups Vegetable Beef Stew (p. 136)
278 CALORIES

- 1 whole wheat dinner roll
76 CALORIES

- spread with 1 teaspoon reduced-fat margarine spread
FREE FOOD

- 1 big green salad (see Free Foods Chart on p. 45) with 1 tablespoon reduced-fat salad dressing
FREE FOOD

- 1 cup fat-free milk
86 CALORIES

LUNCH TOTAL: 440 CALORIES

DINNER & DESSERT:

- 1 serving Chicken Marsala (p. 160)
247 CALORIES

- 1 serving Savory Asparagus (p. 244)
74 CALORIES

- 1/2 cup cooked long-grain white rice
103 CALORIES

- 1 Marbled Chocolate Cheesecake Bar (p. 270)
95 CALORIES

- 1 cup of coffee (with sugar substitute and 1 tablespoon liquid nondairy creamer if desired)
FREE FOOD

DINNER TOTAL: 519 CALORIES

SNACKS:

- 1/2 cup sliced fresh strawberries with 2 tablespoons reduced-fat whipped topping
47 CALORIES

- 1/3 cup 1% cottage cheese with 1/4 cup unsweetened pineapple tidbits
81 CALORIES

WEEK 3, DAY 2 TOTAL: 1,388 CALORIES

day 3

BREAKFAST:

- 1 Lemon-Blueberry Oat Muffin (p. 96)
166 CALORIES

- 1 medium banana
100 CALORIES

- 1 cup fat-free milk
86 CALORIES

BREAKFAST TOTAL: 352 CALORIES

LUNCH:

- 1 Taco Salad Wrap (p. 136)
345 CALORIES

- 8 white corn tortilla chips
93 CALORIES

- with 1/4 cup salsa
FREE FOOD

- 1 can diet soft drink
FREE FOOD

LUNCH TOTAL: 438 CALORIES

DINNER & DESSERT:

- 1 serving Glazed Pork Medallions (p. 162)
200 CALORIES

- 3/4 cup Stir-Fried Carrots (p. 258)
106 CALORIES

- 1 big green salad (see Free Foods Chart on p. 45)
with 1 tablespoon reduced-fat salad dressing
FREE FOOD

- 1 glass ice water
FREE FOOD

- 1 piece Fudgy Chocolate Dessert (p. 290)
200 CALORIES

DINNER TOTAL: 506 CALORIES

SNACKS:

- 1/2 cup Spiced Honey Pretzels (p. 72)
98 CALORIES

- 1 small orange
45 CALORIES

- 1/2 piece string cheese
40 CALORIES

WEEK 3, DAY 3 TOTAL: 1,381 CALORIES

For a lovely lighter dessert, top off slices of angel food cake with fresh fruit and a dollop of reduced-fat whipped topping or frozen yogurt.

day 4

BREAKFAST:

- 1 container yogurt (6-ounce nonfat fruit variety)
160 CALORIES

- topped with 1/4 cup Toasted Almond Granola (p. 109)
106 CALORIES

- 1 slice whole wheat bread, toasted
69 CALORIES

- spread with 1 teaspoon reduced-fat margarine
FREE FOOD

- 1 cup hot tea (with sugar substitute if desired)
FREE FOOD

BREAKFAST TOTAL: 335 CALORIES

LUNCH:

- 1-1/2 cups Zippy Corn Chowder (p. 120)
285 CALORIES

- 4 saltine crackers
52 CALORIES

- 1 big green salad (see Free Foods Chart on p. 45)
with 1 tablespoon reduced-fat salad dressing
FREE FOOD

- 1 medium pear
96 CALORIES

- 1 bottle flavored water
FREE FOOD

LUNCH TOTAL: 432 CALORIES

DINNER & DESSERT:

- 1 serving Easy Chicken Potpie (p. 208)
342 CALORIES

- 1 glass ice water
FREE FOOD

- 1 Tiramisu Parfait (p. 287)
189 CALORIES

- 1 cup of coffee (with sugar substitute and
1 tablespoon liquid nondairy creamer if desired)
FREE FOOD

DINNER TOTAL: 531 CALORIES

SNACKS:

- 1 miniature bagel with 1 tablespoon reduced-fat chive and onion cream cheese
63 CALORIES

- 1 medium plum
40 CALORIES

WEEK 3, DAY 4 TOTAL: 1,402 CALORIES

meal plan | THE COMFORT FOOD DIET

day 5

BREAKFAST:

- 1 serving Mushroom Spinach Omelet (p. 99)
  110 CALORIES
- 2 slices Baked Canadian-Style Bacon (p. 87)
  97 CALORIES
- 1 slice whole wheat bread, toasted
  69 CALORIES
- spread with 1 tablespoon no-sugar-added jam
  FREE FOOD
- 1/2 cup cubed fresh pineapple
  37 CALORIES
- 1 cup hot tea (with sugar substitute if desired)
  FREE FOOD

BREAKFAST TOTAL: 313 CALORIES

LUNCH:

- 1 serving Cantaloupe Chicken Orzo Salad (p. 141)
  345 CALORIES
- 1 whole wheat dinner roll
  76 CALORIES
- spread with 1 teaspoon reduced-fat margarine
  FREE FOOD
- 1 glass ice water
  FREE FOOD

LUNCH TOTAL: 421 CALORIES

DINNER & DESSERT:

- 1 serving Southwest Pasta Bake (p. 224)
  328 CALORIES
- Steamed fresh broccoli florets topped with 1 teaspoon reduced-fat margarine
  FREE FOOD
- 1 cup fat-free milk
  86 CALORIES
- 2 Banana Chocolate Chip Cookies (p. 269)
  132 CALORIES

DINNER TOTAL: 546 CALORIES

SNACKS:

- 1/2 English muffin topped with 1 slice tomato and 1 tablespoon shredded part-skim mozzarella cheese, broiled
  87 CALORIES
- 1 cup prepared sugar-free flavored gelatin
  8 CALORIES
- 1/2 cup baby carrots
  25 CALORIES

WEEK 3, DAY 5 TOTAL: 1,400 CALORIES

day 6

BREAKFAST:

- 1 Poppy Seed Doughnut (p. 92)
  199 CALORIES
- 1 serving Peach Smoothie (p. 93)
  120 CALORIES

BREAKFAST TOTAL: 319 CALORIES

LUNCH:

- 1 slice Baked Deli Focaccia Sandwich (p. 122)
  250 CALORIES
- 20 baked potato chips
  200 CALORIES
- 1 can mineral water
  FREE FOOD

LUNCH TOTAL: 450 CALORIES

DINNER & DESSERT:

- 1 serving Chicken with Mustard Gravy (p. 226)
  262 CALORIES
- 2/3 cup Caramelized Onion Mashed Potatoes (p. 262)
  200 CALORIES
- 1 big green salad (see Free Foods Chart on p. 45) with 1 tablespoon reduced-fat salad dressing
  FREE FOOD
- 1 Wonton Sundae (p. 268)
  83 CALORIES
- 1 cup hot tea (with sugar substitute if desired)
  FREE FOOD

DINNER TOTAL: 545 CALORIES

SNACKS:

- 2 medium celery ribs with 1 tablespoon fat-free ranch salad dressing
  40 CALORIES
- 1/2 cup fresh blueberries
  41 CALORIES

WEEK 3, DAY 6 TOTAL: 1,395 CALORIES

Confused about which oils to use in cooking? The Taste of Home Test Kitchen uses olive and canola oils in lighter recipes since they give the best results. Plus, they contain high levels of monounsaturated fats, which scientists believe may decrease overall cholesterol levels without decreasing levels of HDL (good) cholesterol.

Polyunsaturated fats, such as safflower and corn oils, are also good for cooking since they may help decrease cholesterol. However, polyunsaturated fats many not be as heart-healthy as monounsaturated fats because it's thought that they may decrease HDL (good) cholesterol as well as LDL (bad) cholesterol.

day 7

BREAKFAST:

- 1 serving Ham 'n' Cheese Squares (p. 95)
  141 CALORIES

- 1 Custard Berry Parfait (p. 91)
  119 CALORIES

- 1 slice whole wheat bread, toasted
  69 CALORIES

- spread with 1 teaspoon reduced-fat margarine
  FREE FOOD

- 1 cup of coffee (with sugar substitute and 1 tablespoon liquid nondairy creamer if desired)
  FREE FOOD

BREAKFAST TOTAL: 329 CALORIES

LUNCH:

- 1 Spicy Buffalo Chicken Wrap (p. 134)
  273 CALORIES

- 1 big green salad (see the Free Foods Chart on p. 45)
  FREE FOOD

- with 3 tablespoons of reduced-fat blue cheese salad dressing
  42 CALORIES

- 1 can diet soft drink
  FREE FOOD

LUNCH TOTAL: 315 CALORIES

DINNER & DESSERT:

- 1 serving Swiss Steak (p. 227)
  255 CALORIES

- 1/2 cup cooked long-grain white rice
  103 CALORIES

- Steamed fresh or frozen green beans
  FREE FOOD

- 1 cup brewed iced tea (with sugar substitute if desired)
  FREE FOOD

- 1 slice Yummy Chocolate Cake (p. 286)
  197 CALORIES

- 1 glass ice water
  FREE FOOD

DINNER TOTAL: 555 CALORIES

SNACKS:

- 1 cup Cajun Popcorn (p. 73)
  77 CALORIES

- 1/2 medium pear and 1/2 ounce reduced-fat cheddar cheese
  94 CALORIES

- 1 chocolate kiss
  25 CALORIES

WEEK 3, DAY 7 TOTAL: 1,395 CALORIES

day 1

BREAKFAST:

- 1 Egg 'n' Bacon Sandwich (p. 98)
  179 CALORIES

- 1 cup Gingered Melon (p. 86)
  76 CALORIES

- 1 cup hot tea (with sugar substitute if desired)
  FREE FOOD

BREAKFAST TOTAL: 255 CALORIES

LUNCH:

- 2 cups Crab Pasta Salad (p. 132)
  386 CALORIES

- 1 cup cubed cantaloupe
  54 CALORIES

- 1 cup prepared sugar-free lemonade drink mix
  FREE FOOD

LUNCH TOTAL: 440 CALORIES

DINNER & DESSERT:

- 1 Two-Cheese Turkey Enchilada (p. 228)
  329 CALORIES

- Steamed fresh or frozen pea pods
  FREE FOOD

- 1 big green salad (see Free Foods Chart on p. 45) with 1 tablespoon reduced-fat salad dressing
  FREE FOOD

- 1 cup fat-free milk
  86 CALORIES

- 1 piece Raspberry Custard Tart (p. 288)
  198 CALORIES

DINNER TOTAL: 613 CALORIES

SNACKS:

- 1/3 cup red grapes
  43 CALORIES

- 1 slice reduced-calorie wheat bread, toasted
  48 CALORIES

- spread with 1 tablespoon no-sugar-added jam
  FREE FOOD

WEEK 4, DAY 1 TOTAL: 1,399 CALORIES

In order to best fit your schedule, feel free to move days around on this meal planner.

day 2

BREAKFAST:

- 1 Raspberry Streusel Muffin (p. 98)
  181 CALORIES

- 1 cup Berry Best Smoothies (p. 94)
  108 CALORIES

- 1 cup brewed iced tea
  (with sugar substitute if desired)
  FREE FOOD

  BREAKFAST TOTAL: 289 CALORIES

LUNCH:

- 1-1/2 cups Turkey Vegetable Soup (p. 138)
  272 CALORIES

- 1 whole wheat dinner roll
  76 CALORIES

- spread with 1 teaspoon reduced-fat margarine
  FREE FOOD

- 1 piece of string cheese
  80 CALORIES

- 1 can diet soft drink
  FREE FOOD

  LUNCH TOTAL: 428 CALORIES

DINNER & DESSERT:

- 1 serving Oven Fish 'n' Chips (p. 230)
  358 CALORIES

- Served with 1 tablespoon ketchup
  FREE FOOD

- 1 dill pickle spear
  FREE FOOD

- Shredded cabbage topped with 1
  tablespoon reduced-fat salad dressing
  FREE FOOD

- 1 cup fat-free milk
  86 CALORIES

  DINNER TOTAL: 444 CALORIES

SNACKS:

- 1 medium apple
  72 CALORIES

- 4 pieces Marshmallow Fudge (p. 267)
  164 CALORIES

  WEEK 4, DAY 2 TOTAL: 1,397 CALORIES

day 3

BREAKFAST:

- 2 wedges Garden Frittata (p. 93)
  252 CALORIES

- 1 cup cubed fresh pineapple
  74 CALORIES

- 1 cup of coffee (with sugar substitute and 1
  tablespoon liquid nondairy creamer if desired)
  FREE FOOD

  BREAKFAST TOTAL: 326 CALORIES

LUNCH:

- 1-1/2 cups Pizza Pasta Salad (p. 139)
  383 CALORIES

- 1 medium plum
  40 CALORIES

- 1 bottle flavored water
  FREE FOOD

  LUNCH TOTAL: 423 CALORIES

DINNER & DESSERT:

- 1 serving Gingered Pepper Steak (p. 170)
  235 CALORIES

- 1/2 cup prepared long-grain white rice
  103 CALORIES

- 1 big green salad (see Free Foods Chart on p. 45)
  with 1 tablespoon reduced-fat salad dressing
  FREE FOOD

- 1 glass ice water
  FREE FOOD

- 1 serving Blackberry Cobbler (p. 289)
  199 CALORIES

  DINNER TOTAL: 537 CALORIES

SNACKS:

- 1 Cappuccino Truffle (p. 273)
  43 CALORIES

- 1 piece string cheese
  80 CALORIES

  WEEK 4, DAY 3 TOTAL: 1,409 CALORIES

Not all salads are created equal. Add too many croutons, bacon bits or cheese and your healthy meal becomes a nutritional no-no. Build a better salad by using romaine lettuce or spinach as a base instead of iceberg. When selecting a dressing, aim for less than 50 calories per two-tablespoon serving and ideally try light versions or fat-free ones. Load up on veggies to boost your intake of essential vitamins and minerals.

day 4

BREAKFAST:

- 1 Spicy Scrambled Egg Sandwich (p. 110)
  248 CALORIES

- 1 medium banana
  100 CALORIES

- 1 cup of coffee (with sugar substitute and 1 tablespoon liquid nondairy creamer if desired)
  FREE FOOD

BREAKFAST TOTAL: 348 CALORIES

LUNCH:

- 1 Lime Jalapeno Turkey Wrap (p. 138)
  291 CALORIES

- 8 white corn tortilla chips
  93 CALORIES

- with 1/4 cup salsa
  FREE FOOD

- 1/2 cup baby carrots
  25 CALORIES

- 1 cup brewed iced tea (with sugar substitute if desired)
  FREE FOOD

LUNCH TOTAL: 409 CALORIES

DINNER & DESSERT:

- 1 piece Beef and Spinach Lasagna (p. 214)
  281 CALORIES

- 1 big green salad (see Free Foods Chart on p. 45) with 1 tablespoon reduced-fat salad dressing
  FREE FOOD

- 1 cup fat-free milk
  86 CALORIES

DINNER TOTAL: 367 CALORIES

SNACKS:

- 1/2 cup Strawberry Ice Cream (p. 286)
  153 CALORIES

- 2 tablespoons hummus with 1/4 of a pita and 1/4 of a red bell pepper
  93 CALORIES

WEEK 4, DAY 4 TOTAL: 1,370 CALORIES

> Because they rely on a tasty assortment of herbs and seasonings, ethnic foods often make delicious, low-calorie meal options.

day 5

BREAKFAST:

- 1 serving Orange Oatmeal (p. 108)
  222 CALORIES

- 1 patty Savory Apple-Chicken Sausage (p. 90)
  92 CALORIES

- 1/3 cup red grapes
  43 CALORIES

- 1 cup hot tea (with sugar substitute if desired)
  FREE FOOD

BREAKFAST TOTAL: 357 CALORIES

LUNCH:

- 1 Shredded Beef Barbecue sandwich (p. 140)
  313 CALORIES

- 1 big green salad (see Free Foods Chart on p. 45) with 1 tablespoon reduced-fat salad dressing
  FREE FOOD

- 1 dill pickle spear
  FREE FOOD

- 1 medium apple
  72 CALORIES

- 1 can diet soft drink
  FREE FOOD

LUNCH TOTAL: 385 CALORIES

DINNER & DESSERT:

- 1 cup Creamy Turkey Casserole (p. 211)
  311 CALORIES

- 1 cup fat-free milk
  86 CALORIES

- 1 Cranberry Cheesecake Bar (p. 284)
  142 CALORIES

- 1 cup of coffee (with sugar substitute and 1 tablespoon liquid nondairy creamer if desired)
  FREE FOOD

DINNER TOTAL: 539 CALORIES

SNACKS:

- 1/2 cup sugar-free chocolate pudding (prepared with fat-free milk) topped with a crushed chocolate wafer
  99 CALORIES

- 1/2 cup baby carrots
  25 CALORIES

WEEK 4, DAY 5 TOTAL: 1,405 CALORIES

day 6

BREAKFAST:

- 1 Sausage Breakfast Wrap (p. 108)
  277 CALORIES

- 1/2 cup fresh blueberries
  41 CALORIES

- with 2 tablespoons fat-free frozen whipped topping
  FREE FOOD

- 1 cup hot tea (with sugar substitute if desired)
  FREE FOOD

BREAKFAST TOTAL: 318 CALORIES

LUNCH:

- 2 servings Seafood Salad Pitas (2 filled pita halves) (p. 120)
  324 CALORIES

- 1 medium pear
  96 CALORIES

- 1 cup prepared sugar-free lemonade drink mix
  FREE FOOD

LUNCH TOTAL: 420 CALORIES

DINNER & DESSERT:

- 1 piece Spaghetti Pizza Casserole (p. 218)
  274 CALORIES

- 1 slice reduced-calorie wheat bread
  48 CALORIES

- spread with 1 teaspoon reduced-fat margarine
  FREE FOOD

- 1 big green salad (see Free Foods Chart on p. 45) with 1 tablespoon reduced-fat salad dressing
  FREE FOOD

- 1 cup fat-free milk
  86 CALORIES

DINNER TOTAL: 408 CALORIES

SNACKS:

- 1 slice Lemon Blueberry Cheesecake (p. 290)
  171 CALORIES

- 1/2 small apple with 2 tablespoons fat-free caramel ice cream topping
  93 CALORIES

WEEK 4, DAY 6 TOTAL: 1,410 CALORIES

day 7

BREAKFAST:

- 2 High-Octane Pancakes (p. 99)
  284 CALORIES

- with 2 tablespoons sugar-free syrup
  FREE FOOD

- 1/2 small grapefruit with 1 teaspoon sugar
  48 CALORIES

- 1 cup of coffee (with sugar substitute and 1 tablespoon liquid nondairy creamer if desired)
  FREE FOOD

BREAKFAST TOTAL: 332 CALORIES

LUNCH:

- 1 Chili Potpie (p. 148)
  354 CALORIES

- 1 medium apple
  72 CALORIES

- 1 can mineral water
  FREE FOOD

LUNCH TOTAL: 426 CALORIES

DINNER & DESSERT:

- 1 cup Turkey Fettuccine Skillet (p. 232)
  361 CALORIES

- 3/4 cup minestrone soup
  90 CALORIES

- Steamed fresh broccoli and cauliflower florets topped with 1 teaspoon reduced-fat margarine
  FREE FOOD

- 1 cup fat-free milk
  86 CALORIES

DINNER TOTAL: 537 CALORIES

SNACKS:

- 2 gingersnap cookies spread with 1 tablespoon reduced-fat strawberry cream cheese
  94 CALORIES

- 1 cup prepared sugar-free flavored gelatin
  8 CALORIES

- with 2 tablespoons fat-free frozen whipped topping
  FREE FOOD

WEEK 4, DAY 7 TOTAL: 1,397 CALORIES

Keep fresh sliced mushrooms and washed and peeled carrots on hand. They make easy additions to side dishes and are free foods.

day 1

BREAKFAST:

- 1 wedge Italian Garden Frittata (p. 102)
  183 CALORIES
- 1 Peach Smoothie (p. 93)
  120 CALORIES
- 1/4 cup fresh blueberries
  21 CALORIES

BREAKFAST TOTAL: 324 CALORIES

LUNCH:

- 1 slice Baked Deli Focaccia Sandwich (p. 122)
  240 CALORIES
- 1 serving Grape Tomato Mozzarella Salad (p. 129)
  85 CALORIES
- 1 small orange
  45 CALORIES
- 1 cup fat-free milk
  86 CALORIES

LUNCH TOTAL: 456 CALORIES

DINNER & DESSERT:

- 3 ounces Sweet 'n' Tangy Pot Roast (p. 160)
  249 CALORIES
- 3/4 cup Rosemary Red Potatoes (p. 256)
  153 CALORIES
- 1/2 cup Creamed Spinach (p. 260)
  131 CALORIES
- 1 glass ice water
  FREE FOOD
- 1 Cappuccino Truffle (p. 273)
  43 CALORIES
- 1 cup of coffee (with sugar substitute and
  1 tablespoon liquid nondairy creamer if desired)
  FREE FOOD

DINNER TOTAL: 576 CALORIES

SNACKS:

- 1-1/2 cups air-popped popcorn
  47 CALORIES
- 1 serving Frosted Hazelnuts (p. 83)
  17 CALORIES

WEEK 5, DAY 1, TOTAL: 1,420 CALORIES

To add fiber to your diet, start the day with a bowl of oat cereal or a slice or two of whole wheat toast. Cut back on the amount of ground beef called for in a recipe and replace it with oats, barley or bulgar. Substitute brown rice for white rice. Forgo the potato side dish and make wild rice instead.

day 2

BREAKFAST:

- 2 Buttermilk Buckwheat Pancakes (p. 95)
  195 CALORIES
- with 2 tablespoons of Apple Syrup (p. 89)
  20 CALORIES
- 1 cup Creamy Peaches (p. 105)
  127 CALORIES
- 1 cup of coffee (with sugar substitute and
  1 tablespoon liquid nondairy creamer if desired)
  FREE FOOD

BREAKFAST TOTAL: 342 CALORIES

LUNCH:

- 1-1/2 cups Bean and Pasta Soup (p. 126)
  218 CALORIES
- 6 saltine crackers
  78 CALROIES
- 1/3 cup of red grapes
  43 CALORIES
- 1 cup fat-free milk
  86 CALORIES

LUNCH TOTAL: 425 CALORIES

DINNER & DESSERT:

- 1 cup Turkey Fettuccine Skillet (p. 232)
  361 CALORIES
- 1 big green salad (see Free Foods Chart on p. 45)
  with 1 tablespoon reduced-fat salad dressing
  FREE FOOD
- 1 can diet soft drink
  FREE FOOD
- 1 piece Mixed Berry Pizza (p. 283)
  110 CALORIES
- 1 cup hot tea (with sugar substitute if desired)
  FREE FOOD

DINNER TOTAL: 471 CALORIES

SNACKS:

- 1 cup Six-Vegetable Juice (p. 76)
  66 CALORIES
- 1 Ham 'n' Asparagus Roll-Up (p. 82)
  75 CALORIES

WEEK 5, DAY 2, TOTAL: 1,379 CALORIES

day 3

BREAKFAST:

- 1 Chocolate Chip Banana Muffin (p. 91)
  191 CALORIES
- 1/2 cup cubed fresh pineapple
  37 CALORIES
- 1 cup fat-free milk
  86 CALORIES

BREAKFAST TOTAL: 314 CALORIES

LUNCH:

- 1 piece Antipasto-Stuffed Baguette (p. 129)
  52 CALORIES
- 1 cup Pizza Pasta Salad (p. 139)
  255 CALORIES
- 1 cup cubed cantaloupe
  54 CALORIES
- 1 can diet soft drink
  FREE FOOD

LUNCH TOTAL: 361 CALORIES

DINNER & DESSERT:

- 4 ounces Glazed Pork Medallions (p. 162)
  200 CALORIES
- 3/4 cup Stir-Fried Carrots (p. 258)
  106 CALORIES
- 1/2 cup Seasoned Brown Rice (p. 261)
  118 CALORIES
- 1 glass ice water
  FREE FOOD
- 1 Granola Fudge Cluster (p. 281)
  114 CALORIES

DINNER TOTAL: 538 CALORIES

SNACKS:

- 1 Crunchy Raisin Treat (p. 78)
  86 CALORIES
- 3 Veggie Tortilla Pinwheels (p. 80)
  94 CALORIES

WEEK 5, DAY 3, TOTAL: 1,393 CALORIES

Drinking water has lots of benefits for your body and can keep you from feeling hungry between meals. Here are a few suggestions to help you get into the habit of drinking water:

- Keep a pitcher of water in your refrigerator so it's handy, well-chilled and inviting.
- Keep a big mug or bottle of water with you at work. You'll find yourself reaching for it automatically.
- Perk up plain water with a squeeze of lemon or even lime juice.

day 4

BREAKFAST:

- 1 large scrambled egg
  101 CALORIES
- 1 slice whole wheat bread, toasted
  69 CALORIES
- spread with 1 teaspoon reduced-fat margarine
  FREE FOOD
- 1/2 cup orange juice
  55 CALORIES
- 1/2 cup Grapefruit Orange Medley (p. 97)
  140 CALORIES

BREAKFAST TOTAL: 365 CALORIES

LUNCH:

- 1 Jamaican Jerk Turkey Wrap (p. 133)
  295 CALORIES
- 1 big green salad (see the Free Foods Chart on p. 45)
  FREE FOOD
- with 2 tablespoons of reduced-fat blue cheese salad dressing
  28 CALORIES
- 1 cup fat-free milk
  86 CALORIES

LUNCH TOTAL: 409 CALORIES

DINNER & DESSERT:

- 1 cup Scalloped Potatoes and Ham (p. 161)
  226 CALORIES
- 3/4 cup Garlic Green Beans (p. 247)
  51 CALORIES
- 1 glass ice water
  FREE FOOD
- 1 serving Mocha Pudding Cakes (p. 285)
  227 CALORIES
- 1 cup coffee (with sugar substitute and 1 tablespoon liquid nondairy creamer if desired)
  FREE FOOD

DINNER TOTAL: 504 CALORIES

SNACKS:

- 1 medium peach
  40 CALORIES
- 1 piece string cheese
  80 CALORIES

WEEK 5, DAY 4, TOTAL: 1,398 CALORIES

---

day 5

BREAKFAST:

- 2 Strawberry Crepe Roll-Ups (p. 92)
  137 CALORIES
- 2 Breakfast Patties (p. 85)
  85 CALORIES
- 1 cup hot tea (with sugar substitute if desired)
  FREE FOOD
- 1 medium banana
  100 CALORIES

BREAKFAST TOTAL: **322 CALORIES**

LUNCH:

- 3/4 cup Waldorf Tuna Salad (p. 135)
  340 CALORIES
- 1 whole wheat dinner roll
  76 CALORIES
- 1/2 piece string cheese
  40 CALORIES
- 1 can mineral water
  FREE FOOD

LUNCH TOTAL: **456 CALORIES**

DINNER & DESSERT:

- 1 serving Gingered Pepper Steak (p. 170)
  235 CALORIES
- 1/2 cup prepared long-grain white rice
  103 CALORIES
- 1 cup fat-free milk
  86 CALORIES
- 1 Baklava Tartlet (p. 272)
  76 CALORIES

DINNER TOTAL: **500 CALORIES**

SNACKS:

- 1 serving Lo-Cal Apple Snack (p. 76)
  88 CALORIES
- 1 cup prepared sugar-free flavored gelatin
  8 CALORIES
- with 2 tablespoons fat-free frozen whipped topping
  FREE FOOD

WEEK 5, DAY 5, TOTAL: **1,374 CALORIES**

day 6

BREAKFAST:

- 1 cup Warm 'n' Fruity Breakfast Cereal (p. 100)
  185 CALORIES
- 1/2 cup non-fat fruit yogurt
  107 CALORIES
- 1/2 cup of orange juice
  55 CALORIES

BREAKFAST TOTAL: **347 CALORIES**

LUNCH:

- 1 Ranch Chicken Salad Sandwich (p. 142)
  257 CALORIES
- 10 baked potato chips
  100 CALORIES
- 1 dill pickle spear
  FREE FOOD
- 1 cup fat-free milk
  86 CALORIES

LUNCH TOTAL: **443 CALORIES**

DINNER & DESSERT:

- 1 serving Chicken Marsala (p. 160)
  247 CALORIES
- 3/4 cup Red Potatoes with Beans (p. 247)
  49 CALORIES
- 1 big green salad (see Free Foods Chart on p. 45) with 1 tablespoon reduced-fat salad dressing
  FREE FOOD
- 1 glass ice water
  FREE FOOD
- 1 slice Lemon Blueberry Cheesecake (p. 290)
  171 CALORIES

DINNER TOTAL: **467 CALORIES**

SNACKS:

- 3 Mini Rice Cake Snacks (p. 76)
  81 CALORIES
- 1 cup Spiced Coffee with Cream (p. 83)
  55 CALORIES

WEEK 5, DAY 6, TOTAL: **1,393 CALORIES**

Boost your daily intake of omega-3 fatty acids with fresh seafood, including salmon, tuna and mackerel. Eggs, milk and orange juice fortified with omega-3 fatty acids are also good sources. Another easy trick is to sprinkle ground flax seed on cereal or salads or substitute flax seed oil for other oils.

day 7

BREAKFAST:

- 1 slice Spinach Omelet Brunch Roll (p. 101)
  160 CALORIES
- 1 cup Mango Smoothie (p. 114)
  237 CALORIES

BREAKFAST TOTAL: 397 CALORIES

LUNCH:

- 3 ounces Spicy Pork Tenderloin Salad (p. 137)
  301 CALORIES
- 1 medium pair
  96 CALORIES
- 5 wheat crackers
  45 CALORIES
- 1 cup brewed iced tea
  (with sugar substitute if desired)
  FREE FOOD

LUNCH TOTAL: 442 CALORIES

DINNER & DESSERT:

- 1 Black Bean and Rice Enchilada (p. 194)
  271 CALORIES
- with 2 tablespoons fat-free sour cream
  FREE FOOD
- steamed fresh green beans topped
  with 1 teaspoon reduced-fat margarine
  FREE FOOD
- 1 cup fat-free milk
  86 CALORIES

DINNER TOTAL: 357 CALORIES

SNACKS:

- 1 Sunflower Popcorn Bar (p. 81)
  96 CALORIES
- 4 chocolate kisses
  98 CALORIES

WEEK 5, DAY 7, TOTAL: 1,390 CALORIES

Bad sleep habits can contribute to weight gain. Here are a few tricks to sleep better:

- Don't exercise just before bedtime. Exercise does help people sleep better but it's best to give your body five hours to cool down after exercise to make falling asleep easier.
- Put away the day's stresses before turning in. A warm soothing bath, reading or meditation can have a relaxing effect.
- Try your best to rise at the same time every day. Having a routine helps your body establish a predictable sleep-wake cycle.

day 1

BREAKFAST:

- 1 Fruity French Toast Sandwich (p. 115)
  218 CALORIES
- 1 cup Berry Yogurt Shakes (p. 103)
  136 CALORIES
- 1 cup hot tea (with sugar substitute if desired)
  FREE FOOD

BREAKFAST TOTAL: 354 CALORIES

LUNCH:

- 1 serving Macaroni Salad Tomato Cups (p. 146)
  272 CALORIES
- 1/2 English muffin topped with 1 slice tomato and 1 tablespoon shredded part-skim mozzarella cheese, broiled
  87 CALORIES
- 1 medium banana
  100 CALORIES
- 1 cup prepared sugar-free lemonade drink mix
  FREE FOOD

LUNCH TOTAL: 459 CALORIES

DINNER & DESSERT:

- 1 piece Beef and Spinach Lasagna (p. 214)
  281 CALORIES
- 1 whole wheat dinner roll
  76 CALORIES
- 1 big green salad (see Free Foods Chart on p. 45) with 1 tablespoon reduced-fat salad dressing
  FREE FOOD
- 1 cup fat-free milk
  86 CALORIES

DINNER TOTAL: 443 CALORIES

SNACKS:

- 1 cup whole strawberries
  45 CALORIES
- 2/3 cup Cheerios with 1/4 cup fat-free milk
  93 CALORIES

WEEK 6, DAY 1, TOTAL: 1,394 CALORIES

Keep a bag of fresh spinach on hand. The crispy leaves make it a snap to toss together a salad, but you can also add the greens to soups, use them to top off lean hamburgers or even jazz up spaghetti sauce.

day 2

BREAKFAST:

- 1 Spicy Scrambled Egg Sandwich (p. 110)
  248 CALORIES
- 1 cup Berry Best Smoothie (p. 94)
  108 CALORIES
- 1 cup coffee (with sugar substitute and
  1 tablespoon liquid nondairy creamer if desired)
  FREE FOOD

  BREAKFAST TOTAL: 356 CALORIES

LUNCH:

- 1 Black Bean Burger (p. 150)
  381 CALORIES
- with 1 tablespoon each ketchup and mustard
  FREE FOOD
- 1/2 cup Oven French Fries (p. 259)
  111 CALORIES
- 1 can diet soft drink
  FREE FOOD

  LUNCH TOTAL: 492 CALORIES

DINNER & DESSERT:

- 4 ounces Tasty Italian Chicken (p. 163)
  163 CALORIES
- 1/2 cup cooked whole wheat spaghetti
  88 CALORIES
- 1/2 cup Roasted Italian Vegetables (p. 242)
  68 CALORIES
- 1 big green salad (see Free Foods Chart on p. 45)
  with 1 tablespoon reduced-fat salad dressing
  FREE FOOD
- 1 cup fat-free milk
  86 CALORIES

  DINNER TOTAL: 405 CALORIES

SNACKS:

- 3 Veggie Tortilla Pinwheels (p. 80)
  94 CALORIES
- 1/2 piece string cheese
  40 CALORIES

  WEEK 6, DAY 2, TOTAL: 1,387 CALORIES

day 3

BREAKFAST:

- 1 Lemon-Blueberry Oat Muffin (p. 96)
  166 CALORIES
- 1 cup Frappe Mocha (p. 100)
  114 CALORIES
- 1 medium apple
  72 CALORIES

  BREAKFAST TOTAL: 352 CALORIES

LUNCH:

- 1 serving Cantaloupe Chicken-Orzo Salad (p. 141)
  345 CALORIES
- 1 piece of string cheese
  80 CALORIES
- 1 glass ice water
  FREE FOOD

  LUNCH TOTAL: 425 CALORIES

DINNER & DESSERT:

- 1 serving Italian Beef (p. 237)
  386 CALORIES
- 1/2 cup Southwestern Macaroni Salad (p. 257)
  109 CALORIES
- 1 cup brewed iced tea (with sugar substitute
  if desired)
  FREE FOOD

  DINNER TOTAL: 549 CALORIES

SNACKS:

- 3/4 cup baby carrots
  60 CALORIES
- 1 cup Six-Vegetable Juice (p. 76)
  66 CALORIES

  WEEK 6, DAY 3, TOTAL: 1,398 CALORIES

Did you know stress can actually make you gain weight? Stress triggers the release of cortisol, a chemical in the brain that stimulates appetite.

Stress also triggers the release of insulin, which can make you even more ravenous. But here's the knockout punch: together, cortisol and insulin can actually prevent your body from burning fat.

Go easy on foods loaded with sugar or high in fat. Instead, turn to high-quality protein like fish, chicken and turkey. Whole-grain pastas and fiber-rich fruits and vegetables are healthy choices. Don't stack all your calories in the later afternoon or evening hours. Be sure to eat a good breakfast and lunch.

Limit your intake of caffeine. It can make you edgy or irritable, which doesn't help your stress level. Other things you can do to reduce stress are exercise, laugh, slow down, listen to music or build quiet time into your day.

week 6

day 4

BREAKFAST:
- 1 serving Orange Oatmeal (p. 108) — 222 CALORIES
- 1 cup fat-free milk — 86 CALORIES
- BREAKFAST TOTAL: 308 CALORIES

LUNCH:
- 1 Chicken Gyro (p. 153) — 367 CALORIES
- 1 medium plum — 40 CALORIES
- 1/2 piece string cheese — 40 CALORIES
- 1 can diet soft drink — FREE FOOD
- LUNCH TOTAL: 447 CALORIES

DINNER & DESSERT:
- 1 Crumb-Topped Sole (p. 186) — 267 CALORIES
- 1 cup Summer Garden Medley (p. 252) — 113 CALORIES
- 1 glass ice water — FREE FOOD
- 2 Chocolate Mint Crisps (p. 278) — 149 CALORIES
- DINNER TOTAL: 529 CALORIES

SNACKS:
- 1/2 cup baby carrots — 25 CALORIES
- 1 cup Sweet 'n' Salty Popcorn (p. 75) — 76 CALORIES

WEEK 6, DAY 4, TOTAL: 1,385 CALORIES

Eating more fruits and vegetables doesn't mean you have to completely change your lifestyle. Sometimes, it's an easy decision—like topping your cereal with sliced bananas or fresh berries—that makes the difference.

Sidestep sweet or salty snacks like cookies or potato chips, for more beneficial choices, such as baby carrots, celery sticks, apple or pear slices or raisins.

When you're out to eat, check out the salad bar. It provides an excellent opportunity to stock up on leafy greens and other fresh veggies.

When eating in, stack up your sandwiches with a generous layering of sliced cucumber, tomato, green onions or lettuce (pick up lots of filling ideas that won't add to your daily calorie total on the Free Foods Chart, page 45).

day 5

BREAKFAST:
- 2 Ham and Apricot Crepes (p. 117) — 258 CALORIES
- 1/2 cup Four-Fruit Salad (p. 86) — 63 CALORIES
- 1 cup hot tea (with sugar substitute if desired) — FREE FOOD
- BREAKFAST TOTAL: 321 CALORIES

LUNCH:
- 1 Pineapple Chicken Fajita (p. 147) — 402 CALORIES
- with 1/4 cup salsa — FREE FOOD
- 1 can mineral water — FREE FOOD
- LUNCH TOTAL: 402 CALORIES

DINNER & DESSERT:
- 1 serving Hearty Lentil Spaghetti (p. 231) — 362 CALORIES
- 1 whole wheat dinner roll — 76 CALORIES
- spread with 1 teaspoon reduced-fat margarine spread — FREE FOOD
- 1 big green salad (see Free Foods Chart on p. 45) with 1 tablespoon reduced-fat salad dressing — FREE FOOD
- 1 cup fat-free milk — 86 CALORIES
- 1 Chunky Pecan Bar (p. 275) — 88 CALORIES
- DINNER TOTAL: 524 CALORIES

SNACKS:
- 1 mini bagel with 1 tablespoon reduced-fat chive and onion cream cheese — 63 CALORIES
- 1/2 cup blueberries — 41 CALORIES
- served with 2 tablespoons fat-free frozen whipped topping — FREE FOOD

WEEK 6, DAY 5, TOTAL: 1,351 CALORIES

meal plan | THE COMFORT FOOD DIET

66 THE COMFORT FOOD DIET | www.ComfortFoodDietCookbook.com

day 6

BREAKFAST:

- 1 serving Cheese Tomato Egg Bake (p. 103)
  110 CALORIES
- 1 slice whole wheat bread, toasted
  69 CALORIES
- spread with 1 teaspoon reduced-fat margarine
  FREE FOOD
- 1 cup Strawberry Tofu Smoothie (p. 103)
  152 CALORIES

BREAKFAST TOTAL: 331 CALORIES

LUNCH:

- 1 cup Shrimp Pasta Salad (p. 151)
  261 CALORIES
- 1/3 cup red grapes
  43 CALORIES
- 1 cup fat-free milk
  86 CALORIES

LUNCH TOTAL: 390 CALORIES

DINNER & DESSERT:

- 1 serving Rosemary Turkey Breast (p. 179)
  166 CALORIES
- 2/3 cup Cranberry Cornmeal Dressing (p. 265)
  205 CALORIES
- Steamed fresh broccoli and cauliflower florets topped with 1 teaspoon reduced-fat margarine
  FREE FOOD
- 1/2 cup Strawberry Ice Cream (p. 286)
  153 CALORIES
- 1 glass ice water
  FREE FOOD

DINNER TOTAL: 524 CALORIES

SNACKS:

- 1/2 cup baby carrots
  25 CALORIES
- 1/3 cup chocolate soy milk
  40 CALORIES
- 1 serving Crunchy Raisin Treats (p. 78)
  86 CALORIES

WEEK 6, DAY 6, TOTAL: 1,396 CALORIES

When shopping for fresh uncooked shrimp, choose those that have a firm texture with a mild aroma.

day 7

BREAKFAST:

- 2 Pumpkin Pancakes (p. 112)
  240 CALORIES
- 1 piece Baked Canadian-Style Bacon (p. 87)
  49 CALORIES
- 1 cup fat-free milk
  86 CALORIES

BREAKFAST TOTAL: 375 CALORIES

LUNCH:

- 2 Tuna Artichoke Melts (p. 135)
  335 CALORIES
- 1 medium pear
  96 CALORIES
- 1 cup brewed iced tea (with sugar substitute if desired)
  FREE FOOD

LUNCH TOTAL: 431 CALORIES

DINNER & DESSERT:

- 4 ounces Savory Pork Roast (p. 177)
  219 CALORIES
- 2/3 cup Caramelized Onion Mashed Potatoes (p. 262)
  200 CALORIES
- Steamed fresh or frozen green beans topped with 1 tablespoon reduced-fat margarine
  FREE FOOD
- 1 big green salad (see Free Foods Chart on p. 45) with 1 tablespoon reduced-fat salad dressing
  FREE FOOD
- 1 glass ice water
  FREE FOOD
- 1 Wonton Sundae (p. 268)
  83 CALORIES

DINNER TOTAL: 502 CALORIES

SNACKS:

- 1 small orange
  45 CALORIES
- 1 serving Frosted Hazelnuts (p. 83)
  17 CALORIES
- 1/2 piece string cheese
  40 CALORIES

WEEK 6, DAY 7, TOTAL: 1,410 CALORIES

my long-awaited
MAKEOVER!

By exercising and watching what I ate, I was able to monitor my weight loss journey all the way to single digits.

By Jennifer Marcinkevic

before

I spent the majority of my high school years as a chubby teen. I was the size 12 cheerleader that didn't quite match up with the stick-thin girls standing next to me. Once I started going to college, I found that my weight only increased.

Right after graduation, my fiancé, Keith, proposed to me, and I lost 35 pounds in determination not to look like a marshmallow walking down the aisle. I weighed 165 pounds the day I said "I do," which was the thinnest I had been since my early teens. Needless to say, I felt great.

That feeling didn't last for long though, and after my wedding I gained the weight back. I moved to a new city to start my life with Keith, and while he worked every day, I struggled to make new friends as I went to graduate school two days a week. I was lonely, bored and, unfortunately, I let myself slip back into my previous eating habits.

Six years and two pregnancies later, I gained even more weight. After

being confronted with a surprise medical issue, I knew it was time for a change, and I lost about 60 pounds before I became pregnant with my third child. While I gained 30 pounds back during the pregnancy, I continued to exercise under my doctor's supervision for the duration of the pregnancy. After my daughter was born, I got right back into a serious fitness routine.

By the time my daughter was 7 months old, I had lost a total of 125 pounds. I reached my goal of becoming healthy and was wearing a size 4! By exercising regularly and

after

watching what I ate, I was able to monitor my weight-loss journey all the way down to the single-digit dress sizes.

Although I'm not a big fan of fruits and vegetables, I learned how to prepare them in a healthy yet tasty way. Not only did my new and improved cooking techniques help me, but my husband also lost 20 pounds as a result of the changes to our meal plans. Dinner has now become my favorite meal because I've learned how to cook in a more health-conscience way for my family.

To really keep my weight-loss on track, I paired my improved eating habits with a workout plan. After my children were asleep, I went to the gym and took advantage of the elliptical and treadmill machines. I also used weight-training machines about twice a week.

Each time I worked out I made sure to burn 1,000 calories. In the beginning it would take me about two hours to reach my calorie goal but as my body toned and I got into better shape, it took me less time to work out because I could move faster. I stayed fairly consistent with my routine because I enjoyed using the machines that burned the most calories.

Throughout my weight-loss process I made overall health my biggest priority and focus. I promised myself I would no longer feel guilty for being away from my children to exercise because I knew my well-being would only help them in the long run. Now, I am happier and less stressed, and I have set a great example for my children of how to live a healthy and active life.

When people ask how I lost so much weight, I answer with two theories: First, the timing was right for me. I wasn't stressed and the other areas of my life were in order and structured. Secondly, my family never left my side. My children Cole, Alec and Claire have been my strongest inspirations for losing the weight. Along with my husband, they have never complained and have always supported me.

Together we take family walks and hikes regularly, which only furthers my success and leads all of us toward healthier lives. Although I was never the chubby cheerleader in their eyes, I like to think that when they look at me now, they see me at the top of the pyramid.

KNOWING WHEN THE
TIME IS RIGHT

Think your weight gain only affects your physical appearance? Think again…it could save your life.

I always knew I was overweight, but what I didn't completely realize was that my health was also suffering. During the last two months of my second pregnancy, I experienced severe pain. After a trip to the emergency room, I was told that the pain was caused by the baby shoving his arm or leg under my ribcage. To my surprise, I had the same pain again, this time however, it was two weeks after my son was born.

An emergency ultrasound helped diagnose that I had a gallstone the size of a golf ball, and that it needed to be removed. My son was only five-weeks-old when I went in for surgery, and all I could think about was losing time with my children because of my health issues. I learned that the negative choices I was making about my health could eventually result in spending less time with my beautiful family.

It was this realization that kicked in and motivated me to make a change in my life. I wanted to lose the weight for myself but, most important, I wanted to make a difference in my family's lives as well.

—Jennifer Marcinkevic

snacks

Healthy snacks like those suggested in this colorful chapter will keep you on track between meals. If you're a woman, shoot for two snacks per day, totaling about 100 calories. Men should eat two snacks totaling 200 calories.

75

72

74

Checkout the snack list at right for effortless ideas that are low-calorie yet deliciously satisfying. Or, simply prepare your own nib-bles with the 100-calorie or less recipes that follow on pages 72 to 83. For guilt-free munching on-the-go, see the list of low-calorie ideas on page 77.

Whether you're looking for something SAVORY or SWEET or even a treat that's a bit more SUBSTANTIAL, the following ideas will help you SNACK SMART.

50 CALORIES OR LESS

- **1 cup prepared sugar-free flavored gelatin,** 8 calories

- **1/2 cup baby carrots,** 25 calories

- **1/2 cup cubed fresh pineapple,** 37 calories

- **1 medium plum,** 40 calories

- **2 medium celery ribs with 1 tablespoon fat-free ranch salad dressing,** 40 calories

- **1/3 cup chocolate soy milk,** 40 calories

- **1/2 piece string cheese,** 40 calories

- **2 tablespoons roasted pumpkin seeds,** 40 calories

- **1/2 cup blueberries,** 41 calories

- **1/3 cup red grapes,** 43 calories

- **1 small orange,** 45 calories

- **1/2 (22 g package) crisp rice cereal bar,** 45 calories

- **1-1/2 cups air-popped popcorn,** 47 calories

- **1/2 cup sliced strawberries with 2 tablespoons reduced-fat frozen whipped topping,** 47 calories

- **3 chocolate-covered miniature pretzel twists,** 47 calories

- **1/2 small grapefruit with 1 teaspoon sugar,** 48 calories

- **1 cup mixed greens with 1 tablespoon crumbled blue cheese and 1 tablespoon fat-free Italian salad dressing,** 49 calories

- **2 chocolate kisses,** 49 calories

- **1 cup reduced-sodium V8 juice,** 50 calories

- **1/2 medium banana,** 50 calories

- **1/2 slice toast with 1 teaspoon apple butter,** 50 calories

51-100 CALORIES

- **3/4 cup skinny latte (made with fat-free milk),** 60 calories

- **1 miniature bagel with 1 tablespoon reduced-fat chive and onion cream cheese,** 63 calories

- **2 tablespoons soy nuts,** 70 calories

- **2 California roll slices,** 75 calories

- **4 reduced-sodium saltine crackers topped with 1 tablespoon reduced-sugar orange marmalade,** 77 calories

- **1 roasted chicken drumstick, skin removed,** 77 calories

- **1/4 cup dried apricots,** 78 calories

- **1 hard-cooked egg,** 78 calories

- **1/3 cup 1% cottage cheese with 1/4 cup unsweetened pineapple tidbits,** 81 calories

- **1/2 small baked potato with 3 tablespoons salsa,** 81 calories

- **1/2 cup unsweetened applesauce with 1/2 piece whole wheat toast,** 87 calories

- **1/2 English muffin topped with 1 slice tomato and 1 tablespoon shredded part-skim mozzarella cheese, broiled,** 87 calories

- **1/3 cup canned baked beans,** 89 calories

- **3 pieces snack rye bread topped with 1 tablespoon reduced-fat garden vegetable cream cheese and 6 cucumber slices,** 89 calories

- **3/4 cup minestrone soup,** 90 calories

- **1 slice cinnamon-raisin toast with 1 teaspoon honey,** 91 calories

- **3 vanilla wafers and 1/2 cup fat-free milk,** 91 calories

- **3/4 cup sugar-free hot cocoa prepared with fat-free milk,** 92 calories

- **1/2 small apple with 2 tablespoons fat-free caramel ice cream topping,** 93 calories

- **2/3 cup Cheerios with 1/4 cup fat-free milk,** 93 calories

- **2 tablespoons hummus with 1/4 of a pita and 1/4 of a small red pepper,** 93 calories

- **2 gingersnap cookies with 1 tablespoon reduced-fat strawberry cream cheese,** 93 calories

- **1/2 medium pear and 1/2 ounce reduced-fat cheddar cheese,** 94 calories

- **3 (2-1/2-inch squares) graham crackers,** 98 calories

- **1/2 cup sugar-free chocolate pudding (prepared with fat-free milk) topped with a crushed chocolate wafer,** 99 calories

100 CALORIES

BANANA BERRY DRINK

spiced honey pretzels

Mary Lou Moon | BEAVERTON, OREGON

If your tastes run to sweet and spicy, you'll love these zesty pretzels with a twist. The coating is so yummy, you won't need a fattening dip to enjoy them! They're a great snack for munching, and you won't feel a bit guilty.

4　cups thin pretzel sticks
3　tablespoons honey
2　teaspoons butter, melted
1　teaspoon onion powder
1　teaspoon chili powder

- Line a 15-in. x 10-in. x 1-in. baking pan with foil; coat the foil with cooking spray. Place pretzels in a large bowl.

- In a small bowl, combine honey, butter, onion powder and chili powder. Pour over pretzels; toss to coat evenly. Spread into prepared pan.

- Bake at 350° for 8 minutes, stirring once. Cool on a wire rack, stirring gently several times to separate.

YIELD: 8 servings.

NUTRITION FACTS: 1/2 cup equals 98 calories, 1 g fat (1 g saturated fat), 3 mg cholesterol, 487 mg sodium, 20 g carbohydrate, 1 g fiber, 2 g protein. **DIABETIC EXCHANGE:** 1-1/2 starch.

SPICED HONEY PRETZELS

98 CALORIES

banana berry drink

Eric Knoben | EDGEWOOD, WASHINGTON

This cold, refreshing beverage is a great substitute for breakfast when you're in a hurry. It makes a fun snack anytime.

3/4　cup orange juice, chilled
1/3　cup pineapple juice, chilled
1　cup frozen blueberries
1/2　cup frozen sweetened sliced strawberries
1/2　cup plain yogurt
1　small ripe banana, sliced

- Place half of each ingredient in a blender; cover and process until smooth. Pour into chilled glasses. Repeat with remaining ingredients. Serve immediately.

YIELD: 5 servings.

NUTRITION FACTS: 3/4 cup equals 100 calories, 1 g fat (1 g saturated fat), 3 mg cholesterol, 13 mg sodium, 22 g carbohydrate, 2 g fiber, 2 g protein. **DIABETIC EXCHANGE:** 1-1/2 fruit.

pretty gelatin molds

Dixie Terry | GOREVILLE, ILLINOIS

Revive extra cranberry sauce in this good and easy salad. This is one of the recipes I made for the first Thanksgiving dinner I cooked years ago and has become a seasonal favorite at our house. It's a satisfying snack when hunger strikes between meals.

    1 package (3 ounces) orange gelatin
    3/4 cup boiling water
    3/4 cup whole-berry cranberry sauce
    1 medium navel orange, peeled and finely chopped
    4 lettuce leaves

- In a large bowl, dissolve gelatin in boiling water. Stir in cranberry sauce and orange. Pour into four 1/2-cup molds coated with cooking spray. Chill for 3-4 hours or until set. Unmold onto lettuce-lined plates.

YIELD: 4 servings.

NUTRITION FACTS: 1/2 cup equals 93 calories, trace fat (trace saturated fat), 0 cholesterol, 49 mg sodium, 22 g carbohydrate, 1 g fiber, 2 g protein.

PRETTY GELATIN MOLDS

CAJUN POPCORN

cajun popcorn

Ruby Williams | BOGALUSA, LOUISIANA

Authentic Cajun popcorn is actually deep-fried crawfish tails seasoned with peppery spices. But we like this lighter, simpler version made with real popcorn. It's our favorite TV snack.

    1 teaspoon salt
    1/2 teaspoon ground cumin
    1/2 teaspoon garlic powder
    1/2 teaspoon dried basil
    1/2 teaspoon dried thyme
    1/2 teaspoon paprika
    1/4 teaspoon pepper
    1/8 teaspoon cayenne pepper
    2 tablespoons canola oil
    3 quarts popped popcorn

- In a small bowl, combine the first eight ingredients; set aside. In a small saucepan, heat oil over medium for 1 minute; add seasonings. Cook and stir over low heat for 1 minute. Place the popcorn in a large bowl; add seasoning mixture and toss to coat. Serve immediately.

YIELD: 3 quarts.

NUTRITION FACTS: 1 cup equals 77 calories, 5 g fat (1 g saturated fat), 0 cholesterol, 294 mg sodium, 7 g carbohydrate, 1 g fiber, 1 g protein.

80 CALORIES

SANGRIA GELATIN RING

sangria gelatin ring

Nicole Nemeth | KOMOKA, ONTARIO

This gelatin is enjoyed by everyone because you just can't go wrong with delicious berries.

- 2 packages (3 ounces *each*) lemon gelatin
- 1-1/2 cups boiling white wine *or* white grape juice
- 2 cups club soda, chilled
- 1 cup sliced fresh strawberries
- 1 cup fresh *or* frozen blueberries
- 1 cup fresh *or* frozen raspberries
- 1/2 cup green grapes, halved

- In a large bowl, dissolve gelatin in boiling wine or grape juice; cool for 10 minutes. Stir in club soda; refrigerate until set but not firm, about 45 minutes.
- Fold in the berries and grapes. Pour into a 6-cup ring mold coated with cooking spray. Refrigerate for 4 hours or until set. Invert and unmold onto a serving platter.

YIELD: 10 servings.

NUTRITION FACTS: 1 slice equals 80 calories, trace fat (trace saturated fat), 0 cholesterol, 32 mg sodium, 14 g carbohydrate, 2 g fiber, 1 g protein.

92 CALORIES

blueberry orange smoothies

Nella Parker | HERSEY, MICHIGAN

Any time is the right time for one of these refreshing smoothies using fat-free dairy products and blueberries. It's a snack you'll enjoy and feel good about.

- 2 medium navel oranges
- 1 cup fat-free plain yogurt

- 1/4 cup fat-free milk
- 2/3 cup fresh *or* frozen blueberries
- 4 teaspoons sugar
- 1 to 1-1/3 cups ice cubes

- Peel and remove the white pith from oranges; separate into sections. Place in a blender; add the yogurt, milk, blueberries and sugar. Cover and process until smooth. Add ice; cover and process until smooth. Pour into chilled glasses; serve immediately.

YIELD: 4 servings.

NUTRITION FACTS: 1 cup equals 92 calories, trace fat (trace saturated fat), 2 mg cholesterol, 43 mg sodium, 21 g carbohydrate, 2 g fiber, 4 g protein. **DIABETIC EXCHANGE:** 1-1/2 fruit.

herbed tortilla chips

Angela Case | MONTICELLO, ARKANSAS

I created this recipe when I found several packages of tortilla shells while cleaning out my freezer. It's an inexpensive, low-calorie snack for my husband and me.

- 2 teaspoons grated Parmesan cheese
- 1/2 teaspoon dried oregano
- 1/2 teaspoon dried parsley flakes
- 1/2 teaspoon dried rosemary, crushed
- 1/4 teaspoon garlic powder
- 1/8 teaspoon kosher salt
- Dash pepper
- 2 flour tortillas (6 inches)
- 2 teaspoons olive oil

HERBED TORTILLA CHIPS

94 CALORIES

- In a small bowl, combine the first seven ingredients. Brush tortillas with oil; cut each tortilla into six wedges. Arrange in a single layer on a baking sheet coated with cooking spray.

- Arrange in a single layer on a baking sheet coated with cooking spray.

- Sprinkle wedges with seasoning mixture. Bake at 425° for 5-7 minutes or until golden brown. Cool for 5 minutes.

YIELD: 3 servings.

NUTRITION FACTS: 4 chips equals 94 calories, 5 g fat (1 g saturated fat), 1 mg cholesterol, 245 mg sodium, 9 g carbohydrate, trace fiber, 3 g protein. **DIABETIC EXCHANGES:** 1 fat, 1/2 starch.

fresh strawberry smoothies

Helene Rock | LOS ALTOS, CALIFORNIA

A tantalizing combination of strawberries and orange juice, this smoothie gets its shake-like texture from buttermilk. Try the recipe with whatever other fresh berries you enjoy most.

1/2	cup buttermilk
1/4	cup orange juice
1-1/2	cups sliced fresh strawberries

Sugar substitute equal to 2 tablespoons sugar

- Place all ingredients in a blender; cover and process for 1-2 minutes or until smooth. Pour into chilled glasses; serve immediately.

YIELD: 2 servings.

NUTRITION FACTS: 1 cup equals 82 calories, 1 g fat (trace saturated fat), 2 mg cholesterol, 66 mg sodium, 16 g carbohydrate, 3 g fiber, 3 g protein.

sweet 'n' salty popcorn

Hilary Kerr | HAWKS, MICHIGAN

This popcorn is a family favorite on weekend movie nights, thanks to the classic salty and sweet flavor combination!

10	cups air-popped popcorn
1	tablespoon butter
5	tablespoons instant vanilla pudding mix
1/3	cup light corn syrup

| 1 | teaspoon vanilla extract |

Dash salt

- Place popcorn in a large bowl. In a small microwave-safe bowl, melt butter; whisk in the pudding mix, corn syrup, vanilla and salt until smooth.

- Microwave, uncovered, for 45 seconds or until bubbly. Pour over popcorn; toss to coat. Spread in a 15-in. x 10-in. x 1-in. baking pan coated with cooking spray.

- Bake at 250° for 25-30 minutes or until crisp, stirring once. Remove popcorn from pan to waxed paper to cool. Break into clusters. Store in airtight containers.

YIELD: 12 cups.

EDITOR'S NOTE: This recipe was tested in a 1,100-watt microwave.

NUTRITION FACTS: 1 cup equals 76 calories, 1 g fat (1 g saturated fat), 3 mg cholesterol, 70 mg sodium, 16 g carbohydrate, 1 g fiber, 1 g protein. **DIABETIC EXCHANGE:** 1 starch.

SWEET 'N' SALTY POPCORN

six-vegetable juice

Deborah Moyer | LIBERTY, PENNSYLVANIA

Our family and friends enjoy my vegetable garden by the glassfuls. My husband likes spicy foods, and after one sip, he proclaimed this juice perfect. For more delicate palates, you can leave out the hot peppers.

- 5 pounds ripe tomatoes, peeled and chopped
- 1/2 cup water
- 1/4 cup chopped green pepper
- 1/4 cup chopped carrot
- 1/4 cup chopped celery
- 1/4 cup lemon juice
- 2 tablespoons chopped onion
- 1 tablespoon salt
- 1 to 1-1/2 small serrano peppers

- In a large Dutch oven or soup kettle, combine the first eight ingredients. Remove stems and seeds if desired from peppers; add to tomato mixture. Bring to a boil; reduce heat. Cover and simmer for 30 minutes or until vegetables are tender. Cool. Press mixture through a food mill or fine sieve. Refrigerate or freeze. Shake or stir juice well before serving.

YIELD: 2 quarts.

EDITOR'S NOTE: When cutting hot peppers, disposable gloves are recommended. Avoid touching your face.

NUTRITION FACTS: 1 serving (1 cup) equals 66 calories, 1 g fat (trace saturated fat), 0 cholesterol, 915 mg sodium, 15 g carbohydrate, 3 g fiber, 3 g protein.

SIX-VEGETABLE JUICE

66 CALORIES

81 CALORIES

MINI RICE CAKE SNACKS

mini rice cake snacks

Our Test Kitchen staff had a ball dressing up sweet bite-size rice cakes with a simple spread and colorful fruits. Try them with a combination of your favorite flavors.

- 3 ounces reduced-fat cream cheese
- 1/4 cup orange marmalade
- 24 miniature honey-nut *or* cinnamon-apple rice cakes
- 2 medium fresh strawberries, sliced
- 3 tablespoons fresh blueberries
- 3 tablespoons mandarin orange segments
- 3 tablespoons pineapple tidbits

- In a small bowl, combine cream cheese and marmalade until blended. Spread over rice cakes; top with fruit.

YIELD: 2 dozen.

NUTRITION FACTS: One serving (3 rice cakes) equals 81 calories, 2 g fat (1 g saturated fat), 6 mg cholesterol, 57 mg sodium, 15 g carbohydrate, 1 g fiber, 2 g protein. **DIABETIC EXCHANGES:** 1-1/2 starch, 1/2 fruit.

88 CALORIES lo-cal apple snack

Nancy Horan | SIOUX FALLS, SOUTH DAKOTA

This quick snack is often requested as an office treat. It's a simple and harvest-fresh way to serve autumn's best apples—kids also love it.

- 4 medium Golden Delicious apples, peeled, cored and cut into rings
- 1/2 cup apple juice

1/4 teaspoon ground cinnamon
1 tablespoon grated lemon peel

- In an ungreased 11-in. x 7-in. microwave-safe dish, arrange apples in two rows. Pour the apple juice over apples. Sprinkle with cinnamon and lemon peel. Cover and microwave on high for 4-1/2 minutes or until apples are tender, turning after 1-1/2 minutes.

YIELD: 4 servings.

EDITOR'S NOTE: This recipe was tested in a 1,100-watt microwave.

NUTRITION FACTS: One serving equals 88 calories, 0.55 g fat (0 saturated fat), 0 cholesterol, 1 mg sodium, 23 g carbohydrate, 0 fiber, 0.55 g protein. **DIABETIC EXCHANGES:** 1-1/2 fruit.

olive pepper pinwheels

Kristin Manley | MONTESANO, WASHINGTON

These zippy pinwheels are surprisingly simple to prepare ahead of time and have on hand whenever hunger hits. They're also attractive to serve as appetizers for guests.

1 package (8 ounces) reduced-fat cream cheese
1 teaspoon fat-free milk

OLIVE PEPPER PINWHEELS

1/3 cup *each* finely chopped sweet red, green and yellow pepper
1 can (4-1/4 ounces) chopped ripe olives, drained
2 tablespoons ranch salad dressing mix
6 flour tortillas (6 inches)

- In a bowl, beat cream cheese and milk until smooth; stir in the peppers, olives and dressing mix. Spread over tortillas. Roll up jelly-roll style; wrap tightly in plastic wrap.

- Refrigerate for 2 hours or until firm. Just before serving, cut into 1-in. pieces.

YIELD: 3 dozen.

NUTRITION FACTS: One serving (2 pieces) equals 68 calories, 4 g fat (1 g saturated fat), 7 mg cholesterol, 226 mg sodium, 6 g carbohydrate, 0.55 g fiber, 2 g protein. **DIABETIC EXCHANGES:** 1 vegetable, 1/2 starch.

GREAT SNACKS ON-THE-GO

Here are some single-serving snacks. Keep them in mind when hunger hits.

- **Quaker Chewy Chocolate Chunk Granola Bar,** 90 calories
- **Dairy Queen Fudge Bar,** 50 calories
- **Weight Watchers Lemon Cake with Lemon Icing,** 80 calories
- **Hunts Fat-Free Snack Pack Tapioca Pudding,** 80 calories
- **Weight Watchers Berries 'n Cream Yogurt,** 100 calories
- **Kashi Cherry Dark Chocolate Chewy Granola Bar,** 120 calories
- **South Beach Diet Whole Wheat Snack Crackers,** 100 calories
- **Haagen-Dazs Raspberry & Vanilla Fat-Free Sorbet & Yogurt Bar,** 100 calories
- **Dole Diced Peaches in Light Syrup,** 80 calories
- **Weight Watchers Giant Chocolate Fudge Ice Cream Bar,** 110 calories
- **Peach (medium),** 40 calories
- **Whole Strawberries (1 cup),** 45 calories
- **Raspberries (1 cup),** 60 calories

58 CALORIES

GARLIC-KISSED TOMATOES

garlic-kissed tomatoes

Margaret Zickert | DEERFIELD, WISCONSIN

Everyone I know loves this recipe—even my husband who normally doesn't like garlic! These tomatoes are a hit at potlucks...folks always ask for the recipe.

        6 medium tomatoes
    1/4 cup canola oil
        3 tablespoons lemon juice
        2 garlic cloves, thinly sliced
    1/2 teaspoon salt
    1/2 teaspoon dried oregano
    1/8 teaspoon pepper

- Peel and cut tomatoes in half horizontally. Squeeze tomatoes lightly to release seeds. Discard seeds and juices. Place tomato halves in a container with a tight-fitting lid.

- In a small bowl, combine the oil, lemon juice, garlic, salt, oregano and pepper. Pour over tomatoes. Seal lid and turn to coat. Refrigerate for at least 4 hours or up to 2 days, turning occasionally.

YIELD: 12 servings.

NUTRITION FACTS: 1 serving (1 each) equals 58 calories, 5 g fat (1 g saturated fat), 0 cholesterol, 105 mg sodium, 4 g carbohydrate, 1 g fiber, 1 g protein.

86 CALORIES

crunchy raisin treats

Bernice Morris | MARSHFIELD, MISSOURI

Peanuts give an extra crunch to these crispy treats dotted with raisins. As an evening snack, they are irresistible with a tall, cold glass of milk.

        4 cups miniature marshmallows
    1/4 cup butter
    5-1/2 cups crisp rice cereal
    1-1/2 cups raisins
        1 cup salted dry roasted peanuts

- In a large saucepan or microwave-safe bowl, melt the marshmallows and butter; stir until smooth. Add cereal, raisins and peanuts; mix well. Pat into a greased 13-in. x 9-in. pan. Cool completely; cut into squares.

YIELD: 3 dozen.

NUTRITION FACTS: 1 serving (1 each) equals 86 calories, 3 g fat (1 g saturated fat), 3 mg cholesterol, 72 mg sodium, 14 g carbohydrate, 1 g fiber, 2 g protein.

22 CALORIES

SPICY MINT TEA

spicy mint tea

Ione Banks | JEFFERSON, OREGON

In the old days, a steaming cup of mint tea was said to dispel headaches, heartburn and indigestion. I don't know about that, but I do know that this tea refreshes me every time.

        6 cups water
        2 cinnamon sticks
        4 whole cloves
        4 whole allspice
        2 cups fresh mint leaves
Honey, optional

- Bring the water, cinnamon, cloves and allspice to a boil. Boil for 1 minute. Stir in mint leaves. Remove from heat and steep for 5 minutes. Strain into cups. Sweeten with honey if desired.

YIELD: 4 servings.

NUTRITION FACTS: 1 serving (1 cup) equals 22 calories, trace fat (trace saturated fat), 0 cholesterol, 14 mg sodium, 4 g carbohydrate, 3 g fiber, 2 g protein.

70 CALORIES

CRANBERRY CHUTNEY

cranberry chutney

Karyn Gordon | ROCKLEDGE, FLORIDA

You can serve this chunky chutney over cream cheese or Brie with crackers, or as a condiment with roast pork or poultry. Either way, its slightly tart flavor and deep red hue lend a festive flair to the table.

- 4 cups (1 pound) fresh *or* frozen cranberries
- 1 cup sugar
- 1 cup water
- 1/2 cup packed brown sugar
- 2 teaspoons ground cinnamon
- 1-1/2 teaspoons ground ginger
- 1/2 teaspoon ground cloves
- 1/4 teaspoon ground allspice
- 1 cup chopped tart apple
- 1/2 cup golden raisins
- 1/2 cup diced celery

- In a large saucepan, combine the first eight ingredients. Bring to a boil. Reduce heat; simmer, uncovered, for 20 minutes, stirring occasionally. Add the apple, raisins and celery. Simmer, uncovered, until thickened, about 15 minutes. Cool. Chill until serving.

YIELD: 3 cups.

NUTRITION FACTS: 1 serving (2 tablespoons) equals 70 calories, trace fat (trace saturated fat), 0 cholesterol, 5 mg sodium, 18 g carbohydrate, 1 g fiber, trace protein.

pineapple smoothie beverage

Margery Bryan | ROYAL CITY, WASHINGTON

I got this recipe over 20 years ago. I've tried several healthy smoothie recipes, and this is one of the best.

- 1 can (20 ounces) unsweetened pineapple chunks, undrained
- 1 cup buttermilk
- 2 teaspoons vanilla extract
- 2 teaspoons sugar substitute

Mint leaves, optional

- Drain the pineapple, reserving 1/2 cup juice. Freeze pineapple chunks. Place the juice, buttermilk, vanilla, sugar substitute and frozen pineapple into a blender container. Beat until smooth. Pour into glasses and garnish with mint if desired. Serve immediately.

YIELD: 5 servings.

NUTRITION FACTS: 3/4 cup equals 80 calories, trace fat (trace saturated fat), 2 mg cholesterol, 61 mg sodium, 17 g carbohydrate, 1 g fiber, 2 g protein. **DIABETIC EXCHANGES:** 1/2 fruit, 1/2 fat-free milk.

PINEAPPLE SMOOTHIE BEVERAGE

80 CALORIES

veggie tortilla pinwheels

Doris Ann Yoder | ARTHUR, ILLINOIS

These bite-size snacks are delicious anytime of the day. Simply combine cream cheese, dried beef, chopped vegetables and salad dressing mix, then roll into tortillas, refrigerate, slice and serve.

- 1 package (8 ounces) cream cheese, softened
- 4 teaspoons ranch salad dressing mix
- 1 package (2-1/4 ounces) dried beef, chopped
- 1/2 cup chopped fresh broccoli
- 1/2 cup chopped fresh cauliflower
- 1/4 cup chopped green onions
- 1/4 cup sliced pimiento-stuffed olives
- 5 flour tortillas (8 inches), room temperature

Salsa, optional

- In a large bowl, beat cream cheese and salad dressing mix until blended. Stir in beef, broccoli, cauliflower, onions and olives.

- Spread over tortillas; roll up tightly and wrap in plastic wrap. Refrigerate for at least 2 hours.

- Unwrap and cut into 1/2-in. slices. Serve with the salsa if desired.

YIELD: about 5 dozen.

NUTRITION FACTS: 1 serving (3 each) equals 94 calories, 5 g fat (3 g saturated fat), 14 mg cholesterol, 527 mg sodium, 9 g carbohydrate, trace fiber, 3 g protein.

VEGGIE TORTILLA PINWHEELS

94 CALORIES

89 CALORIES

STRAWBERRY WATERMELON SLUSH

strawberry watermelon slush

Patty Howse | GREAT FALLS, MONTANA

Whether you're watching your weight or not, summertime's the perfect time for this refreshing fruit slush.

- 2 cups cubed seedless watermelon
- 1 pint fresh strawberries, halved
- 1/3 cup sugar
- 1/3 cup lemon juice
- 2 cups ice cubes

- In a blender, combine watermelon, strawberries, sugar and lemon juice; cover and process on high until smooth. While processing, gradually add the ice cubes; process until slushy. Pour into chilled glasses; serve immediately.

YIELD: 5 cups.

NUTRITION FACTS: 1 serving (1 cup) equals 89 calories, trace fat (trace saturated fat), 0 cholesterol, 3 mg sodium, 24 g carbohydrate, 2 g fiber, 1 g protein.

sunflower popcorn bars

Karen Ann Bland | GOVE, KANSAS

Flavored with peanut butter and a hint of vanilla, these change-of-pace bars can't be beat.

- 1 cup sugar
- 1/2 cup light corn syrup
- 1/2 cup honey
- 1/2 cup peanut butter
- 1/4 cup butter, softened
- 1 teaspoon vanilla extract
- 1 cup salted sunflower kernels
- 4 quarts popped popcorn

- In a large saucepan over medium heat, bring the sugar, corn syrup and honey to a boil, stirring often. Boil for 2 minutes. Remove from the heat; stir in the peanut butter, butter and vanilla until smooth. Add sunflower kernels.

- Place popcorn in a large bowl. Add syrup and stir to coat. Press into two greased 13-in. x 9-in. pans. Cut into bars. Store in an airtight container.

YIELD: 4 dozen.

EDITOR'S NOTE: Reduced-fat or generic brands of peanut butter are not recommended for this recipe.

NUTRITION FACTS: 1 serving (1 each) equals 96 calories, 5 g fat (1 g saturated fat), 3 mg cholesterol, 76 mg sodium, 13 g carbohydrate, 1 g fiber, 2 g protein.

SUNFLOWER POPCORN BARS

96 CALORIES

TORTILLA SNACK STRIPS

88 CALORIES

tortilla snack strips

Karen Riordan | FERN CREEK, KENTUCKY

These crispy, zippy strips are a super homemade alternative to commercial snack chips.

- 2 tablespoons butter, melted
- 6 flour tortillas (8 inches)
- 1/2 teaspoon ground cumin
- 1/2 teaspoon garlic powder
- 1/2 teaspoon onion salt *or* onion powder

Dash to 1/8 teaspoon cayenne pepper, optional

- Brush butter over one side of each tortilla. Combine the seasonings; lightly sprinkle 1/4 teaspoon over each tortilla. Make two stacks of tortillas, with three in each stack. Using a serrated knife, cut each stack into nine thin strips.

- Place in an ungreased 15-in. x 10-in. x 1-in. baking pan. Bake at 400° for 8-10 minutes or until lightly browned. Serve warm.

YIELD: 1-1/2 dozen.

NUTRITION FACTS: Two strips (prepared with onion powder, reduced-fat margarine and fat-free tortillas) equals 88 calories, 2 g fat (0 saturated fat), 0 cholesterol, 256 mg sodium, 16 g carbohydrate, 0 fiber, 2 g protein. **DIABETIC EXCHANGES:** 1 starch.

77 CALORIES

TEXAS CAVIAR

texas caviar

Kathy Faris | LYTLE, TEXAS

My neighbor gave me a container of this zippy, tangy salsa one Christmas, and I had to have the recipe. I fix it regularly for potlucks and get-togethers and never have leftovers. I take copies of the recipe with me whenever I take the salsa.

1	can (15-1/2 ounces) black-eyed peas, rinsed and drained
3/4	cup chopped sweet red pepper
3/4	cup chopped green pepper
1	medium onion, chopped
3	green onions, chopped
1/4	cup minced fresh parsley
1	jar (2 ounces) diced pimientos, drained
1	garlic clove, minced
1	bottle (8 ounces) fat-free Italian salad dressing

Tortilla chips

- In a large bowl, combine peas, peppers, onions, parsley, pimientos and garlic. Pour the salad dressing over pea mixture; stir gently to coat. Cover and refrigerate for 24 hours. Serve with tortilla chips.

YIELD: 4 cups.

NUTRITION FACTS: 1/2 cup (calculated without chips) equals 77 calories, trace fat (trace saturated fat), 1 mg cholesterol, 482 mg sodium, 15 g carbohydrate, 3 g fiber, 4 g protein.
DIABETIC EXCHANGES: 1 starch.

ham 'n' asparagus roll-ups

Mary Steiner | WEST BEND, WISCONSIN

These light snacks go together in a jiffy, so they're perfect when unexpected guests drop by. They also make a nice side dish in spring.

16	fresh asparagus spears (about 1 pound), trimmed
1	tablespoon water
16	thin slices fully cooked ham (about 3/4 pound)

DILL SAUCE:

1	cup (8 ounces) plain yogurt
1/2	cup diced seeded and peeled cucumber
1	teaspoon dill weed
1	teaspoon lemon juice

- Place asparagus and water in a microwave-safe 11-in. x 7-in. dish. Cover and cook on high for 2-3 minutes or until crisp-tender. Immediately place asparagus in ice water; drain and pat dry.

- Wrap each asparagus spear with a slice of ham. Just before serving, combine sauce ingredients. Serve with roll-ups.

YIELD: 8 servings.

EDITOR'S NOTE: This recipe was tested in a 1,100-watt microwave.

NUTRITION FACTS: 1 serving (2 each) equals 75 calories, 3 g fat (1 g saturated fat), 19 mg cholesterol, 541 mg sodium, 5 g carbohydrate, 1 g fiber, 10 g protein.

HAM 'N' ASPARAGUS ROLL-UPS

75 CALORIES

parmesan-garlic popcorn snack

Sharon Skildum | MAPLE GROVE, MINNESOTA

This is my husband's favorite late night snack. He thinks it's great while watching TV.

- 2-1/2 quarts popped popcorn, buttered
- 1/4 cup grated Parmesan cheese
- 1 teaspoon garlic powder
- 1 teaspoon dried parsley flakes
- 1/2 teaspoon dill weed

- Place popcorn in a large bowl. In a small bowl, combine the Parmesan cheese, garlic powder, parsley and dill; sprinkle over popcorn and toss lightly. Serve immediately.

YIELD: 2-1/2 quarts.

NUTRITION FACTS: 1 serving (1 cup) equals 65 calories, 4 g fat (1 g saturated fat), 2 mg cholesterol, 135 mg sodium, 7 g carbohydrate, 1 g fiber, 2 g protein.

frosted hazelnuts

Kathleen Lutz | STEWARD, ILLINOIS

These yummy nuts will be the hit of any party spread. They add perfect sweetness in conjunction with other saltier snacks.

- 2 egg whites
- 1 cup sugar
- 2 tablespoons water
- 1 teaspoon salt
- 1/2 teaspoon *each* ground cloves, cinnamon and allspice
- 4 cups hazelnuts

- In a large bowl, beat egg whites until foamy. Add the sugar, water, salt and spices; beat well. Let stand for 5 minutes or until sugar is dissolved. Gently fold in the hazelnuts until well coated.

- Spread into two greased 15-in. x 10-in. x 1-in. baking pans. Bake at 275° for 50-60 minutes or until crisp. Remove to waxed paper to cool. Store in airtight containers.

YIELD: 6 cups.

NUTRITION FACTS: 1 serving (2 tablespoons) equals 17 calories, trace fat (trace saturated fat), 0 cholesterol, 52 mg sodium, 4 g carbohydrate, trace fiber, trace protein.

spiced coffee with cream

Alpha Wilson | ROSWELL, NEW MEXICO

This recipe was a wonderful discovery made 50 years ago. I serve it to company or as a treat for my husband and me.

- 1/4 cup evaporated milk
- 2-1/4 teaspoons confectioners' sugar
- 1/4 teaspoon ground cinnamon
- 1/8 teaspoon vanilla extract
- 1 cup hot strong brewed coffee

Ground nutmeg

- 2 cinnamon sticks

- Pour the milk into a small bowl; place mixer beaters in the bowl. Cover and freeze for 30 minutes or until ice crystals begin to form.

- Add the sugar, cinnamon and vanilla; beat until thick and fluffy. Pour about 1/2 cup into each cup. Add coffee; sprinkle with nutmeg. Serve immediately; garnish with cinnamon sticks.

YIELD: 2 servings.

NUTRITION FACTS: 1 cup equals 55 calories, 2 g fat (2 g saturated fat), 10 mg cholesterol, 32 mg sodium, 7 g carbohydrate, trace fiber, 2 g protein.

SPICED COFFEE WITH CREAM

breakfasts

It's so important to start your day with a good breakfast. This meal helps boost your metabolism so you burn more calories throughout the day, and you'll be less inclined to reach for high-fat and high-calorie snacks before lunch. Shoot for about 350 calories for this meal.

102   111   115

The first section in this chapter has lower-calorie items you might pair with a bowl of cereal, yogurt, etc. The middle and last sections are higher-calorie, more complete dishes that need just a beverage. See the chart on page 87 for the calorie counts of some typical breakfast foods.

100 calories or less

85 CALORIES

BREAKFAST PATTIES

breakfast patties

Jo Ann Honey | LONGMONT, COLORADO
While looking for lower-fat, high-protein breakfast options, I took an old sausage recipe and made it new again. I love these savory patties.

      2 pounds lean ground turkey
 1-1/2 teaspoons salt
      1 teaspoon dried sage leaves
      1 teaspoon pepper
  1/2   teaspoon ground ginger
  1/2   teaspoon cayenne pepper

- Crumble turkey into a large bowl. Add salt, sage, pepper, ginger and cayenne. Shape into sixteen 2-1/2-in. patties.
- In a large skillet, cook patties over medium heat for 4-6 minutes on each side or until meat is no longer pink.

YIELD: 16 patties.

NUTRITION FACTS: 2 patties equals 85 calories, 5 g fat (1 g saturated fat), 45 mg cholesterol, 275 mg sodium, trace carbohydrate, trace fiber, 10 g protein. **DIABETIC EXCHANGES:** 2 very lean meat, 1/2 fat.

sweet berry bruschetta

Patricia Nieh | PORTOLA VALLEY, CALIFORNIA
I've made this recipe by toasting the bread on a grill at cookouts, but any way I serve it, I never have any leftovers. The bruschetta is sweet instead of savory as is often expected, and visitors enjoy that change.

     10 slices French bread (1/2 inch thick)
      5 teaspoons sugar, *divided*
      6 ounces fat-free cream cheese
   1/2   teaspoon almond extract
   3/4   cup fresh blackberries
   3/4   cup fresh raspberries
   1/4   cup slivered almonds, toasted
      2 teaspoons confectioners' sugar

- Place bread on an ungreased baking sheet; lightly coat with cooking spray. Sprinkle with 2 teaspoons sugar. Broil 3-4 in. from the heat for 1-2 minutes or until lightly browned.
- In a small bowl, combine cream cheese, almond extract and remaining sugar. Spread over toasted bread. Top with berries and almonds; dust with confectioners' sugar.

YIELD: 10 pieces.

NUTRITION FACTS: 1 piece equals 92 calories, 2 g fat (trace saturated fat), 1 mg cholesterol, 179 mg sodium, 14 g carbohydrate, 2 g fiber, 4 g protein. **DIABETIC EXCHANGES:** 1 starch, 1/2 fat.

SWEET BERRY BRUSCHETTA

92 CALORIES

GINGERED MELON

76 CALORIES

gingered melon

Patricia Richardson | VERONA, ONTARIO

When I have guests, I like to let them spoon melon from a large serving bowl and add their own toppings. You can also combine the fruit with ice cream or frozen yogurt and ginger ale to make a melon float!

- 1/2 medium honeydew, cut into 1-inch cubes
- 1/4 cup orange juice
- 1-1/2 teaspoons ground ginger
- 1/2 to 1 cup whipped cream
- 1/4 cup fresh *or* frozen unsweetened raspberries

- In a small bowl, combine the melon, orange juice and ginger; cover and refrigerate for 5-10 minutes. Spoon into tall dessert glasses or bowls. Top with whipped cream and raspberries.

YIELD: 4 servings.

NUTRITION FACTS: 1 cup equals 76 calories, 2 g fat (1 g saturated fat), 6 mg cholesterol, 22 mg sodium, 15 g carbohydrate, 1 g fiber, 1 g protein.

63 CALORIES **four-fruit salad**

Debbie Fite | FORT MYERS, FLORIDA

Almost any type of fruit will work in this recipe. The first time I made it, I just used the fruits I had on hand in my refrigerator. It's always great.

- 2 cups fresh strawberries, sliced
- 2 cups green grapes, halved
- 1 small cantaloupe, cut into chunks
- 1 to 2 medium firm bananas, sliced
- 1/3 cup orange juice

- In a large bowl, combine the fruit. Pour juice over fruit and toss to coat. Cover and refrigerate for 4 hours. Stir just before serving.

YIELD: 10 servings.

NUTRITION FACTS: 1/2 cup equals 63 calories, trace fat (trace saturated fat), 0 cholesterol, 5 mg sodium, 15 g carbohydrate, 2 g fiber, 1 g protein.

homemade egg substitute

June Formanek | BELL PLAINE, IOWA

This tasty alternative to whole eggs is perfect for folks who are watching their diets, and it scrambles up fluffy and oh-so delicious.

- 3 egg whites
- 2 tablespoons instant nonfat dry milk powder
- 1 teaspoon water
- 2 to 3 drops yellow food coloring, optional

- In a small bowl, combine all the ingredients. Use as a substitute for eggs.

YIELD: 1 serving (equivalent to 2 eggs).

NUTRITION FACTS: 1 serving equals 64 calories, 0.55 g fat (0 saturated fat), 2 mg cholesterol, 156 mg sodium, 5 g carbohydrate, 0 fiber, 10 g protein. **DIABETIC EXCHANGES:** 1 very lean meat, 1/2 fat-free milk.

HOMEMADE EGG SUBSTITUTE

64 CALORIES

baked canadian-style bacon

97 CALORIES

Myra Innes | AUBURN, KANSAS

Brown sugar, pineapple juice and ground mustard nicely season slices of Canadian bacon. You can easily double the recipe when entertaining a crowd.

- 1 pound sliced Canadian bacon
- 1/4 cup packed brown sugar
- 1/4 cup pineapple juice
- 1/4 teaspoon ground mustard

- Place the bacon in a greased 11-in. x 7-in. baking dish. In a bowl, combine the brown sugar, pineapple juice and mustard. Pour over the bacon. Cover and bake at 325° for 25-30 minutes or until heated through.

YIELD: 8 servings.

NUTRITION FACTS: 2 pieces equals 97 calories, 3 g fat (1 g saturated fat), 21 mg cholesterol, 555 mg sodium, 8 g carbohydrate, trace fiber, 9 g protein.

orange sauce

Cloris Wilkinson | KOKOMO, INDIANA

The cheery color and pleasing flavor of this sauce will wake you up in the morning. It's tasty over pancakes or waffles. It's a refreshing, lower-calorie alternative to maple syrup.

- 2 tablespoons sugar
- 1/2 teaspoon cornstarch
- 1/8 teaspoon grated orange peel
- 1/3 cup orange juice
- 1 teaspoon butter

- In a small saucepan, combine the sugar, cornstarch and orange peel. Stir in orange juice until smooth. Bring to a boil; cook and stir for 1-2 minutes or until thickened to a syrup consistency. Remove from the heat; whisk in butter.

YIELD: 1/3 cup.

NUTRITION FACTS: 2 tablespoons equals 34 calories, 1 g fat (trace saturated fat), 2 mg cholesterol, 8 mg sodium, 7 g carbohydrate, trace fiber, trace protein.

ORANGE SAUCE

34 CALORIES

Here are some typical breakfast foods and the number of calories they contain. Use this list as a reference for what foods you might combine to stay within your goal of a 350-calorie breakfast.

- 3/4 cup oats, quick, instant and regular, cooked with water, 109 calories

- 1 plain mini bagel (2-1/2" diameter), 72 calories

- 1 tablespoon whipped cream cheese, 35 calories

- 1 frozen waffle (1 square), 98 calories

- 1 pancake (6" diameter prepared from dry, complete pancake mix), 149 calories

- 1 large scrambled egg, 101 calories

- 1 cup Cheerios, 111 calories

- 1 cup Wheaties, 107 calories

- 1 cup fat-free milk, 86 calories

- 1 container yogurt (6-ounce nonfat fruit variety), 160 calories

- 1 cup orange juice, 110 calories

- 1 cup skinny latte (made with fat-free milk), 80 calories

- 1 slice whole wheat toast, 69 calories

For additional calorie calculations, check the Nutrition Facts labels on food packages.

69 CALORIES

ASPARAGUS HAM ROLL-UPS

berry yogurt cups

Shannon Mink | COLUMBUS, OHIO

Blueberries and strawberries jazz up plain yogurt in this easy dish that's perfect as a breakfast item or no-bake snack. Use this combination or any of your favorite fruits!

1-1/2	cups sliced fresh strawberries
1-1/2	cups fresh blueberries
1	carton (6 ounces) vanilla yogurt
1	teaspoon sugar
1/8 to 1/4	teaspoon ground cinnamon

• Divide strawberries and blueberries among four individual serving dishes. In a small bowl, combine the yogurt, sugar and cinnamon; spoon over fruit.

YIELD: 4 servings.

NUTRITION FACTS: 3/4 cup fruit with 3 tablespoons yogurt equals 98 calories, 2 g fat (1 g saturated fat), 4 mg cholesterol, 29 mg sodium, 20 g carbohydrate, 3 g fiber, 3 g protein. **DIABETIC EXCHANGES:** 1 fruit, 1/2 milk.

BERRY YOGURT CUPS

98 CALORIES

asparagus ham roll-ups

Rhonda Struthers | OTTAWA, ONTARIO

Havarti cheese, asparagus and red peppers make these tasty roll-ups ideal for a spring celebration. Fresh chive ties give them a fussed-over look, but they're a cinch to assemble!

16	fresh asparagus spears, trimmed
1	medium sweet red pepper, cut into 16 strips
8	ounces Havarti cheese, cut into 16 strips
8	thin slices deli ham *or* prosciutto, cut in half lengthwise
16	whole chives

• In a large skillet, bring 1 in. of water to a boil. Add the asparagus; cover and cook for 3 minutes. Drain and immediately place asparagus in ice water. Drain and pat dry.

• Place an asparagus spear, red pepper strip and cheese strip on each slice of ham. Roll up tightly; tie with a chive. Refrigerate until serving.

YIELD: 16 servings.

NUTRITION FACTS: 1 roll-up equals 69 calories, 5 g fat (3 g saturated fat), 18 mg cholesterol, 180 mg sodium, 2 g carbohydrate, trace fiber, 6 g protein. **DIABETIC EXCHANGES:** 1 fat, 1/2 vegetable.

sage breakfast patties

78 CALORIES

Laura McDowell | LAKE VILLA, ILLINOIS

You'll want to skip store-bought breakfast patties when you try this simple recipe. It combines ground turkey and pork with plenty of sage and other seasonings for terrific flavor. No one will believe that it's low in calories and only has 6 grams of fat.

    2 teaspoons rubbed sage
    2 teaspoons minced chives
  3/4 teaspoon salt
  3/4 teaspoon white pepper
  1/4 teaspoon onion powder
  1/4 teaspoon chili powder
  1/8 teaspoon dried thyme
    1 pound ground turkey
  1/2 pound ground pork

- In a large bowl, combine the first seven ingredients.
- Crumble turkey and pork over mixture and mix well.
- Shape into eighteen 2-in. patties. In a large skillet, cook patties over medium heat for 6-8 minutes or until meat is no longer pink, turning once. Drain on paper towels.

YIELD: 1-1/2 dozen.

NUTRITION FACTS: 1 patty equals 78 calories, 6 g fat (2 g saturated fat), 26 mg cholesterol, 131 mg sodium, trace carbohydrate, trace fiber, 6 g protein. **DIABETIC EXCHANGES:** 1 lean meat, 1/2 fat.

apple syrup

Barbara Hill | OIL SPRINGS, ONTARIO

This delicious alternative to maple syrup makes a great change-of-pace topper for breakfast entrees. We try to eat light, and my husband doesn't feel deprived when I serve this syrup with his waffles and pancakes.

    1 tablespoon cornstarch
  1/4 teaspoon ground cinnamon
  1/4 teaspoon ground nutmeg
1-1/4 cups unsweetened apple juice
Sugar substitute equivalent to 4 teaspoons sugar

- In a small saucepan, combine the cornstarch, cinnamon, nutmeg and apple juice until smooth. Bring to a boil;

20 CALORIES

APPLE SYRUP

cook and stir for 2 minutes or until thickened. Remove from the heat; stir in sugar substitute.

YIELD: 1-1/4 cups.

NUTRITION FACTS: 2 tablespoons equals 20 calories, trace fat (trace saturated fat), 0 cholesterol, 1 mg sodium, 5 g carbohydrate, trace fiber, trace protein. **DIABETIC EXCHANGE:** Free food.

mint berry blast

65 CALORIES

Diane Harrison | MECHANICSBURG, PENNSYLVANIA

What's better than a bowl of fresh-picked berries? A bowl of berries enhanced with mint, lemon juice and a dollop of whipped topping. This treat is quick, easy and so refreshing for brunch!

  1 cup *each* fresh raspberries, blackberries, blueberries and halved strawberries
  1 tablespoon minced fresh mint
  1 tablespoon lemon juice
Whipped topping, optional

- In a large bowl, combine the berries, mint and lemon juice; gently toss to coat. Cover and refrigerate until serving. Garnish with whipped topping if desired.

YIELD: 4 servings.

NUTRITION FACTS: 1 cup (calculated without whipped topping) equals 65 calories, 1 g fat (trace saturated fat), 0 cholesterol, 1 mg sodium, 16 g carbohydrate, 6 g fiber, 1 g protein. **DIABETIC EXCHANGE:** 1 fruit.

92 CALORIES

SAVORY APPLE-CHICKEN SAUSAGE

savory apple-chicken sausage

Angela Buchanan | LONGMONT, COLORADO

These easy, healthy sausages taste great, and they make an elegant brunch dish. The recipe is also versatile. It can be doubled or tripled for a crowd, and the sausage freezes well either cooked or raw.

        1 large tart apple, peeled and diced
        2 teaspoons poultry seasoning
        1 teaspoon salt
      1/4 teaspoon pepper
        1 pound ground chicken

- In a large bowl, combine the apple, poultry seasoning, salt and pepper. Crumble chicken over mixture and mix well. Shape into eight 3-in. patties.

- In a large skillet coated with cooking spray, cook patties over medium heat for 5-6 minutes on each side or until no longer pink. Drain if necessary.

YIELD: 8 patties.

NUTRITION FACTS: 1 patty equals 92 calories, 5 g fat (1 g saturated fat), 38 mg cholesterol, 328 mg sodium, 4 g carbohydrate, 1 g fiber, 9 g protein. **DIABETIC EXCHANGES:** 1 lean meat, 1/2 fruit.

101-200 calories

overnight yeast waffles

Mary Balcomb | CROOKED RIVER RANCH, OREGON

Starting the day with an appealing eye-opener is a step in the right direction when you're trying to eat right.

        1 package (1/4 ounce) active dry yeast
      1/2 cup warm water (110° to 115°)
        1 teaspoon sugar
        2 cups warm fat-free milk (110° to 115°)
        2 eggs, *separated*
        2 tablespoons butter, melted
        1 tablespoon canola oil
    1-3/4 cups all-purpose flour
        1 teaspoon salt

- In a large mixing bowl, dissolve yeast in warm water. Add sugar; let stand for 5 minutes. Add the milk, egg yolks, butter and oil (refrigerate egg whites). Combine flour and salt; stir into milk mixture. Cover bowl and refrigerate overnight.

- Let egg whites stand at room temperature for 30 minutes. In a small mixing bowl, beat egg whites until stiff peaks form. Stir batter; fold in egg whites.

- For each waffle, pour the batter by 1/4 cupfuls into a preheated waffle iron; bake according to manufacturer's directions until golden brown.

YIELD: 10 servings.

NUTRITION FACTS: 2 waffles equals 148 calories, 5 g fat (2 g saturated fat), 50 mg cholesterol, 298 mg sodium, 20 g carbohydrate, 1 g fiber, 5 g protein. **DIABETIC EXCHANGES:** 1 starch, 1 fat.

OVERNIGHT YEAST WAFFLES

148 CALORIES

119 CALORIES

CUSTARD BERRY PARFAITS

custard berry parfaits

Trisha Kruse | EAGLE, IDAHO
Here's a low-fat breakfast treat that captures the classic flavors of berries and cream. The homemade custard comes together in minutes but seems like you fussed.

1/4	cup sugar
4	teaspoons cornstarch
1/4	teaspoon salt
1-2/3	cups 1% milk
2	egg yolks, lightly beaten
3/4	teaspoon vanilla extract
3	cups mixed fresh berries

- In a small saucepan, combine the sugar, cornstarch and salt. Stir in milk until smooth. Cook and stir over medium-high heat until thickened and bubbly. Reduce heat; cook and stir 2 minutes longer. Remove from the heat.

- Stir a small amount of hot filling into egg yolks; return all to the pan, stirring constantly. Bring to a gentle boil; cook and stir 2 minutes longer. Remove from the heat.

- Gently stir in vanilla. Cool to room temperature without stirring. Transfer to a bowl; press plastic wrap onto surface of custard. Refrigerate for at least 1 hour.

- Just before serving, spoon 1/4 cup of berries into each parfait glass; top with 2 tablespoons of custard. Repeat the layers.

YIELD: 6 servings.

NUTRITION FACTS: 1/2 cup berries with 1/4 cup custard equals 119 calories, 3 g fat (1 g saturated fat), 74 mg cholesterol, 137 mg sodium, 21 g carbohydrate, 3 g fiber, 4 g protein. **DIABETIC EXCHANGES:** 1 fruit, 1/2 starch, 1/2 fat.

chocolate chip banana muffins

Lauren Heyn | OAK CREEK, WISCONSIN
Lots of banana flavor and chocolate chips disguise the whole wheat taste in these moist muffins. They're perfect for breakfast or an anytime snack.

3/4	cup all-purpose flour
3/4	cup whole wheat flour
1/2	cup wheat bran
1/2	cup packed brown sugar
1	teaspoon baking powder
3/4	teaspoon baking soda
1/2	teaspoon salt
2	eggs, lightly beaten
1/4	cup fat-free milk
1-1/3	cups mashed ripe bananas (2 to 3 medium)
1/3	cup unsweetened applesauce
1	teaspoon vanilla extract
1/2	cup miniature chocolate chips
1/3	cup chopped pecans

- In a large bowl, combine the first seven ingredients. In another bowl, combine the eggs and milk; stir in the bananas, applesauce and vanilla. Stir into dry ingredients just until moistened. Stir in chocolate chips.

- Coat muffin cups with cooking spray or use paper liners; fill three-fourths full with batter. Sprinkle batter with pecans. Bake at 375° for 18-22 minutes or until a toothpick inserted near the center comes out clean. Cool for 5 minutes before removing from pan to a wire rack.

YIELD: 1 dozen.

NUTRITION FACTS: 1 muffin equals 191 calories, 6 g fat (2 g saturated fat), 36 mg cholesterol, 236 mg sodium, 33 g carbohydrate, 4 g fiber, 4 g protein. **DIABETIC EXCHANGES:** 2 starch, 1/2 fat.

CHOCOLATE CHIP BANANA MUFFINS

191 CALORIES

137
CALORIES

STRAWBERRY CREPE ROLL-UPS

strawberry crepe roll-ups

Cheryl Erikson | GRASS VALLEY, CALIFORNIA

I grew up enjoying these sweet crepes, which my grandmother, aunts and uncles always called "Swedish pancakes." My husband, Chuck, sometimes makes this delicious lighter version for me on weekends.

1-1/4 cups fat-free milk
3/4 cup egg substitute
3/4 teaspoon vanilla extract
1 cup all-purpose flour
1 teaspoon sugar
1/4 teaspoon salt
2/3 cup strawberry spreadable fruit
3 cups chopped fresh strawberries
2 teaspoons confectioners' sugar

- In a large bowl, combine the milk, egg substitute and vanilla. Combine the flour, sugar and salt; add to milk mixture and mix well. Cover and refrigerate for 1 hour.

- Coat a 7- or 8-in. nonstick skillet with cooking spray. Heat skillet over medium heat. Pour about 2 tablespoons batter into the center of skillet. Lift and tilt pan to evenly coat bottom. Cook until top appears dry; turn and cook 15-20 seconds longer. Remove to plate; keep warm. Repeat with the remaining batter, coating skillet with additional cooking spray as needed.

- Spread each crepe with about 2 teaspoons spreadable fruit. Top with about 3 tablespoons strawberries. Roll up. Sprinkle with confectioners' sugar.

YIELD: 8 servings.

NUTRITION FACTS: 2 filled crepes equals 137 calories, trace fat (trace saturated fat), 1 mg cholesterol, 145 mg sodium, 28 g carbohydrate, 3 g fiber, 6 g protein. **DIABETIC EXCHANGES:** 1 starch, 1 fruit.

199 CALORIES

poppy seed doughnuts

This scrumptious doughnut recipe, from our Test Kitchen, freezes well so you can make a batch and save the extras. It's nice to know that even while eating healthy, you can still enjoy a sweet doughnut now and then!

1 cup all-purpose flour
1/2 cup sugar
1 tablespoon poppy seeds
3/4 teaspoon baking powder
3/4 teaspoon baking soda
1/4 teaspoon salt
1 egg
1/3 cup buttermilk
1/3 cup reduced-fat plain yogurt
1 tablespoon canola oil
2 teaspoons lemon juice
1 teaspoon grated lemon peel
1/2 teaspoon vanilla extract
2 teaspoons confectioners' sugar, *divided*

- In a small bowl, combine first six ingredients. Combine the egg, buttermilk, yogurt, oil, lemon juice, peel and vanilla; stir into dry ingredients just until moistened.

- Coat six 4-in. tube pans with cooking spray and dust with 1 teaspoon confectioners' sugar. Divide batter among pans.

- Bake at 400° for 10-12 minutes or until a toothpick inserted near the center comes out clean. Cool for 5 minutes before removing from pans to wire racks. Dust with remaining confectioners' sugar.

YIELD: 6 servings.

NUTRITION FACTS: 1 doughnut equals 199 calories, 4 g fat (1 g saturated fat), 37 mg cholesterol, 341 mg sodium, 36 g carbohydrate, 1 g fiber, 5 g protein. **DIABETIC EXCHANGES:** 2 starch, 1/2 fruit.

120 CALORIES

PEACH SMOOTHIES

peach smoothies

Martha Polasek I MARKHAM, TEXAS

Whip up this creamy concoction as a quick chilled breakfast or refreshing and nutritious snack. Because you can use frozen fruit, you don't have to wait until peaches are in season to enjoy this delicious drink.

- 1/2 cup peach *or* apricot nectar
- 1/2 cup sliced fresh *or* frozen peaches
- 1/4 cup fat-free vanilla yogurt
-   2 ice cubes

- In a blender, combine all ingredients. Cover and process until blended. Pour into chilled glasses; serve immediately.

YIELD: 2 servings.

NUTRITION FACTS: 1 serving equals 120 calories, trace fat (trace saturated fat), 1 mg cholesterol, 29 mg sodium, 29 g carbohydrate, 2 g fiber, 2 g protein. Diabetic Exchanges: 2 fruit.

garden frittata

Catherine Michel I O'FALLON, MISSOURI

I created this dish one day to use up some fresh yellow squash, zucchini and tomato. It's so easy to make because you don't have to fuss with a crust. Give it a different twist by trying it with whatever veggies you have on hand.

-   1 small yellow summer squash, thinly sliced
-   1 small zucchini, thinly sliced

-   1 small onion, chopped
-   1 cup (4 ounces) shredded part-skim mozzarella cheese
-   1 medium tomato, sliced
- 1/4 cup crumbled feta cheese
-   4 eggs
-   1 cup fat-free milk
-   2 tablespoons minced fresh basil
-   1 garlic clove, minced
- 1/2 teaspoon salt
- 1/4 teaspoon pepper
- 1/4 cup shredded Parmesan cheese

- In a microwave-safe bowl, combine the squash, zucchini and onion. Cover and microwave on high for 7-9 minutes or until the vegetables are tender; drain well.

- Transfer to a 9-in. pie plate coated with cooking spray. Top with the mozzarella, tomato and feta cheese.

- In a large bowl, whisk the eggs, milk, basil, garlic, salt and pepper; pour over the cheese and tomato layer. Sprinkle with Parmesan cheese.

- Bake, uncovered, at 375° for 45-50 minutes or until a knife inserted near the center comes out clean. Let stand for 10 minutes before serving.

YIELD: 8 servings.

NUTRITION FACTS: 1 serving equals 126 calories, 7 g fat (4 g saturated fat), 121 mg cholesterol, 316 mg sodium, 6 g carbohydrate, 1 g fiber, 11 g protein. **DIABETIC EXCHANGES:** 1 lean meat, 1 vegetable, 1 fat.

GARDEN FRITTATA

126 CALORIES

160 CALORIES

SPECIAL BRUNCH BAKE

special brunch bake

Nicki Woods | SPRINGFIELD, MISSOURI

This delicious, cheesy bake features buttermilk biscuits. You could even try it with turkey bacon instead of Canadian bacon. My son puts it together by himself, and the entire family devours it. This versatile recipe really works for any meal of the day.

- 2 tubes (4 ounces *each*) refrigerated buttermilk biscuits
- 3 cartons (8 ounces *each*) frozen egg substitute, thawed
- 7 ounces Canadian bacon, chopped
- 1 cup (4 ounces) shredded reduced-fat cheddar cheese
- 1 cup (4 ounces) shredded reduced-fat mozzarella cheese
- 1/2 cup chopped fresh mushrooms
- 1/2 cup finely chopped onion
- 1/4 teaspoon pepper

- Arrange the biscuits in a 13-in. x 9-in. baking dish coated with cooking spray. In a bowl, combine the remaining ingredients; pour over biscuits.

- Bake, uncovered, at 350° for 30-35 minutes or until a knife inserted near the center comes out clean.

YIELD: 12 servings.

NUTRITION FACTS: 1 biscuit section equals 160 calories, 5 g fat (3 g saturated fat), 20 mg cholesterol, 616 mg sodium, 13 g carbohydrate, 1 g fiber, 15 g protein. **DIABETIC EXCHANGES:** 2 lean meat, 1 starch.

berry best smoothies

Pamela Klim | BETTENDORF, IOWA

This fun recipe is a wonderful way to use up over-ripened bananas and help my family get five daily servings of fruit. It's so quick, easy and filling—and my kids absolutely love it!

- 3 tablespoons orange juice concentrate
- 3 tablespoons fat-free half-and-half
- 12 ice cubes
- 1 cup fresh strawberries, hulled
- 1 medium ripe banana, cut into chunks
- 1/2 cup fresh *or* frozen blueberries
- 1/2 cup fresh *or* frozen raspberries

- In a blender, combine all ingredients; cover and process for 30-45 seconds or until smooth. Pour into chilled glasses; serve immediately.

YIELD: 3 servings.

NUTRITION FACTS: 1 cup equals 108 calories, 1 g fat (trace saturated fat), 0 cholesterol, 14 mg sodium, 26 g carbohydrate, 4 g fiber, 2 g protein. **DIABETIC EXCHANGE:** 1-1/2 fruit.

BERRY BEST SMOOTHIES

108 CALORIES

BUTTERMILK BUCKWHEAT PANCAKES

buttermilk buckwheat pancakes

This recipe, from our Taste of Home Test Kitchen, uses buckwheat flour instead of the wheat-based variety to produce light, tender pancakes.

 1 cup buckwheat flour
 2 tablespoons brown sugar
 1 teaspoon baking powder
1/2 teaspoon baking soda
1/2 teaspoon salt
1/8 teaspoon *each* ground cinnamon, nutmeg and cloves
 1 egg
 1 cup 1% buttermilk
 1 tablespoon butter, melted

- In a large bowl, combine the flour, brown sugar, baking powder, baking soda, salt, cinnamon, nutmeg and cloves. Whisk the egg, buttermilk and butter; stir into the dry ingredients just until moistened.

- Pour batter by 1/4 cupfuls onto a hot nonstick griddle coated with cooking spray. Turn when bubbles form on top of pancakes; cook until second side is golden brown.

YIELD: 4 servings.

NUTRITION FACTS: 2 pancakes equals 195 calories, 6 g fat (3 g saturated fat), 63 mg cholesterol, 667 mg sodium, 31 g carbohydrate, 3 g fiber, 7 g protein. **DIABETIC EXCHANGES:** 2 starch, 1 fat.

ham 'n' cheese squares

Sue Ross | CASA GRANDE, ARIZONA
So easy to prepare, this appetizing egg dish is loaded with ham, Swiss cheese and caraway flavor. It cuts nicely into squares, making it an ideal addition to a brunch buffet.

1-1/2 cups cubed fully cooked ham
  1 carton (6 ounces) plain yogurt
 1/4 cup crushed saltines (about 6)
 1/4 cup shredded Swiss cheese
  2 tablespoons butter, melted
  2 teaspoons caraway seeds
  6 eggs

- In a large bowl, combine the first six ingredients. In a small mixing bowl, beat the eggs until thickened and lemon-colored; fold into ham mixture. Transfer to a greased 8-in. square baking dish.

- Bake at 375° for 20-25 minutes or until a knife inserted near the center comes out clean. Let stand for 5 minutes before cutting.

YIELD: 9 servings.

NUTRITION FACTS: 1 piece equals 141 calories, 9 g fat (4 g saturated fat), 166 mg cholesterol, 404 mg sodium, 3 g carbohydrate, trace fiber, 10 g protein.

HAM 'N' CHEESE SQUARES

187 CALORIES

SPINACH CHEESE PHYLLO SQUARES

spinach cheese phyllo squares

Julie Remer | GAHANNA, OHIO

A higher-fat version of this casserole was a big hit when my aunt and I ran a gourmet carryout business. Now, I'm trying to lighten things up a bit.

- 6 sheets phyllo dough (14 inches x 9 inches)
- 1 package (10 ounces) frozen chopped spinach, thawed and squeezed dry
- 2-1/2 cups (10 ounces) shredded part-skim mozzarella cheese
- 1-1/2 cups (6 ounces) shredded reduced-fat cheddar cheese
- 1-1/2 cups (12 ounces) fat-free cottage cheese
- 4 eggs
- 1-1/2 teaspoons dried parsley flakes
- 3/4 teaspoon salt
- 6 egg whites
- 1-1/2 cups fat-free milk

- Layer three phyllo sheets in a 13-in. x 9-in. baking dish coated with cooking spray, lightly spraying the top of each sheet with cooking spray.

- In a large bowl, combine the spinach, cheese, 2 eggs, parsley flakes and salt; spread over the phyllo dough. Top with the remaining phyllo sheets, lightly spraying the top of each sheet with cooking spray. Using a sharp knife, cut into 12 squares; cover and chill for 1 hour. In a small bowl, beat the egg whites, milk and remaining eggs until blended; pour over the casserole. Cover and refrigerate overnight.

- Remove from the refrigerator 1 hour before baking. Bake, uncovered, at 375° for 40-50 minutes or until a knife inserted near the center comes out clean and top is golden brown. Let stand for 10 minutes before cutting.

YIELD: 12 servings.

NUTRITION FACTS: 1 piece equals 187 calories, 9 g fat (5 g saturated fat), 97 mg cholesterol, 593 mg sodium, 9 g carbohydrate, 1 g fiber, 19 g protein. **DIABETIC EXCHANGES:** 2 lean meat, 1/2 starch, 1/2 fat.

120 CALORIES

orange strawberry smoothies

Jan Gilreath | WINNEBAGO, MINNESOTA

My family and friends were so surprised when I told them that this refreshing, healthy drink has a secret ingredient…tofu! My dad often requests it.

- 2-1/4 cups orange juice
- 1 package (12.3 ounces) silken reduced-fat firm tofu
- 3 cups halved frozen unsweetened strawberries
- 1-1/2 cups sliced ripe bananas

- In a food processor, combine the orange juice, tofu, strawberries and bananas; cover and pulse until blended. Pour into chilled glasses; serve immediately.

YIELD: 6 servings.

NUTRITION FACTS: 1 cup equals 120 calories, 1 g fat (trace saturated fat), 0 cholesterol, 51 mg sodium, 25 g carbohydrate, 3 g fiber, 5 g protein. **DIABETIC EXCHANGES:** 1-1/2 fruit, 1 very lean meat.

166 CALORIES

lemon-blueberry oat muffins

Jamie Brown | WALDEN, COLORADO

These yummy oatmeal muffins showcase juicy blueberries and zesty lemon flavor. They're a perfect breakfast on-the-go.

- 1 cup quick-cooking oats
- 1 cup all-purpose flour
- 1/2 cup sugar
- 3 teaspoons baking powder
- 1/4 teaspoon salt
- 1 egg
- 1 egg white

1 cup fat-free milk

2 tablespoons butter, melted

1 teaspoon grated lemon peel

1 teaspoon vanilla extract

1 cup fresh *or* frozen blueberries

TOPPING:

1/2 cup quick-cooking oats

2 tablespoons brown sugar

1 tablespoon butter, softened

- In a large bowl, combine the first five ingredients. In another bowl, combine the egg, egg white, milk, butter, lemon peel and vanilla. Add to dry ingredients just until moistened. Fold in berries.

- Coat muffin cups with cooking spray or use paper liners; fill two-thirds full. Combine topping ingredients; sprinkle over batter.

- Bake at 400° for 20-22 minutes or until a toothpick inserted in the muffin comes out clean. Cool 5 minutes before removing from pan to a wire rack to cool completely.

YIELD: 1 dozen.

EDITOR'S NOTE: If using frozen blueberries, do not thaw before adding to batter.

NUTRITION FACTS: 1 muffin equals 166 calories, 4 g fat (2 g saturated fat), 26 mg cholesterol, 158 mg sodium, 28 g carbohydrate, 2 g fiber, 4 g protein. **DIABETIC EXCHANGES:** 1-1/2 starch, 1 fat.

grapefruit orange medley

The natural fruit flavors shine through in this refreshing recipe from our Test Kitchen.

2 tablespoons sugar

1 tablespoon cornstarch

1/2 cup lemon-lime soda

2 cans (11 ounces *each*) mandarin oranges, drained

2 medium grapefruit, peeled and sectioned

1-1/2 cups green grapes

- In a small saucepan, combine sugar and cornstarch. Whisk in soda until smooth. Bring to a boil; cook and stir for 1 minute or until thickened. Cover and refrigerate until cool.

- In a large bowl, combine the oranges, grapefruit and grapes. Add sauce; stir to coat.

YIELD: 5 servings.

NUTRITION FACTS: 1/2 cup equals 140 calories, trace fat (trace saturated fat), 0 cholesterol, 8 mg sodium, 36 g carbohydrate, 2 g fiber, 1 g protein.

french omelet

Bernice Morris | MARSHFIELD, MISSOURI

This cheesy, chock-full-of-flavor omelet is modeled after one I tasted and loved in a restaurant. Mine is so hearty and rich-tasting that folks never guess it's lower in fat.

2 eggs, lightly beaten

1/2 cup egg substitute

1/4 cup fat-free milk

1/8 teaspoon salt

1/8 teaspoon pepper

1/4 cup cubed fully cooked lean ham

1 tablespoon chopped onion

1 tablespoon chopped green pepper

1/4 cup shredded reduced-fat cheddar cheese

- In a small bowl, combine the eggs, egg substitute, milk, salt and pepper. Coat a 10-in. nonstick skillet with cooking spray and place over medium heat. Add egg mixture. As eggs set, lift edges, letting uncooked portion flow underneath.

- When eggs are set, sprinkle ham, onion, green pepper and cheese over one side; fold omelet over filling. Cover and let stand for 1 minute or until cheese is melted.

YIELD: 2 servings.

NUTRITION FACTS: 1/2 omelet equals 180 calories, 9 g fat (4 g saturated fat), 230 mg cholesterol, 661 mg sodium, 4 g carbohydrate, trace fiber, 20 g protein. **DIABETIC EXCHANGES:** 3 lean meat, 1 fat.

FRENCH OMELET

181 CALORIES

RASPBERRY STREUSEL MUFFINS

raspberry streusel muffins

Kristin Stank | INDIANAPOLIS, INDIANA

These muffins always receive rave reviews. Pecans, brown sugar and a sweet, yummy glaze make them seem anything but light.

- 1-1/2 cups all-purpose flour
- 1/4 cup sugar
- 1/4 cup packed brown sugar
- 2 teaspoons baking powder
- 1 teaspoon ground cinnamon
- 1/4 teaspoon salt
- 1 egg, lightly beaten
- 1/2 cup plus 2 tablespoons fat-free milk
- 2 tablespoons butter, melted
- 1-1/4 cups fresh *or* frozen raspberries
- 1 teaspoon grated lemon peel

TOPPING:

- 1/4 cup chopped pecans
- 1/4 cup packed brown sugar
- 2 tablespoons all-purpose flour
- 1 teaspoon ground cinnamon
- 1 teaspoon grated lemon peel
- 1 tablespoon butter, melted

GLAZE:

- 1/4 cup confectioners' sugar
- 1-1/2 teaspoons lemon juice

- In a large bowl, combine first six ingredients. Combine egg, milk and butter; stir into dry ingredients until just moistened. Fold in raspberries and lemon peel. Coat muffin cups with cooking spray or use paper liners; fill three-fourths full with batter.

- Combine the topping ingredients; sprinkle about 1 tablespoon over each muffin. Bake at 350° for 18-22

minutes or until a toothpick comes out clean. Cool for 5 minutes before removing from pan to a wire rack. Combine glaze ingredients; drizzle over warm muffins.

YIELD: 1 dozen.

EDITOR'S NOTE: If using frozen raspberries, do not thaw before adding to batter.

NUTRITION FACTS: 1 muffin equals 181 calories, 5 g fat (2 g saturated fat), 26 mg cholesterol, 133 mg sodium, 31 g carbohydrate, 2 g fiber, 3 g protein. **DIABETIC EXCHANGES:** 2 starch, 1 fat.

egg 'n' bacon sandwiches

Sharon Pickett | AURORA, INDIANA

Here's a healthy, homemade take on a fast-food favorite. My son-in-law created this recipe so my grandchildren could have a quick yet nutritious breakfast before school.

- 2 eggs
- 1 teaspoon fat-free milk
- 1/4 teaspoon salt
- 1/8 teaspoon pepper
- 2 slices Canadian bacon (1/2 ounce *each*)
- 1 English muffin, split and toasted
- 2 tablespoons shredded reduced-fat cheddar cheese

- In a small bowl, whisk the eggs, milk, salt and pepper. Divide between two 10-oz. microwave-safe custard cups coated with cooking spray. Microwave, uncovered, on high for 20 seconds. Stir; microwave 20-25 seconds longer or until center of egg is almost set.

EGG 'N' BACON SANDWICHES

179 CALORIES

- Place a slice of bacon on each muffin half; top with the egg and sprinkle with cheese. Microwave, uncovered, for 10-13 seconds or until cheese is melted. Let stand for 20-30 seconds before serving.

YIELD: 2 servings.

EDITOR'S NOTE: This recipe was tested in a 1,100-watt microwave.

NUTRITION FACTS: 1 sandwich equals 179 calories, 8 g fat (3 g saturated fat), 223 mg cholesterol, 673 mg sodium, 14 g carbohydrate, 1 g fiber, 12 g protein. **DIABETIC EXCHANGES:** 1 starch, 1 lean meat.

mushroom spinach omelet

Arlene Hammonds | GRAY, TENNESSEE

I lightened up this savory dish by using olive oil, one whole egg and three egg whites. For a change of pace, I like to mix in diced celery and parsley and use different types of cheeses.

1	egg
3	egg whites
1	tablespoon grated Parmesan cheese
1	tablespoon shredded cheddar cheese
1/4	teaspoon salt
1/8	teaspoon crushed red pepper flakes
1/8	teaspoon garlic powder
1/8	teaspoon pepper
1/2	cup sliced fresh mushrooms
2	tablespoons finely chopped green pepper
1	tablespoon finely chopped onion
1/2	teaspoon olive oil
1	cup torn fresh spinach

- In a small bowl, beat the egg and egg whites. Add cheeses, salt, pepper flakes, garlic powder and pepper; mix well. Set aside.

- In an 8-in. nonstick skillet, saute the mushrooms, green pepper and onion in oil for 4-5 minutes or until tender. Add spinach; cook and stir until spinach is wilted. Add egg mixture. As eggs set, lift edges, letting uncooked portion flow underneath. Cut into wedges. Serve immediately.

YIELD: 2 servings.

NUTRITION FACTS: 1 serving equals 110 calories, 6 g fat (2 g saturated fat), 112 mg cholesterol, 489 mg sodium, 4 g carbohydrate, 1 g fiber, 11 g protein. **DIABETIC EXCHANGES:** 1-1/2 lean meat, 1 vegetable.

high-octane pancakes

Kelly Hanlon | STRASBURG, COLORADO

Fluffy and health-packed, these hotcakes are what I rely on to jump-start the morning and keep me fueled up all day long. They're scrumptious.

1/3	cup plus 1 tablespoon all-purpose flour
1/4	cup quick-cooking oats
3	tablespoons toasted wheat germ
2	teaspoons sugar
1-1/4	teaspoons baking powder
1/8	teaspoon salt
2/3	cup fat-free milk
1/4	cup fat-free plain yogurt
1	tablespoon canola oil

- In a small bowl, combine the first six ingredients. In another bowl, combine the milk, yogurt and oil. Stir into dry ingredients just until moistened.

- Pour batter by 1/3 cupfuls onto a hot nonstick griddle coated with cooking spray. Turn when bubbles form on top of pancake; cook until second side is golden brown.

YIELD: 4 pancakes.

NUTRITION FACTS: 1 pancake equals 142 calories, 5 g fat (trace saturated fat), 1 mg cholesterol, 229 mg sodium, 20 g carbohydrate, 1 g fiber, 6 g protein. **DIABETIC EXCHANGES:** 1-1/2 starch, 1/2 fat.

HIGH-OCTANE PANCAKES

frappe mocha

Beverly Coyde | GASPORT, NEW YORK

Using coffee ice cubes adds body to this special drink. What a treat!

1	teaspoon instant coffee granules
1/4	cup boiling water
1	cup milk
4-1/2	teaspoons chocolate syrup
1/2	cup crushed ice

Whipped topping and additional chocolate syrup, optional

- In a small bowl, dissolve coffee granules in water. Pour into an ice cube tray; freeze.
- In a blender, combine milk, chocolate syrup and coffee ice cubes. Cover and process until smooth. Add crushed ice; blend. Pour into chilled glasses; serve immediately. Garnish with whipped topping and additional chocolate syrup if desired.

YIELD: 2 servings.

NUTRITION FACTS: 1 cup (calculated without garnishes) equals 114 calories, 4 g fat (3 g saturated fat), 17 mg cholesterol, 67 mg sodium, 15 g carbohydrate, trace fiber, 4 g protein.

FRAPPE MOCHA

WARM 'N' FRUITY BREAKFAST CEREAL

warm 'n' fruity breakfast cereal

John Vale | HARDIN, MONTANA

We love the heartiness of this nutritious cooked cereal, seasoned with cinnamon and loaded with chopped fruit and nuts. We like it served with plain yogurt and sliced bananas or blueberries. It will start your day right!

5	cups water
2	cups seven-grain cereal
1	medium apple, peeled and chopped
1	cup unsweetened apple juice
1/4	cup dried apricots, chopped
1/4	cup dried cranberries
1/4	cup raisins
1/4	cup chopped dates
1/4	cup maple syrup
1	teaspoon ground cinnamon
1/2	teaspoon salt

Chopped walnuts, optional

- In a 5-qt. slow cooker, combine the first 11 ingredients. Cover and cook on low for 6-7 hours or until fruits are softened. Sprinkle the individual servings with the walnuts if desired.

YIELD: 10 cups.

NUTRITION FACTS: 1 cup (calculated without walnuts) equals 185 calories, 3 g fat (trace saturated fat), 0 cholesterol, 120 mg sodium, 37 g carbohydrate, 5 g fiber, 5 g protein. **DIABETIC EXCHANGES:** 1 starch, 1 fruit, 1/2 fat.

160 CALORIES

SPINACH OMELET BRUNCH ROLL

spinach omelet brunch roll

Laine Beal | TOPEKA, KANSAS

This recipe uses the combination of veggies from one of my favorite recipes and the rolling technique of another. The result is this stunning presentation, which tastes as good as it looks.

- 2 cups egg substitute
- 4 eggs
- 1/2 teaspoon salt
- 1/8 teaspoon hot pepper sauce
- 1 package (10 ounces) frozen chopped spinach, thawed and squeezed dry
- 1/4 cup chopped red onion
- 1 teaspoon Italian seasoning
- 5 turkey bacon strips, diced and cooked, *divided*
- 1 pound sliced fresh mushrooms
- 2 teaspoons canola oil
- 1 cup (4 ounces) shredded part-skim mozzarella cheese, *divided*

- Line a 15-in. x 10-in. x 1-in. baking pan with parchment paper; coat paper with cooking spray and set aside. In a large bowl, whisk the egg substitute, eggs, salt and pepper sauce. Stir in the spinach, onion, Italian seasoning and 1/4 cup bacon.

- Pour into prepared pan. Bake at 375° for 15-20 minutes or until set. Meanwhile, in a large nonstick skillet, saute mushrooms in oil for 6-8 minutes or until tender. Drain on paper towels; blot to remove excess moisture. Keep warm.

- Turn omelet onto a work surface; peel off parchment paper. Sprinkle omelet with mushrooms and 3/4 cup cheese; roll up jelly-roll style, starting with a short side.

- Place on a serving platter. Sprinkle with remaining cheese and bacon.

YIELD: 8 servings.

NUTRITION FACTS: 1 slice equals 160 calories, 8 g fat (3 g saturated fat), 122 mg cholesterol, 505 mg sodium, 6 g carbohydrate, 2 g fiber, 17 g protein. **DIABETIC EXCHANGES:** 2 lean meat, 1 vegetable, 1/2 fat.

broccoli bacon quiches

Charlotte Green | IOTA, LOUISIANA

A hint of Swiss cheese plus plenty of bacon and broccoli enhance these cute, fluffy quiches.

- 1/2 cup fresh *or* frozen broccoli florets, thawed and drained
- 1/2 cup reduced-fat shredded Swiss cheese
- 1 bacon strip, cooked and crumbled
- 1/2 cup egg substitute
- 1/2 cup half-and-half cream
- 1/8 teaspoon salt

Dash garlic powder

Dash lemon-pepper seasoning

- Divide the broccoli, cheese and bacon between two 5-in. pie plates coated with cooking spray. In a small bowl, whisk the egg substitute, cream, salt, garlic powder and lemon-pepper. Pour over bacon.

- Bake, uncovered, at 350° for 15-20 minutes or until a knife inserted near the center comes out clean.

YIELD: 2 servings.

NUTRITION FACTS: 1 quiche equals 192 calories, 9 g fat (6 g saturated fat), 45 mg cholesterol, 481 mg sodium, 5 g carbohydrate, 1 g fiber, 19 g protein.

BROCCOLI BACON QUICHES

192 CALORIES

183 CALORIES

ITALIAN GARDEN FRITTATA

italian garden frittata

Sally Maloney | DALLAS, GEORGIA
I like to serve this pretty frittata with melon wedges for a delicious breakfast or brunch.

       6   egg whites
       4   eggs
   1/2   cup grated Romano cheese, *divided*
       1   tablespoon minced fresh sage
   1/2   teaspoon salt
   1/4   teaspoon pepper
       1   small zucchini, sliced
       2   green onions, sliced
       1   teaspoon olive oil
       2   plum tomatoes, thinly sliced

- In a large bowl, whisk the egg whites, eggs, 1/4 cup Romano cheese, sage, salt and pepper; set aside.

- In a 10-in. ovenproof skillet coated with cooking spray, saute zucchini and onions in oil for 2 minutes. Add egg mixture; cover and cook for 4-6 minutes or until eggs are nearly set.

- Uncover; top with tomato slices and remaining cheese. Broil 3-4 in. from the heat for 2-3 minutes or until the eggs are completely set. Let stand for 5 minutes. Cut into wedges.

YIELD: 4 servings.

NUTRITION FACTS: 1 wedge equals 183 calories, 11 g fat (5 g saturated fat), 228 mg cholesterol, 655 mg sodium, 4 g carbohydrate, 1 g fiber, 18 g protein.

sweet onion pie

Barbara Reese | CATAWISSA, PENNSYLVANIA
Chock-full of sweet onions, this creamy, quiche-like pie makes a scrumptious addition to a brunch buffet. By using less butter to cook the onions and substituting lighter ingredients, I cut the calories and fat from this tasty dish.

       2   sweet onions, halved and sliced
       1   tablespoon butter
       1   unbaked pastry shell (9 inches)
       1   cup egg substitute
       1   cup fat-free evaporated milk
       1   teaspoon salt
   1/4   teaspoon pepper

- In a large nonstick skillet, cook onions in butter over medium-low heat for 30 minutes or until very tender. Meanwhile, line unpricked pastry shell with a double thickness of heavy-duty foil.

- Bake at 450° for 6 minutes. Remove foil; cool on a wire rack. Reduce heat to 425°.

- Spoon onions into pastry shell. In a small bowl, whisk the egg substitute, milk, salt and pepper; pour over onions. Bake for 20-25 minutes or until a knife inserted near the center comes out clean. Let stand for 5-10 minutes before cutting.

YIELD: 8 servings.

NUTRITION FACTS: 1 piece equals 187 calories, 9 g fat (4 g saturated fat), 10 mg cholesterol, 510 mg sodium, 20 g carbohydrate, 1 g fiber, 7 g protein. **DIABETIC EXCHANGES:** 1-1/2 fat, 1 starch, 1 very lean meat.

SWEET ONION PIE

187 CALORIES

110 CALORIES

CHEESE TOMATO EGG BAKE

1-1/2 cups fat-free milk
1 cup unsweetened raspberries
Sugar substitute equivalent to 2 tablespoons sugar

- Place all ingredients in a blender; cover and process until smooth. Pour into chilled glasses; serve immediately.

YIELD: 4 servings.

NUTRITION FACTS: 1 cup equals 152 calories, 2 g fat (1 g saturated fat), 7 mg cholesterol, 161 mg sodium, 25 g carbohydrate, 2 g fiber, 9 g protein. **DIABETIC EXCHANGES:** 1 starch, 1 reduced-fat milk.

cheese tomato egg bake

Jonathan Miller | NAUGATUCK, CONNECTICUT
While making eggs, I wanted something different, so I created this tasty egg bake. We loved it! I hope you will enjoy it just as much.

    3/4 cup egg substitute
    2 tablespoons prepared reduced-fat ranch salad dressing
    1/8 teaspoon garlic powder
    1 plum tomato, seeded and diced
    1 slice process American cheese

- In a large bowl, whisk the egg substitute, salad dressing and garlic powder. Spray the bottom of a 3-cup round baking dish with cooking spray. Pour half of egg mixture into dish; top with tomato and cheese. Pour remaining egg mixture on top.

- Bake at 350° for 22-26 minutes or until completely set and a thermometer reads 160°.

YIELD: 2 servings.

NUTRITION FACTS: 1 serving equals 110 calories, 4 g fat (1 g saturated fat), 7 mg cholesterol, 442 mg sodium, 6 g carbohydrate, trace fiber, 12 g protein.

152 CALORIES

berry yogurt shakes

Jacquie Adams | COLQUITLAM, BRITISH COLUMBIA
We have a few raspberry bushes in our backyard. If my grandchildren don't get the berries first, I use them in recipes like this one. Of course, the kids love the mellow flavor of these shakes. So either way, they win!

    2 cartons (8 ounces *each*) reduced-fat lemon yogurt

strawberry tofu smoothies

Debbie Stepp | OCALA, FLORIDA
This is one sweet way to get more soy in my diet. It's light, satisfying, and I can take it with me in an insulated mug with lid and straw for breakfast on the go.

    1 cup unsweetened apple juice
    1-1/2 cups frozen unsweetened strawberries
    4 ounces silken firm tofu, cubed
    1 teaspoon sugar

- In a blender, combine all ingredients; cover and process for 45-60 seconds or until smooth. Pour into chilled glasses; serve immediately.

YIELD: 2 servings.

NUTRITION FACTS: 1 cup equals 136 calories, 2 g fat (trace saturated fat), 0 cholesterol, 25 mg sodium, 26 g carbohydrate, 3 g fiber, 5 g protein. **DIABETIC EXCHANGES:** 1-1/2 fruit, 1 lean meat.

STRAWBERRY TOFU SMOOTHIES

136 CALORIES

fajita frittata

Mary Ann Gomez | LOMBARD, ILLINOIS

This is a super-flavorful and quick entree. It takes me just a few minutes to prepare. Though you could serve it for breakfast or brunch, whenever I ask my family what they want for dinner, this is the most popular request.

- 1/2 pound boneless skinless chicken breast, cut into strips
- 1 small onion, cut into thin strips
- 1/2 medium green pepper, cut into thin strips
- 1 teaspoon lime juice
- 1/2 teaspoon salt
- 1/2 teaspoon ground cumin
- 1/2 teaspoon chili powder
- 2 tablespoons canola oil
- 2 cups egg substitute, lightly beaten
- 1 cup (4 ounces) shredded reduced-fat Colby-Monterey Jack cheese

Salsa and sour cream, optional

- In a large ovenproof skillet, saute the chicken, onion, green pepper, lime juice, salt, cumin and chili powder in oil until chicken juices run clear.

- Pour the egg substitute over chicken mixture. Cover and cook over medium-low heat for 8-10 minutes or until eggs are nearly set. Uncover; broil 6 in. from the heat for 2-3 minutes or until eggs are set. Sprinkle with cheese.

FAJITA FRITTATA

CRISPY FRENCH TOAST

Cover and let stand for 1 minute or until the cheese is melted. Serve with salsa and sour cream if desired.

YIELD: 8 servings.

NUTRITION FACTS: 1 serving (calculated without salsa and sour cream) equals 137 calories, 7 g fat (2 g saturated fat), 23 mg cholesterol, 393 mg sodium, 3 g carbohydrate, trace fiber, 15 g protein. **DIABETIC EXCHANGES:** 2 lean meat, 1 fat.

crispy french toast

Flo Burtnett | GAGE, OKLAHOMA

I lighten up this golden French toast with egg substitute and skim milk, then flavor it with orange juice, vanilla and a dash of nutmeg. The cornflake coating adds a fun crunch.

- 1/2 cup egg substitute
- 1/2 cup fat-free milk
- 1/4 cup orange juice
- 1 teaspoon vanilla extract

Dash ground nutmeg

- 12 slices day-old French bread (3/4 inch thick)
- 1-1/2 cups crushed cornflakes

- In a shallow dish, combine the egg substitute, milk, orange juice, vanilla and nutmeg. Add bread; soak for 5 minutes, turning once. Coat both sides of each slice with cornflake crumbs.

- Place in a 15-in. x 10-in. x 1-in. baking pan coated with cooking spray. Bake at 425° for 10 minutes; turn. Bake 5-8 minutes longer or until golden brown.

YIELD: 12 slices.

NUTRITION FACTS: 1 slice equals 147 calories, 1 g fat (trace saturated fat), trace cholesterol, 359 mg sodium, 28 g carbohydrate, 1 g fiber, 5 g protein. **DIABETIC EXCHANGES:** 2 starch.

creamy peaches

Don Prokidansky | NEW PORT RICHEY, FLORIDA

Smooth and creamy, this pretty and refreshing breakfast treat is high in protein and virtually fat-free. Best of all, it's very good and goes together in minutes.

- 1 can (15 ounces) sliced peaches in extra-light syrup, drained
- 1-1/2 cups (12 ounces) fat-free cottage cheese
- 4 ounces fat-free cream cheese, cubed

Sugar substitute equivalent to 1 tablespoon sugar

- Thinly slice four peach slices; set aside for garnish. Place the remaining peaches in a food processor; add the cottage cheese. Cover and process until blended. Add the cream cheese and sugar substitute; cover and process until blended.

- Spoon into four serving dishes. Top with reserved peaches. Refrigerate until serving.

YIELD: 4 servings.

EDITOR'S NOTE: This recipe was tested with Splenda no-calorie sweetener.

NUTRITION FACTS: 1 cup equals 127 calories, trace fat (trace saturated fat), 6 mg cholesterol, 443 mg sodium, 15 g carbohydrate, 1 g fiber, 15 g protein. **DIABETIC EXCHANGES:** 2 very lean meat, 1/2 starch, 1/2 fruit.

CREAMY PEACHES

PARADISE GRANOLA

paradise granola

Robyn Larabee | LUCKNOW, ONTARIO

Even our son, who isn't fond of dried fruit, enjoys this granola. It's low-fat, full of fiber and just plain delicious.

- 2 cups old-fashioned oats
- 1/2 cup flaked coconut
- 1/2 cup toasted wheat germ
- 1/4 cup oat bran
- 1/4 cup sunflower kernels
- 1/4 cup slivered almonds
- 1/4 cup chopped pecans
- 2 tablespoons sesame seeds
- 1/4 cup honey
- 2 tablespoons canola oil
- 2 tablespoons grated orange peel
- 1 teaspoon vanilla extract
- 1/2 teaspoon salt
- 1 cup dried cranberries
- 3/4 cup chopped dates
- 1/2 cup chopped dried figs
- 1/2 cup chopped dried apricots
- 3 tablespoons raisins

- In a large bowl, combine the first eight ingredients. In a small bowl, whisk the honey, oil, orange peel, vanilla and salt; pour over oat mixture and mix well. Spread evenly into an ungreased 15-in. x 10-in. x 1-in. baking pan.

- Bake at 350° for 20-25 minutes or until golden brown, stirring once. Cool completely on a wire rack. Stir in dried fruits. Store in an airtight container.

YIELD: 7 cups.

NUTRITION FACTS: 1/4 cup equals 132 calories, 5 g fat (1 g saturated fat), 0 cholesterol, 57 mg sodium, 23 g carbohydrate, 3 g fiber, 3 g protein. **DIABETIC EXCHANGES:** 1 starch, 1/2 fruit, 1/2 fat.

184 CALORIES

EGG WHITE FRITTATA

egg white frittata

Linda Lapresle | GLENDORA, CALIFORNIA
This egg dish is very satisfying and nutritious, too. Whether I serve it for Saturday breakfast or for Sunday supper, it's always a hit.

1-1/4   cups sliced fresh mushrooms
1/2   medium onion, diced
1/2   small sweet red pepper, sliced
1/2   small green pepper, diced
1/4   teaspoon salt
1/4   teaspoon dried oregano
Dash pepper
1   tablespoon olive oil
8   egg whites, beaten
1   tablespoon grated Parmesan cheese

- In a 10-in. ovenproof skillet, saute mushrooms, onion, red pepper, green pepper, salt, oregano and pepper in oil until vegetables are tender. Beat egg whites until foamy; pour into skillet. Cook for 3 minutes over medium-low heat or until puffed and lightly browned on bottom. Sprinkle with cheese.

- Bake, uncovered, at 375° for 8-10 minutes or until egg whites are set. Loosen edges and bottom of frittata with a rubber spatula. Invert onto a serving plate; cut into four wedges. Serve immediately.

YIELD: 2 servings.

NUTRITION FACTS: 2 wedges equals 184 calories, 8 g fat (1 g saturated fat), 2 mg cholesterol, 565 mg sodium, 12 g carbohydrate, 2 g fiber, 17 g protein. **DIABETIC EXCHANGES:** 2 lean meat, 2 vegetable, 1/2 fat.

201-300 calories

fruit-filled puff pancake

Leanne Senger | OREGON CITY, OREGON
My husband and I often make a meal of this fruity puff pancake. The combination of cinnamon, blueberries and bananas is wonderful.

1   tablespoon butter
1/3   cup all-purpose flour
3   tablespoons sugar, *divided*
1/4   teaspoon salt
3   eggs, lightly beaten
1/2   cup milk
1-1/2   cups fresh *or* frozen blueberries
1   medium ripe banana, sliced
1/4   teaspoon ground cinnamon

- Place butter in a 9-in. pie plate. Bake at 400° for 4-5 minutes or until melted. Meanwhile, in a large bowl, combine the flour, 1 tablespoon sugar and salt. Add eggs and milk; whisk until smooth.

- Pour into hot pie plate. Bake at 400° for 10-12 minutes or until edges are puffed and golden brown. Meanwhile, combine blueberries and banana.

- In a small bowl, combine cinnamon and remaining sugar. Spoon the fruit mixture onto pancake; sprinkle with the cinnamon-sugar. Cut into wedges.

YIELD: 4 servings.

NUTRITION FACTS: 1 piece equals 232 calories, 8 g fat (4 g saturated fat), 171 mg cholesterol, 240 mg sodium, 34 g carbohydrate, 2 g fiber, 8 g protein.

FRUIT-FILLED PUFF PANCAKE

232 CALORIES

spiced oatmeal mix

210 CALORIES

Loretta Kleinjan | VOLGA, SOUTH DAKOTA

The microwave makes this warm and cozy treat a snap to whip up. Adapt the ingredients to suit your taste. Try it as a quick pick-me-up any time of day.

- 8 cups quick-cooking oats
- 1-1/2 cups chopped mixed dried fruit
- 1/2 cup sugar
- 1/2 cup packed brown sugar
- 2-1/2 teaspoons ground cinnamon
- 1 teaspoon salt
- 1/2 teaspoon ground nutmeg

- In a large bowl, combine all of the ingredients. Store in an airtight container for up to 1 month.

- **TO PREPARE OATMEAL:** Contents of mix may settle during storage. When preparing recipe, spoon the mix into measuring cup. In a deep microwave-safe bowl, combine 1/2 cup oatmeal mix and 1 cup water. Microwave, uncovered, on high for 1-2 minutes or until bubbly, stirring every 30 seconds. Let stand for 1-2 minutes before serving.

YIELD: 18 servings.

EDITOR'S NOTE: This recipe was tested in a 1,100-watt microwave.

NUTRITION FACTS: 1 cup prepared oatmeal equals 210 calories, 3 g fat (trace saturated fat), 0 cholesterol, 137 mg sodium, 42 g carbohydrate, 4 g fiber, 6 g protein. **DIABETIC EXCHANGES:** 2 starch, 1/2 fruit.

no-fry doughnuts

Susie Baldwin | COLUMBIA, TENNESSEE

We have four boys and these doughnuts never last long at our house. I like them because I don't have to clean up a greasy mess.

- 2 packages (1/4 ounce *each*) active dry yeast
- 1/4 cup warm water (110° to 115°)
- 1-1/2 cups warm milk (110° to 115°)
- 1/3 cup shortening
- 1/2 cup sugar
- 2 eggs
- 1 teaspoon salt
- 1 teaspoon ground nutmeg
- 1/4 teaspoon ground cinnamon
- 4-1/2 to 5 cups all-purpose flour
- 1/4 cup butter, melted

GLAZE:
- 1/2 cup butter
- 2 cups confectioners' sugar
- 5 teaspoons water
- 2 teaspoons vanilla extract

- In a large bowl, dissolve yeast in water. Add the milk and shortening; stir for 1 minute. Add the sugar, eggs, salt, nutmeg, cinnamon and 2 cups flour; beat on low speed until smooth. Stir in enough remaining flour to form a soft dough (do not knead). Cover and let rise in a warm place until doubled, about 1 hour.

- Punch dough down. Turn onto a floured surface; roll out to 1/2-in. thickness. Cut with a 2-3/4-in. doughnut cutter; place 2 in. apart on greased baking sheets. Brush with the butter. Cover and let rise in a warm place until doubled, about 30 minutes.

- Bake at 350° for 20 minutes or until lightly browned. Meanwhile, for glaze, melt butter in a saucepan. Add the confectioners' sugar, water and vanilla; cook over low heat until smooth (do not boil). Keep warm. Dip warm doughnuts, one at a time, into glaze and turn to coat. Drain on a wire rack. Serve immediately.

YIELD: 2 dozen.

NUTRITION FACTS: 1 doughnut equals 233 calories, 10 g fat (5 g saturated fat), 35 mg cholesterol, 170 mg sodium, 33 g carbohydrate, 1 g fiber, 4 g protein.

NO-FRY DOUGHNUTS

233 CALORIES

orange oatmeal

Bernice Haack | MILWAUKEE, WISCONSIN

I like to make this for breakfast because it's quick yet out of the ordinary. The orange flavor adds a little something extra to a weekday breakfast.

1	cup water
3/4	cup orange juice
1/8	teaspoon salt
1	cup quick-cooking oats
1/4	teaspoon grated orange peel
1	tablespoon brown sugar

- In a saucepan, bring the water, orange juice and salt to a boil. Stir in oats and cook for 1 minute or until oatmeal reaches desired consistency. Stir in orange peel. Serve with brown sugar.

YIELD: 2 servings.

NUTRITION FACTS: 1 serving equals 222 calories, 3 g fat (trace saturated fat), 0 cholesterol, 151 mg sodium, 43 g carbohydrate, 4 g fiber, 7 g protein. **DIABETIC EXCHANGES:** 2 starch, 1 fruit.

ORANGE OATMEAL

broccoli-ham cheese pie

Nancy Granaman | BURLINGTON, IOWA

Sheets of easy-to-use phyllo dough create a crisp buttery-tasting crust for this entree. The egg and vegetable pie always gets thumbs-up approval.

12	sheets phyllo dough (14 inches x 9 inches)

Refrigerated butter-flavored spray

1	package (16 ounces) frozen broccoli cuts, thawed and patted dry
1	cup cubed fully cooked lean ham
1	cup (4 ounces) shredded reduced-fat cheddar cheese
1	small onion, chopped
2	tablespoons minced fresh parsley
2	garlic cloves, minced
1/2	teaspoon dried thyme
1/2	teaspoon salt
1/2	teaspoon pepper
1	cup egg substitute
1	cup fat-free evaporated milk
2	tablespoons grated Parmesan cheese

- Spritz one sheet of phyllo dough with butter-flavored spray. Place in a 9-in. pie plate coated with cooking spray; allow one end of dough to overhang edge of plate by 3-4 in. (Until ready to use, keep phyllo dough covered with plastic wrap and a damp towel to prevent drying out.) Repeat with remaining phyllo, overlapping the sheets (staggering the points around the plate) and spritzing with butter-flavored spray between each layer.

- In a large bowl, combine the broccoli, ham, cheese, onion, parsley, garlic, thyme, salt and pepper; spoon into crust. Combine egg substitute and milk; pour over the broccoli mixture. Fold edges of dough over filling toward center of pie plate. Spritz edges with butter-flavored spray.

- Cover edge of crust with foil. Bake at 375° for 40 minutes. Remove foil. Sprinkle with Parmesan cheese. Bake 30-35 minutes longer or until a knife inserted near the center comes out clean. Let stand for 10 minutes before cutting.

YIELD: 6 servings.

EDITOR'S NOTE: This recipe was tested with I Can't Believe It's Not Butter Spray.

NUTRITION FACTS: 1 piece equals 232 calories, 6 g fat (3 g saturated fat), 25 mg cholesterol, 882 mg sodium, 24 g carbohydrate, 3 g fiber, 21 g protein. **DIABETIC EXCHANGES:** 1-1/2 starch, 1 lean meat, 1 vegetable, 1 fat.

sausage breakfast wraps

Ed Rysdyk, Jr. | WYOMING, MICHIGAN

I love breakfast burritos—but they're typically high in fat and cholesterol. So I created my own healthier version. Since my wraps freeze beautifully, they make a perfect anytime meal. Let the sausage mixture cool before assembling and freezing the wraps.

1	pound turkey Italian sausage links, casings removed

277 CALORIES

SAUSAGE BREAKFAST WRAPS

- 1 medium sweet red pepper, diced
- 1 small onion, diced
- 4 cartons (8 ounces *each*) frozen egg substitute, thawed
- 1 can (4 ounces) chopped green chilies
- 1 teaspoon chili powder
- 10 flour tortillas (8 inches), warmed
- 1-1/4 cups salsa

- In a nonstick skillet, cook sausage over medium heat until no longer pink; drain. Transfer to a 13-in. x 9-in. baking dish coated with cooking spray. Sprinkle with red pepper and onion. Combine the egg substitute, green chilies and chili powder; pour over sausage mixture.

- Bake, uncovered, at 350° for 30-35 minutes or until set. Break up sausage mixture with a spoon. Place 2/3 cup down the center of each tortilla; top with salsa. Fold one end over sausage mixture, then fold two sides over.

YIELD: 10 servings.

NUTRITION FACTS: 1 wrap equals 277 calories, 7 g fat (1 g saturated fat), 27 mg cholesterol, 893 mg sodium, 30 g carbohydrate, 2 g fiber, 21 g protein. **DIABETIC EXCHANGES:** 2 starch, 2 lean meat, 1/2 fat.

toasted almond granola

Tracy Weakly | ALOHA, OREGON

I combined several granola recipes to come up with this crunchy, cranberry-and-apricot-flavored treat. The possibilities are endless when you vary the kinds of fruits and nuts.

- 3 cups old-fashioned oats
- 2 cups crisp rice cereal
- 1/2 cup toasted wheat germ
- 1/2 cup nonfat dry milk powder
- 1/3 cup slivered almonds
- 1/4 cup packed brown sugar
- 2 tablespoons sunflower kernels
- 1/4 teaspoon salt
- 1/2 cup orange juice
- 1/4 cup honey
- 2 teaspoons canola oil
- 2 teaspoons vanilla extract
- 1/2 teaspoon almond extract
- 1 cup golden raisins
- 1 cup chopped dried apricots
- 1/2 cup dried cranberries

Fat-free plain yogurt, optional

- In a large bowl, combine the oats, cereal, wheat germ, milk powder, almonds, sugar, sunflower kernels and salt. In a saucepan, combine the orange juice, honey and oil. Heat for 3-4 minutes over medium heat until honey is dissolved. Remove from the heat; stir in the extracts. Pour over the oat mixture; stir to coat.

- Transfer to a 15-in. x 10-in. x 1-in. baking pan coated with cooking spray. Bake at 350° for 20-25 minutes or until crisp, stirring every 10 minutes. Remove and cool completely on a wire rack. Stir in dried fruits. Store in an airtight container. Serve with yogurt if desired.

YIELD: 8 cups.

NUTRITION FACTS: 1/2 cup equals 212 calories, 4 g fat (trace saturated fat), 0 cholesterol, 88 mg sodium, 41 g carbohydrate, 3 g fiber, 6 g protein.

TOASTED ALMOND GRANOLA

212 CALORIES

248 CALORIES

SPICY SCRAMBLED EGG SANDWICHES

spicy scrambled egg sandwiches

Helen Vail | GLENSIDE, PENNSYLVANIA

I take family breakfasts in hand with these energy-building muffins-to-go. They're packed with veggies, flavor and easy-to-swallow nutrition!

- 1/3 cup chopped green pepper
- 1/4 cup chopped onion
- 3 eggs
- 4 egg whites
- 1 tablespoon water
- 1/4 teaspoon salt
- 1/4 teaspoon ground mustard
- 1/8 teaspoon pepper
- 1/8 teaspoon hot pepper sauce
- 1/3 cup fresh *or* frozen corn, thawed
- 1/4 cup real bacon bits
- 4 English muffins, split and toasted

- In a 10-in. skillet coated with cooking spray, cook the green pepper and onion over medium heat until tender, about 8 minutes.

- In a large bowl, whisk the eggs, egg whites, water, salt, mustard, pepper and hot pepper sauce. Pour into skillet. Add corn and bacon; cook and stir until the eggs are completely set. Spoon onto the English muffin bottoms; replace tops. Serve immediately.

YIELD: 4 servings.

NUTRITION FACTS: 1 sandwich equals 248 calories, 6 g fat (2 g saturated fat), 164 mg cholesterol, 739 mg sodium, 31 g carbohydrate, 2 g fiber, 16 g protein. **DIABETIC EXCHANGES:** 2 starch, 2 lean meat.

raspberry key lime crepes

Wolfgang Hanau | WEST PALM BEACH, FLORIDA

Key lime juice turns cream cheese into the refreshing filling for these berry crepes. Sometimes, I even pipe the sweet filling into phyllo-dough cones that I bake separately for a fun snack.

- 3 tablespoons key lime juice
- 1 package (12.3 ounces) silken firm tofu, crumbled
- 6 ounces reduced-fat cream cheese, cubed
- 2/3 cup confectioners' sugar, *divided*
- 2-1/2 teaspoons grated lime peel
- Dash salt
- Dash ground nutmeg
- 6 prepared crepes (9 inches)
- 1-1/2 cups fresh raspberries

- In a blender, combine lime juice, tofu and cream cheese; cover and process until smooth. Set aside 1 teaspoon confectioners' sugar. Add the lime peel, salt, nutmeg and remaining confectioners' sugar; cover and process until blended. Cover and refrigerate for at least 1 hour.

- Spread cream cheese mixture over crepes. Sprinkle with raspberries; roll up. Dust with reserved confectioners' sugar.

YIELD: 6 servings.

NUTRITION FACTS: 1 filled crepe equals 222 calories, 9 g fat (5 g saturated fat), 26 mg cholesterol, 247 mg sodium, 28 g carbohydrate, 3 g fiber, 8 g protein. **DIABETIC EXCHANGES:** 1-1/2 starch, 1 lean meat, 1 fat, 1/2 fruit.

RASPBERRY KEY LIME CREPES

222 CALORIES

WAFFLES WITH PEACH-BERRY COMPOTE

waffles with peach-berry compote

Brandi Waters | FAYETTEVILLE, ARKANSAS

This recipe was created one summer Sunday morning when I was looking for a more healthful alternative to butter and maple syrup to top my waffles. I was amazed at the results!

 1   cup fresh *or* frozen peeled peach slices, chopped
1/2   cup orange juice
 2   tablespoons brown sugar
1/4   teaspoon ground cinnamon
 1   cup fresh *or* frozen blueberries
1/2   cup sliced fresh *or* frozen strawberries

BATTER:
1-1/4   cups all-purpose flour
1/2   cup whole wheat flour
 2   tablespoons flaxseed
 1   teaspoon baking powder
 1   teaspoon baking soda
1/2   teaspoon ground cinnamon
 1   cup buttermilk
3/4   cup orange juice
 1   tablespoon canola oil
 1   teaspoon vanilla extract

- In a small saucepan, combine the peaches, orange juice, brown sugar and cinnamon; bring to a boil over medium

heat. Add the berries; cook and stir for 8-10 minutes or until thickened.

- In a large bowl, combine the flours, flaxseed, baking powder, baking soda and cinnamon. Combine buttermilk, orange juice, oil and vanilla; stir into dry ingredients just until moistened.

- Bake in a preheated waffle iron according to manufacturer's directions until golden brown. Serve with compote.

YIELD: 12 waffles (1-1/2 cups compote).

NUTRITION FACTS: 2 waffles with 1/4 cup compote equals 251 calories, 4 g fat (1 g saturated fat), 2 mg cholesterol, 324 mg sodium, 47 g carbohydrate, 4 g fiber, 7 g protein. **DIABETIC EXCHANGES:** 2-1/2 starch, 1/2 fruit, 1/2 fat.

breakfast bake

Howard Rogers | EL PASO, TEXAS

I wanted to have scrambled eggs and hash browns one morning, and this is the dish I created. My wife loved it...and now I'm making breakfast more often!

1-1/2   cups egg substitute
1/2   cup fat-free milk
3-1/2   cups frozen O'Brien hash brown potatoes, thawed
1-1/3   cups shredded reduced-fat cheddar cheese, *divided*
1/2   cup chopped sweet onion
 4   tablespoons crumbled cooked bacon, *divided*
1/2   teaspoon salt
1/2   teaspoon salt-free seasoning blend
1/4   teaspoon chili powder
 4   green onions, chopped

- In a large bowl, whisk the egg substitute and milk. Stir in the hash browns, 1 cup cheese, onion, 2 tablespoons bacon, salt, seasoning blend and chili powder. Pour into an 8-in. square baking dish coated with cooking spray.

- Bake at 350° for 45-50 minutes or until a knife inserted near the center comes out clean. Sprinkle with the remaining cheese and bacon. Bake 3-5 minutes longer or until cheese is melted. Sprinkle with green onions. Let stand for 5 minutes before cutting.

YIELD: 6 servings.

NUTRITION FACTS: 1 piece equals 219 calories, 6 g fat (4 g saturated fat), 22 mg cholesterol, 682 mg sodium, 25 g carbohydrate, 3 g fiber, 17 g protein. **DIABETIC EXCHANGES:** 2 lean meat, 1-1/2 starch.

confetti scrambled egg pockets

D. Terry | GOREVILLE, ILLINOIS

These scrambled egg pockets are a colorful crowd-pleaser. My eight grandchildren often enjoy these egg-packed pitas for Saturday morning brunch or with a light salad for supper.

- 1 cup fresh *or* frozen corn
- 1/4 cup chopped green pepper
- 2 tablespoons chopped onion
- 1 jar (2 ounces) diced pimientos, drained
- 1 tablespoon butter
- 1-1/4 cups egg substitute
- 3 eggs
- 1/4 cup fat-free evaporated milk
- 1/2 teaspoon seasoned salt
- 1 medium tomato, seeded and chopped
- 1 green onion, sliced
- 3 whole wheat pita breads (6 inches), halved

- In a large nonstick skillet, saute the corn, green pepper, onion and pimientos in butter for 5-7 minutes or until the vegetables are tender.

- In a large bowl, combine the egg substitute, eggs, milk and salt; pour into skillet. Cook and stir over medium heat until the eggs are completely set. Stir in the tomato and green onion. Spoon about 2/3 cup into each pita half.

YIELD: 6 servings.

NUTRITION FACTS: 1 filled pita half equals 207 calories, 6 g fat (2 g saturated fat), 112 mg cholesterol, 538 mg sodium, 28 g carbohydrate, 4 g fiber, 13 g protein. **DIABETIC EXCHANGES:** 1-1/2 starch, 1 lean meat, 1 vegetable, 1/2 fat.

CONFETTI SCRAMBLED EGG POCKETS

207 CALORIES

240 CALORIES

PUMPKIN PANCAKES

pumpkin pancakes

Vicki Floden | STORY CITY, IOWA

I created these light pumpkin-flavored pancakes with two kinds of flour and a blend of spices for a delightful taste. Serve them for brunch as a hearty eye-opener or for a deliciously different meatless dinner.

- 1-1/2 cups all-purpose flour
- 1/2 cup whole wheat flour
- 2 tablespoons brown sugar
- 2 teaspoons baking powder
- 1 teaspoon ground cinnamon
- 1/2 teaspoon salt
- 1/2 teaspoon ground ginger
- 1/2 teaspoon ground nutmeg
- 1-1/2 cups fat-free milk
- 1/2 cup canned pumpkin
- 1 egg white, lightly beaten
- 2 tablespoons canola oil

- In a large bowl, combine the first eight ingredients. In a small bowl, combine the milk, pumpkin, egg white and oil; stir into dry ingredients just until moistened.

- Pour batter by 1/4 cupfuls onto a hot griddle coated with cooking spray; turn when bubbles form on top. Cook until second side is golden brown.

YIELD: 6 servings.

NUTRITION FACTS: 2 pancakes equals 240 calories, 5 g fat (1 g saturated fat), 1 mg cholesterol, 375 mg sodium, 41 g carbohydrate, 3 g fiber, 8 g protein. **DIABETIC EXCHANGES:** 2-1/2 starch, 1 fat.

toasted granola

Susan Lajeunesse | COLCHESTER, VERMONT

We like this granola in so many ways. We sprinkle it over yogurt and ice cream, we eat it with milk like cereal, and we love to just snack on it right from the container.

- 1 cup packed brown sugar
- 1/3 cup water
- 4 cups old-fashioned oats
- 2 cups bran flakes
- 1 jar (12 ounces) toasted wheat germ
- 2 tablespoons all-purpose flour
- 3/4 teaspoon salt
- 1/3 cup canola oil
- 2 teaspoons vanilla extract

- In a large saucepan, bring brown sugar and water to a boil. Cook and stir until sugar is dissolved. Remove from the heat; set aside. In a large bowl, combine the oats, bran flakes, wheat germ, flour and salt. Stir oil and vanilla into sugar mixture; pour over oat mixture and toss to coat.

- Transfer to two 15-in. x 10-in. x 1-in. baking pans coated with cooking spray. Bake at 250° for 1-1/4 to 1-1/2 hours or until dry and lightly browned, stirring every 15 minutes. Cool completely on wire racks. Store in an airtight container.

YIELD: 10-1/2 cups.

NUTRITION FACTS: 1/2 cup equals 202 calories, 6 g fat (1 g saturated fat), 0 cholesterol, 118 mg sodium, 32 g carbohydrate, 4 g fiber, 8 g protein. **DIABETIC EXCHANGES:** 2 starch, 1 fat.

TOASTED GRANOLA

202 CALORIES

297 CALORIES

MIXED BERRY FRENCH TOAST BAKE

mixed berry french toast bake

Amy Berry | POLAND, MAINE

I love this recipe. Perfect for fuss-free holiday breakfasts or company, it's scrumptious and so easy to put together the night before.

- 1 loaf (1 pound) French bread, cubed
- 6 egg whites
- 3 eggs
- 1-3/4 cups fat-free milk
- 1 teaspoon sugar
- 1 teaspoon ground cinnamon
- 1 teaspoon vanilla extract
- 1/4 teaspoon salt
- 1 package (12 ounces) frozen unsweetened mixed berries
- 2 tablespoons cold butter
- 1/3 cup packed brown sugar

- Place bread cubes in a 13-in. x 9-in. baking dish coated with cooking spray. In a large bowl, combine egg whites, eggs, milk, sugar, cinnamon, vanilla and salt; pour over bread. Cover and refrigerate for 8 hours or overnight.

- Thirty minutes before baking, remove the berries from the freezer and set aside, and remove the baking dish from the refrigerator. Bake, covered, at 350° for 30 minutes.

- In a small bowl, cut the butter into the brown sugar until crumbly. Sprinkle berries and brown sugar mixture over French toast. Bake, uncovered, for 15-20 minutes or until a knife inserted near the center comes out clean.

YIELD: 8 servings.

NUTRITION FACTS: 1 serving equals 297 calories, 7 g fat (3 g saturated fat), 88 mg cholesterol, 545 mg sodium, 46 g carbohydrate, 3 g fiber, 12 g protein.

223 CALORIES

FLORENCE-INSPIRED SOUFFLE

florence-inspired souffle

Jenny Flake | GILBERT, ARIZONA

This souffle is not only absolutely delicious, but it's light and beautiful. Your guests will be impressed every time this brunch dish is served. So grab your fork and dig in to this little taste of Florence!

        6 egg whites
      3/4 cup onion and garlic salad croutons
        1 small onion, finely chopped
      1/4 cup finely chopped sweet red pepper
        2 ounces thinly sliced prosciutto, chopped
        1 garlic clove, minced
        2 teaspoons olive oil
        2 cups fresh baby spinach
      1/3 cup all-purpose flour
      1/2 teaspoon salt
      1/4 teaspoon pepper
    1-1/4 cups fat-free milk
        1 egg yolk, beaten
      1/4 teaspoon cream of tartar
      1/4 cup shredded Italian cheese blend

- Let the egg whites stand at room temperature for 30 minutes. Place croutons in a food processor; cover and process until ground. Sprinkle evenly onto the bottom and 1 in. up the sides of a 2-qt. baking dish coated with cooking spray; set aside.

- In a large saucepan, saute onion, red pepper, prosciutto and garlic in oil for 3-5 minutes or until vegetables are crisp-tender. Add the spinach; cook just until wilted. Stir in flour, salt and pepper until blended; gradually add milk. Bring to a boil; cook and stir for 2 minutes or until thickened. Transfer to a large bowl.

- Stir a small amount of hot mixture into egg yolk; return all to the bowl, stirring constantly. Allow to cool slightly.

- In a large bowl, beat the egg whites and cream of tartar until stiff peaks form. Fold into the vegetable mixture. Transfer to prepared dish; sprinkle with cheese. Bake at 350° for 35-40 minutes or until the top is puffed and center appears set. Serve immediately.

YIELD: 4 servings.

NUTRITION FACTS: 1 serving equals 223 calories, 9 g fat (3 g saturated fat), 73 mg cholesterol, 843 mg sodium, 20 g carbohydrate, 2 g fiber, 16 g protein. **DIABETIC EXCHANGES:** 2 lean meat, 1-1/2 starch.

mango smoothies

Treat yourself to this yummy tropical blend of mango, pineapple and banana with a touch of honey. It only has two grams of fat! Our home economists adore it!

      1/2 cup unsweetened pineapple juice
        2 cups frozen chopped peeled mangos
      1/2 medium ripe banana
      1/2 cup reduced-fat plain yogurt
        1 tablespoon honey

- In a blender, combine all the ingredients; cover and process until smooth. Pour into chilled glasses; serve immediately.

YIELD: 2 servings.

NUTRITION FACTS: 1 cup equals 237 calories, 2 g fat (1 g saturated fat), 4 mg cholesterol, 48 mg sodium, 56 g carbohydrate, 4 g fiber, 5 g protein.

MANGO SMOOTHIES

237 CALORIES

MEDITERRANEAN BREAKFAST PITAS

mediterranean breakfast pitas

Josie-Lynn Belmont | WOODBINE, GEORGIA

These pretty low-fat pitas, made with egg substitute, are great for any time of day, not just breakfast. They're full of flavor and healthy ingredients.

- 1/4 cup chopped sweet red pepper
- 1/4 cup chopped onion
- 1 cup egg substitute
- 1/8 teaspoon salt
- 1/8 teaspoon pepper
- 1 small tomato, chopped
- 1/2 cup torn fresh baby spinach
- 1-1/2 teaspoons minced fresh basil
- 2 whole gyro-style pitas (6 inches)
- 2 tablespoons crumbled feta cheese

- In a small nonstick skillet coated with cooking spray, cook and stir red pepper and onion over medium heat for 3 minutes. Add egg substitute, salt and pepper; cook over medium heat until the eggs are completely set, stirring occasionally.

- Combine the tomato, spinach and basil; spoon onto pitas. Top with egg mixture and sprinkle with feta cheese. Serve immediately.

YIELD: 2 servings.

NUTRITION FACTS: 1 pita equals 267 calories, 2 g fat (1 g saturated fat), 4 mg cholesterol, 798 mg sodium, 41 g carbohydrate, 3 g fiber, 20 g protein. **DIABETIC EXCHANGES:** 2 starch, 2 very lean meat, 1 vegetable.

fruity french toast sandwiches

Jessica Walston | GRANBURY, TEXAS

I know you'll find that these pretty little breakfast sandwiches are quick, easy and taste like they came straight from a French kitchen. This recipe is a great way to use up leftover French bread and is easily doubled to serve guests.

- 4 fresh strawberries, sliced
- 1/2 medium firm banana, sliced
- 4 slices French bread (3/4 inch thick)
- 1 egg
- 2 tablespoons half-and-half cream
- 1/4 teaspoon ground cinnamon
- 1/4 teaspoon vanilla extract
- 1 teaspoon canola oil
- 1 teaspoon confectioners' sugar

- In a bowl, combine the strawberry and banana slices. Place 1/4 cup on two slices of bread, arranging fruit in a single layer; top with remaining bread. Set remaining fruit aside.

- In a shallow bowl, beat the egg, cream, cinnamon and vanilla. Dip both sides of sandwiches into egg mixture. Heat oil on a griddle; cook French toast for 3-4 minutes on each side or until golden brown. Sprinkle with confectioners' sugar. Serve with reserved fruit.

YIELD: 2 servings.

NUTRITION FACTS: 1 sandwich equals 218 calories, 8 g fat (2 g saturated fat), 114 mg cholesterol, 253 mg sodium, 30 g carbohydrate, 3 g fiber, 7 g protein. **DIABETIC EXCHANGES:** 1 starch, 1 fruit, 1 fat, 1/2 lean meat.

FRUITY FRENCH TOAST SANDWICHES

spring vegetable quiche

Sandi Tuttle | HAYWARD, WISCONSIN

Brown rice makes up the crust for this different but very healthy, nutritious and totally delicious meatless dish. Best of all, it tastes just as delightful reheated the next morning.

7	egg whites, *divided*
2	cups cooked brown rice
1	tablespoon all-purpose flour
1	cup evaporated fat-free milk
1	egg
1	cup (4 ounces) shredded part-skim mozzarella cheese
1	cup chopped fresh asparagus
1/2	cup fresh *or* frozen corn, thawed
1	jar (4-1/2 ounces) sliced mushrooms, drained
1/3	cup finely chopped carrot
1/4	cup finely chopped red onion
2	tablespoons minced fresh parsley
3/4	teaspoon dried basil
1/2	teaspoon salt
1/4	teaspoon dried oregano
2	tablespoons grated Parmesan cheese

- In a small bowl, whisk 1 egg white. Add rice; stir until blended. Press onto the bottom and up the sides of a 9-in. deep-dish pie plate coated with cooking spray.

SPRING VEGETABLE QUICHE

- In a large bowl, whisk flour and milk until smooth. Whisk in egg and remaining egg whites. Stir in the mozzarella cheese, asparagus, corn, mushrooms, carrot, onion, parsley, basil, salt and oregano. Pour into crust; sprinkle with Parmesan cheese.

- Bake at 375° for 45-50 minutes or until a knife inserted near the center comes out clean. Let stand for 10 minutes before cutting.

YIELD: 6 servings.

NUTRITION FACTS: 1 piece equals 225 calories, 5 g fat (3 g saturated fat), 49 mg cholesterol, 538 mg sodium, 28 g carbohydrate, 3 g fiber, 17 g protein. **DIABETIC EXCHANGES:** 1-1/2 starch, 1 lean meat, 1 vegetable.

silver dollar oat pancakes

Margaret Wilson | HEMET, CALIFORNIA

I combined two of my grandson Joshua's favorite foods—applesauce and oatmeal—into these wholesome little pancakes. He likes the smaller serving size.

1/2	cup all-purpose flour
1/2	cup quick-cooking oats
1-1/2	teaspoons sugar
1	teaspoon baking powder
1/2	teaspoon baking soda
1/2	teaspoon salt
1	egg
3/4	cup buttermilk
1/2	cup cinnamon applesauce
2	tablespoons butter, melted

Maple syrup *or* topping of your choice

- In a large bowl, combine the dry ingredients. In a small bowl, beat the egg, buttermilk, applesauce and butter; stir into dry ingredients just until moistened.

- Pour batter by 2 tablespoonfuls onto a hot griddle coated with cooking spray; turn when bubbles form on top. Cook until second side is golden brown. Serve with syrup.

YIELD: 4 servings.

NUTRITION FACTS: 5 pancakes (calculated without syrup) equals 211 calories, 8 g fat (4 g saturated fat), 70 mg cholesterol, 660 mg sodium, 29 g carbohydrate, 2 g fiber, 6 g protein. **DIABETIC EXCHANGES:** 2 starch, 1-1/2 fat.

ham and apricot crepes

Candy Evavold | SAMAMMISH, WASHINGTON

A sweet apricot sauce nicely complements these savory ham crepes.

- 1-1/2 cups milk
- 2 eggs, lightly beaten
- 1 tablespoon butter, melted
- 1 cup all-purpose flour
- 20 thin slices deli ham

SAUCE:

- 1 can (15-1/4 ounces) apricot halves
- 2/3 cup sugar
- 2 tablespoons cornstarch
- 1/8 teaspoon salt
- 2 cans (5-1/2 ounces *each*) apricot nectar
- 2 tablespoons butter
- 2 teaspoons lemon juice

- In a large bowl, beat the milk, eggs and butter. Add flour until and beat until well combined. Cover and refrigerate for 1 hour.

- Heat a lightly greased 8-in. nonstick skillet; pour 2 tablespoons batter into the center of skillet. Lift and tilt pan to evenly coat bottom. Cook until top appears dry; turn and cook 15-20 seconds longer. Remove to a wire rack. Repeat with remaining batter, greasing skillet as needed. When cool, stack crepes with waxed paper or paper towels in between.

- Place a slice of ham on each crepe; roll up. Place in two greased 13-in. x 9-in. baking dishes. Bake, uncovered, at 350° for 20 minutes.

- Meanwhile, drain the apricots, reserving syrup. Cut the apricots into 1/4-in. slices; set aside. In a large saucepan, combine the sugar, cornstarch and salt. Add the apricot nectar and reserved syrup; stir until smooth. Bring to a boil; cook and stir for 1-2 minutes or until thickened. Remove from the heat; stir in the butter, lemon juice and apricot slices. Serve with crepes.

YIELD: 10 servings.

NUTRITION FACTS: 2 crepes with 1/4 cup sauce equals 258 calories, 7 g fat (3 g saturated fat), 76 mg cholesterol, 493 mg sodium, 39 g carbohydrate, 1 g fiber, 12 g protein.

BLUEBERRY FRENCH TOAST

blueberry french toast

The original recipe for this French toast called for heavy cream and whole eggs, but here is a lighter version that still keeps the delectable taste. Our home economists think you'll adore this recipe.

- 1/2 cup sugar
- 2-1/2 teaspoons cornstarch
- 1 teaspoon ground cinnamon
- 1/4 teaspoon ground allspice
- 3/4 cup water
- 4 cups fresh *or* frozen blueberries
- 1 cup egg substitute
- 1 cup fat-free milk
- 1 teaspoon vanilla extract
- 1/2 teaspoon salt
- 12 slices French bread (1 inch thick)

- In a large bowl, combine sugar, cornstarch, cinnamon and allspice; stir in water until smooth. Add blueberries; mix well. Transfer to a 13-in. x 9-in. baking dish coated with cooking spray.

- In a large bowl, beat the egg substitute, milk, vanilla and salt. Dip each slice of bread into egg mixture; arrange slices over berries.

- Bake at 400° for 20-25 minutes or until toast is golden brown and blueberries are bubbly.

YIELD: 6 servings.

NUTRITION FACTS: 2 slices with about 1/2 cup blueberries equals 285 calories, 2 g fat (trace saturated fat), 1 mg cholesterol, 575 mg sodium, 58 g carbohydrate, 4 g fiber, 10 g protein.

lunches

A satisfying midday meal can keep you going until supper. If you need an afternoon snack, see pages 71-83 for low-calorie, high-flavor suggestions. Shoot for about 450 calories for lunch.

122   156   148

The first section in this chapter has lower-calorie items you might pair with a salad, soup, fruit or one another. The other sections are higher-calorie, more complete dishes that just need a beverage. See the chart on page 125 for the calorie counts of some typical lunch foods.

250 calories or less

89 CALORIES

ZUCCHINI TOMATO SOUP

zucchini tomato soup

Nancy Johnson | LAVERNE, OKLAHOMA

There's garden-fresh flavor in every spoonful of this easy-to-make soup. I like it for a low-calorie lunch, along with a roll and fruit for dessert. It serves just two, but it can be easily doubled or tripled to serve a bigger group.

      2 small zucchini, coarsely chopped
    1/4 cup chopped red onion
  1-1/2 teaspoons olive oil
    1/8 teaspoon salt
      1 cup spicy hot V8 juice
      1 small tomato, cut into thin wedges
Dash *each* pepper and dried basil
      2 tablespoons shredded cheddar cheese, optional
      1 to 2 tablespoons crumbled cooked bacon, optional

- In a large skillet, saute the zucchini and onion in oil until crisp-tender. Sprinkle with salt. Add the V8 juice, tomato, pepper and basil; cook until heated through. Sprinkle with cheese and bacon if desired.

YIELD: 2 servings.

NUTRITION FACTS: 1 serving (calculated without cheese and bacon) equals 89 calories, 4 g fat (1 g saturated fat), 0 cholesterol, 545 mg sodium, 12 g carbohydrate, 3 g fiber, 3 g protein. **DIABETIC EXCHANGES:** 2 vegetable, 1/2 fat.

zesty greek salad

Angela Leinenbach | MECHANICSVILLE, VIRGINIA

Feta cheese and olives give this salad such great flavor, you'd never guess it's as light as it is. It's a nice change of pace for lunch and is even a colorful side dish with all kinds of meat.

      2 cups torn red leaf lettuce
      1 small tomato, cut into wedges
      4 cucumber slices, halved
      2 radishes, sliced
      1 red onion slice, quartered
      2 tablespoons sliced ripe olives
      1 tablespoon crumbled feta cheese
DRESSING:
      1 tablespoon red wine vinegar
      2 teaspoons water
      2 teaspoons olive oil
      1 garlic clove, minced
    1/4 teaspoon sugar
    1/8 teaspoon salt
Dash pepper

- In a small bowl, combine the lettuce, tomato, cucumber, radishes, onion, olives and feta cheese. In a jar with a tight-fitting lid, combine the dressing ingredients; shake well. Drizzle over salad and toss to coat. Serve immediately.

YIELD: 2 servings.

NUTRITION FACTS: 1-1/3 cups equals 89 calories, 6 g fat (1 g saturated fat), 2 mg cholesterol, 265 mg sodium, 7 g carbohydrate, 2 g fiber, 2 g protein. **DIABETIC EXCHANGES:** 1 vegetable, 1 fat.

ZESTY GREEK SALAD

89 CALORIES

234 CALORIES

VEGGIE MACARONI SALAD

veggie macaroni salad

Lynn Cole | SAGLE, IDAHO

When I bring this super salad to church dinners, there is usually nothing to take home. Add 2 or 3 cups leftover turkey or chicken to create a filling main-dish salad. The dressing is so good that we use it on potato salads and even lettuce salads!

- 2 cups uncooked elbow macaroni
- 1 large tomato, seeded and chopped
- 1 cup frozen peas, thawed
- 1/2 cup shredded reduced-fat cheddar cheese
- 1/2 cup chopped celery
- 1 hard-cooked egg, chopped
- 2 green onions, sliced

DRESSING:

- 3/4 cup reduced-fat mayonnaise
- 1 cup fat-free plain yogurt
- 2 tablespoons sugar
- 1 tablespoon prepared mustard
- 1/8 teaspoon celery seed

- Cook the macaroni according to package directions; drain and rinse in cold water. In a large bowl, combine macaroni, tomato, peas, cheese, celery, egg and onions.

- In a small bowl, combine the dressing ingredients. Pour over macaroni mixture and toss to coat. Refrigerate until serving.

YIELD: 10 servings.

NUTRITION FACTS: 3/4 cup equals 234 calories, 8 g fat (2 g saturated fat), 31 mg cholesterol, 246 mg sodium, 32 g carbohydrate, 2 g fiber, 8 g protein. **DIABETIC EXCHANGES:** 2 starch, 1-1/2 fat.

---

190 CALORIES

zippy corn chowder

Kera Bredin | VANCOUVER, BRITISH COLUMBIA

This spicy colorful chowder was so well received the first time I made it that I didn't have the leftovers I anticipated. Now I make the filling soup often.

- 1 medium onion, chopped
- 1 medium green pepper, chopped
- 2 tablespoons butter
- 1 can (14-1/2 ounces) chicken *or* vegetable broth
- 2 large red potatoes, cubed
- 1 jalapeno pepper, chopped
- 2 teaspoons Dijon mustard
- 1 teaspoon salt
- 1/2 teaspoon paprika
- 1/4 to 1/2 teaspoon crushed red pepper flakes
- 3 cups frozen corn
- 4 green onions, chopped
- 3 cups milk, *divided*
- 1/4 cup all-purpose flour

- In a large saucepan, saute the onion and green pepper in butter until tender. Add broth and potatoes. Bring to a boil. Reduce heat; cover and simmer for 15 minutes or until potatoes are almost tender. Stir in jalapeno, mustard, salt, paprika and red pepper flakes. Add corn, green onions and 2-1/2 cups milk. Bring to a boil.

- Combine the flour and remaining milk until smooth; gradually add to soup. Bring to a boil. Cook and stir for 2 minutes or until thickened and bubbly.

YIELD: 8 servings (2 quarts).

EDITOR'S NOTE: When cutting or seeding hot peppers, use rubber or plastic gloves to protect your hands. Avoid touching your face.

NUTRITION FACTS: 1 cup equals 190 calories, 7 g fat (4 g saturated fat), 20 mg cholesterol, 617 mg sodium, 28 g carbohydrate, 3 g fiber, 7 g protein.

---

seafood salad pitas

Linda Evancoe-Coble | LEOLA, PENNSYLVANIA

You can make this lovely and interesting sandwich as a great light lunch. It's so tasty and colorful. Or pair it with a hearty soup for a change-of-pace supper.

- 2 cups chopped imitation crabmeat (about 10 ounces)

162 CALORIES

SEAFOOD SALAD PITAS

1/2 pound cooked medium shrimp, peeled, deveined and chopped (about 1 cup)

2 celery ribs, chopped

1/2 cup thinly sliced green onions

3/4 cup fat-free mayonnaise

3/4 teaspoon seafood seasoning

1/4 teaspoon salt

1/8 teaspoon pepper

4 whole wheat pita breads (6 inches), halved

- In a large bowl, combine the crab, shrimp, celery and onions. In a small bowl, combine the mayonnaise, seafood seasoning, salt and pepper. Pour over the crab mixture; toss to coat. Cover and refrigerate for at least 2 hours. Spoon into the pita halves.

YIELD: 8 servings.

NUTRITION FACTS: 1 filled pita half equals 162 calories, 2 g fat (trace saturated fat), 27 mg cholesterol, 755 mg sodium, 28 g carbohydrate, 3 g fiber, 10 g protein. DIABETIC EXCHANGES: 2 starch, 1 very lean meat.

chicken club brunch ring

Rebecca Clark | WARRIOR, ALABAMA

A few tubes of reduced-fat crescent rolls make this impressive recipe a snap. I fill the ring with chicken salad and serve warm slices with mustard-flavored mayonnaise. Shredded lettuce adds more color.

1/2 cup fat-free mayonnaise

1 tablespoon minced fresh parsley

2 teaspoons Dijon mustard

1-1/2 teaspoons finely chopped onion

1-3/4 cups cubed cooked chicken breast (1/2-inch cubes)

2 bacon strips, cooked and crumbled

1 cup (4 ounces) shredded reduced-fat Swiss cheese, *divided*

2 tubes (8 ounces *each*) refrigerated reduced-fat crescent rolls

2 plum tomatoes

2 cups shredded lettuce

- In a large bowl, combine the mayonnaise, parsley, mustard and onion. Stir in the chicken, bacon and 3/4 cup cheese.

- Unroll crescent dough; separate into 16 triangles. Arrange on an ungreased 12-in. round pizza pan, forming a ring with the pointed ends facing the outer edge of the pan and wide ends overlapping.

- Spoon chicken mixture over wide ends; fold points over filling and tuck under wide ends (filling will be visible). Chop half of a tomato; set aside. Slice the remaining tomatoes; place over filling and tuck into dough.

- Bake at 375° for 20-25 minutes or until golden brown. Sprinkle with remaining cheese. Let stand for 5 minutes. Place lettuce in the center of the ring; sprinkle with chopped tomato.

YIELD: 16 servings.

NUTRITION FACTS: 1 piece equals 153 calories, 6 g fat (2 g saturated fat), 17 mg cholesterol, 368 mg sodium, 14 g carbohydrate, trace fiber, 9 g protein. DIABETIC EXCHANGES: 1 starch, 1 very lean meat, 1 fat.

CHICKEN CLUB BRUNCH RING

153 CALORIES

open-faced crab salad sandwiches

Lanie Kappe | SANTA ANA, CALIFORNIA

Everyone loved the crab salad my mother-in-law contributed to a family gathering, so I reduced the calories in her recipe for this version. Serve it hot or cold or as a spread for crackers.

1/2	cup reduced-fat mayonnaise
1/8	teaspoon salt
1/8	teaspoon pepper
2	packages (8 ounces *each*) imitation crabmeat, chopped
1	cup (4 ounces) shredded part-skim mozzarella cheese
1/4	cup chopped sweet red pepper
1/4	cup chopped green onions
1/4	cup chopped celery
1	loaf (8 ounces) unsliced French bread, halved lengthwise

- In a large bowl, combine mayonnaise, salt and pepper. Stir in the crab, cheese, red pepper, onions and celery. Spoon over bread halves.

- Place on a baking sheet. Broil 5 in. from the heat for 7-8 minutes or until lightly browned. Cut into 3-in. pieces.

YIELD: 8 servings.

NUTRITION FACTS: 1 piece equals 236 calories, 9 g fat (3 g saturated fat), 44 mg cholesterol, 420 mg sodium, 24 g carbohydrate, 1 g fiber, 13 g protein.

OPEN-FACED CRAB SALAD SANDWICHES

236 CALORIES

240 CALORIES

BAKED DELI FOCACCIA SANDWICH

baked deli focaccia sandwich

Mary Humeniuk-Smith | PERRY HALL, MARYLAND

Pesto and focaccia bread make this pretty sandwich deliciously different from most deli specialties.

1	loaf (12 ounces) focaccia bread
1/4	cup prepared pesto
1/4	pound sliced deli ham
1/4	pound sliced deli smoked turkey
1/4	pound sliced deli pastrami
5	slices process American cheese
1/3	cup thinly sliced onion
1	small tomato, sliced
1/4	teaspoon Italian seasoning

- Cut focaccia horizontally in half; spread pesto over cut sides. On bread bottom, layer the ham, turkey, pastrami, cheese, onion and tomato. Sprinkle with Italian seasoning. Replace bread top; wrap in foil.

- Place on a baking sheet. Bake at 350° for 20-25 minutes or until heated through. Let stand for 10 minutes.

YIELD: 8 servings.

NUTRITION FACTS: 1 slice equals 240 calories, 9 g fat (3 g saturated fat), 30 mg cholesterol, 817 mg sodium, 26 g carbohydrate, 1 g fiber, 15 g protein.

crunchy peanut coleslaw

Judy Madsen | ELLIS, IDAHO

When entertaining my large family, I like to offer a buffet of tasty food. This salad has been enjoyed by all. They like its peanutty crunch and tangy dressing.

1	cup (8 ounces) reduced-fat sour cream
1/2	cup fat-free mayonnaise

1 tablespoon sugar

1 tablespoon tarragon vinegar

1/2 teaspoon salt

1/4 teaspoon white pepper

4 cups finely chopped cabbage

1 cup coarsely chopped cauliflower

1 cup chopped celery

1/4 cup finely chopped onion

1/4 cup chopped green pepper

1/4 cup finely chopped cucumber

1/2 cup chopped peanuts

- For dressing, in a small bowl, combine the sour cream, mayonnaise, sugar, vinegar, salt and pepper until blended. In a large bowl, combine the cabbage, cauliflower, celery, onion, green pepper and cucumber. Add dressing and toss to coat. Sprinkle with peanuts.

YIELD: 8 servings.

NUTRITION FACTS: 3/4 cup equals 121 calories, 7 g fat (2 g saturated fat), 12 mg cholesterol, 323 mg sodium, 14 g carbohydrate, 3 g fiber, 4 g protein. **DIABETIC EXCHANGES:** 1 vegetable, 1 fat, 1/2 starch.

CRUNCHY PEANUT COLESLAW

mock caesar salad

Sue Yaeger | BOONE, IOWA

This lightened-up version of the all-time classic is a tasty complement to a soup or a main dish. Best of all, the thick, creamy dressing has all of the flavor you would expect.

1/3 cup fat-free plain yogurt

1/4 cup reduced-fat mayonnaise

1 tablespoon red wine vinegar

2 teaspoons Dijon mustard

1 teaspoon Worcestershire sauce

1/4 teaspoon garlic powder

1/8 teaspoon pepper

6 cups torn romaine

1/2 cup fat-free salad croutons

2 tablespoons shredded Parmesan cheese

- In a small bowl, whisk together the first seven ingredients. In a salad bowl, combine the romaine, croutons and cheese. Drizzle with dressing; toss to coat.

YIELD: 5 servings.

NUTRITION FACTS: 1-1/4 cups equals 90 calories, 5 g fat (1 g saturated fat), 7 mg cholesterol, 299 mg sodium, 9 g carbohydrate, 1 g fiber, 4 g protein. **DIABETIC EXCHANGES:** 1 fat, 1/2 starch.

special clam chowder

Joy Schuster | GLENTANA, MONTANA

I serve this cheesy chowder every Christmas or New Year's. Throughout the year, I substitute the potatoes and clams with broccoli and find that even the grandchildren enjoy the taste.

4 cups cubed red potatoes

3 cups water

1 medium carrot, grated

1 small onion, chopped

2 teaspoons chicken bouillon granules

1 teaspoon dried parsley flakes

1/2 teaspoon pepper

2 tablespoons all-purpose flour

1/2 cup cold water

3 cans (6-1/2 ounces *each*) chopped clams, drained

2/3 cup cubed process cheese (Velveeta)

1 can (12 ounces) evaporated milk

- In a large saucepan, combine the first seven ingredients. Bring to a boil. Reduce heat; cover and simmer for 20 minutes or until potatoes are tender.

- In a small bowl, combine flour and cold water until smooth. Stir into potato mixture. Bring to a boil; cook and stir for 2 minutes or until thickened. Reduce heat. Add clams and cheese; cook and stir until cheese is melted. Stir in milk; heat through.

YIELD: 9 servings (about 2 quarts).

NUTRITION FACTS: 1 cup equals 170 calories, 6 g fat (4 g saturated fat), 26 mg cholesterol, 502 mg sodium, 19 g carbohydrate, 2 g fiber, 9 g protein.

183 CALORIES

PIZZA POCKETS

pizza pockets

Robin Werner | BRUSH PRAIRIE, WASHINGTON

Stuffed with a pizza-style filling, these special sandwiches surprise you with a burst of flavor in every bite.

- 1 package (1/4 ounce) active dry yeast
- 1 cup warm water (120° to 130°)
- 1 tablespoon sugar
- 1 tablespoon butter, melted
- 1 teaspoon salt
- 3 to 3-1/4 cups all-purpose flour
- 1 can (8 ounces) pizza sauce
- 12 slices pepperoni
- 1 package (2-1/2 ounces) thinly sliced fully cooked pastrami, chopped
- 1 package (2-1/2 ounces) thinly sliced fully cooked ham, chopped
- 3/4 cup shredded part-skim mozzarella cheese
- 1 egg, lightly beaten

- In a large bowl, dissolve yeast in warm water. Add sugar, butter, salt and 2-1/4 cups flour. Beat until smooth. Stir in enough remaining flour to form a soft dough.

- Turn onto a floured surface; knead for 6-8 minutes. Roll the dough into a 14-in. x 10-in. rectangle. Cut with a 3-in. round cookie cutter. Reroll scraps to cut a total of 24 circles. Place 1 teaspoon pizza sauce and slice of pepperoni in center of 12 circles.

- In a large bowl, combine pastrami, ham and cheese; place equal amounts over pepperoni. Top with 1/2 teaspoon

of pizza sauce if desired. (Save remaining sauce for another use or use for dipping.) Cover with remaining dough circles; pinch edges or press with a fork to seal.

- Place on greased baking sheets. Brush with egg. bake at 400° for 20-25 minutes or until golden brown.

YIELD: 12 servings.

NUTRITION FACTS: 1 pizza pocket equals 183 calories, 5 g fat (2 g saturated fat), 33 mg cholesterol, 429 mg sodium, 27 g carbohydrate, 1 g fiber, 8 g protein.

249 CALORIES

falafalas

Jodie Sykes | LAKE WORTH, PENNSYLVANIA

My husband loves this recipe, which is of Greek origin. I save any leftovers for his lunch the following day, and he says it tastes as good the second time around. Best of all, it's nutritious.

- 2 cans (15 ounces *each*) garbanzo beans, rinsed and drained
- 2 green onions, minced
- 1 cup canned bean sprouts
- 1/4 cup hulled sunflower kernels
- 1/4 cup dry bread crumbs
- 1 egg
- 1/2 teaspoon garlic powder
- 1/4 teaspoon pepper
- 2 tablespoons soy sauce
- 2 tablespoons Worcestershire sauce
- 2 tablespoons vegetable oil

YOGURT SAUCE:

- 2 cups (16 ounces) plain yogurt
- 1 green onion, minced
- 1 tablespoon dill weed
- 1 garlic clove, minced
- 9 pita bread halves
- 1 tomato, sliced
- 1 red onion, sliced

Lettuce leaves

- In a food processor, combine the first 11 ingredients. Process until smooth. If mixture is moist, add a few more bread crumbs. Using a 1/3 cup measure, shape the mixture into patties.

- In a large skillet, heat the oil over medium-high. Fry patties until golden brown on both sides. Meanwhile, combine sauce ingredients. Stuff pita halves with patties, tomato, onion and lettuce. Spoon sauce into pitas. Serve immediately.

YIELD: 9 servings.

NUTRITION FACTS: 1 falafalas equals 249 calories, 9 g fat (2 g saturated fat), 31 mg cholesterol, 553 mg sodium, 33 g carbohydrate, 4 g fiber, 10 g protein.

Here are some typical lunch foods and the amount of calories they have. Use this list as a reference for what foods you might use or combine with recipes in this chapter to stay within your goal of a 450-calorie lunch.

- 1 slice whole wheat bread, 69 calories
- 1 slice reduced-calorie wheat bread, 48 calories
- 1 large pita (6-1/2" diameter), 165 calories
- 1 flour tortilla (approximately 6" diameter), 150 calories
- 1 whole wheat dinner roll, 76 calories
- 1 hamburger bun, 79 calories
- 1 hard roll, 83 calories
- 1 slice American cheese (1 ounce), 93 calories
- 1 slice Swiss cheese (1 ounce), 106 calories
- 1 slice cheddar cheese (1 ounce), 113 calories
- 1 slice part-skim mozzarella cheese (1 ounce), 72 calories
- 1 tablespoon shredded Parmesan cheese, 21 calories
- 1 saltine cracker, 13 calories
- 1 wheat cracker, 9 calories
- 2 tablespoons smooth peanut butter, 192 calories
- 1 slice deli ham, 22 calories
- 1 slice deli smoked fat-free turkey breast, 10 calories
- 1 beef hot dog, 147 calories
- 1 medium apple, 72 calories
- 1 medium pear, 96 calories
- 20 baked potato chips, 200 calories
- 3/4 cup miniature pretzel twists, 112 calories

For the calorie counts of other typical lunch side dishes, see the Smart Snacks list on page 71. You might also check the Free Foods Chart on page 45.

For calorie calculations of other foods, see the Nutrition Facts labels on food packages.

147 CALORIES

HONEY-DIJON POTATO SALAD

honey-dijon potato salad

Kristie Kline Jones | DOUGLAS, WYOMING

No matter which recipe I tried, my potato salad always turned out bland. So I came up with this creamy version that has plenty of pizzazz. It's so tangy and flavorful, you wouldn't realize it calls for fat-free honey-Dijon salad dressing. It's a favorite at picnics.

- 2-1/4 pounds red potatoes (about 14 small)
- 3 tablespoons vinegar
- 3/4 cup chopped green pepper
- 1/2 cup chopped onion
- 5 tablespoons chopped dill pickles
- 1 teaspoon salt-free seasoning blend
- 1/4 teaspoon pepper
- 1 cup fat-free mayonnaise
- 1/3 cup fat-free honey-Dijon salad dressing
- 2 tablespoons Dijon mustard
- 2 hard-cooked egg whites, chopped

- Place the potatoes in a large saucepan and cover with water. Bring to a boil. Reduce heat; cover and cook for 15-20 minutes or until tender. Drain and cool.

- Cube the potatoes and place in a large bowl. Sprinkle with vinegar. Add the green pepper, onion, pickles, seasoning blend and pepper.

- In a small bowl, combine mayonnaise, salad dressing, mustard and egg whites. Pour over potato mixture; toss to coat. Cover and refrigerate for at least 1 hour.

YIELD: 8 servings.

NUTRITION FACTS: 3/4 cup equals 147 calories, 1 g fat (trace saturated fat), 3 mg cholesterol, 439 mg sodium, 30 g carbohydrate, 4 g fiber, 4 g protein. **DIABETIC EXCHANGES:** 2 starch, 1 vegetable.

218 CALORIES

BEAN AND PASTA SOUP

bean and pasta soup

Maria Gooding | ST. THOMAS, ONTARIO

We're always on the lookout for great, low-fat recipes and this soup fits the bill. Loaded with veggies and pasta, it's fast, filling and delicious. Once school starts, I make it every week.

- 1   cup uncooked small pasta
- 2   celery ribs, thinly sliced
- 2   medium carrots, thinly sliced
- 1   medium onion, chopped
- 1   garlic clove, minced
- 1   tablespoon olive oil
- 2   cups water
- 1   can (14-1/2 ounces) diced tomatoes, undrained
- 1-1/4   cups reduced-sodium chicken broth *or* vegetable broth
- 1   teaspoon dried basil
- 1/2   teaspoon dried rosemary, crushed
- 1/4   teaspoon salt
- 1/8   teaspoon pepper
- 1   can (15 ounces) white kidney *or* cannellini beans, rinsed and drained
- 2   cups shredded fresh spinach
- 1/4   cup shredded Parmesan cheese

- Cook pasta according to package directions. Meanwhile, in a large nonstick saucepan, saute the celery, carrots, onion and garlic in oil for 5 minutes. Stir in the water, tomatoes, broth, basil, rosemary, salt and pepper. Bring

to a boil. Reduce the heat; cover and simmer for 10 minutes or until carrots are tender.

- Drain pasta; stir into vegetable mixture. Add the beans; heat through. Stir in the spinach; cook until spinach is wilted, about 2 minutes. Sprinkle with Parmesan cheese.

YIELD: 5 servings.

NUTRITION FACTS: 1-1/2 cups equals 218 calories, 5 g fat (1 g saturated fat), 3 mg cholesterol, 588 mg sodium, 35 g carbohydrate, 7 g fiber, 9 g protein. **DIABETIC EXCHANGES:** 2 vegetable, 1-1/2 starch, 1 lean meat.

veggie cheese sandwiches

Beverly Little | MARIETTA, GEORGIA

I try to keep the ingredients on hand for these toasted sandwiches. Add whatever vegetables best fit your taste, or use this recipe the next time you need to clean out the vegetable drawer of your refrigerator.

- 1/2   cup sliced onion
- 1/2   cup julienned green pepper
- 2/3   cup chopped tomato
- 1/2   cup sliced fresh mushrooms
- 8   slices Italian bread (1/2 inch thick)
- 4   slices reduced-fat process American cheese product
- 4   teaspoons butter, softened

- In a small nonstick skillet coated with cooking spray, cook onion and green pepper over medium heat for 2 minutes. Add tomato and mushrooms. Cook and stir until the vegetables are tender; drain.

VEGGIE CHEESE SANDWICHES

168 CALORIES

- Divide the vegetable mixture over four slices of bread; top with cheese and remaining bread. Butter top and bottom of each sandwich. In a skillet, toast sandwiches until lightly browned on both sides.

YIELD: 4 servings.

NUTRITION FACTS: 1 sandwich equals 168 calories, 6 g fat (3 g saturated fat), 15 mg cholesterol, 415 mg sodium, 20 g carbohydrate, 2 g fiber, 8 g protein. **DIABETIC EXCHANGES:** 1 starch, 1 vegetable, 1 fat.

creamy pasta salad

Lorraine Menard | OMAHA, NEBRASKA

I love creating new and tasty foods, including this popular salad. I make it often for my husband and me, especially during the summer months. If you add some cooked chicken breast, you can make this a dinner for two.

- 1 cup cooked spiral pasta
- 1/3 cup grape tomatoes, halved
- 1/4 cup shredded reduced-fat cheddar cheese
- 3 tablespoons chopped onion
- 3 tablespoons chopped cucumber
- 3 tablespoons chopped green pepper
- 2 tablespoons shredded Parmesan cheese
- 2 tablespoons sliced pepperoncinis
- 2 radishes, sliced
- 1/8 teaspoon pepper
- 1/4 cup fat-free ranch salad dressing

- In a small bowl, combine the first 10 ingredients. Drizzle with dressing and toss to coat. Cover and refrigerate for at least 1 hour before serving.

YIELD: 2 servings.

NUTRITION FACTS: 1 cup equals 233 calories, 5 g fat (3 g saturated fat), 14 mg cholesterol, 1,021 mg sodium, 35 g carbohydrate, 2 g fiber, 9 g protein.

anytime turkey chili

Brad Bailey | CARY, NORTH CAROLINA

I created this dish to grab the voters' attention at a chili contest we held in our backyard. With pumpkin, brown sugar and cooked turkey, it's like enjoying an entire Thanksgiving dinner in one bowl.

ANYTIME TURKEY CHILI

- 2/3 cup chopped sweet onion
- 1/2 cup chopped green pepper
- 1-1/2 teaspoons dried oregano
- 2 garlic cloves, minced
- 1 teaspoon ground cumin
- 1 teaspoon olive oil
- 1 can (16 ounces) kidney beans, rinsed and drained
- 1 can (15-1/2 ounces) great northern beans, rinsed and drained
- 1 can (15 ounces) solid-pack pumpkin
- 1 can (15 ounces) crushed tomatoes
- 1 can (14-1/2 ounces) reduced-sodium chicken broth
- 1/2 cup water
- 2 tablespoons brown sugar
- 2 tablespoons chili powder
- 1/2 teaspoon pepper
- 3 cups cubed cooked turkey breast

- In a large saucepan, saute the onion, green pepper, oregano, garlic and cumin in oil until vegetables are tender. Stir in the beans, pumpkin, tomatoes, broth, water, brown sugar, chili powder and pepper; bring to a boil. Reduce heat; cover and simmer for 1 hour. Add turkey; heat through.

YIELD: 8 servings (2 quarts).

NUTRITION FACTS: 1 cup equals 241 calories, 2 g fat (trace saturated fat), 45 mg cholesterol, 478 mg sodium, 32 g carbohydrate, 10 g fiber, 25 g protein. **DIABETIC EXCHANGES:** 3 very lean meat, 1-1/2 starch, 1 vegetable.

111 CALORIES

ASIAN SHRIMP SOUP

asian shrimp soup

Michelle Smith | SYKESVILLE, MARYLAND

I love this soup so much, I sometimes double the recipe. In fact, I've nicknamed it the "House Specialty!" If I have leftover chicken or pork, I sometimes substitute it for the shrimp.

- 1 ounce uncooked thin spaghetti, broken into 1-inch pieces
- 3 cups plus 1 tablespoon water, *divided*
- 3 teaspoons reduced-sodium chicken bouillon granules
- 1/2 teaspoon salt
- 1/2 cup sliced fresh mushrooms
- 1/2 cup fresh *or* frozen corn
- 1 teaspoon cornstarch
- 1-1/2 teaspoons reduced-sodium teriyaki sauce
- 1 cup thinly sliced romaine lettuce
- 1 can (6 ounces) small shrimp, rinsed and drained
- 2 tablespoons sliced green onion

- Cook pasta according to package directions.

- In a large saucepan, combine 3 cups water, bouillon and salt; bring to a boil. Stir in mushrooms and corn. Reduce heat; cook, uncovered, until vegetables are tender.

- Combine the cornstarch, teriyaki sauce and remaining water until smooth; stir into soup. Bring to a boil; cook and stir for 1-2 minutes or until slightly thickened. Reduce heat.

- Drain pasta; add the pasta, lettuce, shrimp and green onion to the soup; heat through.

YIELD: 4 servings.

NUTRITION FACTS: 1 cup equals 111 calories, 1 g fat (trace saturated fat), 74 mg cholesterol, 725 mg sodium, 13 g carbohydrate, 1 g fiber, 12 g protein. **DIABETIC EXCHANGES:** 1 starch, 1 very lean meat.

crab salad pockets

Penny Bokovoy | ULM, MONTANA

This sandwich makes a satifying midday meal. When I'm out of crab, I just use tuna with great results.

- 2 ounces imitation crabmeat, flaked *or* canned crabmeat, drained, flaked and cartilage removed
- 1/4 cup finely chopped cucumber
- 2 tablespoons chopped sweet red pepper
- 2 tablespoons chopped green pepper
- 1 tablespoon sliced green onion
- 1 tablespoon finely chopped celery
- 1/4 teaspoon seafood seasoning
- 2 tablespoons fat-free mayonnaise *or* salad dressing
- 2 whole wheat pita pockets (6 inches), halved and warmed

- In a bowl, combine the crab, cucumber, peppers, onion, celery and seafood seasoning. Stir in mayonnaise. Fill the pita halves with crab mixture.

YIELD: 1 serving.

NUTRITION FACTS: 1 sandwich equals 239 calories, 2 g fat (0 saturated fat), 7 mg cholesterol, 829 mg sodium, 46 g carbohydrate, 6 g fiber, 12 g protein.

CRAB SALAD POCKETS

239 CALORIES

52 CALORIES

ANTIPASTO-STUFFED BAGUETTES

antipasto-stuffed baguettes

Dianne Holmgren | PRESCOTT, ARIZONA

My Italian-style sandwiches can be served as an appetizer, too. A homemade olive paste makes every bite delicious.

1	can (2-1/4 ounces) sliced ripe olives, drained
2	tablespoons olive oil
1	teaspoon lemon juice
1	garlic clove, minced
1/8	teaspoon *each* dried basil, thyme, marjoram and rosemary, crushed
2	French bread baguettes (8 ounces *each*)
1	package (4 ounces) crumbled feta cheese
1/4	pound thinly sliced Genoa salami
1	cup fresh baby spinach
1	jar (7-1/4 ounces) roasted red peppers, drained and chopped
1	can (14 ounces) water-packed artichoke hearts, rinsed and drained

- In a blender, combine the olives, oil, lemon juice, garlic and herbs; cover and process until olives are chopped. Set aside 1/3 cup olive mixture (refrigerate remaining mixture for another use).

- Cut the top third off each baguette; carefully hollow out bottoms, leaving a 1/4-in. shell (discard removed bread or save for another use).

- Spread olive mixture in the bottom of each loaf. Sprinkle with feta cheese. Fold salami slices in half and place over cheese. Top with the spinach, red peppers and artichokes, pressing down as necessary. Replace bread tops. Wrap loaves tightly in foil. Refrigerate for at least 3 hours or overnight.

- Serve cold, or place foil-wrapped loaves on a baking sheet and bake at 350° for 20-25 minutes or until heated through. Cut into slices; secure with a toothpick.

YIELD: 3 dozen.

EDITOR'S NOTE: 1/3 cup purchased tapenade (olive paste) may be substituted for the olive mixture.

NUTRITION FACTS: 1 piece equals 52 calories, 3 g fat (1 g saturated fat), 5 mg cholesterol, 196 mg sodium, 5 g carbohydrate, trace fiber, 2 g protein.

grape tomato mozzarella salad

Linda Haas | TENMILE, OREGON

I created this fuss-free recipe after tasting something similar on a cruise. It makes a speedy and summery lunch that's low in calories.

1/2	large sweet onion, thinly sliced
1	medium cucumber, sliced
2	cups grape tomatoes
1/2	cup loosely packed fresh basil leaves, sliced
4	ounces fresh mozzarella cheese, sliced
1/3	cup prepared fat-free Italian salad dressing

- Arrange onion, cucumber, tomatoes, basil and mozzarella on salad plates. Drizzle with dressing. Serve immediately.

YIELD: 6 servings.

NUTRITION FACTS: 1 serving equals 85 calories, 4 g fat (3 g saturated fat), 15 mg cholesterol, 224 mg sodium, 7 g carbohydrate, 1 g fiber, 5 g protein. **DIABETIC EXCHANGES:** 1 lean meat, 1 vegetable.

GRAPE TOMATO MOZZARELLA SALAD

85 CALORIES

broccoli chowder

Esther Shank | HARRISONBURG, VIRGINIA

My family loves this tasty, filling soup made from a recipe that I developed myself.

      4   cups fresh small broccoli florets
      2   medium potatoes, diced
  1-1/2   cups water
      2   medium carrots, thinly sliced
      1   large onion, chopped
      1   celery rib, finely chopped
      4   cups fat-free milk, *divided*
      2   teaspoons reduced-sodium chicken bouillon
          granules
      1   teaspoon Worcestershire sauce
    3/4   teaspoon salt
    1/2   teaspoon pepper
    1/3   cup all-purpose flour
      1   cup cubed reduced-fat process cheese (Velveeta)

- In a large saucepan, combine the first six ingredients. Bring to a boil. Reduce heat; cover and simmer for 8-10 minutes or until vegetables are tender. Add 3 cups milk, bouillon, Worcestershire sauce, salt and pepper.

BROCCOLI CHOWDER

233 CALORIES

- In a small bowl, combine flour and remaining milk until smooth; gradually stir into soup. Bring to a boil; cook and stir for 2 minutes or until thickened. Remove from the heat; stir in cheese just until melted.

YIELD: 6 servings.

NUTRITION FACTS: 1-1/3 cups equals 233 calories, 3 g fat (2 g saturated fat), 11 mg cholesterol, 838 mg sodium, 39 g carbohydrate, 6 g fiber, 15 g protein. **DIABETIC EXCHANGES:** 1 starch, 1 vegetable, 1 fat-free milk.

141 CALORIES asian linguine salad

Pat Hilmer | OSHKOSH, WISCONSIN

With loads of vegetables and a yummy dressing, this chilled pasta toss offers guilt-free enjoyment.

      8   ounces uncooked linguine
    1/3   cup reduced-sodium soy sauce
    1/4   cup water
      2   tablespoons lemon juice
  1-1/2   teaspoons sesame oil
      2   medium carrots, julienned
    1/2   medium sweet red pepper, julienned
  1-1/2   teaspoons olive oil, *divided*
    1/2   cup fresh snow peas
      1   garlic clove, minced
      1   small zucchini, julienned
    1/2   cup canned bean sprouts
      1   green onion, julienned

- Cook linguine according to package directions; drain and place in a large serving bowl. In a small bowl, whisk the soy sauce, water, lemon juice and sesame oil. Refrigerate 1/4 cup for dressing. Pour remaining mixture over hot linguine; toss to coat evenly.

- In a large nonstick skillet or wok coated with cooking spray, stir-fry carrots and red pepper in 3/4 teaspoon olive oil for 2 minutes. Add snow peas and garlic; stir-fry 2 minutes longer. Add to linguine.

- Stir-fry the zucchini, bean sprouts and onion in remaining olive oil for 2 minutes; add to linguine mixture. Cover and refrigerate for at least 2 hours. Just before serving, add dressing and toss to coat.

YIELD: 8 servings.

NUTRITION FACTS: 3/4 cup equals 141 calories, 2 g fat (trace saturated fat), 0 cholesterol, 415 mg sodium, 25 g carbohydrate, 2 g fiber, 5 g protein. **DIABETIC EXCHANGES:** 1-1/2 starch, 1/2 fat.

81 CALORIES

ASPARAGUS TOMATO SALAD

asparagus tomato salad

Dorothy Buhr | OGDEN, ILLINOIS

This colorful, light salad was a hit at our church's cooking club. It's easy to assemble and delicious, too.

- 1 pound fresh asparagus, trimmed and cut into 1-inch pieces
- 1 small zucchini, halved and cut into 1/4-inch slices
- 1 cup grape *or* cherry tomatoes
- 1/4 cup sliced green onions
- 1/4 cup minced fresh parsley
- 3 tablespoons olive oil
- 2 tablespoons red wine vinegar
- 1 garlic clove, minced
- 1/4 teaspoon seasoned salt
- 1/4 teaspoon Dijon mustard
- 1/4 cup shredded Parmesan cheese, optional
- 2 tablespoons sunflower kernels, toasted, optional

- Place the asparagus and zucchini in a steamer basket; place in a saucepan over 1 in. of water. Bring to a boil; cover and steam for 2 minutes. Rinse in cold water.

- In a large bowl, combine asparagus, zucchini, tomatoes, onions and parsley.

- In a small bowl, whisk the oil, vinegar, garlic, seasoned salt and mustard. Pour over asparagus mixture and toss to coat. Sprinkle with Parmesan cheese and sunflower kernels if desired.

YIELD: 6 servings.

NUTRITION FACTS: 3/4 cup (calculated without Parmesan cheese and sunflower kernels) equals 81 calories, 7 g fat (1 g saturated fat), 0 cholesterol, 78 mg sodium, 4 g carbohydrate, 1 g fiber, 2 g protein. **DIABETIC EXCHANGES:** 1 vegetable, 1 fat.

zesty sloppy joes

Sharon Mckee | DENTON, TEXAS

My mother-in-law created this recipe in the early 1950s. It's a real classic that never fails to satisfy.

- 2 pounds lean ground beef
- 1 large green pepper, chopped
- 2 cans (14-1/2 ounces *each*) diced tomatoes, undrained
- 2 cans (8 ounces *each*) tomato sauce
- 1 can (6 ounces) tomato paste
- 2 tablespoons Worcestershire sauce
- 1 tablespoon sugar
- 2 teaspoons celery seed
- 2 teaspoons onion powder
- 1 teaspoon paprika
- 1/4 to 1/2 teaspoon cayenne pepper
- 3 bay leaves
- 16 hamburger buns, split

- In a Dutch oven or large kettle, cook beef and green pepper over medium heat until meat is no longer pink; drain. Stir in the tomatoes, tomato sauce, tomato paste and seasonings. Bring to a boil. Reduce heat; cover and cook over low heat for 30 minutes.

- Uncover; cook 30-40 minutes longer or until thickened. Discard bay leaves. Serve 1/2 cup of meat mixture on each bun.

YIELD: 16 servings.

NUTRITION FACTS: 1 sloppy joe equals 249 calories, 6 g fat (2 g saturated fat), 28 mg cholesterol, 547 mg sodium, 31 g carbohydrate, 4 g fiber, 16 g protein.

ZESTY SLOPPY JOES

249 CALORIES

251-350 calories

291 CALORIES

BEEF FAJITA SALAD

beef fajita salad

Ardeena Harris | ROANOKE, ALABAMA

The beef in this salad marinates for only 10 minutes, but it gets great flavor from the lime juice, cilantro and chili powder.

- 1/4 cup lime juice
- 2 tablespoons minced fresh cilantro
- 1 garlic clove, minced
- 1 teaspoon chili powder
- 3/4 pound boneless beef sirloin steak, cut into thin strips
- 1 medium green pepper, julienned
- 1 medium sweet red pepper, julienned
- 1 medium onion, sliced and halved
- 1 teaspoon olive oil
- 1 can (16 ounces) kidney beans, rinsed and drained
- 4 cups torn mixed salad greens
- 1 medium tomato, chopped
- 4 tablespoons fat-free sour cream
- 2 tablespoons salsa

- In a large resealable plastic bag, combine the lime juice, cilantro, garlic and chili powder; add beef. Seal bag and turn to coat; refrigerate for 10 minutes, turning once.

- Meanwhile, in a nonstick skillet, cook the peppers and onion in oil over medium-high heat for 5 minutes or until

tender. Remove and keep warm. Add beef with marinade to the skillet; cook and stir for 4-5 minutes or until meat is tender and mixture comes to a boil. Add the beans and pepper mixture; heat through.

- Divide the salad greens among four bowls; top each with 1-1/4 cups beef mixture, 1 tablespoon sour cream and 1-1/2 teaspoons salsa.

YIELD: 4 servings.

NUTRITION FACTS: 1 serving equals 291 calories, 6 g fat (2 g saturated fat), 50 mg cholesterol, 291 mg sodium, 34 g carbohydrate, 9 g fiber, 27 g protein. **DIABETIC EXCHANGES:** 2 lean meat, 2 vegetable, 1-1/2 starch.

crab pasta salad

Heather O'Neill | DUDLEY, MASSACHUSETTS

After enjoying this recipe for years, I lightened it up with fat-free mayonnaise and reduced-fat dressing one day. I was just delighted to find it kept all the flavor!

- 8 ounces uncooked spiral pasta
- 1 package (8 ounces) imitation crabmeat, chopped
- 1 cup frozen peas, thawed
- 1 cup fresh broccoli florets
- 1/2 cup chopped green pepper
- 1/4 cup sliced green onions
- 3/4 cup fat-free mayonnaise
- 1/3 cup reduced-fat Italian salad dressing
- 3 tablespoons grated Parmesan cheese

- Cook pasta according to package directions; drain and rinse in cold water. In a large bowl, combine the pasta,

CRAB PASTA SALAD

251 CALORIES

crab, peas, broccoli, green pepper and onions. Combine the mayonnaise, salad dressing and Parmesan cheese; pour over the pasta mixture; toss to coat. Cover and refrigerate for 2 hours or until chilled.

YIELD: 6 servings.

NUTRITION FACTS: 1-1/3 cups equals 251 calories, 5 g fat (1 g saturated fat), 10 mg cholesterol, 746 mg sodium, 42 g carbohydrate, 3 g fiber, 12 g protein. **DIABETIC EXCHANGES:** 3 starch, 1 lean meat.

creamy chicken and wild rice soup

Bonnie Erickson | HINCKLEY, MINNESOTA

I'm happy to share the recipe for this comforting, cool-weather soup that's chock-full of homey harvest goodness. I'm always being asked to make this recipe.

- 2/3 cup uncooked wild rice
- 2/3 cup chopped onion
- 2/3 cup chopped carrot
-   2 tablespoons butter
-   6 cups reduced-sodium chicken broth
-   2 medium potatoes, peeled and cubed
- 1/2 teaspoon salt
- 1/2 teaspoon pepper
-   1 cup chopped fresh broccoli
-   3 cups cubed cooked chicken breast
- 1/2 cup all-purpose flour
-   1 cup fat-free half-and-half

• Cook rice according to package directions. Meanwhile, in a large saucepan coated with cooking spray, cook onion and carrot in butter for 2 minutes. Stir in broth, potatoes, salt and pepper. Bring to a boil. Reduce heat; cover and simmer for 10 minutes. Add broccoli; cook 3-7 minutes longer or until potatoes are tender.

• Drain rice if necessary; fluff with a fork. Stir chicken and rice into potato mixture; heat through. In a small bowl, combine flour and half-and-half until smooth. Gradually stir into soup. Bring to a boil; cook and stir for 2 minutes or until thickened.

YIELD: 8 servings (2-1/2 quarts).

NUTRITION FACTS: 1-1/4 cups equals 251 calories, 5 g fat (2 g saturated fat), 48 mg cholesterol, 707 mg sodium, 29 g carbohydrate, 2 g fiber, 22 g protein. **DIABETIC EXCHANGES:** 2 starch, 2 very lean meat, 1/2 fat.

jamaican jerk turkey wraps

Mary Ann Dell | PHOENIXVILLE, PENNSYLVANIA

I received this recipe after tasting the spicy wraps at a neighborhood party. The grilled turkey tenderloin and light jalapeno dressing make them tops with my gang.

-   2 cups broccoli coleslaw mix
-   1 medium tomato, seeded and chopped
-   3 tablespoons reduced-fat coleslaw dressing
-   1 jalapeno pepper, seeded and chopped
-   1 tablespoon prepared mustard
- 1-1/2 teaspoons Caribbean jerk seasoning
-   2 turkey breast tenderloins (8 ounces *each*)
-   4 fat-free flour tortillas (8 inches)

• In a large bowl, toss the coleslaw mix, tomato, coleslaw dressing, jalapeno and mustard; set aside. Rub seasoning over turkey tenderloins.

• Coat grill rack with cooking spray before starting the grill. Grill tenderloins, covered, over medium heat for 8-10 minutes on each side or until a meat thermometer reads 170°. Let stand for 5 minutes.

• Grill tortillas, uncovered, over medium heat for 45-55 seconds on each side or until warmed. Thinly slice turkey; place down the center of tortillas. Top with coleslaw mixture and roll up.

YIELD: 4 servings.

EDITOR'S NOTE: When cutting or seeding hot peppers, use rubber or plastic gloves to protect your hands. Avoid touching your face.

NUTRITION FACTS: 1 wrap equals 295 calories, 4 g fat (1 g saturated fat), 59 mg cholesterol, 658 mg sodium, 34 g carbohydrate, 3 g fiber, 31 g protein. **DIABETIC EXCHANGES:** 3 very lean meat, 2 starch, 1 vegetable, 1/2 fat.

JAMAICAN JERK TURKEY WRAPS

259 CALORIES

SPECIAL EGG SALAD

special egg salad

Judy Nissen | SIOUX FALLS, SOUTH DAKOTA

This recipe proves you don't have to sacrifice flavor to eat lighter. These yummy, satisfying egg salad sandwiches are sure to be well-received whenever you serve them.

- 3 ounces reduced-fat cream cheese
- 1/4 cup fat-free mayonnaise
- 1/2 teaspoon sugar
- 1/4 teaspoon onion powder
- 1/4 teaspoon garlic powder
- 1/8 teaspoon salt
- 1/8 teaspoon pepper
- 6 hard-cooked eggs, chopped
- 12 slices whole wheat bread, toasted
- 6 lettuce leaves

- In a small bowl, beat the cream cheese until smooth. Beat in mayonnaise, sugar, onion powder, garlic powder, salt and pepper; fold in the eggs. Cover and refrigerate for 1 hour. Serve on toast with lettuce.

YIELD: 6 servings.

NUTRITION FACTS: 1 serving equals 259 calories, 10 g fat (4 g saturated fat), 225 mg cholesterol, 528 mg sodium, 30 g carbohydrate, 4 g fiber, 13 g protein. **DIABETIC EXCHANGES:** 2 starch, 1-1/2 fat, 1 lean meat.

273 CALORIES

spicy buffalo chicken wraps

Jennifer Beck | RIO RANCHO, NEW MEXICO

This recipe has a real kick and is one of my husband's favorites. It's ready in a flash and is easily doubled.

- 1/2 pound boneless skinless chicken breasts, cubed
- 1/2 teaspoon canola oil

- 2 tablespoons Louisiana-style hot sauce
- 1 cup shredded lettuce
- 2 flour tortillas (6 inches), warmed
- 2 teaspoons prepared reduced-fat ranch salad dressing
- 2 tablespoons crumbled blue cheese

- In a nonstick skillet coated with cooking spray, cook chicken in oil for 6 minutes; drain. Stir in hot sauce. Bring to a boil. Reduce heat; simmer, uncovered, for 3-5 minutes or until sauce is thickened and chicken juices run clear.

- Place lettuce on tortillas; drizzle with ranch dressing. Top with chicken mixture and blue cheese; roll up.

YIELD: 2 servings.

NUTRITION FACTS: 1 wrap equals 273 calories, 11 g fat (3 g saturated fat), 70 mg cholesterol, 453 mg sodium, 15 g carbohydrate, 1 g fiber, 28 g protein. **DIABETIC EXCHANGES:** 3 very lean meat, 1-1/2 fat, 1 starch.

273 CALORIES

old-fashioned lamb stew

Michelle Wise | SPRING MILLS, PENNSYLVANIA

This hearty stew is chock-full of tender lamb chunks and lots of vegetables. Sometimes, I prepare this recipe in my slow cooker.

- 1/4 cup all-purpose flour
- 1 teaspoon salt
- 1/2 teaspoon pepper
- 3 pounds boneless lamb, cut into 3-inch pieces
- 2 tablespoons vegetable oil
- 1 can (28 ounces) diced tomatoes, undrained
- 1 medium onion, cut into eighths
- 1 tablespoon dried parsley flakes
- 2 teaspoons dried rosemary, crushed
- 1/4 teaspoon garlic powder
- 4 large carrots, cut into 1/2-inch pieces
- 4 medium potatoes, peeled and cut into 1-inch pieces
- 1 package (10 ounces) frozen peas
- 1 can (4 ounces) mushroom stems and pieces, drained

- In a large resealable plastic bag, combine flour, salt and pepper; add lamb and toss to coat. In a Dutch oven, brown lamb in oil; drain. Add tomatoes, onion, parsley, rosemary and garlic powder. Cover and simmer for 2 hours.

- Add carrots and potatoes; cover and cook 1 hour longer or until the meat is tender. Add peas and mushrooms; heat through. Thicken if desired.

YIELD: 12 servings.

NUTRITION FACTS: 1 cup equals 273 calories, 8 g fat (2 g saturated fat), 74 mg cholesterol, 426 mg sodium, 22 g carbohydrate, 4 g fiber, 27 g protein.

waldorf tuna salad

Shirley Glaab | HATTIESBURG, MISSISSIPPI

I like this recipe because it dresses up tuna salad deliciously with apple, raisins, dates and walnuts...then coats it all with a tangy yogurt dressing.

2	cans (6 ounces *each*) light water-packed tuna, drained and flaked
1	large red apple, chopped
1/3	cup chopped celery
1/3	cup raisins
1/3	cup chopped dates
1/4	cup chopped walnuts
1/2	cup fat-free plain yogurt
1/4	cup reduced-fat mayonnaise
4	lettuce leaves
1/4	cup shredded reduced-fat Monterey Jack cheese

- In a large bowl, combine the tuna, apple, celery, raisins, dates and walnuts. Combine yogurt and mayonnaise; add

WALDORF TUNA SALAD

340 CALORIES

TUNA ARTICHOKE MELTS

335 CALORIES

to tuna mixture and toss to coat. Serve on lettuce-lined plates; sprinkle with the cheese.

YIELD: 4 servings.

NUTRITION FACTS: 3/4 cup equals 340 calories, 12 g fat (2 g saturated fat), 36 mg cholesterol, 495 mg sodium, 34 g carbohydrate, 4 g fiber, 28 g protein. **DIABETIC EXCHANGES:** 2-1/2 lean meat, 1-1/2 fruit, 1 starch, 1 fat.

tuna artichoke melts

Evelyn Basinger | LINVILLE, VIRGINIA

After sampling a similar open-faced sandwich at a restaurant, I created this lovely lemon-seasoned tuna salad with artichoke hearts. Serve it on the patio for lunch with a friend.

1	can (6 ounces) light water-packed tuna, drained and flaked
1/3	cup coarsely chopped water-packed artichoke hearts
2	tablespoons fat-free mayonnaise
1/2	cup shredded reduced-fat Mexican cheese blend, *divided*
1/4	teaspoon salt-free lemon-pepper seasoning
1/8	teaspoon dried oregano
2	English muffins, split and toasted

- In a small bowl, combine tuna, artichokes, mayonnaise, 1/4 cup cheese, lemon-pepper and oregano. Spread over English muffin halves.

- Place on a baking sheet. Broil 4-6 in. from heat for 3-5 minutes or until heated through. Sprinkle with remaining cheese; broil 1-2 minutes longer or until cheese is melted.

YIELD: 2 servings.

NUTRITION FACTS: 2 open-faced sandwiches equals 335 calories, 8 g fat (4 g saturated fat), 47 mg cholesterol, 989 mg sodium, 31 g carbohydrate, 2 g fiber, 34 g protein. **DIABETIC EXCHANGES:** 4 very lean meat, 2 starch, 1 fat.

278 CALORIES

VEGETABLE BEEF STEW

vegetable beef stew

Ruth Rodriguez | FORT MYERS BEACH, FLORIDA

Here is a great variation of beef stew that I came across. With sweet flavor from apricots and squash, we think it has South American or Cuban flair. The addition of corn makes it even more hearty.

3/4	pound lean beef stew meat, cut into 1/2-inch cubes
2	teaspoons canola oil
1	can (14-1/2 ounces) beef broth
1	can (14-1/2 ounces) stewed tomatoes, cut up
1-1/2	cups cubed peeled butternut squash
1	cup frozen corn, thawed
6	dried apricot *or* peach halves, quartered
1/2	cup chopped carrot
1	teaspoon dried oregano
1/4	teaspoon salt
1/4	teaspoon pepper
2	tablespoons cornstarch
1/4	cup water
2	tablespoons minced fresh parsley

- In a nonstick skillet, cook the beef over medium heat in oil until no longer pink; drain. Transfer to a 3-qt. slow cooker. Add the broth, tomatoes, squash, corn, apricots, carrot, oregano, salt and pepper. Cover and cook on high for 5-6 hours or until vegetables and meat are tender.

- Combine cornstarch and water until smooth; gradually stir into stew. Cover and cook on high for 30 minutes or until gravy is thickened. Stir in parsley.

YIELD: 4 servings.

NUTRITION FACTS: 1-1/2 cups equals 278 calories, 9 g fat (3 g saturated fat), 53 mg cholesterol, 717 mg sodium, 32 g carbohydrate, 5 g fiber, 21 g protein. DIABETIC EXCHANGES: 2 lean meat, 2 vegetable, 1-1/2 starch, 1/2 fat.

taco salad wraps

Marlene Roberts | MOORE, OKLAHOMA

These flavorful Southwestern wraps will be a hit at lunch or even dinner.

1/4	pound lean ground beef
1/3	cup plus 2 tablespoons salsa, *divided*
1/4	cup chili beans, drained
1-1/2	teaspoons Worcestershire sauce
1	teaspoon onion powder
1	teaspoon chili powder
1/8	teaspoon garlic powder

Pepper to taste

2	flour tortillas (8 inches), warmed
1/3	cup shredded lettuce
1	plum tomato, chopped
2	tablespoons shredded cheddar cheese
6	baked tortilla chip scoops, slightly crushed

- In a small nonstick skillet, cook beef over medium heat until no longer pink; drain. Stir in 1/3 cup salsa, beans, Worcestershire sauce, onion powder, chili powder, garlic powder and pepper. Bring to a boil; reduce the heat and simmer, uncovered, for 5 minutes.

- Spoon meat mixture onto each tortilla. Layer with lettuce, tomato, cheese, crushed tortilla chips and remaining salsa; roll up.

YIELD: 2 servings.

NUTRITION FACTS: 1 wrap equals 345 calories, 10 g fat (4 g saturated fat), 35 mg cholesterol, 764 mg sodium, 42 g carbohydrate, 5 g fiber, 20 g protein.

TACO SALAD WRAPS

345 CALORIES

herbed tuna sandwiches

332 CALORIES

Marie Connor | VIRGINIA BEACH, VIRGINIA

A delightful combination of herbs and reduced-fat cheese make this simple tuna sandwich stand out.

2 cans (6 ounces *each*) light water-packed tuna, drained and flaked
2 hard-cooked eggs, chopped
1/3 cup fat-free mayonnaise
1/4 cup minced fresh chives
2 teaspoons minced fresh parsley
1/2 teaspoon dried basil
1/4 teaspoon onion powder
8 slices whole wheat bread, toasted
1/2 cup shredded reduced-fat cheddar cheese

• In a small bowl, combine the first seven ingredients. Place four slices of toast on an ungreased baking sheet; top with tuna mixture and sprinkle with cheese.

• Broil 3-4 in. from the heat for 1-2 minutes or until cheese is melted. Top with remaining toast.

YIELD: 4 servings.

NUTRITION FACTS: 1 sandwich equals 332 calories, 9 g fat (4 g saturated fat), 144 mg cholesterol, 864 mg sodium, 30 g carbohydrate, 4 g fiber, 34 g protein. **DIABETIC EXCHANGES:** 4 very lean meat, 2 starch, 1 fat.

spicy pork tenderloin salad

Pat Sellon | MONTICELLO, WISCONSIN

Since it's a meal-in-one, this salad is perfect for lunch, weeknight dinners and entertaining.

4-1/2 teaspoons lime juice
1-1/2 teaspoons orange juice
1-1/2 teaspoons Dijon mustard
1/2 teaspoon curry powder
1/4 teaspoon salt
1/8 teaspoon pepper
2 tablespoons olive oil
SPICE RUB:
1/2 teaspoon salt
1/2 teaspoon ground cumin

301 CALORIES

SPICY PORK TENDERLOIN SALAD

1/2 teaspoon ground cinnamon
1/2 teaspoon chili powder
1/4 teaspoon pepper
1 pork tenderloin (1 pound)
2 teaspoons olive oil
1/3 cup packed brown sugar
6 garlic cloves, minced
1-1/2 teaspoons hot pepper sauce
1 package (6 ounces) fresh baby spinach

• In a small bowl, whisk the first six ingredients; gradually whisk in oil. Cover and refrigerate vinaigrette. Combine the salt, cumin, cinnamon, chili powder and pepper; rub over meat.

• In a ovenproof skillet, brown meat on all sides in oil, about 8 minutes. Combine the brown sugar, garlic and hot pepper sauce; spread over meat.

• Bake at 350° for 25-35 minutes or until a meat thermometer reads 160°. Let pork stand for 5 minutes before slicing.

• Toss spinach with vinaigrette. Arrange spinach on four salad plates; top with sliced pork. Drizzle with pan juices.

YIELD: 4 servings.

NUTRITION FACTS: 3 ounces cooked pork with 1-3/4 cups spinach equals 301 calories, 13 g fat (3 g saturated fat), 63 mg cholesterol, 591 mg sodium, 22 g carbohydrate, 2 g fiber, 24 g protein. **DIABETIC EXCHANGES:** 3 lean meat, 1 starch, 1 vegetable, 1/2 fat.

turkey vegetable soup

Bonnie LeBarron | FORESTVILLE, NEW YORK

Low-sodium ingredients don't diminish the full flavor of this brothy soup. The ground turkey and colorful vegetables give it a heartiness everyone will welcome on a cold, blustery day.

1	pound lean ground turkey
1	cup chopped celery
1/2	cup chopped onion
2	to 3 garlic cloves, minced
2	cans (14-1/2 ounces *each*) reduced-sodium beef broth
2-1/2	cups reduced-sodium tomato juice
1	can (14-1/2 ounces) diced tomatoes, drained
1	cup sliced fresh mushrooms
3/4	cup frozen French-style green beans
1/2	cup sliced carrots
1-1/2	teaspoons Worcestershire sauce
1	teaspoon dried parsley flakes
1	teaspoon dried thyme
1/2	teaspoon sugar
1/2	teaspoon dried basil
1/4	teaspoon pepper
1	bay leaf

- In a Dutch oven coated with cooking spray, saute turkey, celery, onion and garlic until meat is no longer pink; drain.

TURKEY VEGETABLE SOUP

272 CALORIES

291 CALORIES

LIME JALAPENO TURKEY WRAPS

- Stir in remaining ingredients. Bring to a boil. Reduce heat; cover and simmer for 1 hour or until vegetables are tender. Discard bay leaf. Soup may be frozen for up to 3 months.

YIELD: 4 servings.

NUTRITION FACTS: 1-1/2 cups equals 272 calories, 10 g fat (3 g saturated fat), 94 mg cholesterol, 783 mg sodium, 20 g carbohydrate, 5 g fiber, 25 g protein. **DIABETIC EXCHANGES:** 2-1/2 lean meat, 1 starch, 1 vegetable, 1/2 fat.

lime jalapeno turkey wraps

Mary Jo Amos | NOEL, MISSOURI

My grandfather enjoyed burritos filled with leftover turkey, lime and chilies. I've tweaked the recipe a little to better suit our tastes.

3	lettuce leaves
1	cup shredded cooked turkey breast (6 ounces)
2	tablespoons chopped seeded tomato
1	green onion, thinly sliced
1	teaspoon lime juice
1-1/2	teaspoons finely chopped jalapeno pepper
1/8	teaspoon sugar
1/8	teaspoon salt
1/8	teaspoon garlic powder
1/8	teaspoon pepper
2	flour tortillas (8 inches), room temperature
2	red onion rings (1/4 to 1/2 inch thick)
2	pitted ripe *or* stuffed olives, optional

- Chop one lettuce leaf; set aside remaining leaves. In a medium bowl, combine the next nine ingredients and chopped lettuce.
- Place one lettuce leaf on each tortilla. Spoon half the filling off center on each. Fold one end over filling and roll up. Slide each wrap through the middle of an onion ring. Secure roll-up with a toothpick near the onion ring; top each with an olive if desired.

YIELD: 2 servings.

EDITOR'S NOTE: When cutting or seeding hot peppers, use rubber or plastic gloves to protect your hands. Avoid touching your face.

NUTRITION FACTS: 1 wrap equals 291 calories, 4 g fat (1 g saturated fat), 71 mg cholesterol, 483 mg sodium, 31 g carbohydrate, 0 fiber, 0 protein. **DIABETIC EXCHANGES:** 4 very lean meat, 2 starch.

creamy chicken salad

261 CALORIES

Kristi Abernathy | LEWISTOWN, MONTANA

I modified the original recipe for this chicken salad to make it healthier. The ingredients are so flavorful that my changes didn't take away from the taste. This refreshing salad never lasts long at our house.

- 2 cups cubed cooked chicken breast
- 1 cup cooked small ring pasta
- 1 cup halved seedless red grapes
- 1 can (11 ounces) mandarin oranges, drained
- 3 celery ribs, chopped
- 1/2 cup sliced almonds
- 1 tablespoon grated onion
- 1 cup reduced-fat mayonnaise
- 1 cup reduced-fat whipped topping
- 1/4 teaspoon salt

Lettuce leaves, optional

- In a bowl, combine the chicken, pasta, grapes, oranges, celery, almonds and onion.
- In another bowl, combine mayonnaise, whipped topping and salt. Add to the chicken mixture; stir to coat. Serve in a lettuce-lined bowl if desired.

YIELD: 6 servings.

NUTRITION FACTS: 1 cup equals 261 calories, 13 g fat (0 saturated fat), 38 mg cholesterol, 307 mg sodium, 25 g carbohydrate, 2 g fiber, 11 g protein. **DIABETIC EXCHANGES:** 1-1/2 fat, 1 starch, 1 meat, 1/2 fruit.

pizza pasta salad

Danielle Carpenter | VIENNA, WEST VIRGINIA

I wanted to make over my pizza pasta salad, which is very popular with my kids, to make it healthier for us. This version has half the fat, and the cholesterol and calories were cut by one-third, but it's still a kid-pleasing favorite.

- 8 ounces uncooked spiral pasta
- 1/2 teaspoon cornstarch
- 1/3 cup water
- 1/4 cup Parmesan cheese
- 1/2 cup red wine vinegar
- 2 tablespoons olive oil
- 1 teaspoon dried oregano
- 1/2 teaspoon salt
- 1/2 teaspoon garlic powder
- 1/8 teaspoon pepper
- 1-1/2 cups halved cherry tomatoes
- 3/4 cup shredded reduced-fat cheddar cheese
- 3/4 cup shredded part-skim mozzarella cheese
- 1/2 cup sliced green onions
- 1/2 cup sliced turkey pepperoni (about 1-1/2 ounces)

- Cook pasta according to package directions. In a small saucepan, combine cornstarch and water until smooth. Bring to a boil; cook and stir for 1-2 minutes or until thickened. Remove from the heat; stir in the Parmesan cheese, vinegar, oil, oregano, salt, garlic powder and pepper. Drain pasta; rinse in cold water. In a large bowl, combine the remaining ingredients. Add pasta and dressing; toss to coat. Cover and refrigerate for at least 1 hour before serving.

YIELD: 7 servings.

NUTRITION FACTS: 1 cup equals 255 calories, 11 g fat (5 g saturated fat), 26 mg cholesterol, 403 mg sodium, 25 g carbohydrate, 2 g fiber, 14 g protein. **DIABETIC EXCHANGES:** 1-1/2 starch, 1-1/2 fat, 1 lean meat.

PIZZA PASTA SALAD

255 CALORIES

307 CALORIES

GRILLED BEAN BURGERS

grilled bean burgers

Marguerite Shaeffer | SEWELL, NEW JERSEY

I swear by these moist and delicious salsa-topped burgers. They can hold their own against any veggie burger you'd buy at the supermarket. They're wonderful! If you like the heat of chili powder, use 2 teaspoons; for a milder version, use 1 teaspoon.

- 1 large onion, finely chopped
- 4 garlic cloves, minced
- 1 tablespoon olive oil
- 1 medium carrot, shredded
- 1 to 2 teaspoons chili powder
- 1 teaspoon ground cumin
- 1 can (15 ounces) pinto beans, rinsed and drained
- 1 can (15 ounces) black beans, rinsed and drained
- 1-1/2 cups quick-cooking oats
- 2 tablespoons Dijon mustard
- 2 tablespoons reduced-sodium soy sauce
- 1 tablespoon ketchup
- 1/4 teaspoon pepper
- 8 whole wheat hamburger buns, split
- 8 lettuce leaves
- 8 tablespoons salsa

- In a large nonstick skillet coated with cooking spray, saute onion and garlic in oil for 2 minutes. Stir in the carrot, chili powder and cumin; cook 2 minutes longer or until the carrot is tender. Remove from the heat; set aside.

- In a large bowl, mash the pinto beans and black beans. Stir in the oats. Add the mustard, soy sauce, ketchup, pepper and carrot mixture; mix well. Shape into eight 3-1/2-in. patties.

- Coat grill rack with cooking spray before starting the grill. Grill patties, covered, over medium heat for 4-5 minutes on each side or until heated through. Serve on buns with lettuce and salsa.

YIELD: 8 servings.

NUTRITION FACTS: 1 burger equals 307 calories, 5 g fat (1 g saturated fat), 0 cholesterol, 723 mg sodium, 53 g carbohydrate, 10 g fiber, 12 g protein. **DIABETIC EXCHANGES:** 3-1/2 starch, 1 very lean meat.

313 CALORIES

shredded beef barbecue

Lori Bergquist | WILTON, NORTH DAKOTA

This beef roast simmers for hours in a homemade barbecue sauce, so it's very tender and easy to shred for sandwiches. The mixture freezes well, too.

- 1 boneless beef sirloin tip roast (2-1/2 pounds)
- 1/2 teaspoon salt
- 1/4 teaspoon pepper
- 1 tablespoon canola oil
- 1 cup *each* ketchup and water
- 1/2 cup chopped onion
- 1/3 cup packed brown sugar
- 3 tablespoons Worcestershire sauce
- 2 tablespoons lemon juice
- 2 tablespoons cider vinegar
- 2 tablespoons Dijon mustard
- 2 teaspoons celery seed
- 2 teaspoons chili powder
- 12 kaiser rolls, split

- Sprinkle roast with salt and pepper. In a nonstick skillet, brown roast in oil on all sides over medium-high heat; drain.

- Transfer roast to a 5-qt. slow cooker. Combine ketchup, water, onion, brown sugar, Worcestershire sauce, lemon juice, vinegar, mustard, celery seed and chili powder; pour over roast.

- Cover and cook on low for 8-10 hours or until meat is tender. Remove meat; shred with two forks and return to slow cooker. Spoon 1/2 cup meat mixture onto each roll.

YIELD: 12 servings.

NUTRITION FACTS: 1 sandwich equals 313 calories, 9 g fat (2 g saturated fat), 59 mg cholesterol, 688 mg sodium, 33 g carbohydrate, 2 g fiber, 26 g protein. **DIABETIC EXCHANGES:** 3 lean meat, 2 starch.

282 CALORIES

CHICKEN SPAGHETTI SALAD

chicken spaghetti salad

Holly Siphavong | EUREKA, CALIFORNIA

I make this quick dish when I'm in a hurry and don't want a huge meal.

>   3 ounces uncooked spaghetti
> 1/2 cup shredded cooked chicken breast
> 1/2 cup julienned cucumber
> 1/3 cup julienned carrot
>   1 tablespoon white vinegar
>   1 tablespoon reduced-sodium soy sauce
>   2 teaspoons canola oil
>   1 teaspoon minced fresh gingerroot
> 3/4 teaspoon sugar
> 1/4 teaspoon minced garlic

- Cook spaghetti according to package directions; drain and rinse in cold water. Combine the spaghetti, chicken, cucumber and carrot. In a small saucepan, combine the vinegar, soy sauce, oil, ginger, sugar and garlic. Bring to a boil; remove from the heat. Drizzle over the spaghetti mixture and toss to coat.

YIELD: 2 servings.

NUTRITION FACTS: 1-1/2 cups equals 282 calories, 7 g fat (1 g saturated fat), 36 mg cholesterol, 343 mg sodium, 34 g carbohydrate, 3 g fiber, 19 g protein. **DIABETIC EXCHANGES:** 2 starch, 2 lean meat, 1 vegetable.

cantaloupe chicken-orzo salad

Too hot to cook? Then try a main-dish salad served on cool, refreshing cantaloupe wedges. Our staff recommends it with a grainy muffin or hard roll.

> 1/2 cup uncooked orzo pasta
>   1 snack-size cup (4 ounces) pineapple tidbits
> 1/2 cup fat-free mayonnaise
> 1/3 cup fat-free plain yogurt
>   4 teaspoons lemon juice
>   1 teaspoon minced fresh mint
>   1 teaspoon grated lemon peel
>   1 teaspoon honey
> 1/4 teaspoon salt
> 1/8 teaspoon pepper
>   2 cups cubed cooked chicken breast
> 1/2 cup chopped celery
> 1/3 cup chopped sweet red pepper
> 1/4 cup chopped green onions
>   1 small cantaloupe, quartered and seeded
> 1/4 cup unsalted cashews

- Cook pasta according to package directions. Meanwhile, drain pineapple, reserving juice; set pineapple aside. In a small bowl, whisk the mayonnaise, yogurt, lemon juice, mint, lemon peel, honey, salt, pepper and pineapple juice until smooth.

- Drain pasta and rinse in cold water. Place in a large bowl; add the chicken, celery, red pepper, onions and pineapple. Add the mayonnaise mixture and toss to coat. Serve on cantaloupe wedges. Sprinkle with cashews.

YIELD: 4 servings.

NUTRITION FACTS: 1/4 cantaloupe with 1 cup chicken salad equals 345 calories, 8 g fat (2 g saturated fat), 58 mg cholesterol, 473 mg sodium, 43 g carbohydrate, 4 g fiber, 27 g protein. **DIABETIC EXCHANGES:** 3 very lean meat, 2 starch, 1 fruit, 1 fat.

CANTALOUPE CHICKEN-ORZO SALAD

345 CALORIES

257 CALORIES

RANCH CHICKEN SALAD SANDWICHES

ranch chicken salad sandwiches

Bobbie Scroggie | SCOTT DEPOT, WEST VIRGINIA

Tender chopped chicken, crunchy celery and sweet red pepper are given a creamy coating of ranch dressing, sour cream and mayonnaise in this recipe, which makes a terrific sandwich.

- 1/4 cup reduced-fat mayonnaise
- 3 tablespoons fat-free ranch salad dressing
- 3 tablespoons fat-free sour cream
- 1 tablespoon lemon juice
- 1/8 teaspoon pepper
- 2 cups cubed cooked chicken breast
- 1/2 cup thinly sliced celery
- 2 tablespoons diced sweet red pepper
- 1 tablespoon chopped green onion
- 6 hamburger buns, split
- 6 lettuce leaves
- 6 slices tomato

- In a small bowl, combine mayonnaise, ranch dressing, sour cream, lemon juice and pepper. Stir in chicken, celery, red pepper and onion until combined. Spoon 1/3 cup onto each bun bottom; top with lettuce and tomato. Replace bun tops.

YIELD: 6 servings.

NUTRITION FACTS: 1 sandwich equals 257 calories, 7 g fat (1 g saturated fat), 41 mg cholesterol, 456 mg sodium, 29 g carbohydrate, 2 g fiber, 18 g protein. **DIABETIC EXCHANGES:** 2 starch, 2 very lean meat, 1/2 fat.

ham 'n' chickpea soup

Linda Arnold | EDMONTON, ALBERTA

Chock-full of ham, vegetables, chickpeas and orzo, this robust soup is loaded with good-for-you ingredients.

- 1/2 cup uncooked orzo pasta
- 1 small onion, chopped
- 2 garlic cloves, minced
- 2 teaspoons canola oil
- 1 cup cubed fully cooked lean ham
- 1 teaspoon dried rosemary, crushed
- 1 teaspoon rubbed sage
- 2 cups reduced-sodium beef broth
- 1 can (14-1/2 ounces) diced tomatoes, undrained
- 1 can (15 ounces) chickpeas *or* garbanzo beans, rinsed and drained
- 4 tablespoons shredded Parmesan cheese
- 1 tablespoon minced fresh parsley

- Cook orzo according to package directions. Meanwhile, in a large saucepan, saute onion and garlic in oil for 3 minutes. Add the ham, rosemary and sage; saute 1 minute longer. Stir in broth and tomatoes. Bring to a boil. Reduce heat; simmer, uncovered, for 10 minutes.

- Drain orzo; stir into soup. Add chickpeas; heat through. Sprinkle each serving with Parmesan cheese and parsley.

YIELD: 4 servings.

NUTRITION FACTS: 1-1/2 cups equals 312 calories, 8 g fat (2 g saturated fat), 19 mg cholesterol, 1,015 mg sodium, 43 g carbohydrate, 7 g fiber, 18 g protein. **DIABETIC EXCHANGES:** 2-1/2 starch, 2 very lean meat, 1 vegetable, 1/2 fat.

HAM 'N' CHICKPEA SOUP

312 CALORIES

TANGY TUNA BUNWICHES

336 CALORIES

tangy tuna bunwiches

Brenda Biron | SYDNEY, NOVA SCOTIA

Ketchup and Worcestershire sauce lend a nice, tangy flavor to these quick tuna sandwiches. They're great for casual get-togethers, summer lunches or brown-bagging to work.

- 1 can (6 ounces) light water-packed tuna, drained and flaked
- 3 tablespoons fat-free mayonnaise
- 1 tablespoon ketchup
- 1/2 teaspoon lemon juice
- 1/2 teaspoon Worcestershire sauce
- 2 sandwich buns, split
- 2 lettuce leaves

- In a bowl, combine tuna, mayonnaise, ketchup, lemon juice and Worcestershire sauce. Serve on buns with lettuce.

YIELD: 2 servings.

NUTRITION FACTS: 1 sandwich equals 336 calories, 6 g fat (3 g saturated fat), 28 mg cholesterol, 917 mg sodium, 41 g carbohydrate, 3 g fiber, 29 g protein.

vegetable soup with dumplings

Karen Mau | JACKSBORO, TENNESSEE

Not only is this hearty soup my family's favorite meatless recipe, but it's a complete meal-in-one. It's loaded with vegetables and the fluffy carrot dumplings are a great change of pace.

- 1-1/2 cups chopped onions
- 4 medium carrots, sliced
- 3 celery ribs, sliced
- 2 tablespoons canola oil
- 3 cups vegetable broth
- 4 medium potatoes, peeled and sliced
- 4 medium tomatoes, chopped
- 2 garlic cloves, minced
- 1/2 teaspoon salt
- 1/2 teaspoon pepper
- 1/4 cup all-purpose flour
- 1/2 cup water
- 1 cup chopped cabbage
- 1 cup frozen peas

CARROT DUMPLINGS:
- 2-1/4 cups reduced-fat biscuit/baking mix
- 1 cup shredded carrots
- 1 tablespoon minced fresh parsley
- 1 cup cold water
- 10 tablespoons shredded reduced-fat cheddar cheese

- In a Dutch oven, cook the onions, carrots and celery in oil for 6-8 minutes or until crisp-tender. Stir in the broth, potatoes, tomatoes, garlic, salt and pepper. Bring to a boil. Reduce heat; cover and simmer for 15-20 minutes or until vegetables are tender.

- In a small bowl, combine flour and water until smooth; stir into vegetable mixture. Bring to a boil; cook and stir for 2 minutes or until thickened. Stir in cabbage and peas.

- For dumplings, in a small bowl, combine baking mix, carrots and parsley. Stir in water until moistened. Drop in 10 mounds onto simmering soup. Cover and simmer for 15 minutes or until a toothpick inserted in a dumpling comes out clean (do not lift cover while simmering). Garnish with cheese.

YIELD: 10 servings.

NUTRITION FACTS: 1-1/4 cups soup with 1 dumpling equals 258 calories, 7 g fat (2 g saturated fat), 5 mg cholesterol, 826 mg sodium, 44 g carbohydrate, 5 g fiber, 8 g protein. **DIABETIC EXCHANGES:** 2 starch, 2 vegetable, 1 fat.

VEGETABLE SOUP WITH DUMPLINGS

258 CALORIES

259 CALORIES

BBQ RANCH SALAD

bbq ranch salad

Kim Pohlman | COLDWATER, OHIO

High in protein and low in fat, this scrumptious salad has become one of my husband's and my favorite simple and quick meals.

- 3/4 cup cubed cooked chicken breast
- 3/4 cup canned kidney beans, rinsed and drained
- 1 small tomato, chopped
- 1/3 cup frozen corn, thawed
- 2 tablespoons chopped red onion
- 1/4 cup fat-free ranch salad dressing
- 1 tablespoon barbecue sauce
- 1-1/2 cups torn romaine

- In a small bowl, combine the chicken, kidney beans, tomato, corn and onion. Combine ranch dressing and barbecue sauce; pour over salad and toss to coat. Cover and refrigerate for 30 minutes. Divide romaine between two salad plates; top with salad.

YIELD: 2 servings.

NUTRITION FACTS: 1 cup equals 259 calories, 3 g fat (1 g saturated fat), 41 mg cholesterol, 612 mg sodium, 36 g carbohydrate, 7 g fiber, 24 g protein.

barbecued turkey on buns

Christa Norwalk | LA VALLE, WISCONSIN

I feel good serving these luscious sandwiches that make the most of unsweetened pineapple juice for lunch or dinner. They have such great flavor. Folks never guess they're made with ground turkey.

- 1 pound lean ground turkey
- 1/2 cup chopped onion
- 1/2 cup chopped green pepper
- 1 can (6 ounces) tomato paste
- 1 can (6 ounces) unsweetened pineapple juice
- 1/4 cup water
- 2 teaspoons Dijon mustard
- 1/2 teaspoon garlic powder
- 1/2 teaspoon salt
- 1/8 teaspoon pepper
- 6 whole wheat hamburger buns, split and toasted

- In a large saucepan coated with cooking spray, cook the turkey, onion and green pepper over medium heat until meat is no longer pink; drain.

- Stir in the tomato paste, pineapple juice, water, mustard, garlic powder, salt and pepper. Bring to a boil. Reduce heat; simmer, uncovered, for 20-30 minutes or until sauce is thickened. Spoon 1/3 cup onto each bun.

YIELD: 6 servings.

NUTRITION FACTS: 1 sandwich equals 280 calories, 8 g fat (2 g saturated fat), 60 mg cholesterol, 538 mg sodium, 34 g carbohydrate, 6 g fiber, 18 g protein. **DIABETIC EXCHANGES:** 2 starch, 2 lean meat, 1 vegetable.

BARBECUED TURKEY ON BUNS

280 CALORIES

hearty beef vegetable soup

Mrs. Sherman Snowball | SALT LAKE CITY, UTAH

My husband's stew-like soup is loaded with nutritious ingredients but is still easy to prepare.

- 3 tablespoons all-purpose flour
- 1/2 teaspoon salt
- 1/4 teaspoon pepper
- 1 pound beef stew meat, cut into 1/2-inch cubes

276 CALORIES

HEARTY BEEF VEGETABLE SOUP

- Stir in the remaining ingredients. Bring to a boil. Reduce heat; cover and simmer for 1 hour or until meat and vegetables are tender.

YIELD: 8 servings (about 2-1/2 quarts).

NUTRITION FACTS: 1-1/2 cups equals 276 calories, 8 g fat (2 g saturated fat), 35 mg cholesterol, 638 mg sodium, 38 g carbohydrate, 5 g fiber, 15 g protein.

cucumber chicken salad sandwiches

Eva Wright | GRANT, ALABAMA

I dress up chicken salad with crunchy cucumber and dill for this fresh-tasting and satisfying sandwich. Best of all, it's ready in just 10 minutes.

  1 cup cubed cooked chicken breast
1/3 cup chopped seeded peeled cucumber
1/4 cup fat-free mayonnaise
1/4 teaspoon salt
1/8 teaspoon dill weed
  2 lettuce leaves
  4 slices tomato
  2 sandwich buns, split

- In a small bowl, combine the first five ingredients. Place lettuce and tomato on bun bottoms; top with the chicken salad. Replace bun tops.

YIELD: 2 servings.

NUTRITION FACTS: 1 sandwich equals 350 calories, 8 g fat (3 g saturated fat), 57 mg cholesterol, 930 mg sodium, 42 g carbohydrate, 3 g fiber, 28 g protein. **DIABETIC EXCHANGES:** 3 very lean meat, 2-1/2 starch, 2 vegetable.

CUCUMBER CHICKEN SALAD SANDWICHES

350 CALORIES

  2 tablespoons olive oil
  1 can (14-1/2 ounces) Italian diced tomatoes
  1 can (8 ounces) tomato sauce
  2 tablespoons red wine vinegar
  2 tablespoons Worcestershire sauce
  3 garlic cloves, minced
  1 teaspoon dried oregano
  3 cups hot water
  4 medium potatoes, peeled and cubed
  6 medium carrots, sliced
  2 medium turnips, peeled and cubed
  1 medium zucchini, halved lengthwise and sliced
  1 medium green pepper, julienned
  1 cup sliced fresh mushrooms
  1 medium onion, chopped
  1 can (4 ounces) chopped green chilies
  2 tablespoons sugar

- In a large resealable plastic bag, combine flour, salt and pepper. Add beef, a few pieces at a time, and shake to coat.

- In a soup kettle or Dutch oven, brown beef in oil. Stir in tomatoes, tomato sauce, vinegar, Worcestershire sauce, garlic and oregano. Bring to a boil. Reduce heat; cover and simmer for 1 hour.

301 CALORIES

SHRIMP ROMAINE SALAD

shrimp romaine salad

A refreshing meal awaits when this shrimp-topped entree salad is on the menu. Brown rice increases the nutrition, and citrus flavors make it a delight any time of year. Our Test Kitchen staff suggests serving it with a whole wheat roll.

  2 cups cooked brown rice
  2 cups torn romaine
1-1/2 cups orange segments
  1 cup halved cherry tomatoes
1/2 cup sliced red onion
  3 tablespoons orange juice concentrate
  2 tablespoons cider vinegar
  1 tablespoon olive oil
3/4 teaspoon dried tarragon
1/2 teaspoon garlic powder
1/2 teaspoon salt
1/4 teaspoon pepper
3/4 pound cooked medium shrimp, peeled and deveined

- In a large bowl, combine the rice, romaine, oranges, tomatoes and onion. For dressing, in a small bowl, whisk the orange juice concentrate, vinegar, oil, tarragon, garlic powder, salt and pepper. Set aside 4 teaspoons. Pour remaining dressing over rice mixture and toss to coat. Divide among four plates; top with shrimp. Drizzle with reserved dressing.

YIELD: 4 servings.

NUTRITION FACTS: 1 serving equals 301 calories, 6 g fat (1 g saturated fat), 166 mg cholesterol, 498 mg sodium, 41 g carbohydrate, 5 g fiber, 22 g protein. **DIABETIC EXCHANGES:** 2 very lean meat, 1-1/2 starch, 1 vegetable, 1 fruit, 1/2 fat.

macaroni salad tomato cups

Evelyn Kennell | ROANOKE, ILLINOIS

For a light yet hearty meal for two, I suggest this pasta salad that is flavored with ham and crunchy celery.

3/4 cup uncooked elbow macaroni
  2 large tomatoes
1/2 cup diced deli ham
1/4 cup shredded reduced-fat cheddar cheese
  2 tablespoons chopped celery
  3 tablespoons fat-free mayonnaise
  3 tablespoons reduced-fat sour cream
1/4 teaspoon onion powder
1/8 teaspoon pepper
Lettuce leaves, optional

- Cook macaroni according to package directions. Meanwhile, cut a thin slice off the top of each tomato. Scoop out pulp, leaving a 1/2-in. shell. Invert tomatoes onto paper towels to drain. Drain macaroni and rinse in cold water. In a bowl, combine the macaroni, ham, cheese and celery.

- In a small bowl, combine the mayonnaise, sour cream, onion powder and pepper. Pour over salad and stir to coat. Spoon into tomato cups. Serve on a lettuce-lined plate if desired with any additional salad on the side.

YIELD: 2 servings.

NUTRITION FACTS: 1 serving equals 272 calories, 8 g fat (4 g saturated fat), 36 mg cholesterol, 792 mg sodium, 35 g carbohydrate, 4 g fiber, 17 g protein.

MACARONI SALAD TOMATO CUPS

272 CALORIES

sloppy joes

Suzanne Mckinley | LYONS, GEORGIA

Who isn't looking for quick healthy meal solutions? Here's a sophisticated twist on a family favorite. My daughter Tiffany came up with this lower-fat version of traditional sloppy joes—and we all love it! Best of all, this recipe can be made ahead and frozen for real convenience.

    1   pound ground beef
    1/3 cup chopped onion
    1   garlic clove, minced
    1   can (8 ounces) tomato sauce
    1/2 cup ketchup
    4   teaspoons Worcestershire sauce
    1   teaspoon molasses
    1   teaspoon prepared mustard
    1/2 teaspoon ground mustard
Pinch ground cloves
Pinch cayenne pepper
    1/4 teaspoon grated orange peel, optional
    6   whole wheat buns, split

- In a saucepan, cook beef, onion and garlic over medium heat until meat is no longer pink; drain. Stir in the tomato sauce, ketchup, Worcestershire sauce, molasses, prepared mustard, ground mustard, cloves, cayenne and orange peel if desired. Bring to a boil. Reduce heat; simmer, uncovered, for 5 minutes. Serve on buns.

YIELD: 6 servings.

NUTRITION FACTS: 1 sandwich equals 274 calories, 9 g fat (3 g saturated fat), 37 mg cholesterol, 713 mg sodium, 32 g carbohydrate, 4 g fiber, 18 g protein.

pineapple chicken fajitas

Raymonde Bourgeois | SWASTIKA, ONTARIO

Honey and pineapple add a sweet twist to these fajitas that my family loves. Serve this chicken dish with a bit of sour cream, shredded cheddar cheese and salsa. Forget the tortillas and cut even more calories.

    2   pounds boneless skinless chicken breasts, cut into strips
    1   tablespoon olive oil
    1   *each* medium green, sweet red and yellow pepper, julienned
    1   medium onion, cut into thin wedges

351-450 calories

PINEAPPLE CHICKEN FAJITAS

    2   tablespoons fajita seasoning mix
    1/4 cup water
    2   tablespoons honey
    1   tablespoon dried parsley flakes
    1   teaspoon garlic powder
    1/2 teaspoon salt
    1/2 cup unsweetened pineapple chunks, drained
    8   flour tortillas (10 inches), warmed

- In a large nonstick skillet, cook the chicken in oil for 4-5 minutes. Add the peppers and onion; cook and stir 4-5 minutes longer.

- In a small bowl, combine seasoning mix and water; stir in the honey, parsley, garlic powder and salt. Stir into skillet. Add pineapple. Cook and stir for 1-2 minutes or until chicken juices run clear and vegetables are tender.

- Place chicken mixture on one side of each tortilla; fold tortillas over filling.

YIELD: 8 fajitas.

NUTRITION FACTS: 1 fajita equals 402 calories, 8 g fat (2 g saturated fat), 63 mg cholesterol, 839 mg sodium, 44 g carbohydrate, 7 g fiber, 30 g protein.

354 CALORIES

CHILI POTPIES

chili potpies

Welcome your family in from the cold with these individual potpies. Everyone will enjoy the simple corn bread crust that perfectly complements a filling of tangy chili from our Test Kitchen.

1	medium onion, chopped
1	medium green pepper, chopped
2	teaspoons canola oil
2	cans (14-1/2 ounces *each*) diced tomatoes, drained
1	can (16 ounces) chili beans, undrained
1/4	cup tomato sauce
2	tablespoons chili powder
1	teaspoon brown sugar
1/2	teaspoon ground cumin
1/2	cup all-purpose flour
1/2	cup cornmeal
1/2	teaspoon baking powder
1/4	teaspoon salt
1	tablespoon butter, melted
3	to 4 tablespoons fat-free milk

- In a large saucepan, saute onion and green pepper in oil until tender. Stir in the tomatoes, beans, tomato sauce, chili powder, brown sugar and cumin. Bring to a boil. Reduce heat to low; heat, uncovered, while preparing crust.

- In a small bowl, combine the flour, cornmeal, baking powder and salt. Stir in butter and enough milk to form a ball. On a lightly floured surface, roll dough into a 12-in. circle. Using an inverted 10-oz. baking dish as a guide, score four circles. Cut out circles. Cut a small circle in the center of each pastry (discard or reroll cutouts and use as decoration).

- Coat four 10-oz. baking dishes with cooking spray. Fill with chili; top each with a dough circle. Tuck in edges of dough to seal. Bake at 375° for 13-17 minutes or until edges of crust are lightly browned.

YIELD: 4 servings.

NUTRITION FACTS: 1 potpie equals 354 calories, 7 g fat (3 g saturated fat), 8 mg cholesterol, 930 mg sodium, 67 g carbohydrate, 14 g fiber, 13 g protein. **DIABETIC EXCHANGES:** 3 starch, 3 vegetable, 1 very lean meat, 1 fat.

spicy french dip

Ginny Koeppen | WINNFIELD, LOUISIANA

If I'm cooking for a party or family get-together, I can put this beef in the slow cooker in the morning and then concentrate on other preparations. It's a great time-saver and never fails to get rave reviews.

1	boneless beef sirloin tip roast (about 3 pounds), cut in half
1/2	cup water
1	can (4 ounces) diced jalapeno peppers, drained
1	envelope Italian salad dressing mix
12	crusty rolls (5 inches)

- Place beef in a 5-qt. slow cooker. In a small bowl, combine the water, jalapenos and dressing mix; pour over beef. Cover and cook on low for 8-10 hours or until meat is tender. Remove beef and shred using two forks. Skim fat from cooking juices. Serve beef on buns with juice.

YIELD: 12 servings.

NUTRITION FACTS: 1 sandwich with 3 tablespoons juice equals 357 calories, 9 g fat (4 g saturated fat), 68 mg cholesterol, 877 mg sodium, 37 g carbohydrate, 2 g fiber, 31 g protein. **DIABETIC EXCHANGES:** 3 lean meat, 2 starch.

SPICY FRENCH DIP

357 CALORIES

lunches | 351-450 CALORIES

366 CALORIES

TANGY CHICKEN SALAD

- Drain and discard marinade. Roll chicken in bread crumbs. Place on a baking sheet coated with cooking spray. Bake, uncovered, at 350° for 25-30 minutes or until juices run clear, turning once.

- On two plates, arrange salad greens, tomato, hard-cooked egg whites and cheese. Slice chicken; place on salads. Serve with dressing.

YIELD: 2 servings.

NUTRITION FACTS: 1 serving equals 366 calories, 8 g fat (4 g saturated fat), 92 mg cholesterol, 483 mg sodium, 30 g carbohydrate, 5 g fiber, 41 g protein.

tangy chicken salad

Michelle Tromblay | FAIRFIELD, OHIO

I came up with my own version of chicken salad after tasting a similar one at a restaurant. The simple marinade gives the chicken delicious flavor.

1/2	cup plain fat-free yogurt
1	tablespoon lemon juice
1/4	teaspoon minced garlic
1/8	teaspoon salt
1/8	teaspoon celery seed
1/8	teaspoon paprika
1/8	teaspoon Worcestershire sauce

Dash pepper

2	boneless skinless chicken breast halves (5 ounces *each*)
1/3	cup dry bread crumbs
4	cups torn mixed salad greens
1/2	cup chopped fresh tomato
1/2	cup chopped hard-cooked egg whites
1/3	cup shredded reduced-fat cheddar cheese
1/3	cup prepared fat-free honey Dijon salad dressing

- In a large resealable plastic bag, combine the first eight ingredients; add chicken. Seal bag and turn to coat; refrigerate for 8 hours or overnight.

370 CALORIES

shredded beef sandwiches

Bunny Palmertree | CARROLLTON, MISSISSIPPI

I like to serve these mouth-watering sandwiches with a side of coleslaw. The homemade barbeque sauce is exceptional...and it's wonderful for dipping!

1	can (10-1/2 ounces) condensed beef broth, undiluted
1	cup ketchup
1/2	cup packed brown sugar
1/2	cup lemon juice
3	tablespoons steak sauce
2	garlic cloves, minced
1	teaspoon pepper
1	teaspoon Worcestershire sauce
1	beef eye round roast (3-1/2 pounds), cut in half
1	teaspoon salt
16	sandwich buns, split

Dill pickle slices, optional

- In a small bowl, whisk the first eight ingredients. Pour half of mixture into a 5-qt. slow cooker. Sprinkle beef with salt; add beef to slow cooker and top with remaining broth mixture.

- Cover and cook on low for 10-12 hours or until meat is tender. Shred meat with two forks and return to slow cooker. Using a slotted spoon, place 1/2 cup beef mixture on each bun. Top with pickles if desired.

YIELD: 16 servings.

NUTRITION FACTS: 1 sandwich (calculated without pickles) equals 370 calories, 8 g fat (2 g saturated fat), 46 mg cholesterol, 963 mg sodium, 47 g carbohydrate, 1 g fiber, 28 g protein.

black bean burgers

Clara Honeyager | NORTH PRAIRIE, WISCONSIN

My son encouraged me to come up with a good veggie burger for him, and he gave this recipe a triple A+! Not only are they moist and tasty, but they're also very easy to freeze. Now, like my son, I prefer them over meat burgers.

- 1 cup frozen mixed vegetables, thawed
- 1 small onion, chopped
- 1/2 cup chopped sweet red pepper
- 1 can (15 ounces) black beans, rinsed and drained, *divided*
- 1 tablespoon cornstarch
- 2 tablespoons cold water
- 1 cup mashed potato flakes
- 1/4 cup quick-cooking oats
- 3 tablespoons whole wheat flour
- 2 tablespoons nonfat dry milk powder
- 1 egg, lightly beaten
- 1/2 teaspoon salt
- 1/4 teaspoon pepper
- 4 teaspoons canola oil
- 6 kaiser rolls, split
- 2 cups shredded lettuce
- 3/4 cup salsa

- In a large microwave-safe bowl, combine mixed vegetables, onion and red pepper. Cover and microwave on high for 2 minutes.

BLACK BEAN BURGERS

381 CALORIES

- Coarsely mash 3/4 cup black beans. In a bowl, combine the cornstarch and water until smooth; stir in the mashed beans, potato flakes, oats, flour, milk powder, egg, salt and pepper. Stir in vegetable mixture and remaining black beans. Shape into six 5/8-in.-thick patties.

- In a large nonstick skillet, cook the patties in oil for 4-5 minutes on each side or until lightly browned. Serve on rolls with lettuce and salsa.

YIELD: 6 servings.

EDITOR'S NOTE: This recipe was tested in a 1,100-watt microwave.

NUTRITION FACTS: 1 burger equals 381 calories, 7 g fat (1 g saturated fat), 36 mg cholesterol, 841 mg sodium, 64 g carbohydrate, 9 g fiber, 14 g protein.

384 CALORIES

TURKEY 'N' SWISS SANDWICHES

turkey 'n' swiss sandwiches

Leah Starnes | BEDFORD, TEXAS

Perfect for two, these toasted sandwiches turn boring lunches into exciting meals. They offer a wonderful combination of flavors.

- 4 slices sourdough bread, lightly toasted
- 2 teaspoons Dijon mustard
- 4 slices jellied cranberry sauce (1/4 inch thick)
- 6 ounces thinly sliced deli smoked turkey
- 2 slices reduced-fat Swiss cheese

- Spread two slices of bread with mustard. Top with the cranberry sauce, turkey and cheese. Broil 3-4 in. from the heat for 1-2 minutes or until cheese is melted. Top with remaining bread.

YIELD: 2 servings.

NUTRITION FACTS: 1 sandwich equals 384 calories, 8 g fat (2 g saturated fat), 43 mg cholesterol, 1,315 mg sodium, 54 g carbohydrate, 3 g fiber, 27 g protein.

shrimp pasta salad

Traci Wynne | FALLS CHURCH, VIRGINIA

This salad combines two of my favorite foods: pasta and shrimp. It can be a light main dish for lunch or a side for grilled steak, hamburgers and hot dogs. I've made this many times over the years.

- 4 cups uncooked small pasta shells
- 1 pound frozen cooked small shrimp
- 1-1/2 cups frozen peas, thawed
- 1/2 cup thinly sliced green onions
- 1/4 cup minced fresh parsley
- 1/3 cup reduced-fat mayonnaise
- 1/3 cup reduced-fat plain yogurt
- 2 tablespoons lemon juice
- 1 tablespoon minced fresh dill
- 1/4 teaspoon salt
- 1/4 teaspoon pepper

- Cook pasta according to package directions; drain and rinse in cold water. In a large bowl, combine the shrimp, peas, green onions and parsley. Stir in the pasta.

- In a small bowl, combine the remaining ingredients. Pour over pasta mixture and toss to coat. Cover and refrigerate for at least 1 hour.

YIELD: 6 servings.

NUTRITION FACTS: 1-1/2 cups equals 391 calories, 7 g fat (1 g saturated fat), 153 mg cholesterol, 430 mg sodium, 55 g carbohydrate, 4 g fiber, 27 g protein.

chicken and dumpling soup

Morgan Byers | BERKLEY, MICHIGAN

Like a security blanket for the soul, this chicken and dumpling soup is a true classic. My husband is not very fond of leftovers, but he likes this so much, he says he could eat it every day of the week.

- 3/4 pound boneless skinless chicken breasts, cut into 1-inch cubes
- 1/4 teaspoon salt
- 1/8 teaspoon pepper
- 2 teaspoons olive oil
- 1/4 cup all-purpose flour

- 4 cups reduced-sodium chicken broth, *divided*
- 1 cup water
- 2 cups frozen French-cut green beans
- 1-1/2 cups sliced onions
- 1 cup coarsely shredded carrots
- 1/4 teaspoon dried marjoram
- 2/3 cup reduced-fat biscuit/baking mix
- 1/3 cup cornmeal
- 1/4 cup shredded reduced-fat cheddar cheese
- 1/3 cup fat-free milk

- Sprinkle the chicken with salt and pepper. In a nonstick skillet, saute the chicken in oil until browned and juices run clear.

- In a large saucepan, combine flour and 1/2 cup broth until smooth. Stir in water and remaining broth. Add the beans, onions, carrots, marjoram and chicken. Bring to a boil. Reduce heat; simmer, uncovered, for 10 minutes.

- Meanwhile, in a small bowl, combine the biscuit mix, cornmeal and cheese. Stir in milk just until moistened. Drop batter in 12 mounds onto simmering soup. Cover and simmer for 15 minutes or until a toothpick inserted in a dumpling comes out clean (do not lift the cover while simmering).

YIELD: 4 servings.

NUTRITION FACTS: 1-1/4 cups soup with 3 dumplings equals 353 calories, 8 g fat (2 g saturated fat), 52 mg cholesterol, 1,111 mg sodium, 44 g carbohydrate, 5 g fiber, 28 g protein. **DIABETIC EXCHANGES:** 3 very lean meat, 2 starch, 2 vegetable, 1 fat.

CHICKEN AND DUMPLING SOUP

382 CALORIES

SESAME CHICKEN COUSCOUS SALAD

sesame chicken couscous salad

Tari Ambler | SHOREWOOD, ILLINOIS

I grow lots of the ingredients needed in this recipe. Fresh-tasting and crunchy, it's a perfect salad. Try leaving out the chicken and mixing the veggies with the couscous for a fun side dish.

1-1/2 cups reduced-sodium chicken broth
   3 teaspoons reduced-sodium soy sauce, *divided*
   2 teaspoons sesame oil, *divided*
   1 cup uncooked couscous
   2 green onions, sliced
1-1/2 cups fresh *or* frozen sugar snap peas
 3/4 cup fresh broccoli florets
1-1/2 cups cubed cooked chicken
   1 large sweet red pepper, chopped
 3/4 cup diced zucchini
   2 tablespoons cider vinegar
   1 tablespoon apple juice concentrate
   1 tablespoon water
   2 teaspoons canola oil
 1/2 teaspoon ground ginger
 1/4 teaspoon pepper
   2 tablespoons slivered almonds, toasted
   2 teaspoons sesame seeds, toasted

- In a saucepan, combine the broth, 1 teaspoon soy sauce and 1 teaspoon sesame oil; bring to a boil. Stir in the couscous. Cover and remove from the heat. Let stand for 5 minutes. Fluff with a fork. Stir in green onions. Cover and refrigerate until chilled.

- Place pea pods in a steamer basket in a saucepan over 1 in. of water; bring to a boil. Cover and steam for 1

minute. Add broccoli; cover and steam 2 minutes longer or until crisp-tender. Rinse in cold water; drain. Transfer to a serving bowl; add chicken, red pepper and zucchini.

- In a jar with a tight-fitting lid, combine the vinegar, apple juice concentrate, water, canola oil, ginger, pepper and remaining soy sauce and sesame oil. Shake well. Pour over chicken mixture and toss to coat. Cover and refrigerate for 30 minutes or until chilled. Serve over couscous. Sprinkle with almonds and sesame seeds.

YIELD: 4 servings.

NUTRITION FACTS: 1 cup chicken mixture with 3/4 cup couscous equals 382 calories, 9 g fat (1 g saturated fat), 45 mg cholesterol, 451 mg sodium, 45 g carbohydrate, 6 g fiber, 26 g protein. **DIABETIC EXCHANGES:** 3 lean meat, 2 starch, 2 vegetable.

363 CALORIES

chicken dumpling soup

Brenda White | MORRISON, ILLINOIS

My husband was fooled with this low-fat recipe, and I'm sure your family will be, too! A savory broth, hearty chunks of chicken and thick, chewy dumplings provide plenty of comforting flavor.

   1 pound boneless skinless chicken breasts, cut into 1-1/2-inch cubes
   3 cans (14-1/2 ounces *each*) reduced-sodium chicken broth
   3 cups water
   4 medium carrots, chopped
   1 medium onion, chopped
   1 celery rib, chopped
   1 teaspoon minced fresh parsley
 1/2 teaspoon salt
 1/4 teaspoon garlic powder
 1/4 teaspoon poultry seasoning
 1/4 teaspoon pepper
DUMPLINGS:
   3 egg whites
 1/2 cup 1% cottage cheese
   2 tablespoons water
 1/4 teaspoon salt
   1 cup all-purpose flour

- In a large nonstick skillet coated with cooking spray, brown chicken. Add the broth, water, vegetables and seasonings. Bring to a boil. Reduce the heat simmer, uncovered, for 30 minutes.

- Meanwhile, for dumplings, beat egg whites and cottage cheese in a mixing bowl. Add water and salt. Stir in the flour; mix well.

- Bring soup to a boil. Drop dumplings by tablespoonfuls onto the boiling soup. Reduce heat; cover and simmer for 15 minutes or until a toothpick inserted in dumplings comes out clean (do not lift cover while simmering). Serve immediately.

YIELD: 4 servings.

NUTRITION FACTS: 1-1/2 cups equals 363 calories, 4 g fat (2 g saturated fat), 73 mg cholesterol, 900 mg sodium, 39 g carbohydrate, 4 g fiber, 42 g protein. **DIABETIC EXCHANGES:** 4 lean meat, 2-1/2 starch.

family-pleasing sloppy joes

Jill Zosel | SEATTLE, WASHINGTON

My grandma gave me this recipe years ago, and I made a few adjustments to give the sandwiches more pizzazz.

1	pound lean ground turkey
1/2	cup chopped onion
2	garlic cloves, minced
1	tablespoon sugar
1	tablespoon all-purpose flour
1/4	teaspoon pepper
1	cup ketchup
1	tablespoon prepared mustard
1	tablespoon barbecue sauce
1	tablespoon Worcestershire sauce
6	sandwich buns, split

- In a large nonstick skillet, cook the turkey and onion over medium heat until turkey is no longer pink; drain if necessary. Add garlic; cook for 1-2 minutes or until tender.

- Stir in the sugar, flour and pepper. Add the ketchup, mustard, barbecue sauce and Worcestershire sauce. Bring to a boil. Reduce heat; cover and simmer for 5-10 minutes or until heated through. Serve on buns.

YIELD: 6 servings.

NUTRITION FACTS: 1 sandwich equals 388 calories, 11 g fat (4 g saturated fat), 60 mg cholesterol, 969 mg sodium, 52 g carbohydrate, 3 g fiber, 22 g protein. **DIABETIC EXCHANGES:** 3-1/2 starch, 2 lean meat.

chicken gyros

These yummy Greek specialties are a cinch to prepare at home. Just take tender chicken, coat it in a creamy cucumber-yogurt sauce, then tuck it into pita pockets. Our Test Kitchen staff suggests adding lettuce and diced tomato on top.

1/4	cup lemon juice
2	tablespoons olive oil
3/4	teaspoon minced garlic, *divided*
1/2	teaspoon ground mustard
1/2	teaspoon dried oregano
1/2	pound boneless skinless chicken breasts, cut into 1/2-inch strips
1/2	cup chopped peeled cucumber
1/3	cup plain yogurt
1/4	teaspoon dill weed
2	whole wheat gyro-style pitas (6 inches)
1/2	small red onion, thinly sliced

- In a large resealable plastic bag, combine lemon juice, oil, 1/2 teaspoon garlic, mustard and oregano; add chicken. Seal bag and turn to coat; refrigerate for at least 1 hour. In a small bowl, combine the cucumber, yogurt, dill and remaining garlic; cover and refrigerate until serving.

- Drain and discard marinade. In a large nonstick skillet, saute chicken for 7-8 minutes or until juices run clear. Spoon onto each pita bread. Top with yogurt mixture and onion; fold in half.

YIELD: 2 servings.

NUTRITION FACTS: 1 gyro equals 367 calories, 9 g fat (2 g saturated fat), 68 mg cholesterol, 397 mg sodium, 39 g carbohydrate, 2 g fiber, 30 g protein.

CHICKEN GYROS

grilled beef tenderloin sandwiches

Ruth Lee | TROY, ONTARIO

Sweet-sour onions and mushrooms are perfect over the tender beef and lip-smacking garlic mayonnaise in these sandwiches.

       1 tablespoon brown sugar
       2 garlic cloves, minced
     1/2 teaspoon coarsely ground pepper
     1/4 teaspoon salt
       1 beef tenderloin (1 pound)
       1 whole garlic bulb
     1/2 teaspoon canola oil
     1/4 cup *each* fat-free mayonnaise and plain yogurt

ONION TOPPING:

       1 tablespoon olive oil
       1 large sweet onion, thinly sliced
     1/2 pound sliced fresh mushrooms
       2 tablespoons balsamic vinegar
   1-1/2 teaspoons sugar
     1/8 teaspoon salt
     1/8 teaspoon pepper
       4 slices French bread (3/4 inch thick)
       1 cup fresh arugula

- Combine the first four ingredients; rub over meat. Refrigerate for 2 hours. Remove papery outer skin from garlic (do not peel or separate cloves). Cut top off of

GRILLED BEEF TENDERLOIN SANDWICHES

garlic. Brush with canola oil. Wrap bulb in heavy-duty foil. Bake at 425° for 30-35 minutes or until softened. Cool for 10-15 minutes. Squeeze garlic into food processor; add mayonnaise and yogurt. Process until smooth; chill.

- In a large nonstick skillet, heat the olive oil and saute onion for 5 minutes. Reduce the heat; cook and stir for 10-12 minutes or until onion is golden. Add the mushrooms; cook and stir until tender. Add next four ingredients; cook until reduced slightly.

- Coat grill rack with cooking spray before starting the grill. Grill beef, covered, over medium heat for 5-6 minutes on each side or until meat reaches desired doneness. Let stand for 10 minutes before cutting into 4 slices.

- Serve warm on bread with garlic mayonnaise, arugula and onion mixture.

YIELD: 4 servings.

NUTRITION FACTS: 1 sandwich equals 418 calories, 15 g fat (4 g saturated fat), 75 mg cholesterol, 702 mg sodium, 40 g carbohydrate, 3 g fiber, 31 g protein. **DIABETIC EXCHANGES:** 3 lean meat, 2 starch, 1 vegetable, 1 fat.

379 CALORIES italian grilled chicken salad

Lisa Rawski | MILWAUKEE, WISCONSIN

Simple yet elegant, this entree salad is one of my husband's favorites. We love the juicy chicken, fresh greens and bread that's toasted over an open flame. Add whatever beans your gang prefers.

       3 tablespoons balsamic vinegar
       3 tablespoons olive oil
       1 teaspoon dried rosemary, crushed
       1 garlic clove, minced
     1/2 teaspoon salt
     1/2 teaspoon coarsely ground pepper
       4 boneless skinless chicken breast halves
          (4 ounces *each*)
       4 ounces Italian bread, sliced
       4 cups torn romaine
       2 cups chopped seeded tomatoes
       1 cup white kidney *or* cannellini beans
     1/3 cup minced fresh basil

- In a jar with a tight-fitting lid, combine the first six ingredients; shake well. Remove 1 tablespoon vinegar

380 CALORIES

HEARTY BEEF VEGETABLE STEW

mixture; brush over chicken. Cover and refrigerate for 30 minutes. Set aside remaining vinegar mixture.

- Coat grill rack with cooking spray before starting grill. Grill chicken, covered, over medium heat for 4-6 minutes on each side or until juices run clear. Brush the bread slices with 1 tablespoon reserved vinegar mixture. Grill bread, uncovered, over medium heat for 2 minutes on each side or until toasted. Slice chicken and cut bread into cubes; set aside.

- In a large bowl, combine romaine, tomatoes, beans, basil and bread cubes. Drizzle with remaining vinegar mixture; toss to coat. Arrange on salad plates. Top with chicken.

YIELD: 4 servings.

NUTRITION FACTS: 1-1/2 cups dressed salad with chicken equals 379 calories, 13 g fat (2 g saturated fat), 66 mg cholesterol, 632 mg sodium, 31 g carbohydrate, 5 g fiber, 33 g protein. DIABETIC EXCHANGES: 3 lean meat, 1-1/2 starch, 1-1/2 fat, 1 vegetable.

hearty beef vegetable stew

Angela Nelson | RUTHER GLEN, VIRGINIA

I received this wonderful recipe from a co-worker. It's awesome! It is a hit with everyone, including our two young children. And it's nutritious, too.

- 1 can (28 ounces) crushed tomatoes, undrained
- 3 tablespoons quick-cooking tapioca
- 2 tablespoons dried basil
- 1 tablespoon sugar
- 1/2 teaspoon salt
- 1/8 teaspoon pepper
- 1-1/2 pounds red potatoes, cut into 1-inch cubes

- 3 medium carrots, cut into 1-inch slices
- 1 medium onion, chopped
- 1/2 cup chopped celery
- 1-1/2 pounds lean chuck roast, cut into 1-inch cubes
- 2 teaspoons canola oil

- In a bowl, combine the tomatoes, tapioca, basil, sugar, salt and pepper; let stand for 15 minutes. Place potatoes, carrots, onion and celery in a 5-qt. slow cooker.

- In a large nonstick skillet, brown the meat in oil over medium heat. Drain and transfer meat to slow cooker. Pour tomato mixture over the top. Cover and cook on high for 5-6 hours or until meat and vegetables are tender.

YIELD: 6 servings.

NUTRITION FACTS: 1-1/3 cups equals 380 calories, 8 g fat (3 g saturated fat), 78 mg cholesterol, 458 mg sodium, 46 g carbohydrate, 7 g fiber, 31 g protein. DIABETIC EXCHANGES: 3 lean meat, 2 starch, 2 vegetable.

402 CALORIES

tangy pulled pork sandwiches

Beki Kosydar-Krantz | CLARKS SUMMIT, PENNSYLVANIA

The slow cooker not only makes this an easy meal, but it keeps the pork tender, moist and loaded with flavor. The sandwiches are so comforting, they seem anything but light.

- 1 pork tenderloin (1 pound)
- 1 cup ketchup
- 2 tablespoons plus 1-1/2 teaspoons brown sugar
- 2 tablespoons plus 1-1/2 teaspoons cider vinegar
- 1 tablespoon plus 1-1/2 teaspoons Worcestershire sauce
- 1 tablespoon spicy brown mustard
- 1/4 teaspoon pepper
- 4 kaiser rolls, split

- Cut the tenderloin in half; place in a 3-qt. slow cooker. Combine the ketchup, brown sugar, vinegar, Worcestershire sauce, mustard and pepper; pour over pork.

- Cover and cook on low for 4-5 hours or until meat is tender. Remove meat; shred with two forks. Return to the slow cooker; heat through. Serve on rolls.

YIELD: 4 servings.

NUTRITION FACTS: 1 sandwich equals 402 calories, 7 g fat (2 g saturated fat), 63 mg cholesterol, 1,181 mg sodium, 56 g carbohydrate, 2 g fiber, 29 g protein. DIABETIC EXCHANGES: 3-1/2 starch, 3 very lean meat, 1/2 fat.

353 CALORIES

SANTA FE RICE SALAD

santa fe rice salad

Marilyn Sherwood | FREMONT, NEBRASKA

This warm rice and bean salad served with crunchy tortilla chips turns lunch into a fiesta! My whole family enjoys it. Occasionally I add other ingredients, depending on what I have on hand, but this combination is most popular at our house.

   1 medium green pepper, julienned
   1 medium sweet red pepper, julienned
   1 small onion, thinly sliced
   2 teaspoons canola oil
   2 cups cooked rice
   1 can (16 ounces) kidney beans, rinsed and drained
   1 can (11 ounces) Mexicorn, drained
   1 jar (8 ounces) picante sauce
   6 cups shredded lettuce
 3/4 cup shredded reduced-fat cheddar cheese
   6 tablespoons reduced-fat sour cream
Tortilla chips

- In a nonstick skillet, saute peppers and onion in oil for 6-7 minutes or until tender. Stir in the rice, beans, corn and picante sauce until heated through. Place 1 cup of lettuce on each of six salad plates. Top with 1 cup rice mixture, 2 tablespoons cheese and 1 tablespoon sour cream. Serve with tortilla chips.

YIELD: 6 servings.

NUTRITION FACTS: One serving (1 cup salad with 10 tortilla chips) equals 353 calories, 7 g fat (3 g saturated fat), 15 mg cholesterol, 800 mg sodium, 59 g carbohydrate, 9 g fiber, 15 g protein. **DIABETIC EXCHANGES:** 3 starch, 2 vegetable, 1 lean meat.

cheeseburger soup

Janne Rowe | WICHITA, KANSAS

I don't have a lot of extra time to spend in the kitchen. That's why I appreciate this robust soup. You can even cook the ground beef and rice ahead of time for extra-fast assembly.

   1 cup shredded carrot
   1 cup chopped onion
 1/2 cup chopped celery
   2 cans (14-1/2 ounces *each*) chicken broth
   1 pound ground beef, cooked, crumbled and drained
   2 cups cooked long grain rice
   3 cups milk
   1 pound process cheese (Velveeta), cubed
   1 cup (8 ounces) sour cream

- In a large saucepan, combine the carrot, onion, celery and broth. Bring to a boil. Reduce heat; simmer, uncovered, for 15 minutes or until vegetables are tender.

- Stir in the beef, rice, milk and cheese; simmer, uncovered, until the cheese is melted, stirring occasionally (do not boil). Just before serving, whisk in the sour cream; heat through.

YIELD: 10 servings (about 2-1/2 quarts).

NUTRITION FACTS: 1 serving (1 cup) equals 368 calories, 22 g fat (13 g saturated fat), 77 mg cholesterol, 790 mg sodium, 19 g carbohydrate, 1 g fiber, 22 g protein.

CHEESEBURGER SOUP

368 CALORIES

open-faced crab melts

353 CALORIES

Florence McClelland | FREDONIA, NEW YORK

Not only do these versatile sandwiches make a change-of-pace lunch, but you can serve them at everything from fancy teas to last-minute suppers.

- 4 **English muffins, split**
- 1 **can (6 ounces) crabmeat, drained, flaked and cartilage removed**
- 1/3 **cup mayonnaise**
- 1 **tablespoon lemon juice**
- 1/2 **teaspoon pepper**
- 1/4 **teaspoon dried tarragon**
- 1 **cup (4 ounces) shredded cheddar cheese**

- Broil English muffins 4-6 in. from heat for 2-3 minutes or until golden brown. In a large bowl, combine mayonnaise, lemon juice, pepper and tarragon; stir in the crab. Spread over each muffin half; sprinkle with cheddar cheese. Broil for 2-3 minutes or until cheese is melted.

YIELD: 4 servings.

NUTRITION FACTS: 1 serving (1 each) equals 411 calories, 24 g fat (8 g saturated fat), 75 mg cholesterol, 676 mg sodium, 28 g carbohydrate, 2 g fiber, 19 g protein.

cheesy floret soup

353 CALORIES

Janice Russell | KINGFISHER, OKLAHOMA

Talk about comfort food! I received this recipe from my mom, and my family requests it often. It's especially good with crusty French bread.

- 3 **cups fresh broccoli florets**
- 3 **cups fresh cauliflowerets**
- 3 **celery ribs, sliced**
- 1 **small onion, chopped**
- 2 **cups water**
- 1/2 **teaspoon celery salt**
- 3 **tablespoons butter**
- 3 **tablespoons all-purpose flour**
- 2-1/3 **cups milk**
- 1 **pound process cheese (Velveeta), cubed**

- In a large saucepan, combine the first six ingredients. Bring to a boil. Reduce heat; cover and simmer for 12-15 minutes or until vegetables are tender.

BERRY TURKEY SANDWICH

356 CALORIES

- Meanwhile, in a small saucepan, melt butter; stir in flour until smooth. Gradually stir in milk. Bring to a boil; cook and stir for 2 minutes or until thickened. Reduce heat; add cheese. Cook and stir until cheese is melted. Drain vegetables; add cheese sauce and heat through.

YIELD: 4-6 servings.

NUTRITION FACTS: 1 serving (1 cup) equals 401 calories, 28 g fat (17 g saturated fat), 77 mg cholesterol, 1,169 mg sodium, 19 g carbohydrate, 3 g fiber, 21 g protein.

berry turkey sandwich

Edward Meyer | ARNOLD, MISSOURI

Sliced fresh strawberries, Swiss cheese and a nutty cream cheese spread make this turkey sandwich different. Try it on whole wheat, oatmeal or sunflower seed bread. It's tasty and easy to put together.

- 4 **slices whole wheat bread**
- 2 **lettuce leaves**
- 2 **slices reduced-fat Swiss cheese**
- 1/4 **pound thinly sliced deli turkey breast**
- 4 **fresh strawberries, sliced**
- 2 **tablespoons reduced-fat spreadable cream cheese**
- 2 **teaspoons finely chopped pecans**

- On two slices of bread, layer the lettuce, cheese, turkey and strawberries. Combine cream cheese and pecans; spread over remaining bread. Place over strawberries.

YIELD: 2 servings.

NUTRITION FACTS: One sandwich equals 356 calories, 10 g fat (3 g saturated fat), 39 mg cholesterol, 932 mg sodium, 39 g carbohydrate, 5 g fiber, 28 g protein. **DIABETIC EXCHANGES:** 3 lean meat, 2-1/2 starch.

dinners

Whether you crave meat loaf, lasagna, pork roast or steak, it's all here and more! Watch the number of calories and the serving sizes, and you can still have a satisfying dinner every night. Save a few calories to add a side dish or dessert and shoot for 500 calories for an entire supper.

228   210   199

The first section in this chapter has lower-calorie entrees you might pair with side dishes, a green salad, bread, etc. The other main dish sections are higher-calorie one-dish meals that simply need a beverage for a complete supper.

BALSAMIC-SEASONED STEAK

balsamic-seasoned steak

A tasty marinade from our Test Kitchen makes this sirloin so tender. You'll love its simple preparation and scrumptious Swiss-cheese topping.

- 2 tablespoons balsamic vinegar
- 2 teaspoons steak sauce
- 1 boneless beef sirloin steak (1 pound)
- 1/4 teaspoon coarsely ground pepper
- 2 ounces reduced-fat Swiss cheese, cut into thin strips

- In a small bowl, combine vinegar and steak sauce; set aside. Rub steak with pepper. Place on a broiler pan. Broil 4 in. from the heat for 7 minutes.

- Turn; spoon half of the steak sauce mixture over steak. Broil 5-7 minutes longer or until meat reaches desired doneness (for medium-rare, a meat thermometer should read 145°; medium, 160°; well-done, 170°).

- Remove steak to a cutting board; cut across the grain into 1/4-in. slices. Place on a foil-lined baking sheet; drizzle with juices from cutting board and remaining steak sauce mixture. Top with cheese. Broil for 1 minute or until cheese is melted.

YIELD: 4 servings.

NUTRITION FACTS: 3 ounces cooked beef with 1/2 ounce of cheese equals 188 calories, 8 g fat (3 g saturated fat), 70 mg cholesterol, 116 mg sodium, 2 g carbohydrate, trace fiber, 26 g protein.

southwest turkey stew

Stephanie Wilson | HELIX, OREGON

I prefer main dishes that enable me to stay on my diet but still eat what the rest of the family does. This stew is a hit with my husband and our children.

- 1-1/2 pounds turkey tenderloins, cubed
- 2 teaspoons canola oil
- 1 can (15 ounces) turkey chili with beans, undrained
- 1 can (14-1/2 ounces) diced tomatoes
- 1 medium sweet red pepper, cut into 3/4-inch pieces
- 1 medium green pepper, cut into 3/4-inch pieces
- 3/4 cup chopped onion
- 3/4 cup salsa
- 3 garlic cloves, minced
- 1-1/2 teaspoons chili powder
- 1/2 teaspoon salt
- 1/2 teaspoon ground cumin
- 1 tablespoon minced fresh cilantro, optional

- In a nonstick skillet, brown turkey in oil; transfer to a 3-qt. slow cooker. Stir in the chili, tomatoes, peppers, onion, salsa, garlic, chili powder, salt and cumin. Cover and cook on low for 5-6 hours or until turkey juices run clear. Garnish with cilantro if desired.

YIELD: 6 servings.

NUTRITION FACTS: 1-1/4 cups equals 238 calories, 4 g fat (1 g saturated fat), 65 mg cholesterol, 837 mg sodium, 17 g carbohydrate, 5 g fiber, 33 g protein. **DIABETIC EXCHANGES:** 4 lean meat, 1 vegetable, 1/2 starch.

SOUTHWEST TURKEY STEW

CHICKEN MARSALA

chicken marsala

Nancy Granaman | BURLINGTON, IOWA

Chicken marsala is usually high in fat and calories. But in this version, the flavor really comes from deglazing the skillet with the broth and wine, so even though I eliminated extra oil, the taste is still fantastic.

- 6 boneless skinless chicken breast halves (4 ounces *each*)
- 1 cup fat-free Italian salad dressing
- 1 tablespoon all-purpose flour
- 1 teaspoon Italian seasoning
- 1/2 teaspoon garlic powder
- 1/4 teaspoon paprika
- 1/4 teaspoon pepper
- 2 tablespoons olive oil, *divided*
- 1 tablespoon butter
- 1/2 cup reduced-sodium chicken broth
- 1/2 cup marsala wine *or* 3 tablespoons unsweetened apple juice plus 5 tablespoons additional reduced-sodium chicken broth
- 1 pound sliced fresh mushrooms
- 1/2 cup minced fresh parsley

- Flatten the chicken to 1/2-in. thickness. Place in a large resealable plastic bag; add salad dressing. Seal bag and turn to coat; refrigerate for 8 hours or overnight.

- Drain and discard marinade. Combine the flour, Italian seasoning, garlic powder, paprika and pepper; sprinkle over both sides of chicken. In a large nonstick skillet coated with cooking spray, cook chicken in 1 tablespoon oil and butter for 2 minutes on each side or until browned. Transfer to a 13-in. x 9-in. baking dish coated with cooking spray.

- Gradually add broth and wine or apple juice mixture to skillet, stirring to loosen browned bits. Bring to a boil; cook and stir for 2 minutes. Strain sauce; set aside. In the same skillet, cook mushrooms in remaining oil for 2 minutes; drain. Stir sauce into mushrooms; heat through. Pour over chicken; sprinkle with parsley. Bake, uncovered, at 350° for 25-30 minutes or until chicken juices run clear.

YIELD: 6 servings.

NUTRITION FACTS: 1 chicken breast half with 1/3 cup mushroom mixture equals 247 calories, 9 g fat (3 g saturated fat), 68 mg cholesterol, 348 mg sodium, 9 g carbohydrate, 1 g fiber, 26 g protein. **DIABETIC EXCHANGES:** 3 very lean meat, 1-1/2 fat, 1/2 starch.

sweet 'n' tangy pot roast

Carol Mulligan | HONEOYE FALLS, NEW YORK

I fixed this delicious roast the first time I cooked for my husband-to-be more than 20 years ago.

- 1 boneless beef chuck roast (3 pounds)
- 1/2 teaspoon salt
- 1/2 teaspoon pepper
- 1 cup water
- 1 cup ketchup
- 1/4 cup red wine *or* beef broth
- 1 envelope brown gravy mix
- 2 teaspoons Dijon mustard
- 1 teaspoon Worcestershire sauce
- 1/8 teaspoon garlic powder
- 3 tablespoons cornstarch
- 1/4 cup cold water

- Cut meat in half and place in a 5-qt. slow cooker. Sprinkle with salt and pepper. In a bowl, combine the water, ketchup, wine or broth, gravy mix, mustard, Worcestershire sauce and garlic powder; pour over the meat. Cover and cook on low for 9-10 hours or until meat is tender.

- Combine cornstarch and cold water until smooth. Stir into slow cooker. Cover and cook on high for 30 minutes or until gravy is thickened. Remove the meat from the slow cooker. Slice and serve with gravy.

YIELD: 8 servings.

NUTRITION FACTS: 3 ounces cooked beef with 1/2 cup gravy equals 249 calories, 8 g fat (3 g saturated fat), 89 mg cholesterol, 748 mg sodium, 13 g carbohydrate, 1 g fiber, 30 g protein. **DIABETIC EXCHANGES:** 3 lean meat, 1 starch.

(214 CALORIES)

MEATLESS CHILI MAC

scalloped potatoes and ham

Ruth Ann Stelfox | RAYMOND, ALBERTA

A friend of mine served this scrumptious, comforting dish at her wedding. I liked it so much, I asked for the recipe. The potatoes and ham taste wonderful covered in a creamy cheese sauce. This recipe makes a lot, so it's perfect for feeding a crowd.

- 2 cans (10-3/4 ounces *each*) condensed cream of mushroom soup, undiluted
- 2 cans (10-3/4 ounces *each*) condensed cream of celery soup, undiluted
- 1 can (10-3/4 ounces) condensed cheddar cheese soup, undiluted
- 1 can (12 ounces) evaporated milk
- 10 pounds medium potatoes, peeled and thinly sliced
- 5 pounds fully cooked ham, cubed
- 4 cups (16 ounces) shredded cheddar cheese

- In two large bowls, combine soups and milk. Add the potatoes and ham; toss to coat. Divide among four greased 13-in. x 9-in. baking dishes.

- Cover and bake at 325° for 1-1/4 hours or until the potatoes are tender. Uncover; sprinkle with cheese. Bake 5-10 minutes longer or until cheese is melted.

YIELD: 4 casseroles (10 servings each).

NUTRITION FACTS: 1 cup equals 226 calories, 10 g fat (5 g saturated fat), 46 mg cholesterol, 970 mg sodium, 20 g carbohydrate, 1 g fiber, 15 g protein.

SCALLOPED POTATOES AND HAM

(226 CALORIES)

meatless chili mac

Cindy Ragan | NORTH HUNTINGDON, PENNSYLVANIA

I came across this recipe in a newspaper years ago and it's been a real hit at our house ever since. It's fast and flavorful and appeals to all ages.

- 1 large onion, chopped
- 1 medium green pepper, chopped
- 1 garlic clove, minced
- 1 tablespoon olive oil
- 2 cups water
- 1-1/2 cups uncooked elbow macaroni
- 1 can (15-1/2 ounces) mild chili beans, undrained
- 1 can (15-1/2 ounces) great northern beans, rinsed and drained
- 1 can (14-1/2 ounces) diced tomatoes, undrained
- 1 can (8 ounces) tomato sauce
- 4 teaspoons chili powder
- 1 teaspoon salt
- 1 teaspoon ground cumin
- 1/2 cup fat-free sour cream

- In a large saucepan or Dutch oven, saute the onion, green pepper and garlic in oil until tender. Stir in the water, macaroni, beans, tomatoes, tomato sauce, chili powder, salt and cumin. Bring to a boil. Reduce heat; cover and simmer for 15-20 minutes or until macaroni is tender. Top each serving with 1 tablespoon sour cream.

YIELD: 8 servings (2-1/2 quarts).

NUTRITION FACTS: 1-1/4 cups equals 214 calories, 3 g fat (1 g saturated fat), 3 mg cholesterol, 857 mg sodium, 37 g carbohydrate, 8 g fiber, 10 g protein. **DIABETIC EXCHANGES:** 2 starch, 1 very lean meat, 1 vegetable.

beefy vegetable soup

Jimmy Osmon | UPPER DARBY, PENNSYLVANIA

This chunky soup is loaded with tender beef stew meat, carrots, potatoes and green beans—and it sure is tasty! A little steak sauce and garlic powder season the broth perfectly.

1-1/2	pounds lean beef stew meat
1	tablespoon canola oil
2	cans (14-1/2 ounces *each*) reduced-sodium beef broth
1-1/2	cups water
2	tablespoons reduced-sodium soy sauce
3	medium potatoes, cubed (about 1 pound)
3	medium carrots, cubed
3	celery ribs, chopped
2	tablespoons Worcestershire sauce
2	tablespoons steak sauce
1	tablespoon garlic powder
1/2	teaspoon salt
1/4	teaspoon dried oregano
1/8	teaspoon ground nutmeg
1/8	teaspoon pepper
2	cups fresh corn *or* frozen corn
1-3/4	cups frozen cut green beans

- In a large kettle or Dutch oven, cook beef over medium heat in oil until no longer pink; drain. Add the broth, water and soy sauce. Bring to a boil. Reduce the heat; cover and simmer for 1 hour.

BEEFY VEGETABLE SOUP

227 CALORIES

- Add the potatoes, carrots, celery, Worcestershire sauce, steak sauce and seasonings. Bring to a boil. Reduce heat; cover and simmer for 30-40 minutes or until the vegetables are just tender.
- Add corn and beans. Bring to a boil. Reduce heat; cover and simmer for 5-10 minutes or until vegetables are tender.

YIELD: 9 servings (about 3-1/4 quarts).

NUTRITION FACTS: 1-1/2 cups equals 227 calories, 7 g fat (2 g saturated fat), 49 mg cholesterol, 584 mg sodium, 24 g carbohydrate, 4 g fiber, 19 g protein. **DIABETIC EXCHANGES:** 2 lean meat, 2 vegetable, 1 starch.

glazed pork medallions

Michele Flagel | SHELLSBURG, IOWA

After my husband was told to lower his cholesterol, he was sure he'd never taste good food again. He was so surprised by this entree.

1	pork tenderloin (1-1/4 pounds)
1/4	teaspoon salt
1/3	cup reduced-sugar orange marmalade
2	teaspoons cider vinegar
2	teaspoons Worcestershire sauce
1/2	teaspoon minced fresh gingerroot
1/8	teaspoon crushed red pepper flakes

- Cut pork into 1-in. slices and flatten to 1/4-in. thickness; sprinkle with salt. In a large nonstick skillet coated with cooking spray, cook pork in batches over medium-high heat until juices run clear. Reduce heat to low; return all meat to the pan. Combine the remaining ingredients; pour over pork and turn to coat. Heat through.

YIELD: 4 servings.

NUTRITION FACTS: 4 ounces cooked pork equals 200 calories, 5 g fat (2 g saturated fat), 79 mg cholesterol, 231 mg sodium, 9 g carbohydrate, trace fiber, 28 g protein. **DIABETIC EXCHANGES:** 4 very lean meat, 1/2 fruit, 1/2 fat.

grilled citrus steak

Joan Whyte-Elliott | FENELON FALLS, ONTARIO

We invite someone for dinner almost every weekend, and this recipe has never failed us. It can be prepared in just a few minutes.

243 CALORIES

GRILLED CITRUS STEAK

2/3 cup reduced-sugar orange marmalade

1/3 cup reduced-sodium soy sauce

1/3 cup lemon juice

1 tablespoon canola oil

2 pounds boneless beef top round steak (2 inches thick)

- In a large bowl, combine the orange marmalade, soy sauce, lemon juice and oil. Pour 1 cup marinade into a large resealable plastic bag. Score the surface of the steak with shallow diagonal cuts, making diamond shapes. Add the steak to the marinade. Seal bag and turn to coat; refrigerate for 6-8 hours, turning occasionally. Cover and refrigerate remaining marinade.

- Coat the grill rack with cooking spray before starting the grill for indirect heat. Drain and discard marinade from beef. Grill beef, covered, over direct medium-hot heat for 6-8 minutes or until browned, turning once. Place the beef over indirect heat and continue grilling for 25-30 minutes or until the beef reaches desired doneness (for medium-rare, a meat thermometer should read 145°; medium, 160°; well-done, 170°), basting occasionally with reserved marinade.

YIELD: 6 servings.

NUTRITION FACTS: 4 ounces cooked beef equals 243 calories, 7 g fat (2 g saturated fat), 96 mg cholesterol, 337 mg sodium, 6 g carbohydrate, 0.55 g fiber, 37 g protein. **DIABETIC EXCHANGES:** 4 lean meat, 1/2 fruit.

tasty italian chicken

Beth Ann Stein | RICHMOND, INDIANA

A friend delivered this meal to me and my husband after our first child was born. I've lightened it up, and it still tastes wonderful.

1/2 cup chopped onion

1-1/8 teaspoons paprika, *divided*

3 teaspoons olive oil, *divided*

1-1/4 cups water

1/4 cup tomato paste

1 bay leaf

1/2 teaspoon reduced-sodium chicken bouillon granules

1/2 teaspoon Italian seasoning

1/4 cup all-purpose flour

1-1/2 teaspoons grated Parmesan cheese

1/2 teaspoon salt

1/4 teaspoon garlic powder

1/4 teaspoon dried oregano

1-1/2 pounds chicken tenderloins

- In a small saucepan, saute onion and 1/8 teaspoon paprika in 1 teaspoon oil until tender. Stir in water, tomato paste, bay leaf, bouillon and Italian seasoning. Bring to a boil. Reduce heat; simmer, uncovered, for 10 minutes.

- Meanwhile, in a large resealable plastic bag, combine the flour, Parmesan cheese, salt, garlic powder, oregano and remaining paprika. Add chicken; seal bag and shake to coat.

- In a large nonstick skillet coated with cooking spray, cook half of the chicken in 1 teaspoon oil for 2-3 minutes on each side or until juices run clear. Remove and keep warm; repeat with remaining chicken and oil. Remove bay leaf from sauce. Serve over chicken.

YIELD: 6 servings.

NUTRITION FACTS: 4 ounces cooked chicken with 3 tablespoons sauce equals 163 calories, 3 g fat (trace saturated fat), 67 mg cholesterol, 287 mg sodium, 8 g carbohydrate, 1 g fiber, 27 g protein. **DIABETIC EXCHANGES:** 3 very lean meat, 1/2 starch, 1/2 fat.

TASTY ITALIAN CHICKEN

163 CALORIES

171
CALORIES

OVEN-FRIED FISH NUGGETS

oven-fried fish nuggets

LaDonna Reed | PONCA CITY, OKLAHOMA

I'm happy to share the recipe for these buttery-tasting fish bites, which don't taste light at all. My husband and I love fresh fried fish, but we're both trying to cut back on fats. I made up this recipe and it was a huge hit. He tells me that he likes it as much as deep-fried fish, and that's saying a lot!

  1/3 cup seasoned bread crumbs
  1/3 cup crushed cornflakes
    3 tablespoons grated Parmesan cheese
  1/2 teaspoon salt
  1/4 teaspoon pepper
1-1/2 pounds cod fillets, cut into 1-inch cubes
Butter-flavored cooking spray

• In a shallow bowl, combine the bread crumbs, cornflakes, Parmesan cheese, salt and pepper. Coat the fish with butter-flavored spray, then roll in crumb mixture.

• Place on a baking sheet coated with cooking spray. Bake at 375° for 15-20 minutes or until the fish flakes easily with a fork.

YIELD: 4 servings.

NUTRITION FACTS: 1 serving equals 171 calories, 2 g fat (1 g saturated fat), 66 mg cholesterol, 415 mg sodium, 7 g carbohydrate, trace fiber, 29 g protein. **DIABETIC EXCHANGES:** 5 very lean meat, 1/2 starch.

breaded orange roughy

Joann Frazier Hensley | MCGAHEYSVILLE, VIRGINIA

My family loves fish, so I serve it often. Seasoned pepper really adds to the flavor of these tender fillets.

  1 cup crushed cornflakes
  2 teaspoons seasoned pepper
1/4 teaspoon salt
  4 egg whites
1/4 cup water
  6 fresh *or* frozen orange roughy fillets (4 ounces *each*)
1/4 cup all-purpose flour

• In a shallow dish, combine cornflakes, seasoned pepper and salt. In another shallow dish, beat egg whites and water. In a third shallow bowl, add flour. Coat fish with flour; dip in egg white mixture, then roll in cornflake mixture.

• Place on a baking sheet coated with cooking spray. Bake at 425° for 9-11 minutes or until the fish flakes easily with a fork.

YIELD: 6 servings.

NUTRITION FACTS: 1 fillet equals 158 calories, 1 g fat (0.55 g saturated fat), 23 mg cholesterol, 400 mg sodium, 16 g carbohydrate, 0.55 g fiber, 20 g protein. **DIABETIC EXCHANGES:** 3 very lean meat, 1 starch.

BREADED ORANGE ROUGHY

158
CALORIES

CHILI SAUCE MEAT LOAF

chili sauce meat loaf

Averleen Ressie | RICE LAKE, WISCONSIN

This meat loaf with a zesty chili sauce is a sure way to please a family. My son-in-law is in his glory when I serve the tasty entree. There are never any leftovers.

1/3 cup plus 2 tablespoons chili sauce, *divided*
1 egg white
1 tablespoon Worcestershire sauce
3/4 cup quick-cooking oats
3/4 cup finely chopped onion
2 garlic cloves, minced
1 teaspoon dried thyme
1/2 teaspoon salt
1/2 teaspoon pepper
1-1/2 pounds lean ground beef

- In a large bowl, combine 1/3 cup chili sauce, egg white, Worcestershire sauce, oats, onion, garlic, thyme, salt and pepper. Crumble beef over mixture and mix well.

- Shape into a 9-in. x 4-in. loaf; place in an 11-in. x 7-in. baking dish coated with cooking spray.

- Bake, uncovered, at 350° for 50 minutes. Brush with the remaining chili sauce. Bake 5-10 minutes longer or until a meat thermometer reads 160°. Let stand for 10 minutes before slicing.

YIELD: 6 servings.

NUTRITION FACTS: 2 slices equals 244 calories, 10 g fat (4 g saturated fat), 69 mg cholesterol, 565 mg sodium, 14 g carbohydrate, 2 g fiber, 24 g protein. **DIABETIC EXCHANGES:** 3 lean meat, 1 starch.

slow-cooked pork and beans

Patricia Hager | NICHOLASVILLE, KENTUCKY

I like to get this dish started before leaving for work in the morning. When I get home, my supper's ready! It's a hearty slow cooker meal that is also good for a potluck. A generous helping of tender pork and beans is perfect alongside a slice of warm corn bread.

1 boneless whole pork loin roast (3 pounds)
1 medium onion, sliced
3 cans (15 ounces *each*) pork and beans
1-1/2 cups barbecue sauce
1/4 cup packed brown sugar
1 teaspoon garlic powder

- Cut roast in half; place in a 5-qt. slow cooker. Top with onion. Combine beans, barbecue sauce, brown sugar and garlic powder; pour over meat. Cover and cook on low for 6 hours or until meat is tender.

- Remove roast; shred with two forks. Return meat to slow cooker; heat through.

YIELD: 12 servings.

NUTRITION FACTS: 1 cup equals 217 calories, 6 g fat (2 g saturated fat), 56 mg cholesterol, 404 mg sodium, 16 g carbohydrate, 2 g fiber, 24 g protein.

SLOW-COOKED PORK AND BEANS

hearty spaghetti sauce

Kimberly Rockwell | CHARLOTTE, NORTH CAROLINA

This easy sauce requires just minutes of preparation and simmers until dinnertime.

1-1/2	pounds lean ground beef
1	large onion, chopped
1	large green pepper, chopped
1/2	pound sliced fresh mushrooms
3	cans (15 ounces *each*) crushed tomatoes
1	can (6 ounces) tomato paste
1/2	cup ketchup
1	tablespoon sugar
1	tablespoon chili powder
1	teaspoon salt
1	teaspoon garlic powder
1	teaspoon dried basil
1	teaspoon dried oregano
1	teaspoon Italian seasoning
1	teaspoon Worcestershire sauce
1/2	teaspoon pepper

• In a large saucepan coated with cooking spray, cook the beef, onion and green pepper over medium heat until meat is no longer pink; drain. Add mushrooms; cook and stir for 2 minutes. Stir in remaining ingredients. Bring to a boil. Reduce heat; cover and simmer for 1-1/2 hours.

YIELD: 12 servings.

NUTRITION FACTS: 2/3 cup of sauce equals 163 calories, 5 g fat (2 g saturated fat), 28 mg cholesterol, 516 mg sodium, 18 g carbohydrate, 4 g fiber, 14 g protein. **DIABETIC EXCHANGES:** 2 vegetable, 1 lean meat, 1/2 starch.

HEARTY SPAGHETTI SAUCE

163 CALORIES

222 CALORIES

MUSHROOM CHEESE CHICKEN

mushroom cheese chicken

Anna Free | BRADNER, OHIO

There's a tasty surprise tucked inside this chicken. The flavorful mushroom-mozzarella filling is perked up with chives and pimientos. A golden crumb topping adds a bit of crunch to the tender chicken bundles. They're sure to impress guests.

4	boneless skinless chicken breast halves (5 ounces *each*)
1/2	teaspoon salt

Dash pepper

2	tablespoons all-purpose flour
1/2	cup reduced-fat plain yogurt
1/2	cup shredded part-skim mozzarella cheese
1/2	cup canned mushroom stems and pieces
1	tablespoon diced pimientos
1	tablespoon minced fresh parsley
1	tablespoon minced chives

TOPPING:

1	tablespoon reduced-fat plain yogurt
1	tablespoon dry bread crumbs
1/8	teaspoon paprika

• Flatten chicken to 1/8-in. thickness; sprinkle with salt and pepper. In a small bowl, combine the flour and yogurt until smooth. Stir in the cheese, mushrooms, pimientos, parsley and chives. Spread down the center of each piece of chicken. Roll up and tuck in ends; secure with toothpicks. Place seam side down in an 11-in. x 7-in. baking dish coated with cooking spray.

- Brush yogurt over chicken. Combine bread crumbs and paprika; sprinkle over the top. Bake, uncovered, at 350° for 20-25 minutes or until chicken juices run clear. Discard toothpicks before serving.

YIELD: 4 servings.

NUTRITION FACTS: 1 stuffed chicken breast half equals 222 calories, 5 g fat (2 g saturated fat), 92 mg cholesterol, 544 mg sodium, 4 g carbohydrate, trace fiber, 39 g protein. **DIABETIC EXCHANGE:** 4 lean meat.

honey lemon schnitzel

Carole Fraser | NORTH YORK, ONTARIO

These pork cutlets, coated in a sweet sauce with honey, lemon juice and butter, make a wonderful schnitzel. They're certainly good enough for company but perfect for a quick weeknight meal, too.

- 2 tablespoons all-purpose flour
- 1/2 teaspoon salt
- 1/2 teaspoon pepper
- 4 pork sirloin cutlets (4 ounces *each*)
- 2 tablespoons butter
- 1/4 cup lemon juice
- 1/4 cup honey

- In a large resealable plastic bag, combine the flour, salt and pepper. Add pork, two pieces at a time, and shake to coat. In a large skillet, cook pork in butter over medium heat for 3-4 minutes on each side or until juices run clear. Remove and keep warm.

- Add lemon juice and honey to the skillet; cook and stir for 3 minutes or until thickened. Return pork to pan; cook 2-3 minutes longer or until heated through.

YIELD: 4 servings.

NUTRITION FACTS: 1 cutlet equals 174 calories, 8 g fat (4 g saturated fat), 33 mg cholesterol, 368 mg sodium, 22 g carbohydrate, trace fiber, 6 g protein.

peppery roast beef

Maureen Brand | SOMERS, IOWA

With its spicy coating and creamy horseradish sauce, this tender roast is sure to be the star of any meal, whether it's a sit-down dinner or serve-yourself potluck.

- 1 tablespoon olive oil
- 1 tablespoon seasoned pepper
- 2 garlic cloves, minced
- 1/2 teaspoon dried thyme
- 1/4 teaspoon salt
- 1 boneless beef eye round roast (4 to 5 pounds)

HORSERADISH SAUCE:
- 1 cup (8 ounces) sour cream
- 2 tablespoons lemon juice
- 2 tablespoons milk
- 2 tablespoons prepared horseradish
- 1 tablespoon Dijon mustard
- 1/4 teaspoon salt
- 1/8 teaspoon pepper

- In a small bowl, combine the oil, seasoned pepper, garlic, thyme and salt; rub over roast. Place fat side up on a rack in a shallow roasting pan.

- Bake, uncovered, at 325° for 2-1/2 to 3 hours or until meat reaches desired doneness (for medium-rare, a meat thermometer should read 145°; medium, 160°; well-done, 170°). Let stand for 10 minutes before slicing.

- In a small bowl, combine the sauce ingredients. Serve with roast.

YIELD: 12 servings.

NUTRITION FACTS: 4 ounces cooked beef with 2 tablespoons sauce equals 228 calories, 10 g fat (4 g saturated fat), 83 mg cholesterol, 211 mg sodium, 3 g carbohydrate, trace fiber, 30 g protein.

PEPPERY ROAST BEEF

199 CALORIES

SLOW-COOKED SIRLOIN

slow-cooked sirloin

Vicki Tormaschy | DICKINSON, NORTH DAKOTA

My family of five likes to eat beef, so this recipe is a favorite. I usually serve it with whole wheat bread to soak up the tasty gravy.

- 1 boneless beef sirloin steak (1-1/2 pounds)
- 1 medium onion, cut into 1-inch chunks
- 1 medium green pepper, cut into 1-inch chunks
- 1 can (14-1/2 ounces) reduced-sodium beef broth
- 1/4 cup Worcestershire sauce
- 1/4 teaspoon dill weed
- 1/4 teaspoon dried thyme
- 1/4 teaspoon pepper

Dash crushed red pepper flakes

- 2 tablespoons cornstarch
- 2 tablespoons water

- In a large nonstick skillet coated with cooking spray, brown beef on both sides. Place onion and green pepper in a 3-qt. slow cooker. Top with beef. Combine the broth, Worcestershire sauce, dill, thyme, pepper and pepper flakes; pour over beef. Cover and cook on high for 3-4 hours or until the meat reaches desired doneness and vegetables are crisp-tender.

- Remove beef and keep warm. Combine cornstarch and water until smooth; gradually stir into cooking juices. Cover and cook about 30 minutes longer or until slightly thickened. Return beef to the slow cooker; heat through.

YIELD: 6 servings.

NUTRITION FACTS: 1 serving equals 199 calories, 6 g fat (2 g saturated fat), 68 mg cholesterol, 305 mg sodium, 8 g carbohydrate, 1 g fiber, 26 g protein. **DIABETIC EXCHANGES:** 3 lean meat, 1 vegetable.

seafood soup

Valerie Bradley | BEAVERTON, OREGON

This tempting tomato-based soup is loaded with tender chunks of salmon, shrimp and chopped veggies.

- 1/2 cup chopped onion
- 1/2 cup chopped green pepper
- 3 tablespoons minced fresh parsley
- 1 tablespoon olive oil
- 1 cup chopped carrots
- 1 garlic clove, minced
- 1 can (15 ounces) tomato sauce
- 1 can (14-1/2 ounces) diced tomatoes
- 3/4 cup white wine *or* chicken broth
- 1 bay leaf
- 1/2 teaspoon dried oregano
- 1/4 teaspoon dried basil
- 1/4 teaspoon pepper
- 3/4 pound salmon fillets, skinned and cut into 3/4-inch cubes
- 1/2 pound uncooked medium shrimp, peeled and deveined

- In a large saucepan, saute the onion, green pepper and parsley in oil until tender. Add carrots and garlic; cook and stir for 3 minutes. Stir in tomato sauce, tomatoes, wine or broth and seasonings.

- Bring to a boil. Reduce heat; cover and simmer for 30 minutes. Stir in the salmon and shrimp. Cover and

SEAFOOD SOUP

212 CALORIES

cook 7-10 minutes longer or until fish flakes easily with a fork and shrimp turn pink. Discard bay leaf.

YIELD: 6 servings.

NUTRITION FACTS: 1 cup equals 212 calories, 9 g fat (2 g saturated fat), 87 mg cholesterol, 620 mg sodium, 13 g carbohydrate, 3 g fiber, 19 g protein. **DIABETIC EXCHANGES:** 3 lean meat, 2 vegetable.

229 CALORIES

TUSCAN PORK ROAST

tuscan pork roast

Diane Toomey | METHUEN, MASSACHUSETTS
Treated to a flavorful rub the night before, this herb-crusted roast doesn't need any prep work on the day of your get-together.

3	garlic cloves, minced
2	tablespoons olive oil
1	tablespoon fennel seed, crushed
1	tablespoon dried rosemary, crushed
1	teaspoon salt
1/4	teaspoon pepper
1	boneless pork loin roast (3 pounds)

- In a small bowl, combine the first six ingredients; rub over pork roast. Cover and refrigerate overnight.

- Place the roast on a rack in a shallow roasting pan. Bake, uncovered, at 350° for 1-1/2 hours or until a meat thermometer reads 160°, basting occasionally with pan juices. Let stand for 10 minutes before slicing.

YIELD: 10 servings.

NUTRITION FACTS: 4 ounces cooked pork equals 229 calories, 10 g fat (3 g saturated fat), 80 mg cholesterol, 282 mg sodium, 1 g carbohydrate, 1 g fiber, 31 g protein. **DIABETIC EXCHANGE:** 4 lean meat.

chicken with garlic-tomato sauce

Angela Schellenberg | STEINBACH, MANITOBA
My husband and I came up with this recipe, and we love the way it turned out.

4	boneless skinless chicken breast halves (4 ounces *each*)
1/4	teaspoon pepper
2	teaspoons olive oil, *divided*
2	plum tomatoes, seeded and chopped
2	garlic cloves, minced
2	medium carrots, halved and thinly sliced
1	cup Italian tomato sauce
3/4	cup reduced-sodium chicken broth
1/4	cup tomato paste
1	teaspoon dried rosemary, crushed

Hot cooked pasta

- Sprinkle both sides of chicken with pepper. In a large nonstick skillet over medium-high heat, brown chicken on each side in 1 teaspoon oil. Remove and keep warm.

- In same skillet, saute tomatoes and garlic in remaining oil for 1 minute. Add carrots; saute 2-3 minutes longer. Combine tomato sauce, broth, tomato paste and rosemary; stir into skillet. Bring to a boil.

- Return the chicken to the pan. Reduce heat; cover and simmer for 10-12 minutes or until chicken juices run clear and carrots are crisp-tender. Serve with pasta.

YIELD: 4 servings.

NUTRITION FACTS: 1 chicken breast half with 3/4 cup sauce (calculated without pasta) equals 197 calories, 5 g fat (1 g saturated fat), 63 mg cholesterol, 510 mg sodium, 10 g carbohydrate, 3 g fiber, 26 g protein. **DIABETIC EXCHANGES:** 3 lean meat, 2 vegetable.

CHICKEN WITH GARLIC-TOMATO SAUCE

197 CALORIES

gingered pepper steak

Tracy Youngman | POST FALLS, IDAHO

Seasoned with just the right amount of ginger, this colorful and classic stir-fry is a quick dinner at my house. I got the recipe from my best friend after she made it for me years ago. I loved it then…and still do!

    1/3 cup reduced-sodium soy sauce
      2 tablespoons cider vinegar
      1 tablespoon sugar
    3/4 teaspoon ground ginger
      1 tablespoon cornstarch
      1 beef flank steak (1 pound), cut into thin strips
      1 *each* large green and sweet red pepper, julienned
      1 teaspoon canola oil

Hot cooked rice, optional

- In a small bowl, combine the soy sauce, vinegar, sugar and ginger. In another small bowl, combine the cornstarch and half of the soy sauce mixture until smooth; cover and refrigerate. Pour remaining soy sauce mixture into a large resealable plastic bag; add flank steak. Seal bag and turn to coat; refrigerate for 1-2 hours.

- In a large nonstick skillet or wok coated with cooking spray, stir-fry peppers for 2-3 minutes or until crisp-tender; remove and keep warm.

- Drain and discard marinade. In the same pan, stir-fry beef in hot oil for 3-4 minutes or until no longer pink. Stir

GINGERED PEPPER STEAK

235 CALORIES

reserved soy sauce mixture and stir into skillet. Bring to a boil; cook and stir for 2 minutes or until thickened. Return peppers to the pan; heat through. Serve with rice if desired.

YIELD: 4 servings.

NUTRITION FACTS: 1 cup (calculated without rice) equals 235 calories, 10 g fat (4 g saturated fat), 54 mg cholesterol, 875 mg sodium, 12 g carbohydrate, 2 g fiber, 24 g protein. **DIABETIC EXCHANGES:** 3 lean meat, 1 vegetable, 1/2 starch, 1/2 fat.

wintertime beef soup

238 CALORIES

Carol Tupper | JOPLIN, MISSOURI

Kidney beans, ground beef, green pepper and chopped cabbage make this thick soup hearty and satisfying.

      1 pound lean ground beef
      4 celery ribs, coarsely chopped
      1 medium onion, coarsely chopped
      1 medium green pepper, coarsely chopped
      1 garlic clove, minced
      2 cups water
      2 cups reduced-sodium tomato juice
      1 can (14-1/2 ounces) diced tomatoes, undrained
      1 can (8 ounces) tomato sauce
      2 teaspoons reduced-sodium beef bouillon granules
      2 teaspoons chili powder
    1/2 teaspoon salt
      2 cans (16 ounces *each*) kidney beans, rinsed and drained
      2 cups coarsely chopped cabbage

- In a large saucepan or Dutch oven, cook the beef, celery, onion, green pepper and garlic over medium heat until meat is no longer pink; drain. Stir in the water, tomato juice, tomatoes, tomato sauce, bouillon, chili powder and salt. Bring to a boil. Reduce heat; cover and simmer for 30 minutes.

- Stir in kidney beans; return to a boil. Stir in cabbage. Reduce heat; cover and cook 12 minutes longer or until the cabbage is tender.

YIELD: 8 servings.

NUTRITION FACTS: 1-2/3 cups equals 238 calories, 4 g fat (2 g saturated fat), 28 mg cholesterol, 703 mg sodium, 30 g carbohydrate, 8 g fiber, 20 g protein. **DIABETIC EXCHANGES:** 2 lean meat, 2 vegetable, 1 starch.

203 CALORIES

SPINACH AND MUSHROOM SMOTHERED CHICKEN

spinach and mushroom smothered chicken

Katrina Wagner | GRAIN VALLEY, MISSOURI

Chicken breasts stay nice and moist with a mushroom and spinach topping tucked under a blanket of melted cheese. It's extra special to serve but is not tricky to make.

3	cups fresh baby spinach
1-3/4	cups sliced fresh mushrooms
3	green onions, sliced
2	tablespoons chopped pecans
1-1/2	teaspoons olive oil
4	boneless skinless chicken breast halves (4 ounces *each*)
1/2	teaspoon rotisserie chicken seasoning
2	slices reduced-fat provolone cheese, halved

- In a large skillet, saute the spinach, mushrooms, onions and pecans in oil until mushrooms are tender. Set aside and keep warm.

- Coat grill rack with cooking spray before starting the grill. Sprinkle the chicken with seasoning; grill, covered, over medium heat for 4-5 minutes on each side or until juices run clear.

- Top with cheese. Cover and grill 2-3 minutes longer or until cheese is melted. To serve, top each chicken breast with reserved spinach mixture.

YIELD: 4 servings.

NUTRITION FACTS: 1 chicken breast half equals 203 calories, 9 g fat (2 g saturated fat), 68 mg cholesterol, 210 mg sodium, 3 g carbohydrate, 2 g fiber, 27 g protein. **DIABETIC EXCHANGES:** 3 very lean meat, 1 vegetable, 1 fat.

tenderloin with herb sauce

Monica Shipley | TULARE, CALIFORNIA

Tender pork is treated to a rich and creamy sauce with a slight red-pepper kick.

2	pork tenderloins (1 pound *each*)
1/2	teaspoon salt
4	teaspoons butter
2/3	cup half-and-half cream
2	tablespoons minced fresh parsley
2	teaspoons herbes de Provence
2	teaspoons reduced-sodium soy sauce
1	teaspoon beef bouillon granules
1/2	to 3/4 teaspoon crushed red pepper flakes

- Cut each tenderloin into 12 slices; sprinkle with salt. In a large nonstick skillet coated with cooking spray, brown pork in butter in batches over medium heat for 3-4 minutes on each side. Return all pork to the skillet.

- Combine remaining ingredients; pour over pork. Cook and stir over low heat for 2-3 minutes or until sauce is thickened.

YIELD: 6 servings.

EDITOR'S NOTE: Look for herbes de Provence in the spice aisle of your grocery store. It is also available from Penzeys Spices. Call 1-800/741-7787 or visit www.penzeys.com.

NUTRITION FACTS: 4 ounces cooked pork with 2 tablespoons sauce equals 238 calories, 10 g fat (5 g saturated fat), 104 mg cholesterol, 495 mg sodium, 2 g carbohydrate, trace fiber, 31 g protein. **DIABETIC EXCHANGES:** 4 lean meat, 1 fat.

TENDERLOIN WITH HERB SAUCE

238 CALORIES

148 CALORIES

LIME CHICKEN TACOS

lime chicken tacos

Tracy Gunter | BOISE, IDAHO

Lime adds zest to this yummy filling for tortillas, and leftovers would be a refreshing topping to any taco salad as well. This fun recipe is great and simple for a casual dinner with friends or family.

1-1/2	pounds boneless skinless chicken breasts
3	tablespoons lime juice
1	tablespoon chili powder
1	cup frozen corn
1	cup chunky salsa
12	fat-free flour tortillas (6 inches), warmed

Sour cream, shredded cheddar cheese and shredded lettuce, optional

• Place the chicken in a 3-qt. slow cooker. Combine lime juice and chili powder; pour over chicken. Cover and cook on low for 5-6 hours or until chicken is tender.

• Remove the chicken; cool slightly. Shred and return to the slow cooker. Stir in corn and salsa. Cover and cook on low for 30 minutes or until heated through. Serve in tortillas with sour cream, cheese and lettuce if desired.

YIELD: 12 tacos.

NUTRITION FACTS: 1 taco (calculated without sour cream and cheese) equals 148 calories, 2 g fat (trace saturated fat), 31 mg cholesterol, 338 mg sodium, 18 g carbohydrate, 1 g fiber, 14 g protein. **DIABETIC EXCHANGES:** 2 very lean meat, 1 starch.

three-meat spaghetti sauce

Ellen Stringer | BOURBONNAIS, ILLINOIS

I simmer this hearty sauce in large batches, freeze it and use it for spaghetti, lasagna and pizza. I adapted the original recipe until I came up with the perfect sauce. I've received many compliments on it from friends and family. Sometimes I simmer it in a large electric roaster instead of on the stovetop.

1	pound ground beef
1	pound bulk Italian sausage
1	cup chopped onion
1	can (28 ounces) crushed tomatoes
3	cups water
2	cans (6 ounces *each*) tomato paste
2	jars (4-1/2 ounces *each*) sliced mushrooms, drained
1	cup chopped pepperoni
2	tablespoons grated Parmesan cheese
2	tablespoons Italian seasoning
1	tablespoon sugar
2	teaspoons garlic salt
1	teaspoon pepper
1	teaspoon dried parsley flakes

Hot cooked spaghetti

• In a soup kettle or Dutch oven, cook beef, sausage and onion over medium heat until meat is no longer pink; drain. Stir in tomatoes, water, tomato paste, mushrooms,

THREE-MEAT SPAGHETTI SAUCE

121 CALORIES

pepperoni, Parmesan cheese and seasonings. Bring to a boil. Reduce heat; cover and simmer for 30 minutes. Cool. Freeze in serving-size portions.

YIELD: 11-1/2 cups.

TO USE FROZEN SPAGHETTI SAUCE: Thaw in the refrigerator overnight. Place in a saucepan; heat through. Serve over spaghetti.

NUTRITION FACTS: 1/2 cup sauce equals 121 calories, 8 g fat (3 g saturated fat), 23 mg cholesterol, 467 mg sodium, 6 g carbohydrate, 1 g fiber, 8 g protein.

southwest summer pork chops

Sandy Shortt | CEDARVILLE, OHIO

We always try to be active and eat lighter foods like these tasty pork chops. They get their appeal from a simple combination of herbs and seasonings. We love the seasoning blend on pork, but you can also use it on chicken. It gives foods terrific taste without added salt.

- 4 teaspoons dried minced onion
- 2 teaspoons ground cumin
- 1 teaspoon cornstarch
- 1 teaspoon chili powder
- 1 teaspoon dried minced garlic
- 1/2 teaspoon dried oregano
- 1/2 teaspoon paprika
- 1/4 teaspoon cayenne pepper
- 6 bone-in pork loin chops (about 3/4 inch thick and 7 ounces *each*)
- 1/4 cup barbecue sauce
- 2 tablespoons lemon juice

- In a small bowl, combine first eight ingredients; rub over pork chops. In a large resealable plastic bag, combine barbecue sauce and lemon juice; add pork chops; Seal bag and turn to coat; refrigerate for 1-2 hours.

- Discard marinade. If grilling the pork chops, coat grill rack with cooking spray before starting the grill. Grill chops, covered, over medium heat or broil 6 in. from the heat for 6-8 minutes on each side or until a meat thermometer reads 160°.

YIELD: 6 servings.

NUTRITION FACTS: 1 pork chop equals 234 calories, 8 g fat (3 g saturated fat), 81 mg cholesterol, 202 mg sodium, 8 g carbohydrate, 1 g fiber, 30 g protein. **DIABETIC EXCHANGES:** 4 lean meat, 1/2 starch.

creamy swiss steak

Gloria Carpenter | BANCROFT, MICHIGAN

When I was working, I'd put this Swiss steak in the slow cooker before I left for the day. A creamy mushroom sauce made with canned soup nicely flavors the tender round steak. It's delicious and so easy to make.

- 3/4 cup all-purpose flour
- 1 teaspoon salt
- 1/2 teaspoon pepper
- 2 pounds boneless beef round steak, cut into serving-size portions
- 2 tablespoons butter
- 1/2 cup chopped onion
- 2 cans (10-3/4 ounces *each*) condensed cream of mushroom soup, undiluted
- 1 cup water

Hot cooked noodles

- In a shallow bowl, combine the flour, salt and pepper; dredge beef. In a large skillet, brown beef in butter on both sides. Transfer to a 3-qt. slow cooker; top with onion. Combine soup and water; pour over onion. Cover and cook on low for 8-9 hours or until meat is tender. Serve with noodles.

YIELD: 8 servings.

NUTRITION FACTS: 1 serving (calculated without noodles) equals 243 calories, 8 g fat (4 g saturated fat), 73 mg cholesterol, 624 mg sodium, 13 g carbohydrate, 1 g fiber, 28 g protein.

CREAMY SWISS STEAK

breaded flounder fillets

Michelle Smith | SYKESVILLE, MARYLAND

I use flounder in this recipe, but any fish fillets can be prepared with this tasty coating. It's quick and easy when time is tight.

- 1/4 **cup all-purpose flour**
- 1/4 **cup cornmeal**
-   1 **teaspoon salt**
- 1/2 **teaspoon paprika**
- 1/2 **teaspoon pepper**
-   2 **egg whites**
- 1/4 **cup fat-free milk**
-   4 **flounder fillets (6 ounces** *each***)**
-   1 **tablespoon grated Parmesan cheese**

- In a shallow bowl, combine flour, cornmeal, salt, paprika and pepper. In another shallow bowl, beat egg whites and milk. Coat fish with cornmeal mixture, then dip into egg white mixture. Coat fish again in cornmeal mixture.

- In a 15-in. x 10-in. x 1-in. baking pan coated with cooking spray, arrange fish in a single layer. Sprinkle with Parmesan cheese. Bake, uncovered, at 425° for 8-10 minutes or until fish flakes easily with a fork.

YIELD: 4 servings.

NUTRITION FACTS: 1 fillet equals 236 calories, 3 g fat (1 g saturated fat), 83 mg cholesterol, 789 mg sodium, 14 g carbohydrate, 1 g fiber, 37 g protein. **DIABETIC EXCHANGES:** 5 very lean meat, 1 starch.

BREADED FLOUNDER FILLETS

236 CALORIES

243 CALORIES

HONEY CHICKEN STIR-FRY

honey chicken stir-fry

Caroline Sperry | SHELBY TOWNSHIP, MICHIGAN

I'm a new mom, and my schedule is very dependent upon our young son. So I like meals that can be ready in as little time as possible. This all-in-one meal with a hint of sweetness from honey is a big time-saver.

-   1 **pound boneless skinless chicken breasts, cut into 1-inch pieces**
-   1 **garlic clove, minced**
-   3 **teaspoons olive oil,** *divided*
-   3 **tablespoons honey**
-   2 **tablespoons reduced-sodium soy sauce**
- 1/8 **teaspoon salt**
- 1/8 **teaspoon pepper**
-   1 **package (16 ounces) frozen broccoli stir-fry vegetable blend**
-   2 **teaspoons cornstarch**
-   1 **tablespoon cold water**

Hot cooked rice

- In a large nonstick skillet, stir-fry chicken and garlic in 2 teaspoons oil. Add honey, soy sauce, salt and pepper. Cook and stir until chicken is lightly browned and juices run clear. Remove and keep warm.

- In same pan, stir-fry vegetables in remaining oil for 4-5 minutes or until tender. Return chicken to the pan; stir to coat. Combine cornstarch and cold water until smooth; gradually stir into chicken mixture. Bring to a boil; cook and stir for 1 minute or until thickened. Serve with rice.

YIELD: 4 servings.

NUTRITION FACTS: 1 cup stir-fry mixture (calculated without rice) equals 243 calories, 5 g fat (1 g saturated fat), 66 mg cholesterol, 470 mg sodium, 19 g carbohydrate, 3 g fiber, 28 g protein. **DIABETIC EXCHANGES:** 3 lean meat, 3 vegetable.

mushroom pepper steak

Billie Moss | EL SOBRANTE, CALIFORNIA
A fast marinade flavors and tenderizes the sirloin steak in this colorful stir-fry. Garlic and ginger round out the flavor.

6 tablespoons reduced-sodium soy sauce, *divided*
1/8 teaspoon pepper
1 pound boneless beef sirloin steak, cut into thin strips
1 tablespoon cornstarch
1/2 cup reduced-sodium beef broth
1 garlic clove, minced
1/2 teaspoon minced fresh gingerroot
3 teaspoons canola oil, *divided*
1 cup julienned sweet red pepper
1 cup julienned green pepper
2 cups sliced fresh mushrooms
2 medium tomatoes, cut into wedges
6 green onions, cut into 1/2-inch pieces

Hot cooked rice, optional

241 CALORIES

MUSHROOM PEPPER STEAK

- In a large resealable plastic bag, combine 3 tablespoons soy sauce and pepper; add beef. Seal bag and turn to coat; refrigerate for 30-60 minutes. In a small bowl, combine the cornstarch, broth and remaining soy sauce until smooth; set aside.

- Drain and discard marinade from beef. In a large nonstick skillet or wok, stir-fry the garlic and ginger in 2 teaspoons oil for 1 minute. Add the beef; stir-fry for 4-6 minutes or until no longer pink. Remove beef and keep warm.

- Stir-fry the peppers in remaining oil for 1 minute. Add the mushrooms; stir-fry 2 minutes longer or until peppers are crisp-tender. Stir broth mixture and add to vegetable mixture. Bring to a boil; cook and stir for 2 minutes or until thickened. Return beef to pan; add tomatoes and onions. Cook for 2 minutes or until heated through. Serve over rice if desired.

YIELD: 4 servings.

NUTRITION FACTS: 1-1/4 cups beef mixture (calculated without rice) equals 241 calories, 10 g fat (3 g saturated fat), 64 mg cholesterol, 841 mg sodium, 13 g carbohydrate, 3 g fiber, 25 g protein. **DIABETIC EXCHANGES:** 3 lean meat, 2 vegetable, 1 fat.

Here are some typical dinner foods and the amount of calories so you have an idea of how best to stay within a 500-calorie meal.

- 1 ground sirloin beef patty (4 ounces), broiled, 175 calories
- 4 ounces pork tenderloin, roasted, 131 calories
- 1 prime beef tenderloin steak (4 ounces), broiled, 200 calories

- 1 boneless pork loin chop (4 ounces), broiled, 154 calories
- 1 salmon fillet (4 ounces), broiled, 184 calories
- 4 ounces large shell-on shrimp, peeled, deveined and cooked, 90 calories

- 1 boneless, skinless chicken breast half (4 ounces), broiled, 130 calories
- 4 ounces boneless, skinless turkey breast tenderloin, broiled, 112 calories

Weight given is before cooking.

For additional calorie calculations, check the Nutrition Facts labels on food packages.

212 CALORIES

CHICKEN WITH MUSHROOM SAUCE

chicken with mushroom sauce

Jennifer Pemberton | MUNCIE, INDIANA

It looks impressive, but this mouthwatering dish comes together in no time. I think it rivals that of many full-fat entrees found in fancy restaurants.

- 2 teaspoons cornstarch
- 1/2 cup fat-free milk
- 4 boneless skinless chicken breast halves (4 ounces *each*)
- 1 tablespoon olive oil
- 1/2 pound fresh mushrooms, sliced
- 1/2 medium onion, sliced and separated into rings
- 1 tablespoon reduced-fat butter
- 1/4 cup sherry *or* chicken broth
- 1/2 teaspoon salt
- 1/8 teaspoon pepper

• In a small bowl, combine cornstarch and milk until smooth; set aside. Flatten chicken to 1/4-in. thickness. In a large nonstick skillet, cook chicken in oil over medium heat for 5-6 minutes on each side or until juices run clear. Remove and keep warm.

• In the same skillet, saute the mushrooms and onion in butter until tender. Stir in the sherry or broth, salt and

pepper; bring to a boil. Stir cornstarch mixture and to the pan. Bring to a boil; cook and stir for 2 minutes or until thickened. Serve with chicken.

YIELD: 4 servings.

EDITOR'S NOTE: This recipe was tested with Land O'Lakes light stick butter.

NUTRITION FACTS: 1 chicken breast half with 1/3 cup sauce equals 212 calories, 8 g fat (2 g saturated fat), 68 mg cholesterol, 387 mg sodium, 7 g carbohydrate, 1 g fiber, 26 g protein. **DIABETIC EXCHANGES:** 3 very lean meat, 1 vegetable, 1 fat, 1/2 starch.

dijon-crusted fish

Scott Schmidtke | CHICAGO, ILLINOIS

Dijon mustard, Parmesan cheese and a hint of horseradish give this golden fish lots of zing. The preparation is so easy, it takes just 5 to 7 minutes to get four servings ready for the oven. I like tilapia since it has no fishy taste.

- 3 tablespoons reduced-fat mayonnaise
- 2 tablespoons grated Parmesan cheese, *divided*
- 1 tablespoon lemon juice
- 2 teaspoons Dijon mustard
- 1 teaspoon horseradish
- 4 tilapia fillets (5 ounces *each*)
- 1/4 cup dry bread crumbs
- 2 teaspoons butter, melted

DIJON-CRUSTED FISH

214 CALORIES

- In a small bowl, combine the mayonnaise, 1 tablespoon Parmesan cheese, lemon juice, mustard and horseradish. Place fillets on a baking sheet coated with cooking spray. Spread mayonnaise mixture evenly over fillets.

- In a small bowl, combine the bread crumbs, butter and remaining Parmesan cheese; sprinkle over fillets.

- Bake at 425° for 13-18 minutes or until the fish flakes easily with a fork.

YIELD: 4 servings.

NUTRITION FACTS: 1 fillet equals 214 calories, 8 g fat (3 g saturated fat), 80 mg cholesterol, 327 mg sodium, 7 g carbohydrate, trace fiber, 29 g protein. **DIABETIC EXCHANGES:** 4 very lean meat, 1-1/2 fat, 1/2 starch.

savory pork roast

219 CALORIES

Edith Fisher | LEYDEN, MASSACHUSETTS

Seasoned with a rub of sage, oregano, thyme and nutmeg, this incredible roast is perfect for family occasions. The impressive, satisfying entree has wonderful old-fashioned flavor.

2	teaspoons dried rosemary, crushed
2	teaspoons salt
1-1/2	teaspoons dried oregano
1-1/2	teaspoons dried thyme
1-1/2	teaspoons rubbed sage
1/4	teaspoon ground nutmeg
1/4	teaspoon pepper
1	bone-in pork loin roast (5 pounds)
1	cup sliced onions
1	cup sliced carrots

- In a small bowl, combine the first seven ingredients. With a sharp knife, cut 1/2-in.-deep slits in fat side of roast. Rub spice mixture into slits and over roast. Place roast fat side up in a shallow roasting pan. Place the onion and carrots around roast.

- Bake, uncovered, at 350° for 1-3/4 to 2-1/4 hours or until a meat thermometer reads 160°. Let stand for 10 minutes before carving.

YIELD: 12 servings.

NUTRITION FACTS: 4 ounces cooked pork equals 219 calories, 10 g fat (4 g saturated fat), 83 mg cholesterol, 459 mg sodium, 1 g carbohydrate, 1 g fiber, 29 g protein. **DIABETIC EXCHANGE:** 4 lean meat.

chicken rice dish

Rebecca Vandiver | BETHANY, OKLAHOMA

Fresh early-spring asparagus and a hint of lemon dress up this tasty chicken main dish. To round out the meal, I like to serve a green salad and toasted garlic bread.

2	cups water
2	cups cut fresh asparagus (1-inch diagonal pieces)
1	package (6 ounces) long grain and wild rice mix
1/4	cup reduced-fat butter, *divided*
3/4	pound boneless skinless chicken breasts, cut into 1-inch strips
1	teaspoon minced garlic
1/4	teaspoon salt
1	medium carrot, shredded
2	tablespoons lemon juice
1/2	teaspoon grated lemon peel, optional

- In a large saucepan, combine the water, asparagus, rice mix with contents of seasoning packet and 2 tablespoons butter. Bring to a boil; reduce heat. Cover and simmer for 10-15 minutes or until the water is absorbed.

- Meanwhile, in a large skillet, saute the chicken, garlic and salt in remaining butter until the chicken juices run clear. Add the carrot, lemon juice and lemon peel if desired; cook and stir for 1-2 minutes or until heated through. Stir into rice mixture.

YIELD: 4 servings.

NUTRITION FACTS: 1-1/4 cups equals 247 calories, 7 g fat (4 g saturated fat), 54 mg cholesterol, 668 mg sodium, 29 g carbohydrate, 2 g fiber, 20 g protein. **DIABETIC EXCHANGES:** 2 lean meat, 1-1/2 starch, 1 vegetable.

CHICKEN RICE DISH

247 CALORIES

new england seafood chowder

Kristine Lowel | SOUTHBOROUGH, MASSACHUSETTS

We find many ways to prepare the abundance of fresh seafood available in our area, and this "fish chowdy" is a hearty favorite. Featuring a flavorful combination of haddock, shrimp and scallops, the chowder is great to serve to a group.

4	pounds haddock fillets, cut into 3/4-inch pieces
1/4	pound uncooked medium shrimp, peeled and deveined
1/4	pound bay scallops
4	bacon strips, diced
3	medium onions, quartered and thinly sliced
2	tablespoons all-purpose flour
2	cups diced peeled potatoes
4	cups milk
2	tablespoons butter
1	tablespoon minced fresh parsley
2	teaspoons salt
1/2	teaspoon lemon-pepper seasoning
1/4	teaspoon pepper

- Place the haddock in a Dutch oven; cover with water. Bring to a boil over medium heat. Reduce heat; simmer, uncovered, for 20 minutes. Add the shrimp and scallops; simmer 10 minutes longer. Drain, reserving 2 cups cooking liquid; set liquid and seafood aside.

- In a soup kettle, cook bacon over medium heat until crisp; drain on paper towels. In the drippings, saute onions

NEW ENGLAND SEAFOOD CHOWDER

237 CALORIES

CHICKEN STUFFING BAKE

247 CALORIES

until tender. Stir in flour until blended. Gradually stir in reserved cooking liquid. Bring to a boil; cook and stir for 2 minutes or until thickened. Reduce heat. Add the potatoes; cover and cook for 15-20 minutes or until potatoes are tender.

- Add milk, seafood, butter, parsley, salt, lemon-pepper and pepper; heat through. Sprinkle with bacon.

YIELD: 15 servings (3-3/4 quarts).

NUTRITION FACTS: 1 cup equals 237 calories, 8 g fat (4 g saturated fat), 101 mg cholesterol, 531 mg sodium, 10 g carbohydrate, 1 g fiber, 29 g protein.

chicken stuffing bake

Jena Coffey | SUNSET HILLS, MISSOURI

I love to cook but just don't have much time. This casserole is both good and fast, which makes it my most often prepared recipe. I serve it with a green salad.

1	can (10-3/4 ounces) condensed reduced-fat reduced-sodium cream of mushroom soup, undiluted
1	cup fat-free milk
1	package (6 ounces) stuffing mix
2	cups cubed cooked chicken breast
2	cups fresh broccoli florets, cooked
2	celery ribs, finely chopped
1-1/2	cups (6 ounces) shredded reduced-fat Swiss cheese, *divided*

- In a large bowl, combine soup and milk until blended. Add stuffing mix with contents of seasoning packet, chicken, broccoli, celery and 1 cup cheese. Transfer to a greased 13-in. x 9-in. baking dish.

- Bake, uncovered, at 375° for 20 minutes or until heated through. Sprinkle with the remaining cheese; bake 5 minutes longer or until cheese is melted.

YIELD: 8 servings.

NUTRITION FACTS: 1 cup equals 247 calories, 7 g fat (4 g saturated fat), 42 mg cholesterol, 658 mg sodium, 24 g carbohydrate, 3 g fiber, 22 g protein. **DIABETIC EXCHANGES:** 2 lean meat, 1-1/2 starch.

vegetable beef ragout

Add your favorite vegetables to this tasty convenience item for a quick and delicious meal. Our home economists suggest looking for beef tips and gravy in the meat department.

- 1 **cup sliced fresh mushrooms**
- 1/2 **cup chopped onion**
- 1 **tablespoon canola oil**
- 1 **package (17 ounces) refrigerated beef tips with gravy**
- 1 **package (14 ounces) frozen sugar snap peas, thawed**
- 1 **cup cherry tomatoes, halved**

Hot cooked pasta, optional

- In a large skillet, saute the mushrooms and onion in oil until tender. Add beef tips with gravy, peas and tomatoes; heat through. Serve over pasta if desired.

YIELD: 4 servings.

NUTRITION FACTS: 1 cup beef mixture (calculated without noodles) equals 246 calories, 10 g fat (3 g saturated fat), 47 mg cholesterol, 670 mg sodium, 15 g carbohydrate, 4 g fiber, 21 g protein.

VEGETABLE BEEF RAGOUT

ROSEMARY TURKEY BREAST

rosemary turkey breast

Dorothy Pritchett | WILLS POINT, TEXAS

I perk up turkey with a blend of rosemary, garlic and paprika. Because I rub the mixture directly on the meat under the skin, I can remove the skin before serving and not lose any spices.

- 8 **to 10 garlic cloves**
- 3 **tablespoons chopped fresh rosemary *or* 3 teaspoons dried rosemary, crushed**
- 2 **tablespoons olive oil**
- 1 **teaspoon salt**
- 1 **teaspoon paprika**
- 1/2 **teaspoon coarsely ground pepper**
- 1 **bone-in turkey breast (4 pounds)**

- In a food processor, combine the garlic, rosemary, oil, salt, paprika and pepper; cover and process until garlic is coarsely chopped.

- With your fingers, carefully loosen the skin from both sides of turkey breast. Spread half of the garlic mixture over the meat under the skin. Smooth skin over meat and secure to underside of breast with toothpicks. Spread remaining garlic mixture over turkey skin.

- Place turkey breast on a rack in a shallow roasting pan. Bake, uncovered, at 325° for 1-1/2 to 2 hours or until a meat thermometer reads 170°. Let stand for 10-15 minutes. Discard toothpicks before carving.

YIELD: 11 servings.

NUTRITION FACTS: 4 ounces cooked turkey (calculated without skin) equals 166 calories, 3 g fat (1 g saturated fat), 85 mg cholesterol, 269 mg sodium, 1 g carbohydrate, trace fiber, 31 g protein. **DIABETIC EXCHANGE:** 4 very lean meat.

239 CALORIES

CHICKEN WITH ROASTED RED PEPPER SAUCE

chicken with roasted red pepper sauce

Kelly Cobb | MASON, OHIO

I created this recipe as a way to introduce different vegetables to my family. My son said it was the best chicken he'd ever tasted.

- 3 medium sweet red peppers, cut in half lengthwise and seeded
- 1 large whole garlic bulb
- 1 teaspoon plus 1 tablespoon olive oil, *divided*
- 4 boneless skinless chicken breast halves (4 ounces *each*)
- 1/2 teaspoon salt, *divided*
- 1/4 teaspoon pepper, *divided*
- 1/2 cup sliced leek (white portion only)
- 1/2 cup reduced-sodium chicken broth

Hot cooked pasta, optional

- 1/4 cup shredded Parmesan cheese

- Broil peppers 4 in. from heat until skins blister, about 15 minutes. Immediately place peppers in a bowl; cover and let stand for 15-20 minutes. Peel off and discard the charred skin. Coarsely chop the peppers; transfer to a food processor.

- Remove papery outer skin from the garlic (do not peel or separate cloves); cut top off of garlic bulb. Brush with 1 teaspoon oil. Wrap bulb in heavy-duty foil. Bake at 425° for 30-35 minutes or until softened. Cool for 10-15 minutes. Squeeze softened garlic into the food processor with peppers; cover and process until almost smooth. Set aside.

- Sprinkle both sides of chicken with 1/4 teaspoon salt and 1/8 teaspoon pepper. In a large nonstick skillet, cook the chicken in remaining oil over medium heat for 3-4 minutes on each side or until lightly browned. Remove and keep warm.

- In the same skillet, cook leek for 2 minutes or until leek is lightly browned. Add broth, stirring to loosen any browned bits from pan. Add the red pepper mixture, chicken and remaining salt and pepper. Bring to a boil. Reduce heat; cover and simmer for 3 minutes until chicken juices run clear. Uncover; pepper sauce over pasta if desired. Sprinkle with Parmesan cheese.

YIELD: 4 servings.

NUTRITION FACTS: 1 chicken breast half with 1/3 cup sauce and 1 tablespoon Parmesan cheese (calculated without pasta) equals 239 calories, 8 g fat (2 g saturated fat), 69 mg cholesterol, 537 mg sodium, 12 g carbohydrate, 3 g fiber, 30 g protein. **DIABETIC EXCHANGES:** 3 lean meat, 2 vegetable.

229 CALORIES

chunky chicken soup

Nancy Clow | MALLORYTOWN, ONTARIO

I am a stay-at-home mom who relies on my slow cooker for fast, nutritious meals with minimal cleanup and prep time. I knew this recipe was a hit when I didn't have any leftovers, and my husband asked me to make it again.

- 1-1/2 pounds boneless skinless chicken breasts, cut into 2-inch strips
- 2 teaspoons canola oil
- 2/3 cup finely chopped onion
- 2 medium carrots, chopped
- 2 celery ribs, chopped
- 1 cup frozen corn
- 2 cans (10-3/4 ounces *each*) condensed cream of potato soup, undiluted
- 1-1/2 cups chicken broth
- 1 teaspoon dill weed
- 1 cup frozen peas
- 1/2 cup half-and-half cream

- In a large skillet over medium-high heat, brown chicken in oil. With a slotted spoon, transfer to a 5-qt. slow cooker. Add the onion, carrots, celery and corn. In a small bowl, whisk the soup, broth and dill until blended; stir into slow cooker.

- Cover and cook on low for 4 hours or until vegetables are tender. Stir in peas and cream. Cover and cook 30 minutes longer or until heated through.

YIELD: 7 servings.

NUTRITION FACTS: 1 cup equals 229 calories, 7 g fat (3 g saturated fat), 66 mg cholesterol, 629 mg sodium, 17 g carbohydrate, 3 g fiber, 24 g protein.

potato ham skillet

Sharon Crider | LEBANON, MISSOURI

I use up leftover ham to create this stovetop supper. The delicious combination is great to serve anytime.

4-1/2 teaspoons butter
   3 medium potatoes, peeled and thinly sliced
 1/2 teaspoon salt
 1/4 teaspoon pepper
   7 green onions, chopped
 1/2 cup chopped green pepper
   2 cups diced fully cooked ham
 3/4 cup egg substitute
 1/2 cup shredded reduced-fat cheddar cheese
Minced fresh parsley

- In a 10-in. skillet, melt butter over medium heat. In skillet, layer half of potatoes, salt, pepper, onions, green pepper and ham; repeat layers. Cover; cook over medium heat for 10-15 minutes or until potatoes are tender.

- Pour egg substitute over the top. Cover and cook for 3-5 minutes or until eggs are nearly set. Sprinkle with cheese. Cover and cook 3-5 minutes or until eggs are nearly set. Sprinkle with cheese. Cover and cook 3-5 minutes longer or until cheese is melted and eggs are completely set. Cut into wedges. Sprinkle with parsley.

YIELD: 6 servings.

NUTRITION FACTS: 1 serving equals 189 calories, 7 g fat (4 g saturated fat), 28 mg cholesterol, 821 mg sodium, 16 g carbohydrate, 2 g fiber, 18 g protein. **DIABETIC EXCHANGES:** 2 lean meat, 1 starch.

POTATO HAM SKILLET

189 CALORIES

214 CALORIES

SIRLOIN WITH MUSHROOM SAUCE

sirloin with mushroom sauce

This steak is special enough to make for company, and you can have it ready in no time! We know you'll enjoy the mouthwatering combination of rich, brown mushroom sauce and tender strips of peppery steak in this recipe from our Test Kitchen.

   1 boneless beef sirloin steak (1 pound and 3/4 inch thick)
   1 teaspoon coarse ground pepper
   2 teaspoons canola oil
1-1/2 cups sliced fresh mushrooms
 1/2 cup beef broth
 1/2 cup dry red wine *or* additional beef broth

- Rub steak with pepper. In a heavy ovenproof skillet over medium-high heat, brown steak in oil for about 4 minutes on each side.

- Bake, uncovered, at 450° for 4 minutes or until meat reaches desired doneness (for medium-rare, a meat thermometer should read 145°; medium, 160°; well-done, 170°). Transfer steak to a warm serving platter. Let steak stand for 10 minutes.

- In same skillet, cook mushrooms over medium heat until golden brown. Add broth and wine or additional broth. bring to a boil; cook until liquid is reduced by about half. Thinly slice the steak; top with mushroom sauce.

YIELD: 4 servings.

NUTRITION FACTS: 3 ounces cooked beef with 1/4 cup mushroom sauce equals 214 calories, 9 g fat (3 g saturated fat), 77 mg cholesterol, 161 mg sodium, 1 g carbohydrate, trace fiber, 27 g protein. **DIABETIC EXCHANGES:** 3 lean meat, 1/2 fat.

lemon thyme chicken

Kay Shimonek | CORSICANA, TEXAS

Buttered onions are a great addition to the lemon sauce in this easy supper. Best of all, it takes only a few minutes to brown the lightly breaded chicken in a skillet.

- 3 tablespoons all-purpose flour
- 1/2 teaspoon salt
- 1/4 teaspoon pepper
- 4 boneless skinless chicken breast halves (4 ounces *each*)
- 2 teaspoons olive oil
- 1 medium onion, chopped
- 1 tablespoon butter
- 1/2 teaspoon dried thyme
- 1 cup chicken broth
- 3 tablespoons lemon juice
- 2 tablespoons minced fresh parsley

- In a small bowl, combine the flour, salt and pepper. Set aside 4-1/2 teaspoons for sauce. Sprinkle remaining flour mixture over both sides of chicken. In a large nonstick skillet coated with cooking spray, cook chicken in oil over medium heat for 7-9 minutes on each side or until juices run clear. Remove and keep warm.

- In the same pan, saute onion in butter until tender. Add thyme and reserved flour mixture; stir until blended. Gradually stir in the broth and lemon juice, scraping up any browned bits from bottom of pan. Bring to a boil;

LEMON THYME CHICKEN

213 CALORIES

cook and stir for 2 minutes or until thickened. Serve over chicken. Sprinkle with parsley.

YIELD: 4 servings.

NUTRITION FACTS: 1 chicken breast half with 3 tablespoons sauce equals 213 calories, 8 g fat (3 g saturated fat), 70 mg cholesterol, 614 mg sodium, 10 g carbohydrate, 1 g fiber, 25 g protein. **DIABETIC EXCHANGES:** 3 very lean meat, 1 fat, 1/2 starch.

242 CALORIES

BEEF TENDERLOIN WITH BALSAMIC SAUCE

beef tenderloin with balsamic sauce

This beef tenderloin is quick to prepare—but our home economists think it's special enough to serve to guests.

- 2 tablespoons minced fresh rosemary *or* 2 teaspoons dried rosemary, crushed
- 2 tablespoons minced garlic
- 1-1/2 teaspoons salt
- 1 teaspoon coarsely ground pepper
- 1 beef tenderloin, trimmed (about 2 pounds)

SAUCE:
- 2 cups port wine *or* 1 cup grape juice and 1 cup reduced-sodium beef broth
- 2 tablespoons balsamic vinegar
- 1 teaspoon butter
- 1/4 teaspoon salt
- 1/8 teaspoon pepper

- Combine the rosemary, garlic, salt and pepper; rub evenly over tenderloin. Cover and refrigerate for 2 hours. Place the meat on a rack in shallow roasting pan. Bake, uncovered, at 400° for 50-70 minutes or until the meat reaches desired doneness (for medium-rare, a meat thermometer should read 145°; medium, 160°; well-done, 170°). Let stand for 10 minutes before slicing.

- In a saucepan, bring wine or grape juice and broth to a boil; cook until reduced to 3/4 cup. Add vinegar; cook for 3-4 minutes or until reduced to a sauce consistency. Stir in butter, salt and pepper. Serve with tenderloin.

YIELD: 8 servings.

NUTRITION FACTS: 3 ounces cooked beef with 3-1/2 teaspoons sauce equals 242 calories, 9 g fat (3 g saturated fat), 72 mg cholesterol, 576 mg sodium, 6 g carbohydrate, 0 fiber, 24 g protein. **DIABETIC EXCHANGES:** 3 lean meat, 1 fat.

peppered chicken breasts

194 CALORIES

Jill Morzillo | LOUISVILLE, KENTUCKY

Black pepper is prominent in this succulent poultry entree, yet it doesn't overpower the creamy mustard sauce.

- 4 **boneless skinless chicken breast halves (4 ounces _each_)**
- 2 **teaspoons olive oil**
- 2 **teaspoons pepper**
- 1/4 **teaspoon salt**

MUSTARD SAUCE:

- 2 **teaspoons cornstarch**
- 1/3 **cup reduced-fat sour cream**
- 1 **cup chicken broth**
- 1/4 **cup white grape juice**
- 1/4 **cup chopped green onions**
- 2 **teaspoons Dijon mustard**

Snipped chives

- Rub chicken with oil; sprinkle with pepper and salt. Place in a greased 11-in. x 7-in. baking dish. Bake, uncovered, at 425° for 15-20 minutes or until juices run clear.

- Meanwhile, in a small bowl, combine cornstarch and sour cream until smooth; set aside.

- In a small saucepan, combine the broth, grape juice and onions. Bring to a boil; cook for 4-5 minutes or until the liquid is reduced to 1 cup. Gradually whisk in sour cream mixture. Bring to a boil; cook and stir for 2 minutes or until thickened. Stir in mustard until blended. Serve over chicken. Sprinkle with chives.

YIELD: 4 servings.

NUTRITION FACTS: 1 serving equals 194 calories, 7 g fat (2 g saturated fat), 69 mg cholesterol, 513 mg sodium, 6 g carbohydrate, trace fiber, 25 g protein. **DIABETIC EXCHANGES:** 3 lean meat, 1/2 starch.

braised pork chops

Shirley Antaya | ARAB, ALABAMA

I'm always looking for recipes that are low-calorie and sugar- and salt-free to fix for my husband—he's diabetic and has to watch his blood pressure. We always enjoy these tender chops.

- 1/2 **teaspoon dried marjoram**
- 1/8 **teaspoon onion powder**
- 1/8 **teaspoon garlic powder**
- 1/8 **teaspoon pepper**
- 4 **bone-in pork loin chops (6 ounces _each_ and 3/4 inch thick)**
- 1 **teaspoon olive oil**
- 1/2 **cup water**
- 2 **teaspoons cornstarch**
- 1/4 **cup reduced-sodium chicken broth**

- Combine seasonings; sprinkle over pork chops. In a nonstick skillet, cook chops in oil until browned on both sides. Add water. Bring to a boil. Reduce heat; cover and simmer for 45-60 minutes or until tender. Remove meat and keep warm. Combine cornstarch and broth until smooth; stir into cooking juices. Bring to a boil; cook and stir for 2 minutes or until thickened. Serve over pork chops.

YIELD: 4 servings.

NUTRITION FACTS: 1 pork chop with 2 tablespoons gravy equals 180 calories, 9 g fat (3 g saturated fat), 67 mg cholesterol, 83 mg sodium, 1 g carbohydrate, trace fiber, 23 g protein. **DIABETIC EXCHANGE:** 3 lean meat.

BRAISED PORK CHOPS

180 CALORIES

241 CALORIES

SLOW-COOKED ITALIAN CHICKEN

slow-cooked italian chicken

Deanna d'Auria | BANNING, CALIFORNIA

With its nicely seasoned tomato sauce, this enticing chicken dish is especially good over pasta or rice. My father loved it when I made this for him.

- 4 boneless skinless chicken breast halves (4 ounces *each*)
- 1 can (14-1/2 ounces) reduced-sodium chicken broth
- 1 can (14-1/2 ounces) stewed tomatoes, cut up
- 1 can (8 ounces) tomato sauce
- 1 medium green pepper, chopped
- 1 green onion, chopped
- 1 garlic clove, minced
- 3 teaspoons chili powder
- 1 teaspoon ground mustard
- 1/2 teaspoon garlic powder
- 1/2 teaspoon onion powder
- 1/2 teaspoon pepper
- 1/3 cup all-purpose flour
- 1/2 cup cold water

Hot cooked pasta

- Place chicken in a 3-qt. slow cooker. In a bowl, combine the broth, tomatoes, tomato sauce, green pepper, onion, garlic and seasonings; pour over chicken. Cover; cook on low for 4-5 hours or until a meat thermometer reads 170°.

- Remove the chicken and keep warm. Pour cooking juice into a large saucepan; skim fat. Combine flour and cold water until smooth; stir into juices.

- Bring to a boil; cook and stir for 2 minutes or until thickened. Serve over chicken and pasta.

YIELD: 4 servings.

NUTRITION FACTS: 1 chicken breast half with 1/2 cup sauce (calculated without pasta) equals 241 calories, 2 g fat (trace saturated fat), 66 mg cholesterol, 1,003 mg sodium, 25 g carbohydrate, 4 g fiber, 31 g protein.

220 CALORIES

hearty jambalaya

Mel Miller | PERKINS, OKLAHOMA

It's a pleasure to serve this meaty, satisfying jambalaya. Since it freezes so nicely, I can serve half and put half away for another day when time is tight.

- 1 pound smoked turkey sausage, cut into 1/2-inch slices
- 1 pound boneless skinless chicken breasts, cubed
- 1 large onion, chopped
- 1/2 cup chopped celery
- 1/2 cup chopped green pepper
- 4 garlic cloves, minced
- 2 tablespoons reduced-fat butter
- 1 can (14-1/2 ounces) diced tomatoes, undrained
- 1 can (6 ounces) tomato paste
- 1/2 teaspoon hot pepper sauce
- 1/4 to 1/2 teaspoon cayenne pepper
- 1/8 teaspoon garlic powder
- 1/8 teaspoon white pepper
- 1/8 teaspoon pepper
- 1/2 pound uncooked medium shrimp, peeled and deveined

Hot cooked rice, optional

- In a Dutch oven, saute the sausage, chicken, onion, celery, green pepper and garlic in butter until chicken is browned. Stir in the tomatoes, tomato paste and seasonings. Bring to a boil. Reduce heat; cover and simmer for 6-8 minutes or until chicken is no longer pink.

- Stir in shrimp; cover and simmer for 4 minutes or until shrimp turn pink. Serve over rice if desired; or cool, cover and freeze for up to 2 months.

YIELD: 8 servings.

NUTRITION FACTS: 1 cup (calculated without rice) equals 220 calories, 6 g fat (3 g saturated fat), 101 mg cholesterol, 675 mg sodium, 16 g carbohydrate, 3 g fiber, 24 g protein. **DIABETIC EXCHANGES:** 3 lean meat, 1 starch.

ham 'n' sausage stromboli

Lee Gregory | ASHLAND, OHIO

This hearty stromboli isn't difficult to make and is great for serving a group.

- 1 package (16 ounces) hot roll mix
- 1-1/4 cups warm water (120° to 130°)
- 3 tablespoons olive oil, *divided*
- 1/3 pound sliced deli ham
- 1/3 pound sliced salami
- 4 slices process American cheese, cut into thin strips
- 1 cup (4 ounces) shredded part-skim mozzarella *or* provolone cheese
- 1/4 pound bulk Italian sausage, cooked and crumbled
- 2 tablespoons grated Parmesan cheese
- 1 teaspoon dried oregano
- 1/2 teaspoon garlic powder
- 1/4 teaspoon coarsely ground pepper

- In a bowl, combine the contents of hot roll mix and yeast packet. Stir in warm water and 2 tablespoons oil until dough pulls away from sides of bowl. Turn onto a floured surface; knead until smooth and elastic, about 5 minutes. Cover and let rest for 5 minutes. Press into a lightly greased 15-in. x 10-in. x 1-in. baking pan.

- Layer the ham, salami, American cheese, mozzarella cheese and Italian sausage over dough. Roll up jelly-roll style, starting with a long side; pinch seam to seal. Place diagonally in pan. Brush dough with remaining oil; sprinkle with Parmesan cheese, oregano, garlic powder and pepper.

HAM 'N' SAUSAGE STROMBOLI

200 CALORIES

208 CALORIES

ZESTY GRILLED CHICKEN

- Bake at 375° for 35-40 minutes or until golden brown. Let stand for 10 minutes before slicing.

YIELD: 18 servings.

NUTRITION FACTS: 1 slice equals 200 calories, 9 g fat (3 g saturated fat), 22 mg cholesterol, 575 mg sodium, 19 g carbohydrate, 1 g fiber, 9 g protein.

zesty grilled chicken

Missy Herr | QUARRYVILLE, PENNSYLVANIA

On hot summer days, this yummy chicken dish is a cinch to throw together without heating up the kitchen.

- 6 tablespoons white vinegar
- 3 tablespoons canola oil
- 2 tablespoons ketchup
- 2 teaspoons dried parsley flakes
- 1-1/2 teaspoons garlic salt
- 1/2 teaspoon paprika
- 1/4 teaspoon dried oregano
- 1/8 teaspoon hot pepper sauce
- 1/8 teaspoon Worcestershire sauce
- 1 bay leaf
- 4 boneless skinless chicken breast halves (6 ounces *each*)

- In a large resealable plastic bag, combine the first 10 ingredients; add chicken. Seal bag and turn to coat; refrigerate for 4-8 hours, turning occasionally.

- Drain and discard marinade. Grill chicken, covered, over medium heat for 6-8 minutes on each side or until juices run clear.

YIELD: 4 servings.

NUTRITION FACTS: 1 chicken breast half equals 208 calories, 7 g fat (1 g saturated fat), 94 mg cholesterol, 275 mg sodium, 1 g carbohydrate, trace fiber, 34 g protein. **DIABETIC EXCHANGES:** 5 very lean meat, 1/2 fat.

251-350 calories

259 CALORIES

STOVETOP MEAT LOAVES

stovetop meat loaves

Emily Sund | GENESEO, ILLINOIS

For this convenient recipe, all you need is your stovetop and 35 minutes. It's a fast, easy and low-calorie recipe to make for one or two people.

      3 tablespoons 2% milk
      2 tablespoons quick-cooking oats
      1 tablespoon chopped onion
    1/4 teaspoon salt
    1/2 pound lean ground beef
    1/2 teaspoon cornstarch
    1/2 cup Italian tomato sauce
    1/4 cup cold water

- In a small bowl, combine the milk, oats, onion and salt. Crumble beef over mixture and mix well. Shape into two loaves.

- In a small nonstick skillet, brown loaves on both sides; drain. Combine the cornstarch, tomato sauce and water until smooth. Pour over meat loaves. Bring to a boil. Reduce heat to medium-low; cover and cook for 15-20 minutes or until meat is no longer pink.

YIELD: 2 servings.

NUTRITION FACTS: 1 meat loaf equals 259 calories, 10 g fat (4 g saturated fat), 71 mg cholesterol, 922 mg sodium, 16 g carbohydrate, 2 g fiber, 25 g protein. **DIABETIC EXCHANGES:** 3 lean meat, 1 starch.

cranberry-mustard pork loin

255 CALORIES

Laura Cook | WILDWOOD, MISSOURI

This dressed-up pork loin is so easy that you only have to spend a few minutes in the morning preparing it. It's a family favorite because it is tasty, and it's at the top of my list because it's fast!

      1 boneless whole pork loin roast (2 pounds)
      1 can (16 ounces) whole-berry cranberry sauce
    1/4 cup Dijon mustard
      3 tablespoons brown sugar
      3 tablespoons lemon juice
      1 tablespoon cornstarch
    1/4 cup cold water

- Place roast in a 3-qt. slow cooker. Combine the cranberry sauce, mustard, brown sugar and lemon juice; pour over roast. Cover and cook on low for 4 to 4-1/2 hours or until a meat thermometer reads 160°.

- Remove roast and keep warm. Strain cooking juices into a 2-cup measuring cup; add enough water to measure 2 cups. In a small saucepan, combine cornstarch and cold water until smooth; stir in cooking juices. Bring to a boil; cook and stir for 2 minutes or until thickened. Serve with pork.

YIELD: 8 servings.

NUTRITION FACTS: 3 ounces cooked pork equals 255 calories, 6 g fat (2 g saturated fat), 56 mg cholesterol, 236 mg sodium, 28 g carbohydrate, 1 g fiber, 22 g protein.

crumb-topped sole

Looking for a low-carb supper that's ready in a pinch? Then you'll want to try this buttery sole perfected by our Test Kitchen. The moist fillets are covered with a rich sauce and topped with golden bread crumbs. Try it with a simple salad or a low-calorie rice pilaf.

      3 tablespoons reduced-fat mayonnaise
      3 tablespoons grated Parmesan cheese, *divided*
      2 teaspoons mustard seed
    1/4 teaspoon pepper
      4 sole fillets (6 ounces *each*)
      1 cup soft bread crumbs
      1 green onion, finely chopped

267 CALORIES

CRUMB-TOPPED SOLE

1/2 teaspoon ground mustard
2 teaspoons butter, melted

- Combine the mayonnaise, 2 tablespoons Parmesan cheese, mustard seed and pepper; spread over tops of fillets. Place on a broiler pan coated with cooking spray. Broil 4 in. from the heat for 3-5 minutes or until fish flakes easily with a fork.

- Meanwhile, in a small bowl, combine bread crumbs, onion, ground mustard and remaining Parmesan cheese; stir in butter. Spoon over fillets; spritz topping with cooking spray. Broil 1-2 minutes longer or until golden brown.

YIELD: 4 servings.

NUTRITION FACTS: 1 fillet equals 267 calories, 10 g fat (3 g saturated fat), 94 mg cholesterol, 378 mg sodium, 8 g carbohydrate, 1 g fiber, 35 g protein. **DIABETIC EXCHANGES:** 5 lean meat, 1 fat, 1/2 starch.

weekday lasagna

Karen Mccabe | PROVO, UTAH

My husband requests this satisfying entree. I love it because it's low fat and a real time-saver since you don't cook the noodles before baking.

    1 pound lean ground beef
    1 small onion, chopped
    1 can (28 ounces) crushed tomatoes
1-3/4 cups water
    1 can (6 ounces) tomato paste
    1 envelope spaghetti sauce mix
    1 egg, lightly beaten
    2 cups (16 ounces) fat-free cottage cheese
    2 tablespoons grated Parmesan cheese
    6 uncooked lasagna noodles
    1 cup (4 ounces) shredded part-skim mozzarella cheese

- In a large saucepan, cook the beef and onion over medium heat until meat is no longer pink; drain. Stir in the tomatoes, water, tomato paste and spaghetti sauce mix. Bring to a boil. Reduce heat; cover and simmer for 15-20 minutes, stirring occasionally.

- In a small bowl, combine the egg, cottage cheese and Parmesan cheese. Spread 2 cups meat sauce in a 13-in. x 9-in. baking dish coated with cooking spray. Layer with three noodles, half of cottage cheese mixture and half of remaining meat sauce. Repeat layers.

- Cover and bake at 350° for 50 minutes. Uncover; sprinkle with mozzarella cheese. Bake 10-15 minutes longer or until bubbly and the cheese is melted. Let stand for 15 minutes before cutting.

YIELD: 9 servings.

NUTRITION FACTS: 1 piece equals 280 calories, 7 g fat (3 g saturated fat), 65 mg cholesterol, 804 mg sodium, 29 g carbohydrate, 4 g fiber, 25 g protein. **DIABETIC EXCHANGES:** 3 lean meat, 2 vegetable, 1 starch.

WEEKDAY LASAGNA

280 CALORIES

taco-stuffed pepper cups

Pat Habiger | SPEARVILLE, KANSAS

I'm happy to share the recipe for these pretty stuffed peppers. When green, red or yellow bell peppers are plentiful, they create a colorful container for this spicy taco mixture that's perfect for weeknights.

      2 **medium green peppers**
    1/2 **pound lean ground turkey**
      2 **tablespoons chopped onion**
      1 **can (16 ounces) kidney beans, rinsed and drained**
      1 **can (8 ounces) tomato sauce**
      3 **tablespoons taco seasoning**
    1/4 **cup fat-free sour cream**
    1/4 **cup shredded reduced-fat cheddar cheese**
    1/4 **cup chopped tomato**

- Cut tops off peppers and remove seeds. In a large kettle, cook peppers in boiling water for 3-5 minutes. Drain and rinse in cold water; set aside.

- In a large skillet, cook the turkey and onion over medium heat until meat is no longer pink; drain. Stir in the beans, tomato sauce and taco seasoning; bring to a boil. Reduce the heat; simmer, uncovered, for 5-6 minutes or until heated through.

TACO-STUFFED PEPPER CUPS

- Spoon into peppers. Place in an ungreased 8-in. square baking dish. Bake, uncovered, at 350° for 10-12 minutes or until peppers are tender. Top with the sour cream, cheese and tomatoes.

YIELD: 4 servings.

NUTRITION FACTS: 1 stuffed pepper half (equals 261 calories, 6 g fat (2 g saturated fat), 52 mg cholesterol, 823 mg sodium, 31 g carbohydrate, 7 g fiber, 21 g protein. **DIABETIC EXCHANGES:** 2 lean meat, 2 vegetable, 1-1/2 starch, 1 fat.

apples 'n' onion topped chops

Beverly Mclain | ENDICOTT, NEW YORK

Now that my husband and I are trying to lose weight, I find it a challenge to come up with healthy dishes that are flavorful, quick and appealing to our young daughter. This one fits the bill on all counts.

      4 **boneless pork loin chops (5 ounces *each*)**
      3 **cups sweet onion slices**
      1 **teaspoon canola oil**
      2 **medium Granny Smith apples, peeled and sliced**
    1/2 **cup water**
      2 **tablespoons brown sugar**
      1 **tablespoon cider vinegar**
      1 **teaspoon garlic powder**
    1/2 **teaspoon salt**
    1/4 **to 1/2 teaspoon pepper**
    1/4 **teaspoon dried rosemary, crushed**

- In a large nonstick skillet coated with cooking spray, cook chops for about 3 minutes on each side or until browned. Remove meat; set aside and keep warm.

- In same skillet, cook and stir onion in oil for 7 minutes or until golden brown. Add the apple slices; cook and stir 3 minutes longer.

- Combine the water, brown sugar, vinegar, garlic powder, salt, pepper and rosemary. Stir into skillet. Bring to a boil. Return meat to pan. Reduce heat; cover and simmer for 8-10 minutes or until apples are crisp-tender and a meat thermometer reads 160°.

YIELD: 4 servings.

NUTRITION FACTS: 1 pork chop with 1/2 cup apple-onion mixture equals 326 calories, 11 g fat (4 g saturated fat), 79 mg cholesterol, 344 mg sodium, 25 g carbohydrate, 2 g fiber, 33 g protein. **DIABETIC EXCHANGES:** 4 lean meat, 2 vegetable, 1 fruit.

290 CALORIES

ITALIAN CHICKEN WRAPS

italian chicken wraps

Cathy Hofflander | ADRIAN, MICHIGAN

After enjoying a chicken wrap at a restaurant, I experimented at home to create something similar. This delicious version is as quick as it is simple.

- 1 package (16 ounces) frozen stir-fry vegetable blend
- 2 packages (6 ounces *each*) ready-to-use grilled chicken breast strips
- 1/2 cup fat-free Italian salad dressing
- 3 tablespoons shredded Parmesan cheese
- 6 flour tortillas (8 inches), room temperature

- In a large saucepan, cook the vegetables according to package directions; drain. Stir in the chicken, salad dressing and cheese. Simmer, uncovered, for 3-4 minutes or until heated through. Spoon about 3/4 cup down the center of each tortilla; roll up tightly.

YIELD: 6 servings.

NUTRITION FACTS: 1 wrap equals 290 calories, 6 g fat (2 g saturated fat), 40 mg cholesterol, 1,129 mg sodium, 38 g carbohydrate, 3 g fiber, 20 g protein. **DIABETIC EXCHANGES:** 2 lean meat, 2 vegetable, 1-1/2 starch.

texas ranch-style stew

Sue West | ALVORD, TEXAS

Ground beef, beans and pasta thicken this hearty stew that's perfect for brisk days. The zippy sauce, made with canned vegetable juice, gives the chunky mixture a western flair.

- 1 cup small shell pasta
- 1 pound lean ground beef
- 1 medium onion, chopped
- 1 medium green pepper, chopped
- 2 garlic cloves, minced
- 3 cans (5-1/2 ounces *each*) reduced-sodium V8 juice
- 1 can (15 ounces) ranch-style beans *or* baked beans, undrained
- 1 can (14-1/2 ounces) Southwestern diced tomatoes, undrained
- 1/2 cup frozen corn, thawed
- 1 tablespoon chili powder
- 1/2 teaspoon salt
- 1/4 teaspoon pepper

- Cook pasta according to package directions. Meanwhile, in a large nonstick skillet, cook the beef, onion, green pepper and garlic over medium heat until meat is no longer pink; drain. Stir in the remaining ingredients. Bring to a boil. Reduce heat; simmer, uncovered, for 10 minutes, stirring occasionally. Drain pasta. Stir into stew.

YIELD: 6 servings.

NUTRITION FACTS: 1-1/3 cups equals 307 calories, 7 g fat (3 g saturated fat), 37 mg cholesterol, 886 mg sodium, 37 g carbohydrate, 7 g fiber, 22 g protein. **DIABETIC EXCHANGES:** 3 lean meat, 2 vegetable, 1-1/2 starch.

TEXAS RANCH-STYLE STEW

307 CALORIES

290 CALORIES

HAMBURGER NOODLE CASSEROLE

hamburger noodle casserole

Martha Henson | WINNSBORO, TEXAS

People have a hard time believing this homey and filling casserole uses lighter ingredients. The taste is so rich and creamy…a great weeknight family entree!

5	cups uncooked yolk-free noodles
1-1/4	pounds lean ground beef
2	garlic cloves, minced
3	cans (8 ounces *each*) tomato sauce
1/2	teaspoon sugar
1/2	teaspoon salt
1/8	teaspoon pepper
1	package (8 ounces) reduced-fat cream cheese
1	cup reduced-fat ricotta cheese
1/4	cup fat-free sour cream
3	green onions, thinly sliced, *divided*
2/3	cup shredded reduced-fat cheddar cheese

- Cook noodles according to package directions. Meanwhile, in a large nonstick skillet over medium heat, cook beef and garlic until meat is no longer pink; drain. Stir in the tomato sauce, sugar, salt and pepper; heat through. Drain noodles; stir into beef mixture.

- In a small mixing bowl, beat cream cheese, ricotta cheese and sour cream until blended. Stir in half of the onions.

- Spoon half of noodle mixture into a 13-in. x 9-in. baking dish coated with cooking spray. Top with cheese mixture and remaining noodle mixture.

- Cover and bake at 350° for 30 minutes. Uncover; sprinkle with cheddar cheese. Bake 5-10 minutes longer or until heated through and cheese is melted. Sprinkle with the remaining onions.

YIELD: 10 servings.

NUTRITION FACTS: 1 cup equals 290 calories, 12 g fat (7 g saturated fat), 56 mg cholesterol, 650 mg sodium, 23 g carbohydrate, 2 g fiber, 22 g protein. **DIABETIC EXCHANGES:** 2 lean meat, 1-1/2 starch, 1 fat.

salmon-stuffed potatoes

Carolyn Schmeling | BROOKFIELD, WISCONSIN

Here's a tasty twist on twice-baked potatoes. The spuds are stuffed with a mixture of potato, sour cream and smoked salmon, then sprinkled with chives. They're hearty enough to be served as a main dish alongside a salad or a bowl of soup.

4	medium baking potatoes (about 8 ounces *each*)
1/2	cup reduced-fat sour cream
1/2	cup 1% buttermilk

SALMON-STUFFED POTATOES

307 CALORIES

1 tablespoon butter

1/4 teaspoon salt

1/8 teaspoon pepper

4 ounces smoked salmon, cut into 1/2-inch pieces

4 teaspoons snipped chives

• Scrub and pierce potatoes. Bake at 400° for 40-60 minutes or until tender. Cool until easy to handle. Cut a thin slice off the top of each potato and discard. Scoop out the pulp, leaving a thin shell.

• In a bowl, mash the pulp with sour cream. Stir in the buttermilk, butter, salt and pepper. Gently fold in salmon. Spoon into potato shells. Sprinkle with chives.

YIELD: 4 servings.

NUTRITION FACTS: 1 stuffed potato equals 307 calories, 7 g fat (4 g saturated fat), 26 mg cholesterol, 820 mg sodium, 52 g carbohydrate, 4 g fiber, 11 g protein. **DIABETIC EXCHANGES:** 3 starch, 1 lean meat, 1/2 fat.

spicy seasoned chicken

305 CALORIES

Seasoned with a zesty combination of garlic powder, chili powder and cumin, this specialty can be used as a fabulous filling for tacos and burritos. Our home economists even suggest serving the chicken over a bed of greens for a warm entree salad.

1 pound boneless skinless chicken breasts, cut into strips

1 teaspoon ground cumin

1 teaspoon garlic powder

1 teaspoon chili powder

1/2 teaspoon salt

1 tablespoon canola oil

4 flour tortillas (8 inches), warmed

Shredded cheddar cheese, sliced ripe olives, shredded lettuce, sour cream and salsa, optional

• In a large skillet, saute chicken, cumin, garlic powder, chili powder and salt in oil until chicken is no longer pink. Serve with flour tortillas. Serve with toppings if desired.

YIELD: 4 servings.

NUTRITION FACTS: 1 serving (calculated without optional toppings) equals 305 calories, 9 g fat (2 g saturated fat), 63 mg cholesterol, 606 mg sodium, 26 g carbohydrate, trace fiber, 28 g protein.

onion-apricot pork chops

Phyllis Schmalz | KANSAS CITY, KANSAS

Dressed up with a glossy sauce, these tender chops are ready in a half hour!

4 boneless pork loin chops (4 ounces *each*)

1 tablespoon butter

1 large onion, sliced and separated into rings

1/2 cup chopped dried apricots

1-1/2 cups beef broth

1/4 cup orange marmalade

1 teaspoon minced fresh gingerroot

1 garlic clove, minced

Dash ground nutmeg

1 tablespoon cornstarch

4-1/2 teaspoons cold water

• In a large skillet, brown the pork chops in butter over medium-high heat. Add the onion and apricots. Combine the broth, marmalade, ginger, garlic and nutmeg; pour into skillet. Bring to a boil. Reduce heat; cover and simmer for 12-15 minutes or until meat juices run clear.

• Remove chops and keep warm. Combine cornstarch and water until smooth; stir into skillet. Bring to a boil; cook and stir for 1-2 minutes or until thickened. Spoon over pork chops.

YIELD: 4 servings.

NUTRITION FACTS: 1 chop equals 296 calories, 10 g fat (4 g saturated fat), 62 mg cholesterol, 392 mg sodium, 30 g carbohydrate, 2 g fiber, 23 g protein.

ONION-APRICOT PORK CHOPS

SPAGHETTI PIE

kentucky grilled chicken

Jill Evely | WILMORE, KENTUCKY

This chicken is perfect for an outdoor summer meal, and my family thinks it's fantastic. It takes about an hour on the grill but is worth the wait. I like to really "mop" on the basting sauce.

- 1 **cup cider vinegar**
- 1/2 **cup canola oil**
- 5 **teaspoons Worcestershire sauce**
- 4 **teaspoons hot pepper sauce**
- 2 **teaspoons salt**
- 10 **bone-in chicken breast halves (10 ounces** *each***)**

- In a small bowl, combine first five ingredients; mix well. Pour 1 cup marinade into a large resealable plastic bag; add the chicken. Seal bag and turn to coat; refrigerate for at least 4 hours. Cover and refrigerate the remaining marinade for basting.

- Coat grill rack with cooking spray before starting the grill. Drain and discard marinade from chicken. Grill bone side down, covered, over indirect medium heat for 20 minutes. Turn; grill 20-30 minutes longer or until juices run clear, basting occasionally with reserved marinade.

YIELD: 10 servings.

NUTRITION FACTS: 1 chicken breast half (with skin removed) equals 283 calories, 11 g fat (2 g saturated fat), 113 mg cholesterol, 406 mg sodium, trace carbohydrate, trace fiber, 41 g protein. **DIABETIC EXCHANGES:** 6 very lean meat, 2 fat.

KENTUCKY GRILLED CHICKEN

spaghetti pie

Ellen Thompson | SPRINGFIELD, OHIO

A classic Italian combination is remade into a tasty, family-pleasing casserole in this quick and easy dish. My family never grows tired of it.

- 1 **pound lean ground beef**
- 1/2 **cup finely chopped onion**
- 1/4 **cup chopped green pepper**
- 1 **cup canned diced tomatoes, undrained**
- 1 **can (6 ounces) tomato paste**
- 1 **teaspoon dried oregano**
- 3/4 **teaspoon salt**
- 1/2 **teaspoon garlic powder**
- 1/4 **teaspoon sugar**
- 1/4 **teaspoon pepper**
- 6 **ounces spaghetti, cooked and drained**
- 1 **tablespoon butter, melted**
- 2 **egg whites, lightly beaten**
- 1/4 **cup grated Parmesan cheese**
- 1 **cup (8 ounces) fat-free cottage cheese**
- 1/2 **cup shredded part-skim mozzarella cheese**

- In a nonstick skillet, cook beef, onion and green pepper over medium heat until meat is no longer pink; drain. Stir in tomatoes, tomato paste, oregano, salt, garlic powder, sugar and pepper; set aside.

- In a large bowl, combine the spaghetti, butter, egg whites and Parmesan cheese. Press onto the bottom and up the sides of a 9-in. deep-dish pie plate coated with cooking spray. Top with cottage cheese and beef mixture.

- Bake, uncovered, at 350° for 20 minutes. Sprinkle with mozzarella cheese. Bake 5-10 minutes longer or until cheese is melted and filling is heated through. Let stand for 5 minutes before cutting.

YIELD: 6 servings.

NUTRITION FACTS: 1 piece equals 348 calories, 10 g fat (5 g saturated fat), 52 mg cholesterol, 690 mg sodium, 33 g carbohydrate, 4 g fiber, 29 g protein. **DIABETIC EXCHANGES:** 3 lean meat, 2 vegetable, 1-1/2 starch, 1 fat.

glazed pork tenderloin

Virginia Smith | PEORIA, ILLINOIS

Here's a well-seasoned recipe originally intended for the grill. But we liked it so much that I came up with this version for the oven just so we could enjoy it all year long!

- 2 teaspoons dried oregano
- 1 teaspoon dried parsley flakes
- 1/2 teaspoon dried rosemary, crushed
- 1/2 teaspoon dried thyme
- 1/2 teaspoon garlic powder
- 1/2 teaspoon seasoned salt

Dash pepper

Dash cayenne pepper

- 1 pork tenderloin (3/4 pound)

GLAZE:

- 4-1/2 teaspoons brown sugar
- 4-1/2 teaspoons Dijon mustard
- 1/4 teaspoon honey

- In a small bowl, combine the first eight ingredients. Rub over pork. Place in a large resealable plastic bag. Seal bag and refrigerate overnight.

- Combine the glaze ingredients. Place tenderloin on a rack in a foil-lined shallow roasting pan. Bake, uncovered, at 350° for 40-45 minutes or until a meat thermometer reads 160°, basting occasionally with glaze. Let stand for 5 minutes before slicing.

YIELD: 2 servings.

NUTRITION FACTS: 5 ounces cooked pork equals 263 calories, 7 g fat (2 g saturated fat), 95 mg cholesterol, 737 mg sodium, 14 g carbohydrate, 1 g fiber, 35 g protein. **DIABETIC EXCHANGES:** 5 lean meat, 1 starch.

pepper jack chicken

Dorothy Storms | WINDER, GEORGIA

I'm retired but my husband works, so I have to make easy dinners for two. These grilled chicken breasts topped with zippy cheese and salsa are a favorite.

- 2 boneless skinless chicken breast halves (5 ounces *each*)
- 2 teaspoons olive oil
- 1/2 to 1 teaspoon seasoned pepper
- 1/4 teaspoon garlic powder
- 2 slices reduced-fat pepper Jack cheese (3/4 ounce *each*)
- 1/4 cup salsa

Hot cooked egg noodles, optional

- Brush chicken with oil; sprinkle with seasoned pepper and garlic powder. Grill on an indoor grill coated with cooking spray for 4-5 minutes on each side or until juices run clear.

- Transfer the chicken to serving plates; top with cheese and salsa. Serve with noodles if desired.

YIELD: 2 servings.

NUTRITION FACTS: 1 serving (calculated without noodles) equals 257 calories, 11 g fat (4 g saturated fat), 88 mg cholesterol, 347 mg sodium, 2 g carbohydrate, 1 g fiber, 34 g protein.

PEPPER JACK CHICKEN

325 CALORIES

PHYLLO CHICKEN POTPIE

phyllo chicken potpie

Ribbons of buttery phyllo dough provide a crispy topping for this impressive entree. Our home economists turned to pearl onions, mushrooms, asparagus and chicken as well as a creamy sauce that's flavored with thyme and sherry. It's special.

      6 cups water
      2 cups fresh pearl onions
  1-1/2 pounds boneless skinless chicken breasts, cubed
      2 tablespoons canola oil, *divided*
      2 medium red potatoes, peeled and chopped
      1 cup sliced fresh mushrooms
      1 can (14-1/2 ounces) reduced-sodium chicken broth
    1/2 pound fresh asparagus, trimmed and cut into 1-inch pieces
      3 tablespoons sherry *or* additional reduced-sodium chicken broth
      3 tablespoons cornstarch
    1/2 cup fat-free milk
  1-1/2 teaspoons minced fresh thyme
    1/2 teaspoon salt
    1/4 teaspoon pepper
     10 sheets phyllo dough (14 inches x 9 inches)
Refrigerated butter-flavored spray

- In a Dutch oven, bring water to a boil. Add pearl onions; boil for 3 minutes. Drain and rinse in cold water; peel and set aside.

- In a large skillet, cook chicken in 1 tablespoon oil over medium heat until juices run clear; remove and keep warm. In the same pan, saute potatoes in remaining oil for 5 minutes. Add the onions and mushrooms; saute 3 minutes longer. Add the broth, asparagus and sherry or additional broth. Bring to a boil. Reduce heat; cover and simmer for 5 minutes or until potatoes are tender.

- Combine cornstarch and milk until smooth; stir into skillet. Bring to a boil; cook and stir for 2 minutes or until thickened. Drain chicken; add to onion mixture. Stir in the thyme, salt and pepper. Transfer to an 8-in. square baking dish coated with cooking spray.

- Stack all 10 phyllo sheets. Roll up, starting at a long side; cut into 1/2-in. strips. Place in a large bowl and toss to separate strips. Spritz with butter-flavored spray. Arrange over chicken mixture; spritz again. Bake, uncovered, at 425° for 10-15 minutes or until golden brown.

YIELD: 6 servings.

NUTRITION FACTS: 1 serving equals 325 calories, 8 g fat (1 g saturated fat), 63 mg cholesterol, 542 mg sodium, 33 g carbohydrate, 2 g fiber, 29 g protein. **DIABETIC EXCHANGES:** 3 very lean meat, 2 vegetable, 1-1/2 starch, 1 fat.

black bean and rice enchiladas

Christie Ladd | MECHANICSBURG, PENNSYLVANIA
I love Mexican food, but I'm always looking for ways to make it more healthy. I modified a dish that I have enjoyed in restaurants to suit my taste and lifestyle. No one will even miss the meat.

      1 green pepper, chopped
      1 medium onion, chopped
      3 garlic cloves, minced
      1 tablespoon olive oil
      1 can (15 ounces) black beans, rinsed and drained
      1 can (14-1/2 ounces) diced tomatoes and green chilies
    1/4 cup picante sauce
      1 tablespoon chili powder
      1 teaspoon ground cumin
    1/4 teaspoon crushed red pepper flakes
      2 cups cooked brown rice
      8 flour tortillas (6 inches), warmed
      1 cup salsa

BLACK BEAN AND RICE ENCHILADAS

1 cup (4 ounces) shredded reduced-fat cheddar cheese
3 tablespoons chopped fresh cilantro leaves

- In a large nonstick skillet, saute the green pepper, onion and garlic in oil until tender. Add the beans, tomatoes, picante sauce, chili powder, cumin and red pepper flakes; bring to a boil. Reduce heat; simmer, uncovered, until heated through and mixture thickens. Add rice; cook 5 minutes longer or until heated through.

- Spoon a rounded 1/2 cup down the center of each tortilla. Fold sides over filling and roll up. Place in a 13-in. x 9-in. baking dish coated with cooking spray. Spoon salsa over each tortilla. Cover and bake at 350° for 25 minutes. Uncover; sprinkle with cheese and cilantro. Bake 2-3 minutes longer or until cheese is melted.

YIELD: 8 servings.

NUTRITION FACTS: 1 enchilada equals 271 calories, 6 g fat (2 g saturated fat), 10 mg cholesterol, 638 mg sodium, 43 g carbohydrate, 5 g fiber, 12 g protein. DIABETIC EXCHANGES: 2-1/2 starch, 1 lean meat, 1 vegetable.

ham-stuffed jumbo shells

Leona Reuer | MEDINA, NORTH DAKOTA

This is a good way to use up leftover ham. I made it for a family reunion, and the dish came back empty. I also received a lot of requests for the recipe.

24 jumbo pasta shells
3 tablespoons all-purpose flour

2 cups 1% milk
1/2 pound fresh mushrooms, halved and sliced
1/2 cup chopped onion
1/2 cup chopped green pepper
1 tablespoon canola oil
3 cups cubed fully cooked lean ham
1 cup (4 ounces) shredded reduced-fat Swiss cheese, *divided*
3 tablespoons grated Parmesan cheese
2 tablespoons minced fresh parsley
1/4 teaspoon paprika

- Cook pasta according to package directions. Meanwhile, in a small saucepan, combine flour and milk until smooth. Bring to a boil; cook and stir for 2 minutes or until thickened. Remove from the heat; set aside.

- In a large nonstick skillet, saute the mushrooms, onion and green pepper in oil until tender. Reduce heat; add the ham, 1/2 cup Swiss cheese and Parmesan cheese. Cook and stir until cheese is melted. Remove from the heat. Stir in 1/2 cup of the reserved sauce.

- Drain pasta; stuff each shell with about 3 tablespoons of filling. Place in a 13-in. x 9-in. baking dish coated with cooking spray. Top with remaining sauce. Cover and bake at 350° for 30 minutes or until heated through. Sprinkle with parsley, paprika and remaining Swiss cheese.

YIELD: 8 servings.

NUTRITION FACTS: 3 stuffed shells equals 274 calories, 7 g fat (2 g saturated fat), 26 mg cholesterol, 703 mg sodium, 30 g carbohydrate, 2 g fiber, 23 g protein. DIABETIC EXCHANGES: 2 lean meat, 2 starch.

HAM-STUFFED JUMBO SHELLS

chuck wagon dinner

Dorothy Cowan | FERNDALE, CALIFORNIA

Try serving this mild chili-like dish with tortilla chips or flour tortillas. Since it cooks up in a single pot, it's perfect for camping, too.

1/3	pound lean ground beef
1	small onion, chopped
1/4	cup chopped green pepper
1	garlic clove, minced
1	can (7 ounces) whole kernel corn, drained
3/4	cup kidney beans, rinsed and drained
1/2	cup tomato sauce
1	tablespoon chili powder
1/8	teaspoon pepper

• In a large saucepan, cook the beef, onion, green pepper and garlic over medium heat until meat is no longer pink; drain. Add the corn, beans, tomato sauce and seasonings; cover and cook 5-10 minutes longer or until heated through.

YIELD: 2 servings.

NUTRITION FACTS: 1-1/2 cups equals 300 calories, 7 g fat (3 g saturated fat), 46 mg cholesterol, 509 mg sodium, 38 g carbohydrate, 9 g fiber, 24 g protein. **DIABETIC EXCHANGES:** 2-1/2 lean meat, 2 starch, 1 vegetable.

CHUCK WAGON DINNER

300 CALORIES

304 CALORIES

SUNDAY CHICKEN SUPPER

sunday chicken supper

Ruthann Martin | LOUISVILLE, OHIO

This convenient slow cooker dish makes a hearty supper that's special any day of the week.

2	small carrots, cut into 2-inch pieces
1/2	medium onion, chopped
1/2	celery rib, cut into 2-inch pieces
1	cup cut fresh green beans (2-inch pieces)
2	small red potatoes, halved
2	bone-in chicken breast halves (7 ounces *each*), skin removed
2	bacon strips, cooked and crumbled
3/4	cup hot water
1	teaspoon chicken bouillon granules
1/4	teaspoon salt
1/4	teaspoon dried thyme
1/4	teaspoon dried basil

Pinch pepper

• In a 3-qt. slow cooker, layer the first seven ingredients in the order listed. Combine the water, bouillon, salt, thyme, basil and pepper; pour over the top. Do not stir. Cover and cook on low for 6-8 hours or until vegetables are tender and meat thermometer reads 170°. Remove chicken and vegetables. Thicken cooking juices for gravy if desired.

YIELD: 2 servings.

NUTRITION FACTS: 1 serving equals 304 calories, 7 g fat (2 g saturated fat), 94 mg cholesterol, 927 mg sodium, 21 g carbohydrate, 5 g fiber, 37 g protein. **DIABETIC EXCHANGES:** 5 very lean meat, 1 starch, 1 vegetable, 1/2 fat.

orange-glazed pork stir-fry

Edie Despain | LOGAN, UTAH

To add extra color and tangy flavor, I like to stir drained mandarin orange segments in with the cooked pork. This recipe makes a fast, simple and delicious meal!

1/2	pound pork tenderloin, cut into 1/4-inch slices
2	teaspoons canola oil
1	cup fresh snow peas
1	small onion, sliced and separated into rings
1/4	cup reduced-sugar orange marmalade
1	tablespoon chili sauce

Hot cooked rice, optional

- In a nonstick skillet or wok, stir-fry the pork in oil for 3-4 minutes or until no longer pink. Remove and keep warm. In the same pan, stir-fry the snow peas and onion in marmalade and chili sauce for 3-5 minutes or until crisp-tender.

- Return pork to the pan; cook and stir for 1-2 minutes or until heated through. Serve with rice if desired.

YIELD: 2 servings.

NUTRITION FACTS: 1-1/2 cups pork mixture (calculated without rice) equals 277 calories, 9 g fat (2 g saturated fat), 63 mg cholesterol, 164 mg sodium, 23 g carbohydrate, 3 g fiber, 26 g protein. **DIABETIC EXCHANGES:** 3 lean meat, 1 vegetable, 1 starch, 1 fat.

ORANGE-GLAZED PORK STIR-FRY

277 CALORIES

266 CALORIES

SHRIMP-STUFFED SOLE

shrimp-stuffed sole

Robert Bishop | LEXINGTON, KENTUCKY

If you like stuffed fish, this recipe is the way to go. It's so easy to assemble and cooks in just a few minutes in the microwave.

4	sole fillets, halved lengthwise
1	tablespoon lemon juice
1/8	teaspoon onion powder
1/4	cup reduced-fat butter, melted, *divided*
1	can (6 ounces) small shrimp, rinsed and drained
1/3	cup fat-free milk
1/4	cup finely chopped celery
2	teaspoons minced fresh parsley
1	cup cubed bread, toasted

Dash paprika

- Sprinkle the fillets with the lemon juice and onion salt; set aside. Pour 2 tablespoons butter into an 8-in. square microwave-safe dish. Add the shrimp, milk, celery and parsley. Cover and microwave on high for 1 to 1-1/2 minutes or until celery is tender. Stir in bread cubes.

- Spoon the shrimp mixture onto fillets. Starting with a short side, roll up each and secure with toothpicks. Place in a greased shallow microwave-safe dish. Brush with remaining butter; sprinkle with paprika.

- Cover and microwave on high for 4-6 minutes or until fish flakes easily with a fork. Let stand for 5 minutes before serving. Discard toothpicks.

YIELD: 4 servings.

EDITOR'S NOTE: This recipe was tested in a 1,100-watt microwave.

NUTRITION FACTS: 1 serving equals 266 calories, 8 g fat (5 g saturated fat), 188 mg cholesterol, 769 mg sodium, 6 g carbohydrate, trace fiber, 41 g protein. **DIABETIC EXCHANGES:** 5 very lean meat, 1-1/2 fat, 1 vegetable.

302 CALORIES

GERMAN-STYLE SHORT RIBS

german-style short ribs

Bregitte Rugman | SHANTY BAY, ONTARIO

My husband and our eight children are excited when I plug in the slow cooker to make these fall-off-the-bone-tender ribs. We like them served over rice or even egg noodles.

    3/4 cup dry red wine *or* beef broth
    1/2 cup mango chutney
      3 tablespoons quick-cooking tapioca
    1/4 cup water
      3 tablespoons brown sugar
      3 tablespoons cider vinegar
      1 tablespoon Worcestershire sauce
    1/2 teaspoon salt
    1/2 teaspoon ground mustard
    1/2 teaspoon chili powder
    1/2 teaspoon pepper
      4 pounds bone-in beef short ribs
      2 medium onions, sliced
    Hot cooked egg noodles

- In a 5-qt. slow cooker, combine the first 11 ingredients. Add ribs and turn to coat. Top with onions. Cover and cook on low for 8-10 hours or until meat is tender. Remove ribs from slow cooker. Skim fat from cooking juices; serve with ribs and noodles.

YIELD: 8 servings.

NUTRITION FACTS: 1 serving (calculated without noodles) equals 302 calories, 11 g fat (5 g saturated fat), 55 mg cholesterol, 378 mg sodium, 28 g carbohydrate, 1 g fiber, 19 g protein.

apricot beef stir-fry

Our Test Kitchen staff used apricot preserves to lend sweetness to this tasty beef stir-fry while red pepper flakes provided a bit of kick.

      1 teaspoon cornstarch
    1/4 cup cold water
    1/2 cup apricot preserves
      2 tablespoons reduced-sodium soy sauce
    1/2 teaspoon minced garlic
    1/4 teaspoon salt
    1/4 teaspoon crushed red pepper flakes
      1 pound boneless beef sirloin steak, thinly sliced
      1 tablespoon canola oil
      1 package (16 ounces) frozen asparagus stir-fry vegetable blend
    Hot cooked rice

- In a small bowl, whisk cornstarch and cold water until smooth. Stir in the apricot preserves, soy sauce, garlic, salt and pepper flakes; set aside.

- In a large skillet or wok, stir-fry beef in oil until no longer pink; remove and keep warm. In the same pan, stir-fry vegetable blend according to package directions. Return beef to the pan. Stir apricot mixture and add to beef mixture. Cook and stir until slightly thickened. Serve with rice.

YIELD: 4 servings.

NUTRITION FACTS: 1 cup (calculated without rice) equals 309 calories, 10 g fat (3 g saturated fat), 63 mg cholesterol, 531 mg sodium, 34 g carbohydrate, 3 g fiber, 23 g protein.

APRICOT BEEF STIR-FRY

309 CALORIES

293 CALORIES

CHICKEN PESTO PIZZA

chicken pesto pizza

Heather Thompson | WOODLAND HILLS, CALIFORNIA
Here's a tasty twist on a comforting family classic. Make it a standby for casual nights at home.

- 2 tablespoons active dry yeast
- 1 cup warm water (110 to 115)
- 2-3/4 cups bread flour
- 1 tablespoon plus 2 teaspoons olive oil, *divided*
- 1 tablespoon sugar
- 1-1/2 teaspoon salt, *divided*
- 1/2 pound boneless skinless chicken breasts, cut into 1/2-inch pieces
- 1 small onion, halved and thinly sliced
- 1/2 *each* small green, sweet red and yellow peppers, julienned
- 1/2 cup sliced fresh mushrooms
- 3 tablespoons prepared pesto
- 1-1/2 cups (6 ounces) shredded part-skim mozzarella cheese
- 1/4 teaspoon pepper

- In a bowl, dissolve yeast in warm water. Beat in 1 cup flour, 1 tablespoon oil, sugar and 1 teaspoon salt. Add remaining flour; beat until combined.

- Turn onto a lightly floured surface; knead until smooth and elastic. Place in a bowl coated with cooking spray, turning once to coat top. Cover and let rise in a warm place until doubled, about 1 hour.

- In a nonstick skillet over medium heat, cook chicken, onion, peppers and mushrooms in remaining oil until chicken is no longer pink and vegetables are tender. Remove from the heat; set aside.

- Punch dough down; roll into a 15-in. circle. Transfer to a 14-in. pizza pan. Build up edges slightly. Spread with

pesto. Top with chicken mixture and cheese. Sprinkle with pepper and remaining salt. Bake at 400° for 18-20 minutes or until crust and cheese are lightly browned.

YIELD: 8 slices.

NUTRITION FACTS: 1 slice equals 293 calories, 10 g fat (3 g saturated fat), 30 mg cholesterol, 601 mg sodium, 35 g carbohydrate, 2 g fiber, 18 g protein. **DIABETIC EXCHANGES:** 2 starch, 1 lean meat, 1 fat.

tasty tuna casserole

Elsie Epp | NEWTON, KANSAS
Reduced-fat cream cheese adds a delightful texture to this easy, tomatoey twist on classic tuna casserole.

- 2 cups uncooked elbow macaroni
- 1 can (12 ounces) solid white tuna, drained
- 1 can (8 ounces) tomato sauce
- 4 ounces reduced-fat cream cheese, cubed
- 1 small onion, finely chopped
- 1/4 teaspoon salt
- 1/2 teaspoon dried oregano

- Cook macaroni according to the package directions. Meanwhile, in a large bowl, combine remaining ingredients. Drain macaroni; stir into tuna mixture.

- Transfer to a 2-qt. baking dish coated with cooking spray. Cover and bake at 350° for 20-25 minutes or until heated through.

YIELD: 4 servings.

NUTRITION FACTS: 1-1/2 cups equals 334 calories, 9 g fat (5 g saturated fat), 56 mg cholesterol, 851 mg sodium, 33 g carbohydrate, 2 g fiber, 29 g protein. **DIABETIC EXCHANGES:** 3 very lean meat, 2 starch, 1 fat.

TASTY TUNA CASSEROLE

334 CALORIES

slow-cooked sweet 'n' sour pork

Martha Nickerson | HANCOCK, MAINE

A co-worker gave me this recipe many years ago, and my family still enjoys the satisfying entree.

2	tablespoons plus 1-1/2 teaspoons paprika
1-1/2	pounds boneless pork loin roast, cut into 1-inch strips
1	tablespoon canola oil
1	can (20 ounces) unsweetened pineapple chunks
1	medium onion, chopped
1	medium green pepper, chopped
1/4	cup cider vinegar
3	tablespoons brown sugar
3	tablespoons reduced-sodium soy sauce
1	tablespoon Worcestershire sauce
1/2	teaspoon salt
2	tablespoons cornstarch
1/4	cup cold water

Hot cooked rice, optional

- Place the paprika in a large resealable plastic bag. Add the pork, a few pieces at a time, and shake to coat. In a nonstick skillet, brown the pork in oil in batches over medium-high heat. Transfer to a 3-qt. slow cooker.

- Drain pineapple, reserving juice; refrigerate pineapple. Add the pineapple juice, onion, green pepper, vinegar, brown sugar, soy sauce, Worcestershire sauce and salt

SLOW-COOKED SWEET 'N' SOUR PORK

312 CALORIES

291 CALORIES

SOUTHWESTERN BEEF STRIPS

to slow cooker; mix well. Cover and cook on low for 6-8 hours or until meat is tender.

- Combine cornstarch and water until smooth; stir into pork mixture. Add pineapple. Cover and cook 30 minutes longer or until sauce is thickened. Serve over rice if desired.

YIELD: 6 servings.

NUTRITION FACTS: 1 cup pork mixture (calculated without rice) equals 312 calories, 10 g fat (3 g saturated fat), 73 mg cholesterol, 592 mg sodium, 28 g carbohydrate, 2 g fiber, 27 g protein. **DIABETIC EXCHANGES:** 3 lean meat, 1 fruit, 1/2 starch, 1/2 fat.

southwestern beef strips

This filling main dish, from our home economists, gets its zip from Mexican seasoning. Keep it on hand to season ground beef or turkey for tasty tacos and other Southwestern specialties without adding lots of calories.

1-1/2	pounds boneless beef sirloin steak, cut into thin strips
1	medium onion, sliced
1	medium sweet red pepper, cut into thin strips
2	tablespoons Mexican seasoning
1	teaspoon salt
1/4	teaspoon pepper
2	tablespoons canola oil
1	can (15 ounces) black beans, rinsed and drained
1-1/2	cups frozen corn, thawed
1/2	cup picante sauce
2	teaspoons dried cilantro flakes

Hot cooked fettuccine, optional

- In a large skillet, stir-fry the beef, onion, red pepper, Mexican seasoning, salt and pepper in oil until meat is no longer pink. Stir in the beans, corn, picante sauce and cilantro; heat through. Serve with fettuccine if desired.

YIELD: 6 servings.

EDITORS NOTE: Mexican seasoning is a blend of cumin, chili pepper, onion and garlic. It is found in the spice section of your local grocery store.

NUTRITION FACTS: 1-1/3 cups beef mixture (calculated without fettuccine) equals 291 calories, 11 g fat (3 g saturated fat), 63 mg cholesterol, 777 mg sodium, 22 g carbohydrate, 5 g fiber, 27 g protein.

open-faced chicken sandwiches

276 CALORIES

Lynda Clark | SPOKANE, WASHINGTON

Caramelized onions, mushrooms and two types of cheese make these my favorite sandwiches. I invented them for a last-minute picnic by combining items I had on hand. They've been a hit ever since.

- 1 loaf (8 ounces and 8 inches long) French bread
- 1 pound fresh mushrooms, sliced
- 1 large sweet onion, sliced
- 1 cup fat-free mayonnaise
- 1/2 cup crumbled blue cheese
- 1/4 teaspoon pepper
- 1 pound boneless skinless chicken breasts, grilled and sliced
- 1 cup (4 ounces) shredded part-skim mozzarella cheese

- Cut bread into eight 1-in. slices and toast slices. Meanwhile, in a large nonstick skillet coated with cooking spray, saute mushrooms and onion for 15-20 minutes or until onion is tender and golden brown; set aside.

- In a small bowl, combine mayonnaise, blue cheese and pepper; mix well. Spread blue cheese mixture over each bread slice. Top with chicken, mushroom mixture and mozzarella cheese. Place on a broiler pan. Broil 4-6 in. from the heat for 3-4 minutes or until cheese is melted.

YIELD: 8 servings.

NUTRITION FACTS: 1 open-faced sandwich equals 276 calories, 8 g fat (4 g saturated fat), 66 mg cholesterol, 618 mg sodium, 23 g carbohydrate, 3 g fiber, 27 g protein. **DIABETIC EXCHANGES:** 3 lean meat, 1 starch, 1 vegetable.

berry barbecued pork roast

Doris Heath | FRANKLIN, NORTH CAROLINA

Moist and tender, this elegant pork roast, topped with a thick ruby-red cranberry barbecue sauce, is sure to please everyone at your table.

- 1 boneless rolled pork loin roast (3 pounds)
- 1/4 teaspoon salt
- 1/4 teaspoon pepper
- 4 cups fresh *or* frozen cranberries
- 1 cup sugar
- 1/2 cup orange juice
- 1/2 cup barbecue sauce

- Sprinkle roast with salt and pepper. Place with fat side up on a rack in a shallow roasting pan. Bake, uncovered, at 350° for 45 minutes.

- Meanwhile, in a saucepan, combine cranberries, sugar, orange juice and barbecue sauce. Bring to a boil. Reduce heat to medium-low; cook and stir for 10-12 minutes or until cranberries pop and sauce is thickened.

- Brush some of the sauce over roast. Bake 15-20 minutes longer or until a meat thermometer reads 160°, brushing often with the sauce. Let stand for 10 minutes before slicing. Serve with remaining sauce.

YIELD: 12 servings.

NUTRITION FACTS: 3 ounces cooked pork with 1/4 cup sauce equals 262 calories, 8 g fat (3 g saturated fat), 67 mg cholesterol, 190 mg sodium, 23 g carbohydrate, 1 g fiber, 24 g protein. **DIABETIC EXCHANGES:** 3 lean meat, 1 starch, 1/2 fruit.

BERRY BARBECUED PORK ROAST

262 CALORIES

254 CALORIES

SPICY TWO-BEAN CHILI

spicy two-bean chili

Lesley Pew | LYNN, MASSACHUSETTS

Chili fans will get a kick out of this untraditional recipe. Tomatoes with green chilies, lime juice and kidney and black beans give it an original twist. It's wonderful ladled over steaming rice.

2	pounds ground beef
3	large onions, chopped
6	garlic cloves, minced
2	cans (16 ounces *each*) kidney beans, rinsed and drained
2	cans (15 ounces *each*) black beans, rinsed and drained
2	cans (10 ounces *each*) diced tomatoes and green chilies, undrained
1	can (14-1/2 ounces) chicken broth
1/2	cup lime juice
6	tablespoons cornmeal
1/4	cup chili powder
4	teaspoons dried oregano
3	teaspoons ground cumin
2	teaspoons salt
2	teaspoons rubbed sage
1/2	teaspoon white pepper
1/2	teaspoon paprika
1/2	teaspoon pepper

Hot cooked rice

Shredded cheddar cheese

• In a Dutch oven, cook the beef, onions and garlic over medium heat until meat is no longer pink; drain. Transfer to a 5-qt. slow cooker. Stir in the beans, tomatoes, broth, lime juice, cornmeal and seasonings.

• Cover and cook on low for 8 hours or until heated through. Serve with rice; sprinkle with cheese.

YIELD: 11 servings.

NUTRITION FACTS: 1 cup (calculated without rice and cheese) equals 254 calories, 8 g fat (3 g saturated fat), 40 mg cholesterol, 906 mg sodium, 24 g carbohydrate, 6 g fiber, 21 g protein.

tender turkey meatballs

Jane Thoma | MONROE, MICHIGAN

I changed a traditional meatball dinner to come up with this healthier version. Whether offered as appetizers, packed cold for picnics or served over spaghetti, these moist marjoram-seasoned meatballs are well-received.

1/2	cup chopped onion
1/4	cup egg substitute
1/4	cup toasted wheat germ
1/4	cup chopped green pepper
1/4	cup ketchup
1	teaspoon chili powder
1/2	teaspoon dried marjoram
1/2	teaspoon pepper
1	pound lean ground turkey
1	package (12 ounces) spaghetti
5	cups meatless spaghetti sauce

• In a bowl, combine the first eight ingredients. Crumble turkey over mixture and mix well. Shape into 30 balls, about 1 in. each. Place meatballs on a rack coated with cooking spray in a shallow baking pan. Bake at 400° for 13-16 minutes or until juices run clear; drain.

TENDER TURKEY MEATBALLS

312 CALORIES

- Meanwhile, cook the spaghetti according to the package directions. Transfer meatballs to a large saucepan; add spaghetti sauce. Heat through. Drain spaghetti; top with meatballs and sauce.

YIELD: 6 servings.

NUTRITION FACTS: 5 meatballs with sauce and 1 cup spaghetti equals 312 calories, 7 g fat (2 g saturated fat), 60 mg cholesterol, 1,047 mg sodium, 40 g carbohydrate, 5 g fiber, 22 g protein. **DIABETIC EXCHANGES:** 2-1/2 starch, 2 lean meat.

cran-orange pork medallions

Julie Wesson | WILTON, WISCONSIN

Talk about versatility! This is a long-time family favorite just as it is, but occasionally, I jazz up the recipe with jalapeno peppers and fresh ginger. I've also made it with peach preserves and dried cherries for a delicious change of pace.

1	pork tenderloin (1 pound), cut into 1-inch slices
1/2	teaspoon salt
1/2	teaspoon garlic powder
1/2	teaspoon ground coriander
1/4	teaspoon pepper
2	tablespoons olive oil
1	medium red onion, chopped
1/2	cup orange marmalade
1/4	cup orange juice
1/4	cup orange-flavored dried cranberries
2	tablespoons balsamic vinegar

- Flatten pork slices to 1/4-in. thickness. Combine the salt, garlic powder, coriander and pepper; sprinkle over both sides of pork.

- In a large skillet, saute pork in oil for 3 minutes on each side or until juices run clear. Remove and keep warm.

- In same skillet, saute onion in pan juices for 5 minutes or until tender. Stir in marmalade, orange juice, cranberries and vinegar. Bring to a boil. Reduce heat; return pork to skillet. Simmer, uncovered, for 5 minutes or until sauce is thickened.

YIELD: 4 servings.

NUTRITION FACTS: 3 ounces cooked pork equals 339 calories, 11 g fat (2 g saturated fat), 63 mg cholesterol, 365 mg sodium, 38 g carbohydrate, 1 g fiber, 23 g protein.

italian chicken and penne

Janeen Longfellow | WOLCOTTVILLE, INDIANA

This easy stir-fry combines the pasta with green pepper, mushrooms and tomatoes in an Italian-style sauce. I made up this dish one evening, and it was a big hit with my family.

8	ounces uncooked penne pasta
1	pound boneless skinless chicken breasts, cut into 1/2-inch pieces
1	small green pepper, julienned
1/2	cup chopped onion
1	garlic clove, minced
1	tablespoon olive oil
1	cup sliced fresh mushrooms
1	cup halved cherry *or* grape tomatoes
1	can (8 ounces) pizza sauce
1/2	teaspoon Italian seasoning
1/3	cup shredded part-skim mozzarella cheese

- Cook pasta according to the package directions; drain. In a nonstick wok, stir-fry the chicken, pepper, onion and garlic in oil until chicken is no longer pink. Add pasta, mushrooms, tomatoes, sauce and seasoning; heat through. Remove from heat. Sprinkle with cheese; let stand until melted.

YIELD: 6 servings.

NUTRITION FACTS: 1-1/3 cups equals 288 calories, 5 g fat (1 g saturated fat), 47 mg cholesterol, 96 mg sodium, 36 g carbohydrate, 3 g fiber, 26 g protein. **DIABETIC EXCHANGES:** 3 very lean meat, 2 starch, 1 vegetable, 1/2 fat.

ITALIAN CHICKEN AND PENNE

open-faced swordfish sandwiches

Alicia Montalvo Pagan | NEW BEDFORD, MASSACHUSETTS

Topped with mellow blue cheese salad dressing and a festive combination of carrots, red onion and lime juice, these warm sandwiches are a special way to welcome dinnertime.

- 1 cup canned bean sprouts, rinsed and drained
- 3/4 cup julienned carrots
- 1/4 cup thinly sliced red onion
- 1 tablespoon lime juice
- 1 teaspoon sugar
- 1/2 teaspoon minced fresh gingerroot
- 4 swordfish steaks (5 ounces *each*)
- 1 tablespoon olive oil
- 1/2 teaspoon salt
- 1/8 teaspoon cayenne pepper
- 4 slices sourdough bread (1/2 inch thick), toasted
- 8 teaspoons fat-free blue cheese salad dressing

- In a small bowl, combine bean sprouts, carrots and onion. Combine the lime juice, sugar and ginger; stir into the vegetable mixture. Cover and refrigerate for 30 minutes.

OPEN-FACED SWORDFISH SANDWICHES

- Brush both sides of swordfish steaks with oil; sprinkle with salt and cayenne. If grilling the fish, coat grill rack with cooking spray before starting the grill. Grill the fish, uncovered, over medium-hot heat or broil 4-6 in. from the heat for 6 minutes. Turn; grill or broil 4-7 minutes longer or until fish flakes easily with a fork.

- Place a swordfish steak on each piece of toast; top with 2 teaspoons blue cheese dressing and about 1/2 cup bean sprout mixture.

YIELD: 4 servings.

NUTRITION FACTS: 1 sandwich equals 319 calories, 10 g fat (2 g saturated fat), 52 mg cholesterol, 749 mg sodium, 26 g carbohydrate, 3 g fiber, 30 g protein. DIABETIC EXCHANGES: 4 very lean meat, 1-1/2 starch, 1 vegetable, 1 fat.

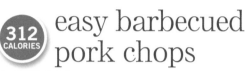

easy barbecued pork chops

Jorie Welch | ACWORTH, GEORGIA

This is my favorite "penny pincher" skillet supper. Sweet red peppers add color and flavor to this main dish, but when I'm watching our budget, I use less expensive green peppers.

- 4 bone-in pork loin chops (6 ounces *each*)
- 2 teaspoons canola oil
- 1 medium green pepper, chopped
- 2/3 cup chopped celery
- 1/3 cup chopped onion
- 1 cup ketchup
- 1/4 cup packed brown sugar
- 1/4 cup reduced-sodium chicken broth
- 2 tablespoons chili powder

- In a large nonstick skillet, brown pork chops in oil over medium-high heat. Remove chops and keep warm. Add green pepper, celery and onion to the skillet; cook and stir until vegetables begin to soften.

- Return pork chops to the pan. In a bowl, combine the ketchup, brown sugar, broth and chili powder. Pour over chops and vegetables. Bring to a boil. Reduce heat; cover and simmer for 30 minutes or until meat is tender.

YIELD: 4 servings.

NUTRITION FACTS: 1 pork chop with 1/3 cup sauce equals 312 calories, 9 g fat (2 g saturated fat), 66 mg cholesterol, 867 mg sodium, 35 g carbohydrate, 3 g fiber, 24 g protein. DIABETIC EXCHANGES: 3 lean meat, 2 starch.

335 CALORIES

SLOW COOKER FAJITAS

slow cooker fajitas

Katie Urso | SENECA, ILLINOIS

I love fajitas served in Mexican restaurants, but when I prepared them at home, the meat was always chewy. Then I tried this recipe in my slow cooker, and my husband and I savored every last bite. Fresh cilantro gives these fajitas the extra punch that makes them taste truly authentic.

- 1 *each* medium green, sweet red and yellow pepper, cut into 1/2-inch strips
- 1 sweet onion, cut into 1/2-inch strips
- 2 pounds boneless beef sirloin steaks, cut into thin strips
- 3/4 cup water
- 2 tablespoons red wine vinegar
- 1 tablespoon lime juice
- 1 teaspoon ground cumin
- 1 teaspoon chili powder
- 1/2 teaspoon salt
- 1/2 teaspoon garlic powder
- 1/2 teaspoon pepper
- 1/2 teaspoon cayenne pepper
- 8 flour tortillas (8 inches), warmed
- 1/2 cup salsa
- 1/2 cup shredded reduced-fat cheddar cheese
- 8 teaspoons minced fresh cilantro

- Place the peppers and onion in a 5-qt. slow cooker. Top with beef. Combine the water, vinegar, lime juice and seasonings; pour over meat. Cover and cook on low for 8-9 hours or until tender.

- Using a slotted spoon, place about 3/4 cup meat mixture down center of each tortilla. Top with 1 tablespoon salsa, 1 tablespoon cheese and 1 teaspoon cilantro; roll up.

YIELD: 8 servings.

NUTRITION FACTS: 1 fajita equals 335 calories, 10 g fat (3 g saturated fat), 69 mg cholesterol, 564 mg sodium, 32 g carbohydrate, 2 g fiber, 29 g protein. **DIABETIC EXCHANGES:** 3 lean meat, 2 starch, 1 vegetable.

stuffing-coated chicken

Rosemary Dibble | SANDY, UTAH

Stuffing mix gives these moist chicken breasts a fast and tasty coating you'll enjoy.

- 1 envelope cream of chicken soup mix
- 1/3 cup hot water
- 3/4 cup stuffing mix
- 2 boneless skinless chicken breast halves (4 ounces *each*)
- 1 tablespoon reduced-fat butter, melted

- In a shallow bowl, combine soup mix and water. Place stuffing mix in another shallow bowl. Dip chicken in soup mixture, then coat with stuffing.

- Place in an 8-in. square baking dish coated with cooking spray. Drizzle with butter. Bake, uncovered, at 375° for 25-30 minutes or until juices run clear.

YIELD: 2 servings.

NUTRITION FACTS: 1 serving equals 269 calories, 8 g fat (4 g saturated fat), 74 mg cholesterol, 913 mg sodium, 20 g carbohydrate, 1 g fiber, 27 g protein. **DIABETIC EXCHANGES:** 3 lean meat, 1 starch.

STUFFING-COATED CHICKEN

269 CALORIES

251 CALORIES

MEAT 'N' POTATO KABOBS

meat 'n' potato kabobs

You'll love this quick recipe created by the staff in our Test Kitchen. The potatoes are cooked in the microwave first, so grilling is super-easy. It's a delicious stick-to-your-ribs meal that keeps calories at bay.

- 1 pound boneless beef sirloin steak, cut into 1-inch cubes
- 1-1/2 teaspoons steak seasoning, *divided*
- 1 teaspoon minced garlic
- 1 cup diet cola
- 3 small red potatoes, cubed
- 1 tablespoon water
- 1 cup cherry tomatoes
- 1 medium sweet orange pepper, cut into 1-inch pieces
- 1 teaspoon canola oil
- 1 cup pineapple chunks

- Sprinkle beef cubes with 1 teaspoon steak seasoning and garlic; place in a large resealable plastic bag. Add cola. Seal bag and turn to coat; set aside.
- Place the potatoes and water in a microwave-safe dish; cover and microwave on high for 4 minutes or until tender. Drain. Add the tomatoes, orange pepper, oil and remaining steak seasoning; toss gently to coat.

- Drain and discard marinade. Alternately thread the beef, vegetables and pineapple onto eight metal or soaked wooden skewers. Grill, covered, over medium-hot heat or broil 4-6 in. from the heat for 4 minutes on each side or until meat reaches desired doneness (for medium-rare, a meat thermometer should read 145°; medium, 160°; well-done, 170°).

YIELD: 4 servings.

EDITOR'S NOTE: This recipe was tested in a 1,100-watt microwave and was tested with McCormick's Montreal Steak Seasoning. Look for it in the spice aisle.

NUTRITION FACTS: 1 kabob equals 251 calories, 7 g fat (2 g saturated fat), 63 mg cholesterol, 311 mg sodium, 23 g carbohydrate, 3 g fiber, 24 g protein. **DIABETIC EXCHANGES:** 3 lean meat, 1 starch, 1/2 fruit.

spinach chicken pockets

Mitzi Sentiff | ANNAPOLIS, MARYLAND

The tender chicken mixture that's tucked into these pita pockets has a cumin zip and refreshing cucumber-and-yogurt sauce. A mainstay at my house, this sandwich is great alone or served with soup or salad.

- 3/4 pound boneless skinless chicken breast halves
- 1/2 cup reduced-fat plain yogurt
- 2 tablespoons reduced-fat mayonnaise
- 1 tablespoon Dijon mustard
- 1/4 teaspoon ground cumin

SPINACH CHICKEN POCKETS

317 CALORIES

1/8 teaspoon cayenne pepper

2 cups fresh baby spinach

1/2 cup chopped seeded cucumber

2 green onions, sliced

4 pita breads (6 inches), halved

- In a large nonstick skillet coated with cooking spray, cook chicken over medium heat for 10-12 minutes on each side or until juices run clear. Remove; thinly slice the chicken and cool.

- Meanwhile, in a small bowl, combine yogurt, mayonnaise, mustard, cumin and cayenne; set aside. In a large bowl, combine the spinach, cucumber, onions and chicken.

- Drizzle with yogurt mixture; toss to coat. Microwave pita breads for 15-20 seconds or until warmed. Fill each half with 1/2 cup chicken mixture.

YIELD: 4 servings.

NUTRITION FACTS: 2 filled pita halves equals 317 calories, 6 g fat (1 g saturated fat), 51 mg cholesterol, 552 mg sodium, 39 g carbohydrate, 2 g fiber, 25 g protein. **DIABETIC EXCHANGES:** 2-1/2 very lean meat, 2 starch, 1 vegetable, 1 fat.

hearty taco casserole

Krista Frank | RHODODENDRON, OREGON

One night when I didn't have time to make homemade tortillas, I used the dough to make the crust of this dish instead. Topped with taco fixings, it was an instant hit.

2/3 cup uncooked brown rice

1-1/3 cups plus 4 to 5 tablespoons water, *divided*

3/4 cup all-purpose flour

3/4 teaspoon baking powder

1/8 teaspoon salt

2 tablespoons cold butter

FILLING:

1/2 pound lean ground beef

1/2 cup chopped onion

1/2 cup chopped green pepper

2 garlic cloves, minced

1 cup water

1 envelope taco seasoning

2 eggs, lightly beaten

1/4 cup minced fresh cilantro

1 cup (4 ounces) shredded reduced-fat cheddar cheese

284 CALORIES

HEARTY TACO CASSEROLE

2 cups shredded lettuce

2 medium tomatoes, chopped

3/4 cup salsa

1/2 cup fat-free sour cream

- In a small saucepan, bring rice and 1-1/3 cups water to a boil. Reduce heat; cover and simmer for 30-35 minutes or until rice is tender and water is absorbed.

- Meanwhile, in a large bowl, combine the flour, baking powder and salt; cut in butter until crumbly. Stir in enough remaining water to form a soft dough. On a floured surface, roll the dough into a 12-in. x 8-in. rectangle. Press into a 13-in. x 9-in. baking dish coated with cooking spray. Bake at 400° for 13-15 minutes or until very lightly browned.

- For filling, in a large nonstick skillet, cook the beef, onion, green pepper and garlic over medium heat until the meat is no longer pink; drain. Add the water, taco seasoning and cooked rice. Bring to a boil. Reduce the heat; simmer, uncovered, for 2-3 minutes or until thickened. Remove from the heat. Stir in eggs and cilantro. Spread over crust.

- Cover and bake for 15-17 minutes or until the filling is set. Cut into squares. Top with the cheese, lettuce and tomatoes. Serve with salsa and sour cream.

YIELD: 8 servings.

NUTRITION FACTS: 1 serving equals 284 calories, 10 g fat (5 g saturated fat), 87 mg cholesterol, 764 mg sodium, 34 g carbohydrate, 3 g fiber, 16 g protein. **DIABETIC EXCHANGES:** 2 starch, 1 lean meat, 1 vegetable, 1 fat.

259 CALORIES

SOUTHWEST LASAGNA ROLLS

southwest lasagna rolls

Trisha Kruse | EAGLE, IDAHO

We love these south-of-the-border lasagna rolls. The cheesy dish comes together fast with a carton of vegetarian chili, and it makes a great entree served with a green salad and baked tortilla chips.

- 1 can (15 ounces) fat-free vegetarian chili
- 1 carton (15 ounces) reduced-fat ricotta cheese
- 1 cup (4 ounces) shredded reduced-fat Mexican cheese blend
- 1 can (4 ounces) chopped green chilies
- 1 teaspoon taco seasoning
- 1/4 teaspoon salt
- 8 lasagna noodles, cooked and drained
- 1 jar (16 ounces) salsa

- In a large bowl, combine the first six ingredients. Spread about 1/2 cup on each noodle; carefully roll up. Place seam side down in a 13-in. x 9-in. baking dish coated with cooking spray.

- Cover and bake at 350° for 25 minutes. Uncover; top with salsa. Bake 10 minutes longer or until heated through.

YIELD: 8 servings.

NUTRITION FACTS: 1 lasagna roll equals 259 calories, 6 g fat (3 g saturated fat), 23 mg cholesterol, 648 mg sodium, 31 g carbohydrate, 6 g fiber, 15 g protein. **DIABETIC EXCHANGES:** 2 starch, 1 lean meat, 1 vegetable.

easy chicken potpie

Martha Evans | OMAHA, NEBRASKA

I turn to baking mix, canned soup and frozen vegetables for this spirit-warming favorite. I like to serve it with cranberry sauce.

- 1 can (10-3/4 ounces) reduced-fat reduced-sodium condensed cream of chicken soup, undiluted
- 1 can (10-3/4 ounces) reduced-fat reduced-sodium condensed cream of mushroom soup, undiluted
- 1/2 cup plus 2/3 cup fat-free milk, *divided*
- 1/2 teaspoon dried thyme
- 1/4 teaspoon pepper
- 1/8 teaspoon poultry seasoning
- 2 packages (16 ounces *each*) frozen mixed vegetables, thawed
- 1-1/2 cups cubed cooked chicken breast
- 1-1/2 cups reduced-fat biscuit/baking mix

- In a large bowl, combine the soups, 1/2 cup milk, thyme, pepper and poultry seasoning. Stir in the vegetables and chicken.

- Transfer to a 13-in. x 9-in. baking dish coated with cooking spray. In a small bowl, stir biscuit mix and remaining milk just until blended. Drop by 12 rounded tablespoonfuls onto chicken mixture. Bake, uncovered, at 350° for 40-50 minutes or until filling is bubbly and biscuits are golden brown.

YIELD: 6 servings.

NUTRITION FACTS: 1-1/3 cups chicken mixture with 2 biscuits equals 342 calories, 5 g fat (2 g saturated fat), 36 mg cholesterol, 871 mg sodium, 53 g carbohydrate, 7 g fiber, 21 g protein. **DIABETIC EXCHANGES:** 3 vegetable, 2-1/2 starch, 2 very lean meat.

EASY CHICKEN POTPIE

342 CALORIES

baked vegetable beef stew

Alice McCabe | CLIMAX, NEW YORK

When my granddaughter was 3, she had a bear that sang a song about "root stew." She thought he was talking about tree roots, so I took her to the store to buy root veggies, and we made this stew.

1-1/2	pounds boneless beef sirloin tip roast, cut into 1-inch cubes
3	cups cubed peeled potatoes
3	celery ribs, cut into 1-inch pieces
1-1/2	cups cubed peeled sweet potatoes
3	large carrots, cut into 1-inch pieces
1	large onion, cut into 12 wedges
1	cup cubed peeled rutabaga
1	envelope reduced-sodium onion soup mix
2	teaspoons dried basil
1/2	teaspoon salt
1/4	teaspoon pepper
1/2	cup water
1	can (14-1/2 ounces) stewed tomatoes

- In a large resealable plastic bag, combine beef, vegetables, soup mix and seasonings. Seal bag; shake to coat evenly.

- Transfer to a Dutch oven or 13-in. 9-in. baking dish coated with cooking spray (pan will be very full). Pour water over beef mixture.

- Cover and bake at 325° for 1-1/2 hours. Stir in tomatoes. Bake, uncovered, for 30-40 minutes, stirring after 25 minutes, or until beef and vegetables are tender.

YIELD: 6 servings.

NUTRITION FACTS: 1-1/3 cups equals 343 calories, 6 g fat (2 g saturated fat), 71 mg cholesterol, 699 mg sodium, 42 g carbohydrate, 5 g fiber, 29 g protein. **DIABETIC EXCHANGES:** 3 lean meat, 3 vegetable, 1-1/2 starch.

turkey tetrazzini

Irene Banegas | LAS CRUCES, NEW MEXICO

Your family will flip over this turkey and mushroom pasta casserole. In fact, the creamy Parmesan-topped tetrazzini is so satisfying that no one will suspect that it's low in fat and light on calories.

1/2	pound uncooked spaghetti
1/4	cup finely chopped onion
1	garlic clove, minced
1	tablespoon butter
3	tablespoons cornstarch
1	can (14-1/2 ounces) reduced-sodium chicken broth
1	can (12 ounces) fat-free evaporated milk
2-1/2	cups cubed cooked turkey breast
1	can (4 ounces) mushroom stems and pieces, drained
1/2	teaspoon seasoned salt

Dash pepper

2	tablespoons grated Parmesan cheese
1/4	teaspoon paprika

- Cook spaghetti according to package directions; drain.

- In a large saucepan, saute the onion and garlic in butter until tender. Combine cornstarch and broth until smooth; stir into the onion mixture. Bring to a boil; cook and stir for 2 minutes or until thickened. Reduce heat to low. Add the milk; cook and stir for 2-3 minutes. Stir in the spaghetti, turkey, mushrooms, seasoned salt and pepper.

- Transfer to an 8-in. square baking dish coated with cooking spray. Cover and bake at 350° for 20 minutes. Uncover; sprinkle with Parmesan cheese and paprika. Bake 5-10 minutes longer or until heated through.

YIELD: 6 servings.

NUTRITION FACTS: 1-1/4 cups equals 331 calories, 5 g fat (2 g saturated fat), 51 mg cholesterol, 544 mg sodium, 41 g carbohydrate, 1 g fiber, 28 g protein. **DIABETIC EXCHANGES:** 3 very lean meat, 2 starch, 1 vegetable, 1/2 fat-free milk.

TURKEY TETRAZZINI

leftover-turkey bake

Alice Slagter | WYOMING, MICHIGAN

Dotted with pretty cranberries, this moist casserole is a wonderful way to finish up extra turkey.

    1-1/2 cups finely chopped onion
      1/2 cup finely chopped celery
        1 can (14-1/2 ounces) reduced-sodium chicken
           broth, *divided*
        2 eggs, lightly beaten
        2 teaspoons poultry seasoning
      1/2 teaspoon salt
      1/4 teaspoon pepper
        3 cups cubed whole grain bread
        3 cups cubed white bread
        2 cups cubed cooked turkey breast
      1/2 cup chopped fresh *or* frozen cranberries

- In a large saucepan, bring the onion, celery and 1/2 cup broth to a boil. Reduce heat; simmer, uncovered, for 5-8 minutes or until vegetables are tender. Remove from the heat. Stir in the eggs, poultry seasoning, salt, pepper and remaining broth until blended. Add the bread cubes, turkey and cranberries; mix well.

- Spoon into a 2-qt. baking dish coated with cooking spray. Cover and bake at 350° for 15 minutes. Uncover; bake 20-25 minutes longer or until lightly browned and a knife inserted near the center comes out clean.

YIELD: 4 servings.

NUTRITION FACTS: 1 serving equals 290 calories, 5 g fat (1 g saturated fat), 154 mg cholesterol, 916 mg sodium, 34 g carbohydrate, 4 g fiber, 27 g protein. **DIABETIC EXCHANGES:** 3 lean meat, 1-1/2 starch, 1 vegetable.

LEFTOVER-TURKEY BAKE

ROUND STEAK SAUERBRATEN

round steak sauerbraten

Linda Bloom | MCHENRY, ILLINOIS

It takes only minutes to ready this round steak for the slow cooker, then it simmers most of the day to a tasty tenderness. The flavorful beef strips and sauce are nice over hot rice, too.

        1 envelope brown gravy mix
        2 tablespoons plus 1-1/2 teaspoons brown sugar
    2-1/2 cups cold water, *divided*
        1 cup chopped onion
        2 tablespoons white vinegar
        2 teaspoons Worcestershire sauce
        4 bay leaves
    2-1/2 pounds boneless beef top round steak, cut into
           3-inch x 1/2-inch strips
        2 teaspoons salt
        1 teaspoon pepper
      1/4 cup cornstarch
       10 cups hot cooked egg noodles

- In a 5-qt. slow cooker, combine the gravy mix, brown sugar, 2 cups water, onion, vinegar, Worcestershire sauce and bay leaves.

- Sprinkle beef with salt and pepper; stir into gravy mixture. Cover and cook on low for 6-1/2 to 7 hours or until meat is tender.

- Combine cornstarch and remaining water until smooth; stir into the beef mixture. Cover and cook on high for 30 minutes or until thickened. Discard bay leaves. Serve over noodles.

YIELD: 10 servings.

NUTRITION FACTS: 3/4 cup beef mixture over 1 cup noodles equals 331 calories, 6 g fat (2 g saturated fat), 96 mg cholesterol, 741 mg sodium, 37 g carbohydrate, 2 g fiber, 32 g protein. **DIABETIC EXCHANGES:** 3 lean meat, 2-1/2 starch.

chicken fajita spaghetti

Heather Brown | FRISCO, TEXAS

This combination of a satisfying pasta dish and fun chicken fajitas is always popular whenever I serve it.

- 8 ounces uncooked spaghetti
- 1 pound boneless skinless chicken breasts, cut into strips
- 1 tablespoon canola oil
- 1 small onion, sliced
- 1 small sweet red pepper, julienned
- 1 small sweet yellow pepper, julienned
- 1 can (4 ounces) chopped green chilies
- 1/2 cup water
- 1/2 cup taco sauce
- 1 envelope fajita seasoning mix

- Cook spaghetti according to package directions. Meanwhile, in a skillet, cook chicken over medium heat in oil for 4-5 minutes on each side or until juices run clear; remove and keep warm.

- In the same skillet, saute the onion and peppers until tender. Add the chicken and remaining ingredients; heat through. Drain spaghetti; toss with chicken mixture.

YIELD: 6 servings.

NUTRITION FACTS: 1-1/4 cups equals 282 calories, 5 g fat (1 g saturated fat), 42 mg cholesterol, 722 mg sodium, 37 g carbohydrate, 2 g fiber, 21 g protein. **DIABETIC EXCHANGES:** 2 starch, 2 lean meat, 1 vegetable.

CHICKEN FAJITA SPAGHETTI

282 CALORIES

CREAMY TURKEY CASSEROLE

311 CALORIES

creamy turkey casserole

Mary Jo O'Brien | HASTINGS, MINNESOTA

I'm happy to share this satisfying supper idea that puts holiday turkey leftovers to terrific use. I sometimes make turkey just so I have the extras for the casserole.

- 1 can (10-3/4 ounces) condensed cream of celery soup, undiluted
- 1 can (10-3/4 ounces) condensed cream of mushroom soup, undiluted
- 1 can (10-3/4 ounces) condensed cream of onion soup, undiluted
- 5 ounces process cheese (Velveeta), cubed
- 1/3 cup mayonnaise
- 4 cups cubed cooked turkey breast
- 1 package (16 ounces) frozen broccoli cuts, thawed
- 1-1/2 cups cooked white rice
- 1-1/2 cups cooked wild rice
- 1 can (8 ounces) sliced water chestnuts, drained
- 1 jar (4 ounces) sliced mushrooms, drained
- 1-1/2 cups salad croutons

- In a large bowl, combine soups, cheese and mayonnaise. Stir in the turkey, broccoli, rice, water chestnuts and mushrooms.

- Transfer to a greased 13-in. x 9-in. baking dish. Bake, uncovered, at 350° for 30 minutes; stir. Sprinkle with croutons. Bake 8-12 minutes longer or until bubbly.

YIELD: 12 servings.

EDITOR'S NOTE: Reduced-fat or fat-free mayonnaise is not recommended for this recipe.

NUTRITION FACTS: 1 cup equals 311 calories, 14 g fat (4 g saturated fat), 52 mg cholesterol, 846 mg sodium, 25 g carbohydrate, 3 g fiber, 20 g protein.

254 CALORIES

BEEF VEGETABLE STIR-FRY

beef vegetable stir-fry

Betsy Larimer | SOMERSET, PENNSYLVANIA

This simple recipe produces a very tasty and quick-to-fix main dish. The soy sauce gives strong flavor to the sliced beef, peppers, onions and mushrooms.

- 4-1/2 teaspoons cornstarch
- 4 tablespoons reduced-sodium soy sauce, *divided*
- 1 pound boneless beef sirloin steak, cut into 2-inch strips
- 2 medium green pepper, cut into strips
- 2 medium onions, halved and thinly sliced
- 1 tablespoon canola oil
- 1/2 pound sliced fresh mushrooms

- In a large bowl, combine cornstarch and 2 tablespoons soy sauce until smooth. Add beef; stir to coat.

- In a large skillet or wok, stir-fry the green peppers and onions in oil for 3 minutes; add beef. Cook and stir for 3 minutes. Add mushrooms. Cook and stir for 3-5 minutes or until the vegetables are tender and meat is no longer pink. Stir in the remaining soy sauce.

YIELD: 4 servings.

NUTRITION FACTS: 1 cup equals 254 calories, 9 g fat (3 g saturated fat), 63 mg cholesterol, 658 mg sodium, 17 g carbohydrate, 3 g fiber, 26 g protein. **DIABETIC EXCHANGES:** 3 lean meat, 3 vegetable, 1/2 fat.

soft fish tacos

Carrie Billups | FLORENCE, OREGON

My husband, Bill, and I created the recipe for these tasty fish tacos. The combination with tilapia and cabbage may seem unusual, but after one bite, everyone's hooked!

- 4 cups coleslaw mix
- 1/2 cup fat-free tartar sauce
- 1/2 teaspoon salt
- 1/2 teaspoon ground cumin
- 1/4 teaspoon pepper
- 1-1/2 pounds tilapia fillets
- 2 tablespoons olive oil
- 1 tablespoon lemon juice
- 10 corn tortillas (6 inches), warmed

Shredded cheddar cheese, chopped tomato and sliced avocado, optional

- In a large bowl, toss the coleslaw mix, tartar sauce, salt, cumin and pepper; set aside. In a large nonstick skillet coated with cooking spray, cook tilapia in oil and lemon juice over medium heat for 4-5 minutes on each side or until fish flakes easily with a fork.

- Place tilapia on tortillas; top with coleslaw mixture. Serve with cheese, tomato and avocado if desired.

YIELD: 5 servings.

NUTRITION FACTS: 2 tacos (calculated without optional toppings) equals 310 calories, 8 g fat (2 g saturated fat), 66 mg cholesterol, 542 mg sodium, 31 g carbohydrate, 4 g fiber, 29 g protein. **DIABETIC EXCHANGES:** 4 very lean meat, 2 starch, 1 fat.

SOFT FISH TACOS

310 CALORIES

311 CALORIES

SAUSAGE PIZZA

sausage pizza

Our home economists used spicy sausage, onions, mushrooms and plenty of cheese to make this pizza a real keeper. It beats the delivery variety every time.

- 1 loaf (1 pound) frozen bread dough, thawed
- 12 ounces Italian turkey sausage links, casings removed
- 1/2 cup sliced onion
- 1/2 cup sliced fresh mushrooms
- 1/2 cup chopped green pepper
- 1/2 cup pizza sauce
- 2 cups (8 ounces) shredded part-skim mozzarella cheese

- With greased fingers, pat dough onto an ungreased 12-in. pizza pan. Prick dough thoroughly with a fork. Bake at 400° for 10-12 minutes or until lightly browned. Meanwhile, in a large skillet, cook the sausage, onion, mushrooms and green pepper over medium heat until sausage is no longer pink; drain.

- Spread pizza sauce over crust. Top with sausage mixture; sprinkle with cheese. Bake at 400° for 12-15 minutes or until golden brown. Or wrap the pizza and freeze for up to 2 months.

- **TO USE FROZEN PIZZA:** Unwrap and place on a pizza pan; thaw in the refrigerator. Bake at 400° for 18-22 minutes or until golden brown.

YIELD: 8 slices.

NUTRITION FACTS: 1 slice equals 311 calories, 11 g fat (4 g saturated fat), 39 mg cholesterol, 754 mg sodium, 33 g carbohydrate, 2 g fiber, 20 g protein. **DIABETIC EXCHANGES:** 2 starch, 1-1/2 lean meat, 1-1/2 fat.

southwestern beef stew

Regina Stock | TOPEKA, KANSAS

This zippy stew seasoned with picante sauce is great on cold evenings. The preparation is so easy using a slow cooker…it's ready in minutes after a busy day at work.

- 2 pounds beef stew meat, cut into 1-inch cubes
- 1 jar (16 ounces) picante sauce
- 2 medium potatoes, peeled and cut into 1/2-inch cubes
- 4 medium carrots, cut into 1/2-inch slices
- 1 large onion, chopped
- 1 teaspoon chili powder
- 1/4 teaspoon salt
- 1/4 teaspoon ground cumin
- 1 tablespoon cornstarch
- 1/4 cup cold water

- In a large nonstick skillet coated with cooking spray, brown beef on all sides; drain. Transfer to a 3-qt. slow cooker. Stir in the picante sauce, potatoes, carrots, onion, chili powder, salt and cumin. Cover and cook on low for 8-9 hours or until meat and vegetables are tender.

- In a small bowl, combine cornstarch and water until smooth; stir into the stew. Cover and cook on high for 15 minutes or until gravy is thickened.

YIELD: 7 servings.

NUTRITION FACTS: 1 cup equals 266 calories, 9 g fat (3 g saturated fat), 81 mg cholesterol, 436 mg sodium, 18 g carbohydrate, 2 g fiber, 26 g protein. **DIABETIC EXCHANGES:** 3 lean meat, 2 vegetable, 1/2 starch.

SOUTHWESTERN BEEF STEW

266 CALORIES

beef and spinach lasagna

Carolyn Schmeling | BROOKFIELD, WISCONSIN

Using no-cook noodles gives you a jump start on assembling this hearty main dish. It cuts nicely after standing for a few minutes, revealing flavorful layers.

- 1 pound lean ground beef
- 1 medium onion, chopped
- 2 jars (26 ounces *each*) meatless spaghetti sauce
- 4 garlic cloves, minced
- 1 teaspoon dried basil
- 1 teaspoon dried oregano
- 1 package (10 ounces) frozen chopped spinach, thawed and squeezed dry
- 2 cups ricotta cheese
- 2 cups (8 ounces) shredded part-skim mozzarella cheese, *divided*
- 9 no-cook lasagna noodles

- In a large skillet, cook the beef and onion over medium heat until meat is no longer pink; drain. Stir in the spaghetti sauce, garlic, basil and oregano. Bring to a boil. Reduce the heat; cover and simmer for 10 minutes. In a bowl, combine spinach, ricotta and 1 cup mozzarella until combined.

- Spread 1-1/2 cups meat sauce into a greased 13-in. x 9-in. baking dish. Top with three noodles. Spread 1-1/2 cups sauce to edges of noodles. Top with half of the spinach mixture. Repeat layers. Top with remaining noodles, sauce and mozzarella.

BEEF AND SPINACH LASAGNA

281 CALORIES

318 CALORIES

CHICKEN CHILI

- Cover and bake at 375° for 30 minutes. Uncover; bake 10-15 minutes longer or until bubbly. Let stand for 10 minutes before cutting.

YIELD: 12 servings.

NUTRITION FACTS: 1 piece equals 281 calories, 11 g fat (6 g saturated fat), 50 mg cholesterol, 702 mg sodium, 26 g carbohydrate, 3 g fiber, 20 g protein.

chicken chili

Our Test Kitchen staff suggests assembling this deliciously seasoned chili at midday, starting your slow cooker, and your dinner will be ready and waiting for you.

- 1-1/2 pounds boneless skinless chicken breasts, cut into 1/2-inch cubes
- 1 cup chopped onion
- 3 tablespoons vegetable oil
- 1 can (15 ounces) cannellini *or* white kidney beans, rinsed and drained
- 1 can (14-1/2 ounces) diced tomatoes, undrained
- 1 can (14-1/2 ounces) diced tomatoes with mild green chilies, undrained
- 1 cup frozen corn
- 1 teaspoon salt
- 1 teaspoon ground cumin
- 1 teaspoon minced garlic
- 1/2 teaspoon celery salt
- 1/2 teaspoon ground coriander
- 1/2 teaspoon pepper

Sour cream and shredded cheddar cheese, optional

- In a large skillet, saute the chicken and onion in oil for 5 minutes or until the chicken is browned. Transfer to a 5-qt. slow cooker. Stir in the beans, tomatoes, corn and seasonings. Cover and cook on low for 5 hours or until chicken is no longer pink. Garnish with sour cream and cheese if desired.

YIELD: 6 servings.

NUTRITION FACTS: 1 cup (calculated without optional toppings) equals 318 calories, 10 g fat (2 g saturated fat), 63 mg cholesterol, 1,092 mg sodium, 28 g carbohydrate, 6 g fiber, 28 g protein.

pork 'n' penne skillet

Dawn Goodison | ROCHESTER, NEW YORK

I enjoy this one-pan skillet supper because it's quick, and the cleanup is easy. But best of all, my family enjoys this flavorful and nutritious dinner. Toss a salad while this is cooking for a complete filling meal.

2	tablespoons all-purpose flour
1	teaspoon chili powder
3/4	teaspoon salt
3/4	teaspoon pepper
1	pound boneless pork loin chops, cut into strips
2	cups sliced fresh mushrooms
1	cup chopped onion
1	cup chopped sweet red pepper
1	teaspoon dried oregano
1	teaspoon minced garlic
1	tablespoon canola oil
1	tablespoon butter
3	cups milk
1	can (15 ounces) tomato sauce
2	cups uncooked penne

- In a large resealable plastic bag, combine the flour, chili powder, salt and pepper. Add pork, a few pieces at a time, and shake to coat.

- In a large skillet, cook the pork, mushrooms, onion, red pepper, oregano and garlic in oil and butter over medium heat for 4-6 minutes or until pork is browned.

- Add the milk, tomato sauce and pasta. Bring to a boil. Reduce heat; simmer, uncovered, for 15-20 minutes or until meat juices run clear and pasta is tender.

YIELD: 8 servings.

NUTRITION FACTS: 1 cup equals 264 calories, 10 g fat (4 g saturated fat), 44 mg cholesterol, 546 mg sodium, 26 g carbohydrate, 2 g fiber, 18 g protein.

ham and noodle casserole

Ruth Hastings | LOUISVILLE, ILLINOIS

Cottage cheese is the secret to this creamy pasta casserole that has lots of colorful frozen veggies and ham. Add a green salad and fruit for dessert for a complete meal.

6	ounces uncooked yolk-free fine noodles
1-1/2	cups (12 ounces) 1% small-curd cottage cheese
1	package (10 ounces) frozen mixed vegetables, thawed and drained
1	cup cubed fully cooked lean ham
3/4	cup reduced-fat sour cream
1/4	cup fat-free milk
3	tablespoons grated Parmesan cheese
2	teaspoons all-purpose flour
1	teaspoon dill weed *or* 1 tablespoon snipped fresh dill
1/4	teaspoon salt

- Cook noodles according to package directions; drain. In a large bowl, combine the remaining ingredients. Add noodles and toss to coat. Transfer to a 2-qt. baking dish coated with cooking spray.

- Cover and bake at 350° for 30 minutes. Uncover; bake 5-10 minutes longer or until heated through. Let stand for 5 minutes before serving.

YIELD: 4 servings.

NUTRITION FACTS: 1-1/2 cups equals 266 calories, 5 g fat (3 g saturated fat), 21 mg cholesterol, 702 mg sodium, 32 g carbohydrate, 3 g fiber, 21 g protein. **DIABETIC EXCHANGES:** 2 lean meat, 1-1/2 starch, 1 vegetable.

HAM AND NOODLE CASSEROLE

- In a large bowl, combine the carrot, onion, egg substitute, 2 tablespoons tomato soup, 2 tablespoons vegetable soup, 1 tablespoon Italian seasoning, cayenne, pepper and rice. Crumble turkey over mixture and mix well. Place about 1/3 cupful on each cabbage leaf. Overlap the cut ends of leaf; fold in sides, beginning from the cut end. Roll up completely to enclose filling.

- Place the rolls seam side down in an 11-in. x 7-in. baking dish coated with cooking spray. Combine the remaining soups; pour over cabbage rolls. Sprinkle with remaining Italian seasoning. Cover and bake at 350° for 50-60 minutes or until the cabbage is tender and a meat thermometer reads 165°.

YIELD: 5 servings.

NUTRITION FACTS: 2 cabbage rolls equals 293 calories, 10 g fat (3 g saturated fat), 74 mg cholesterol, 582 mg sodium, 29 g carbohydrate, 4 g fiber, 22 g protein. **DIABETIC EXCHANGES:** 3 lean meat, 1-1/2 starch, 1 vegetable.

(293 CALORIES)

ITALIAN-STYLE CABBAGE ROLLS

italian-style cabbage rolls

Erika Niehoff | EVELETH, MINNESOTA

Here's a great way to get your family to eat their vegetables. Not only is this one of my gang's favorite dinners, but my son loves to help me roll the turkey filling into the cabbage leaves.

- 1/3 cup uncooked brown rice
- 1 medium head cabbage
- 1/2 cup shredded carrot
- 1/4 cup finely chopped onion
- 1/4 cup egg substitute
- 1 can (10-3/4 ounces) reduced-sodium condensed tomato soup, undiluted, *divided*
- 1 can (10-3/4 ounces) reduced-fat reduced-sodium condensed vegetable beef soup, undiluted, *divided*
- 2 tablespoons Italian seasoning, *divided*
- 1/4 teaspoon cayenne pepper
- 1/4 teaspoon pepper
- 1 pound lean ground turkey

- Cook rice according to package directions. Meanwhile, cook cabbage in boiling water just until leaves fall off head. Set aside 10 large leaves for rolls. (Refrigerate the remaining cabbage for another use.) Cut out the thick vein from the bottom of each reserved leaf, making a V-shaped cut.

honey pineapple chicken

(302 CALORIES)

Carol Gillespie | CHAMBERSBURG, PENNSYLVANIA

Sweet pineapple and savory soy sauce season this flavorful chicken dish. I adapted the recipe for my slow cooker because it's so much easier to prepare it hours in advance, then let it simmer all day.

- 3 pounds boneless skinless chicken breast halves
- 2 tablespoons canola oil
- 1 can (8 ounces) unsweetened crushed pineapple, undrained
- 1 cup packed brown sugar
- 1/2 cup honey
- 1/3 cup lemon juice
- 1/4 cup butter, melted
- 2 tablespoons prepared mustard
- 2 teaspoons soy sauce

- In a skillet, brown chicken in oil in batches on both sides; transfer to a 5-qt. slow cooker. Combine remaining ingredients; pour over chicken. Cover and cook on low for 3-4 hours or until chicken is no longer pink. Strain pan juices, reserving pineapple. Serve pineapple over chicken.

YIELD: 12 servings.

NUTRITION FACTS: 1 serving equals 302 calories, 9 g fat (3 g saturated fat), 73 mg cholesterol, 180 mg sodium, 33 g carbohydrate, trace fiber, 23 g protein.

open-faced turkey tacos

Mrs. Dale Jenne | MARENGO, ILLINOIS

I like to serve this filling, open-faced tortilla with a side of cold applesauce. Add extra salsa if you like things spicy.

- 1 pound lean ground turkey
- 1 medium onion, chopped
- 1 can (16 ounces) fat-free refried beans
- 1 jar (16 ounces) salsa
- 10 flour tortillas (6 inches), warmed
- 2 cups shredded lettuce
- 2 medium tomatoes, chopped
- 2 medium green peppers, chopped
- 2 medium sweet red peppers, chopped
- 10 tablespoons fat-free sour cream

- In a large skillet, cook turkey and onion over medium heat until meat is no longer pink; drain. Add beans and salsa; cook and stir until heated through. Spread 1/2 cup turkey mixture over each tortilla. Top with the lettuce, tomatoes, peppers and sour cream.

YIELD: 10 servings.

NUTRITION FACTS: 1 taco equals 265 calories, 7 g fat (1 g saturated fat), 38 mg cholesterol, 674 mg sodium, 32 g carbohydrate, 6 g fiber, 16 g protein. **DIABETIC EXCHANGES:** 2 starch, 2 lean meat, 1 vegetable.

OPEN-FACED TURKEY TACOS

SWISS CHICKEN SUPREME

swiss chicken supreme

Even though this recipe is slimmed down from the classic version with reduced-fat ingredients, it is still supreme. Our Test Kitchen staff suggests serving it with carrot coins.

- 4 boneless skinless chicken breast halves (4 ounces *each*)
- 1 tablespoon dried minced onion
- 1/2 teaspoon garlic powder
- 1/4 teaspoon salt
- 1/8 teaspoon pepper
- 4 slices (3/4 ounce *each*) reduced-fat Swiss cheese
- 1 can (10-3/4 ounces) reduced-fat reduced-sodium condensed cream of chicken soup, undiluted
- 1/3 cup reduced-fat sour cream
- 1/2 cup fat-free milk
- 1/3 cup crushed reduced-fat butter-flavored crackers (about 8 crackers)
- 1 teaspoon butter, melted

- Place chicken in a 13-in. x 9-in. baking dish coated with cooking spray. Sprinkle with the minced onion, garlic powder, salt and pepper. Top each with a slice of cheese.

- In a small bowl, combine soup, sour cream and milk; pour over chicken. Toss cracker crumbs and butter; sprinkle over chicken. Bake, uncovered, at 350° for 30-40 minutes or until chicken juices run clear and crumbs are golden.

YIELD: 4 servings.

NUTRITION FACTS: 1 serving equals 310 calories, 11 g fat (5 g saturated fat), 89 mg cholesterol, 567 mg sodium, 17 g carbohydrate, trace fiber, 34 g protein. **DIABETIC EXCHANGES:** 3 very lean meat, 2 fat, 1 starch.

spaghetti pizza casserole

Kim Neer | MANSFIELD, OHIO

I first tried this great-tasting dish at an office Christmas party. It quickly became everyone's favorite. It makes a wonderful alternative to ordinary spaghetti.

1	package (7 ounces) spaghetti
1/2	cup egg substitute
1/4	cup grated Parmesan cheese
1	pound lean ground beef
1	medium onion, chopped
1/2	cup chopped green pepper
1/2	cup chopped sweet yellow pepper
2	garlic cloves, minced
1	jar (26 ounces) meatless spaghetti sauce
1	teaspoon Italian seasoning
1	teaspoon dried basil
1/2	teaspoon salt
1/4	teaspoon pepper
1/2	pound sliced fresh mushrooms
1-1/2	cups (6 ounces) shredded part-skim mozzarella cheese

- Cook spaghetti according to package directions. Rinse with cold water and drain. In a large bowl, toss the spaghetti with egg substitute and Parmesan cheese. Spread evenly into a 15-in. x 10-in. x 1-in. baking pan coated with cooking spray; set aside.

- In a large nonstick skillet, cook the beef, onion and peppers over medium heat until meat is no longer pink;

SPAGHETTI PIZZA CASSEROLE

274 CALORIES

drain. Add garlic; cook 1 minute longer. Stir in the spaghetti sauce and seasonings; heat through.

- Spoon over spaghetti. Top with mushrooms and cheese. Bake, uncovered, at 350° for 25-30 minutes or until lightly browned. Let stand for 5 minutes before serving.

YIELD: 9 servings.

NUTRITION FACTS: 1 piece equals 274 calories, 8 g fat (4 g saturated fat), 37 mg cholesterol, 685 mg sodium, 29 g carbohydrate, 3 g fiber, 22 g protein. **DIABETIC EXCHANGES:** 2 lean meat, 1-1/2 starch, 1 vegetable.

326 CALORIES

ITALIAN BEEF ON ROLLS

italian beef on rolls

Jami Hilker | FAIR GROVE, MISSOURI

This is one of my all-time favorite slow cooker recipes! With 28 grams of protein per serving, it's a great way to meet your daily protein needs!

1	boneless beef sirloin tip roast (2 pounds)
1	can (14-1/2 ounces) diced tomatoes, undrained
1	medium green pepper, chopped
1/2	cup water
1	tablespoon sesame seeds
1-1/2	teaspoons garlic powder
1	teaspoon fennel seed, crushed
1/2	teaspoon salt
1/2	teaspoon pepper
8	hard rolls, split

- Place the roast in a 3-qt. slow cooker. In a small bowl, combine tomatoes, green pepper, water and seasonings;

pour over roast. Cover and cook on low for 8-9 hours or until meat is very tender.

- Remove roast; cool slightly. Skim fat from cooking juices; shred beef and return to the slow cooker. Serve on rolls.

YIELD: 8 servings.

NUTRITION FACTS: 2/3 cup beef mixture on 1 roll equals 326 calories, 8 g fat (2 g saturated fat), 60 mg cholesterol, 572 mg sodium, 34 g carbohydrate, 3 g fiber, 28 g protein. **DIABETIC EXCHANGES:** 3 lean meat, 2 starch.

beef burgundy

Mary Jo Nikolaus | MANSFIELD, OHIO

To save time, the night before serving this tasty dish, I trim the meat, cut up the vegetables and store them in the fridge in separate containers. Prep takes only minutes the next morning. At supper, I simply cook the noodles to complete this warm, hearty, fuss-free meal!

1-1/2   pounds beef stew meat, cut into 1-inch cubes
1/2   pound whole fresh mushrooms, halved
4   medium carrots, chopped
1   can (10-3/4 ounces) condensed golden mushroom soup, undiluted
1   large onion, cut into thin wedges
1/2   cup Burgundy wine *or* beef broth
1/4   cup quick-cooking tapioca
1/2   teaspoon salt
1/4   teaspoon dried thyme
1/4   teaspoon pepper
Hot cooked egg noodles

- In a 5-qt. slow cooker, combine the first 10 ingredients. Cover and cook on low for 5-1/2 to 6-1/2 hours or until meat is tender. Serve over noodles.

YIELD: 6 servings.

NUTRITION FACTS: 1 cup (calculated without noodles) equals 273 calories, 9 g fat (3 g saturated fat), 73 mg cholesterol, 642 mg sodium, 19 g carbohydrate, 3 g fiber, 24 g protein.

chops 'n' kraut

Ruth Tamul | MOREHEAD CITY, NORTH CAROLINA

Diced tomatoes lend color to this satisfying entree, and brown sugar sweetens the sauerkraut.

6   bone-in pork loin chops (3/4 inch thick and 7 ounces *each*)
1/4   teaspoon salt
1/4   teaspoon pepper
3   teaspoons canola oil, *divided*
1   medium onion, thinly sliced
2   garlic cloves, minced
1   can (14-1/2 ounces) petite diced tomatoes, undrained
1   can (14 ounces) sauerkraut, rinsed and well drained
1/3   cup packed brown sugar
1-1/2   teaspoons caraway seeds

- Sprinkle both sides of pork chops with salt and pepper. In a large nonstick skillet coated with cooking spray, cook three chops in 1 teaspoon oil for 2-3 minutes on each side or until browned; drain. Repeat with the remaining chops and 1 teaspoon oil.

- Place pork chops in a 13-in. x 9-in. baking dish coated with cooking spray; set aside. In the same skillet, cook onion and garlic in remaining oil until tender. Stir in the tomatoes, sauerkraut, brown sugar and caraway seeds. Cook and stir until mixture comes to a boil.

- Carefully pour over the chops. Cover and bake at 350° for 20-25 minutes or until meat is tender.

YIELD: 6 servings.

NUTRITION FACTS: 1 pork chop with 2/3 cup sauerkraut mixture equals 311 calories, 11 g fat (3 g saturated fat), 86 mg cholesterol, 691 mg sodium, 21 g carbohydrate, 3 g fiber, 32 g protein. **DIABETIC EXCHANGES:** 4 lean meat, 1 vegetable, 1/2 starch, 1/2 fat.

CHOPS 'N' KRAUT

313 CALORIES

BAKED SPAGHETTI

baked spaghetti

Pat Walter | PINE ISLAND, MINNESOTA

This is a wonderful casserole for a potluck. Wherever I take it, people really enjoy it. It has the classic combination of ground beef, pasta, tomato sauce and cheese.

- 1 package (16 ounces) spaghetti
- 1-1/2 pounds lean ground beef
- 1 medium onion, chopped
- 1/2 cup chopped green pepper
- 1 can (10-3/4 ounces) condensed cream of mushroom soup, undiluted
- 1 can (10-3/4 ounces) condensed tomato soup, undiluted
- 1 can (8 ounces) tomato sauce
- 1 cup water
- 2 tablespoons brown sugar
- 1 teaspoon salt
- 1 teaspoon dried basil
- 1 teaspoon dried oregano
- 1/2 teaspoon dried marjoram
- 1/2 teaspoon dried rosemary, crushed
- 1/8 teaspoon garlic salt
- 1 cup (4 ounces) shredded part-skim mozzarella cheese, *divided*

- Break spaghetti in half; cook according to the package directions. Meanwhile, in a Dutch oven, cook the beef, onion and green pepper over medium heat until meat is no longer pink; drain. Stir in the soups, tomato sauce, water, brown sugar and seasonings.

- Drain spaghetti; stir into meat sauce. Add 1/2 cup cheese. Transfer to a greased 13-in. x 9-in. baking dish. Cover and bake at 350° for 30 minutes. Uncover; sprinkle with remaining cheese. Bake 10-15 minutes longer or until cheese is melted.

YIELD: 12 servings.

NUTRITION FACTS: 1 cup equals 313 calories, 9 g fat (4 g saturated fat), 36 mg cholesterol, 706 mg sodium, 39 g carbohydrate, 2 g fiber, 18 g protein.

pork tenderloin stew

Janet Allen | DECATUR, ILLINOIS

This thick, creamy stew is one my family requests often. It does an especially good job of warming us up on cold winter days.

- 2 pork tenderloins (1 pound *each*), cut into 1-inch cubes
- 1 tablespoon olive oil
- 1 medium onion, chopped

PORK TENDERLOIN STEW

293 CALORIES

1 garlic clove, minced

1 can (14-1/2 ounces) reduced-sodium chicken broth

2 pounds red potatoes, peeled and cubed

1 cup sliced fresh carrots

1 cup sliced celery

1/2 pound sliced fresh mushrooms

2 tablespoons cider vinegar

2 teaspoons sugar

1-1/2 teaspoons dried tarragon

1 teaspoon salt

2 tablespoons all-purpose flour

1/2 cup fat-free milk

1/2 cup reduced-fat sour cream

293 CALORIES

- In a large nonstick skillet, cook pork in oil until no longer pink; remove and keep warm. In the same pan, saute onion and garlic until crisp-tender. Add the broth, vegetables, vinegar, sugar, tarragon and salt; bring to a boil. Reduce heat; cover and simmer for 25-30 minutes or until the vegetables are tender.

- Combine the flour and milk until smooth; gradually stir into vegetable mixture. Bring to a boil; cook and stir for 2 minutes or until thickened. Add pork and heat through. Reduce heat; stir in sour cream just before serving.

YIELD: 8 servings.

NUTRITION FACTS: 1-1/4 cups equals 293 calories, 7 g fat (3 g saturated fat), 68 mg cholesterol, 521 mg sodium, 28 g carbohydrate, 3 g fiber, 28 g protein. **DIABETIC EXCHANGES:** 3 lean meat, 1 starch, 1 vegetable, 1/2 fat.

chipotle turkey chili

Christie Ladd | MECHANICSBURG, PENNSYLVANIA

I combined a few chili recipes I had and came up with this spicy, low-calorie variety. It's great served with crusty rolls or baked tortilla chips.

1 can (7 ounces) chipotle peppers in adobo sauce

1-1/4 pounds lean ground turkey

3 medium carrots, chopped

1 medium green pepper, chopped

1/2 cup chopped onion

4 garlic cloves, minced

1 can (28 ounces) crushed tomatoes

1 can (14-1/2 ounces) reduced-sodium chicken broth

CHIPOTLE TURKEY CHILI

1 can (8 ounces) tomato sauce

1-1/2 teaspoons dried oregano

1-1/2 teaspoons dried basil

1 teaspoon chili powder

1/2 teaspoon ground cumin

1 can (16 ounces) kidney beans, rinsed and drained

1 can (15 ounces) garbanzo beans *or* chickpeas, rinsed and drained

- Drain chipotle peppers; set aside 2 tablespoons adobo sauce. Seed and chop three peppers; set aside. (Save remaining peppers and sauce for another use.)

- In a large Dutch oven or soup kettle coated with cooking spray, cook turkey, carrots, green pepper, onion, garlic and reserved peppers over medium heat until meat is no longer pink; drain if necessary. Stir in the tomatoes, broth, tomato sauce, oregano, basil, chili powder, cumin and reserved adobo sauce. Bring to a boil. Reduce the heat; cover and simmer for 1 hour.

- Stir in the beans. Cover and simmer for 15-20 minutes or until heated through.

YIELD: 8 servings.

EDITOR'S NOTE: When cutting or seeding hot peppers, use rubber or plastic gloves to protect your hands. Avoid touching your face.

NUTRITION FACTS: 1 cup equals 293 calories, 8 g fat (2 g saturated fat), 56 mg cholesterol, 844 mg sodium, 35 g carbohydrate, 9 g fiber, 22 g protein. **DIABETIC EXCHANGES:** 3 lean meat, 3 vegetable, 1 starch.

ground chicken gumbo

Our home economists suggest substituting ground turkey or even pork in this recipe. It has lots of down-south goodness and zippy seasoning.

- 1 cup uncooked long grain rice
- 1 pound ground chicken
- 1 cup chopped celery
- 1 cup chopped green pepper
- 1/2 cup chopped onion
- 2 tablespoons olive oil
- 1 can (28 ounces) crushed tomatoes
- 1 cup sliced fresh okra
- 1 cup chicken broth
- 1 teaspoon Cajun seasoning
- 1 teaspoon salt
- 1 teaspoon dried oregano
- 1 teaspoon ground thyme
- 1/4 teaspoon hot pepper sauce

- Cook rice according to package directions. Meanwhile, in a Dutch oven or soup kettle, cook the chicken, celery, green pepper and onion in oil over medium heat for 8 minutes or until chicken is no longer pink; drain.

- Stir in the remaining ingredients. Bring to a boil. Reduce heat; cover and simmer for 20 minutes or until heated through. Serve over rice.

YIELD: 6 servings.

NUTRITION FACTS: 1 cup gumbo with 1/2 cup rice equals 322 calories, 11 g fat (2 g saturated fat), 50 mg cholesterol, 900 mg sodium, 40 g carbohydrate, 5 g fiber, 18 g protein.

GROUND CHICKEN GUMBO

322 CALORIES

320 CALORIES

DOWN-HOME BARBECUED CHICKEN

down-home barbecued chicken

Mary Kaye Rackowitz | MARYSVILLE, WASHINGTON

When summer barbecue season is here, you'll love grilling this family-pleasing favorite. Hot pepper sauce adds a little zip to the tender chicken.

- 1/2 cup ketchup
- 1/4 cup water
- 2 tablespoons brown sugar
- 1 tablespoon lemon juice
- 1 tablespoon cider vinegar
- 1 teaspoon Worcestershire sauce
- 1 teaspoon prepared mustard
- 1 garlic clove, minced

Dash salt
- 1/4 to 1/2 teaspoon hot pepper sauce
- 1 bay leaf
- 2 bone-in chicken breast halves (8 ounces *each*), skin removed

- In small saucepan, combine first 11 ingredients; bring to a boil, stirring occasionally. Reduce heat; cover and simmer for 30 minutes. Discard bay leaf. Reserve 1/3 cup sauce for basting. Cover and refrigerate remaining sauce.

- Prepare grill for indirect heat, using a drip pan. Place the chicken over drip pan. Grill, covered, over indirect medium heat for 20-25 minutes on each side or until juices run clear, basting occasionally with reserved sauce. Serve with remaining sauce.

YIELD: 2 servings.

NUTRITION FACTS: 1 chicken breast half with 1/4 cup sauce equals 320 calories, 5 g fat (1 g saturated fat), 101 mg cholesterol, 938 mg sodium, 32 g carbohydrate, 1 g fiber, 38 g protein. **DIABETIC EXCHANGES:** 5 very lean meat, 1 starch, 1 fruit.

maple-orange pot roast

Christina Marquis | ORLANDO, FLORIDA

Served with fresh bread, this easy-to-prepare, tender roast is a wonderful reminder of New England's autumn flavors. It always brings back memories of a friend's maple sap house in New Hampshire, where I'm originally from.

1	boneless beef rump roast (3 pounds)
1/2	cup orange juice
1/4	cup sugar-free maple-flavored syrup
1/4	cup white wine *or* chicken broth
2	tablespoons balsamic vinegar
1	tablespoon Worcestershire sauce
1	teaspoon grated orange peel
1	bay leaf
1/2	teaspoon salt
1/4	teaspoon pepper
1-1/2	pounds red potatoes, cut into large chunks
5	medium carrots, cut into 2-inch pieces
2	celery ribs, cut into 2-inch pieces
2	medium onions, cut into wedges
4	teaspoons cornstarch
1/4	cup cold water

- In a large nonstick skillet coated with cooking spray, brown roast on all sides; drain. Place in a roasting pan coated with cooking spray.
- In same skillet, combine orange juice, syrup, wine or broth, vinegar, Worcestershire sauce, orange peel, bay leaf, salt and pepper. Bring to a boil, stirring frequently; pour over meat. Place the potatoes, carrots, celery and onions around roast. Cover and bake at 325° for 3 hours or until meat is tender.
- Remove meat and vegetables and keep warm. Pour pan juices into a measuring cup. Discard bay leaf and skim fat.
- Pour into a small saucepan. In a small bowl, combine cornstarch and water until smooth. Gradually stir into juices. Bring to a boil; cook and stir for 2 minutes or until thickened. Serve with pot roast and vegetables.

YIELD: 8 servings.

NUTRITION FACTS: 3 ounces cooked beef with 3/4 cup vegetables and 2 tablespoons gravy equals 335 calories, 8 g fat (3 g saturated fat), 102 mg cholesterol, 264 mg sodium, 27 g carbohydrate, 4 g fiber, 36 g protein. **DIABETIC EXCHANGES:** 3 lean meat, 2 vegetable, 1 starch.

MAPLE-ORANGE POT ROAST

spicy beans 'n' rice

298 CALORIES

Ranae Jones | FORT RUCKER, ALABAMA

Savory Cajun flavor zips up this quick skillet dish that's loaded with beans, tomatoes, rice and seasonings. It's delicious served with corn bread muffins.

1/2	cup coarsely chopped green pepper
1/2	cup coarsely chopped onion
2	garlic cloves, minced
1	tablespoon canola oil
1	can (14-1/2 ounces) stewed tomatoes, cut up
1	can (8 ounces) tomato sauce
1/2	teaspoon Italian seasoning
1/4	teaspoon cayenne pepper
1/8	teaspoon fennel seed, crushed
1	can (16 ounces) kidney beans, rinsed and drained
1	can (15-1/4 ounces) butter beans, rinsed and drained
2-1/2	cups cooked rice

- In a nonstick skillet, saute the green pepper, onion and garlic in oil until tender. Stir in the stewed tomatoes, tomato sauce, Italian seasoning, cayenne and fennel seed. Bring to a boil. Reduce heat; cover and simmer for 10 minutes. Stir in the beans. Cover and simmer 5-10 minutes longer or until beans are heated through. Serve with rice.

YIELD: 5 servings.

NUTRITION FACTS: 1 cup bean mixture with 1/2 cup rice equals 298 calories, 3 g fat (trace saturated fat), 0 cholesterol, 888 mg sodium, 59 g carbohydrate, 10 g fiber, 14 g protein.

328 CALORIES

SOUTHWEST PASTA BAKE

southwest pasta bake

Carol Lepak | SHEBOYGAN, WISCONSIN

Fat-free cream cheese and reduced-fat cheddar make this creamy casserole lower in fat and calories. It's a good way to get our kids to eat spinach in "disguise."

- 8 ounces uncooked penne pasta
- 1 package (8 ounces) fat-free cream cheese, cubed
- 1/2 cup fat-free milk
- 1 package (10 ounces) frozen chopped spinach, thawed and squeezed dry
- 1 teaspoon dried oregano
- 1 pound lean ground beef
- 2 garlic cloves, minced
- 1 jar (16 ounces) picante sauce
- 1 can (8 ounces) no-salt-added tomato sauce
- 1 can (6 ounces) no-salt-added tomato paste
- 2 teaspoons chili powder
- 1 teaspoon ground cumin
- 1 cup (4 ounces) shredded reduced-fat cheddar cheese
- 1 can (2-1/4 ounces) sliced ripe olives, drained
- 1/4 cup sliced green onions

- Cook pasta according to package directions. Meanwhile, in a small bowl, beat cream cheese until smooth. Beat in milk. Stir in spinach and oregano; set aside.

- In a nonstick skillet, cook beef and garlic over medium heat until meat is no longer pink; drain. Stir in picante sauce, tomato sauce, tomato paste, chili powder and cumin; bring to a boil. Reduce heat; simmer, uncovered, for 5 minutes. Drain pasta; stir into meat mixture.

- In a 13-in. x 9-in. baking dish coated with cooking spray, layer half of the meat mixture and all of the spinach mixture. Top with remaining meat mixture.

- Cover and bake at 350° for 30 minutes. Uncover; sprinkle with cheese. Bake 5 minutes longer or until the cheese is melted. Sprinkle with olives and onions. Let stand for 10 minutes before serving.

YIELD: 8 servings.

NUTRITION FACTS: 1 serving equals 328 calories, 9 g fat (4 g saturated fat), 40 mg cholesterol, 855 mg sodium, 36 g carbohydrate, 4 g fiber, 25 g protein. **DIABETIC EXCHANGES:** 3 lean meat, 2 vegetable, 1-1/2 starch.

338 CALORIES

italian turkey skillet

Patricia Kile | NOKOMIS, FLORIDA

With lots of colorful veggies, pasta and seasonings, this turkey dish makes a satisfying supper.

- 1 package (1 pound) linguine
- 3/4 cup sliced fresh mushrooms
- 1/2 cup chopped onion
- 1/2 cup chopped celery
- 1/2 cup chopped green pepper
- 2 tablespoons canola oil
- 2 cups cubed cooked turkey
- 1 can (14-1/2 ounces) diced tomatoes, drained
- 1 can (10-3/4 ounces) condensed tomato soup, undiluted
- 1 tablespoon Italian seasoning
- 1 tablespoon minced fresh parsley
- 1/4 teaspoon pepper
- 1/8 teaspoon salt
- 1 cup (4 ounces) shredded cheddar cheese, optional

- Cook linguine according to package directions. Meanwhile, in a large skillet, saute the mushrooms, onion, celery and green pepper in oil over medium heat until tender. Stir in the turkey, tomatoes, soup, Italian seasoning, parsley, pepper and salt.

- Drain linguine; stir into turkey mixture. Sprinkle with cheese if desired. Cover and cook for 3-4 minutes or until mixture is heated through and cheese is melted.

YIELD: 8 servings.

NUTRITION FACTS: 1 cup (calculated without cheese) equals 338 calories, 7 g fat (1 g saturated fat), 27 mg cholesterol, 362 mg sodium, 51 g carbohydrate, 4 g fiber, 19 g protein.

easy chicken and dumplings

Nancy Tuck | ELK FALLS, KANSAS

Perfect for cool nights, this main course is speedy, low in calories and a delicious one-dish meal. Try it when you have a craving for a chicken potpie.

3	celery ribs, chopped
1	cup sliced fresh carrots
3	cans (14-1/2 ounces *each*) reduced-sodium chicken broth
1/2	teaspoon poultry seasoning
1/8	teaspoon pepper
3	cups cubed cooked chicken breast
1-2/3	cups reduced-fat biscuit/baking mix
2/3	cup fat-free milk

- In a Dutch oven coated with cooking spray, saute celery and carrots for 5 minutes. Stir in broth, poultry seasoning and pepper. Bring to a boil. Reduce the heat; simmer, uncovered. Add the chicken.

- For the dumplings, combine the biscuit mix and milk. Drop by tablespoonfuls onto simmering broth. Cover and simmer for 10-15 minutes or until a toothpick inserted into a dumpling comes out clean (do not lift cover while simmering).

YIELD: 6 servings.

NUTRITION FACTS: 1 cup chicken mixture with 3 dumplings equals 282 calories, 5 g fat (1 g saturated fat), 60 mg cholesterol, 1,022 mg sodium, 29 g carbohydrate, 1 g fiber, 28 g protein. **DIABETIC EXCHANGES:** 3 very lean meat, 1-1/2 starch, 1 vegetable, 1/2 fat.

EASY CHICKEN AND DUMPLINGS

282 CALORIES

MEXICAN LASAGNA

341 CALORIES

mexican lasagna

Sheree Swistun | WINNIPEG, MANITOBA

I was hungry for something different, so I gave my Italian-style lasagna a Mexican accent. It's packed with tempting seasonings, and the cheese, green onions and ripe olives make an attractive topping.

1	pound lean ground beef
1	can (16 ounces) fat-free refried beans
2	teaspoons dried oregano
1	teaspoon ground cumin
3/4	teaspoon garlic powder
9	uncooked lasagna noodles
1	jar (16 ounces) salsa
2	cups water
2	cups (16 ounces) reduced-fat sour cream
1	can (2-1/4 ounces) sliced ripe olives, drained
1	cup (4 ounces) shredded reduced-fat Mexican-blend cheese
1/2	cup thinly sliced green onions

- In a nonstick skillet, cook beef over medium heat until no longer pink; drain. Add the refried beans, oregano, cumin and garlic powder; heat through.

- Place three noodles in a 13-in. x 9-in. baking dish coated with cooking spray; cover with half of the meat mixture. Repeat layers. Top with remaining noodles. Combine salsa and water; pour over noodles.

- Cover and bake at 350° for 60-70 minutes or until the noodles are tender. Spread with sour cream. Sprinkle with olives, cheese and onions.

YIELD: 9 servings.

NUTRITION FACTS: 1 piece equals 341 calories, 13 g fat (7 g saturated fat), 49 mg cholesterol, 680 mg sodium, 31 g carbohydrate, 4 g fiber, 24 g protein. **DIABETIC EXCHANGES:** 2 starch, 2 lean meat, 1-1/2 fat.

baked pork chimichangas

LaDonna Reed | PONCA CITY, OKLAHOMA

Because this recipe makes a lot, I can freeze extras for those nights when I don't feel like cooking.

1	pound dried pinto beans
1	boneless pork loin roast (3 pounds), trimmed
3	cans (4 ounces *each*) chopped green chilies
1	large onion, chopped
1/3	cup chili powder
1/2	cup reduced-sodium chicken broth
30	flour tortillas (6 inches)
4	cups (16 ounces) shredded reduced-fat cheddar cheese
2	cups picante sauce
1	egg white
2	teaspoons water

- Place the beans in a soup kettle; add water to cover by 2 in. Bring to a boil; boil for 2 minutes. Remove from the heat; cover and let stand for 1 hour. Drain and rinse beans, discarding liquid.

- Place roast in a Dutch oven. In a bowl, combine chilies, onion, chili powder and beans. Spoon over roast. Cover and bake at 325° for 1-1/2 hours. Stir in broth; cover and bake 30-45 minutes longer or until a meat thermometer reads 160°. Increase oven temperature to 350°.

BAKED PORK CHIMICHANGAS

276 CALORIES

- Remove meat and shred with two forks; set aside. Mash bean mixture; stir in shredded pork. Spoon 1/3 cup mixture down the center of each tortilla; top with picante sauce. Fold sides and ends over the filling and roll up. Place seam side down on two 15-in. x 10-in. x 1-in. baking pans coated with cooking spray.

- In a bowl, whisk egg white and water; brush over top. Bake, uncovered, at 350° for 25-30 minutes or until heated through. Serve immediately or cool, wrap and freeze for up to 3 months.

YIELD: 2-1/2 dozen.

NUTRITION FACTS: 1 chimichanga equals 276 calories, 8 g fat (4 g saturated fat), 36 mg cholesterol, 475 mg sodium, 30 g carbohydrate, 6 g fiber, 20 g protein. **DIABETIC EXCHANGES:** 2 starch, 2 lean meat.

262 CALORIES chicken with mustard gravy

A rich gravy made with honey mustard and sour cream drapes nicely over these golden-brown chicken breasts from our Test Kitchen.

4	boneless skinless chicken breast halves (6 ounces *each*)
1/2	teaspoon salt, *divided*
1/4	teaspoon pepper, *divided*
2	tablespoons reduced-fat butter
4	teaspoons honey mustard
1	tablespoon milk
1/2	teaspoon dried basil
1/2	teaspoon dried parsley flakes
1/2	cup reduced-fat sour cream

- Rub chicken with 1/4 teaspoon salt and 1/8 teaspoon pepper. In a large skillet over medium heat, cook chicken in butter for 6-8 minutes on each side or until no longer pink. Remove and keep warm.

- In the same skillet, combine the mustard, milk, basil, parsley, and remaining salt and pepper. Cook and stir over low heat until heated through. Remove from the heat; stir in sour cream. Serve with chicken.

YIELD: 4 servings.

NUTRITION FACTS: 1 chicken breast half with 2 tablespoons gravy equals 262 calories, 10 g fat (5 g saturated fat), 115 mg cholesterol, 476 mg sodium, 5 g carbohydrate, trace fiber, 37 g protein. **DIABETIC EXCHANGES:** 4 very lean meat, 2-1/2 fat.

SWISS STEAK

swiss steak

Betty Richardson | SPRINGFIELD, ILLINOIS

Here's a low-cal dinner that takes up very little time. We like it with mashed potatoes, rice or noodles. Add a green salad and supper is set.

- 4 **beef cube steaks (4 ounces *each*)**
- 1 **tablespoon canola oil**
- 1 **medium onion, chopped**
- 1 **celery rib with leaves, chopped**
- 1 **garlic clove, minced**
- 1 **can (14-1/2 ounces) stewed tomatoes, cut up**
- 1 **can (8 ounces) tomato sauce**
- 1 **teaspoon beef bouillon granules**
- 1 **tablespoon cornstarch**
- 2 **tablespoons cold water**

- In a large nonstick skillet, brown cube steaks on both sides in oil over medium-high heat; remove and set aside. In the same skillet, saute the onion, celery and garlic for 3-4 minutes or until tender. Add the tomatoes, tomato sauce and bouillon. Return steaks to the pan. Bring to a boil. Reduce heat; cover and simmer for 1-1/4 to 1-3/4 hours or until meat is tender.

- Combine cornstarch and water until smooth; stir into tomato mixture. Bring to a boil; cook and stir for 2 minutes or until thickened.

YIELD: 4 servings.

NUTRITION FACTS: 1 steak with 3/4 cup sauce equals 255 calories, 8 g fat (2 g saturated fat), 65 mg cholesterol, 746 mg sodium, 18 g carbohydrate, 3 g fiber, 28 g protein. **DIABETIC EXCHANGES:** 3 lean meat, 3 vegetable, 1/2 fat.

sausage spaghetti pie

Sue Ann O'Buck | SINKING SPRING, PENNSYLVANIA

This is a recipe that I adapted to our healthy lifestyle, with ingredients my family prefers. It is just wonderful and has been a big hit with my family and all who have tried it.

- 4 **ounces uncooked spaghetti**
- 1/2 **pound smoked turkey kielbasa, diced**
- 1 **cup garden-style spaghetti sauce**
- 1 **cup reduced-fat ricotta cheese**
- 3 **egg whites**
- 1/3 **cup grated Parmesan cheese**
- 1/4 **cup shredded part-skim mozzarella cheese**

- Cook spaghetti according to package directions. Meanwhile, in a small nonstick skillet, saute sausage for 3-4 minutes or until browned; stir in spaghetti sauce.

- In a small bowl, combine ricotta cheese and 1 egg white; set aside. Drain spaghetti; add Parmesan cheese and remaining egg whites. Press onto the bottom and up the sides of a 9-in. deep-dish pie plate coated with cooking spray. Spoon ricotta mixture into crust. Top with the sausage mixture.

- Bake, uncovered, at 350° for 20 minutes. Sprinkle with mozzarella cheese. Bake 5 minutes longer or until cheese is melted and filling is heated through. Let stand for 5 minutes before slicing.

YIELD: 4 servings.

NUTRITION FACTS: 1 piece equals 341 calories, 9 g fat (4 g saturated fat), 47 mg cholesterol, 980 mg sodium, 38 g carbohydrate, 2 g fiber, 24 g protein. **DIABETIC EXCHANGES:** 3 lean meat, 2 starch, 1 vegetable.

SAUSAGE SPAGHETTI PIE

346 CALORIES

SPINACH TUNA CASSEROLE

spinach tuna casserole

Karla Hamrick | WAPAKONETA, OHIO

A thick, gooey casserole has been a family favorite for years, but now we enjoy this lighter version.

- 5 cups uncooked egg noodles
- 1 cup (8 ounces) reduced-fat sour cream
- 1/2 cup fat-free mayonnaise
- 2 to 3 teaspoons lemon juice
- 2 tablespoons butter
- 1/4 cup all-purpose flour
- 2 cups fat-free milk
- 1/3 cup plus 2 tablespoons shredded Parmesan cheese, *divided*
- 1 package (10 ounces) frozen chopped spinach, thawed and squeezed dry
- 1 package (6 ounces) reduced-sodium chicken stuffing mix
- 1/3 cup seasoned bread crumbs
- 2 cans (6 ounces *each*) light water-packed tuna, drained and flaked

- Cook the noodles according to package directions. Meanwhile, in a small bowl, combine the sour cream, mayonnaise and lemon juice; set aside.

- In a large saucepan or Dutch oven, melt butter. Stir in flour until blended. Gradually stir in milk. Bring to a boil;

cook and stir for 2 minutes or until thickened. Reduce heat; stir in 1/3 cup Parmesan cheese until melted. Remove from the heat; stir in the sour cream mixture. Add the spinach, stuffing mix, bread crumbs and tuna; mix well.

- Drain noodles and place in a 13-in. x 9-in. baking dish coated with cooking spray. Top with the tuna mixture; sprinkle with remaining Parmesan cheese.

- Cover and bake at 350° for 35 minutes. Uncover; bake 5-10 minutes longer or until lightly browned and heated through.

YIELD: 8 servings.

NUTRITION FACTS: 1 serving equals 346 calories, 9 g fat (5 g saturated fat), 50 mg cholesterol, 734 mg sodium, 41 g carbohydrate, 2 g fiber, 24 g protein. **DIABETIC EXCHANGES:** 2-1/2 starch, 2 very lean meat, 1-1/2 fat.

two-cheese turkey enchiladas

Shelly Platten | AMHERST, WISCONSIN

Sour cream and cream cheese create a creamy filling for these yummy turkey enchiladas. The entree is always a huge hit with my family.

- 1 pound extra-lean ground turkey
- 1 large onion, chopped

TWO-CHEESE TURKEY ENCHILADAS

329 CALORIES

1/2 cup chopped green pepper

1 teaspoon brown sugar

1 teaspoon garlic powder

1 teaspoon ground cumin

1 teaspoon chili powder

1 can (28 ounces) crushed tomatoes, *divided*

1 package (8 ounces) reduced-fat cream cheese

1/4 cup fat-free sour cream

1 can (4 ounces) chopped green chilies

1 cup salsa

8 fat-free flour tortillas (8 inches), warmed

1/2 cup shredded reduced-fat cheddar cheese

- Crumble turkey into a large nonstick skillet; add the onion, green pepper, brown sugar and seasonings. Cook and stir over medium heat until turkey is no longer pink. Stir in 1 cup crushed tomatoes. Reduce heat; simmer, uncovered, for 10 minutes, stirring occasionally.

- In a small bowl, beat cream cheese, sour cream and chilies until blended; set aside. Combine salsa and remaining tomatoes; spread 1 cup into a 13-in. x 9-in. baking dish coated with cooking spray.

- Spoon about 3 tablespoons cream cheese mixture and 1/3 cup turkey mixture down the center of each tortilla. Roll up and place seam side down in baking dish. Top with remaining salsa mixture; sprinkle with cheddar cheese. Bake, uncovered, at 350° for 20-25 minutes or until bubbly.

YIELD: 8 servings.

NUTRITION FACTS: 1 enchilada equals 329 calories, 9 g fat (5 g saturated fat), 49 mg cholesterol, 776 mg sodium, 39 g carbohydrate, 5 g fiber, 24 g protein. **DIABETIC EXCHANGES:** 2 starch, 2 very lean meat, 2 vegetable, 1-1/2 fat.

ranch ham 'n' cheese pasta

Even though this pasta dish is lower in calories and fat than you'd expect, it is still rich-tasting, cheesy and satisfying. Our home economists relied on light ingredients and just a pinch of butter.

1 package (16 ounces) penne pasta

1 tablespoon butter

1 tablespoon all-purpose flour

1 cup fat-free milk

2 teaspoons dried parsley flakes

1 teaspoon garlic salt

1 teaspoon salt-free lemon-pepper seasoning

1/2 teaspoon garlic powder

1/2 teaspoon dried minced onion

1/2 teaspoon dill weed

1/4 teaspoon onion powder

1/8 teaspoon pepper

1 cup (8 ounces) reduced-fat sour cream

2 cups cubed fully cooked lean ham

1-1/2 cups (6 ounces) shredded reduced-fat Mexican cheese blend

1/4 cup shredded Parmesan cheese

- Cook pasta according to package directions; drain. In a Dutch oven, melt butter; whisk in flour until smooth. Gradually add milk and seasonings. Bring to a boil; cook and stir for 2 minutes or until thickened. Reduce heat; fold in sour cream until blended. Add ham and pasta; cook and stir until heated through. Remove from the heat; stir in Mexican cheese blend until melted. Sprinkle with Parmesan cheese.

YIELD: 10 servings.

NUTRITION FACTS: 1 cup equals 306 calories, 9 g fat (5 g saturated fat), 27 mg cholesterol, 612 mg sodium, 38 g carbohydrate, 2 g fiber, 20 g protein. **DIABETIC EXCHANGES:** 2-1/2 starch, 2 lean meat.

RANCH HAM 'N' CHEESE PASTA

306 CALORIES

351-450 calories

351 CALORIES

EASY ARROZ CON POLLO

easy arroz con pollo

Debbie Harris | TUCSON, ARIZONA

My children really look forward to dinner when they know I'm serving this. It's so simple to make, we enjoy it often at our house.

    1-3/4 cups uncooked instant rice
        6 boneless skinless chicken breast halves
Garlic salt and pepper to taste
        1 can (14-1/2 ounces) chicken broth
        1 cup picante sauce
        1 can (8 ounces) tomato sauce
      1/2 cup chopped onion
      1/2 cup chopped green pepper
      1/2 cup shredded Monterey Jack cheese
      1/2 cup shredded cheddar cheese

• Spread the rice in a greased 13-in. x 9-in. baking dish. Sprinkle both sides of the chicken with garlic salt and pepper; place over rice. In a bowl, combine the broth, picante sauce, tomato sauce, onion and green pepper; pour over the chicken.

• Cover and bake at 350° for 55 minutes or until the rice is tender and the chicken juices run clear. Sprinkle with

---

cheeses. Bake, uncovered, 5 minutes longer or until cheese is melted.

YIELD: 6 servings.

NUTRITION FACTS: 1 serving equals 351 calories, 9 g fat (5 g saturated fat), 91 mg cholesterol, 791 mg sodium, 30 g carbohydrate, 1 g fiber, 35 g protein.

oven fish 'n' chips

Janice Mitchell | AURORA, COLORADO

Crunchy fillets with a kick of cayenne and crispy potatoes are a quick and tasty light meal for two.

        1 tablespoon olive oil
      1/4 teaspoon pepper, *divided*
        2 medium potatoes, peeled
        3 tablespoons all-purpose flour
        1 egg
        1 tablespoon water
      1/3 cup crushed cornflakes
    1-1/2 teaspoons grated Parmesan cheese
Dash cayenne pepper
      1/2 pound fresh *or* frozen haddock fillets, thawed
Tartar sauce, optional

• In a large bowl, combine oil and 1/8 teaspoon pepper. Cut potatoes lengthwise into 1/2-in. strips. Add to oil mixture and toss to coat. Place on a baking sheet coated with cooking spray. Bake at 425° for 25-30 minutes or until golden brown and crisp.

• Meanwhile, in a shallow bowl, combine the flour and remaining pepper. In another shallow bowl, beat egg

OVEN FISH 'N' CHIPS

358 CALORIES

and water. In a third bowl, combine the cornflakes, Parmesan cheese and cayenne. Dredge fillets in flour, then dip in egg mixture and coat with crumbs.

- Place on a baking sheet coated with cooking spray. Bake at 425° for 10-15 minutes or until fish flakes easily with a fork. Serve with chips and tartar sauce if desired.

YIELD: 2 servings.

NUTRITION FACTS: 1 serving (calculated without tartar sauce) equals 358 calories, 10 g fat (2 g saturated fat), 131 mg cholesterol, 204 mg sodium, 39 g carbohydrate, 2 g fiber, 28 g protein. **DIABETIC EXCHANGES:** 3 very lean meat, 2-1/2 starch, 2 fat.

CREAMY PORK CHOP DINNER

creamy pork chop dinner

Joyce Valentine I SANFORD, COLORADO

Hearty and comforting, this meat-and-potatoes meal is full of homemade goodness...and it's easy to prepare. Sometimes I use chicken thighs instead of pork chops.

2	medium potatoes, peeled and cut into 1/4-inch slices
2	medium carrots, sliced
2	boneless pork loin chops (3/4 inch thick and 4 ounces *each*)
1	tablespoon onion soup mix
1-1/2	teaspoons cornstarch
1	can (10-3/4 ounces) ready-to-serve creamy chicken soup

- Place potatoes and carrots in a 1-qt. baking dish coated with cooking spray. In a skillet coated with cooking spray, brown pork chops on both sides. Place over vegetables.

- In a small bowl, combine the soup mix, cornstarch and soup until blended. Pour over pork chops. Cover and bake at 350° for 1 hour or until potatoes are tender.

YIELD: 2 servings.

NUTRITION FACTS: 1 serving equals 360 calories, 11 g fat (3 g saturated fat), 57 mg cholesterol, 807 mg sodium, 40 g carbohydrate, 6 g fiber, 27 g protein.

hearty lentil spaghetti

Marie Bender I HENDERSON, NEVADA

You won't miss the meat with this spaghetti sauce. Packed full of lentils and Italian flavors, the sauce is thick, hearty and zippy.

3/4	cup chopped onion
2	garlic cloves, minced
1	tablespoon olive oil
1-1/2	cups dried lentils, rinsed
4	cups vegetable broth
1/2	teaspoon pepper
1/4	teaspoon cayenne pepper
1	can (14-1/2 ounces) Italian diced tomatoes
1	can (6 ounces) tomato paste
1	teaspoon white vinegar
1-1/2	teaspoons dried basil
1-1/2	teaspoons dried oregano
12	ounces uncooked spaghetti
1/4	cup shredded Parmesan cheese

- In a large saucepan coated with cooking spray, cook onion and garlic in oil until tender. Stir in the lentils, broth, pepper and cayenne. Bring to a boil. Reduce heat; cover and simmer for 20-30 minutes or until lentils are tender.

- Stir in the tomatoes, tomato paste, vinegar, basil and oregano. Return to a boil. Reduce the heat; cover and simmer for 40-45 minutes.

- Cook spaghetti according to package directions; drain. Serve with lentil sauce. Sprinkle with Parmesan cheese.

YIELD: 8 servings.

NUTRITION FACTS: 3/4 cup sauce with 3/4 cup spaghetti equals 362 calories, 4 g fat (1 g saturated fat), 2 mg cholesterol, 764 mg sodium, 65 g carbohydrate, 14 g fiber, 19 g protein.

turkey fettuccine skillet

Kari Johnston | MARWAYNE, ALBERTA

I came up with this simple dish as a way to use leftover turkey after Thanksgiving and Christmas dinners. My children really enjoy it. Even with lighter ingredients, it's still comfort food at its best.

- 8 ounces uncooked fettuccine
- 1/2 cup chopped onion
- 1/2 cup chopped celery
- 4 garlic cloves, minced
- 1 teaspoon canola oil
- 1 cup sliced fresh mushrooms
- 2 cups fat-free milk
- 1 teaspoon salt-free seasoning blend
- 1/4 teaspoon salt
- 2 tablespoons cornstarch
- 1/2 cup fat-free half-and-half
- 1/3 cup grated Parmesan cheese
- 3 cups cubed cooked turkey breast
- 3/4 cup shredded part-skim mozzarella cheese

SHEPHERD'S PIE

390 CALORIES

TURKEY FETTUCCINE SKILLET

361 CALORIES

- Cook fettuccine according to package directions. Meanwhile, in a large ovenproof skillet coated with cooking spray, saute onion, celery and garlic in oil for 3 minutes. Add mushrooms; cook and stir until vegetables are tender. Stir in milk, seasoning blend and salt. Bring to a boil.
- Mix cornstarch and half-and-half until smooth; stir into skillet. Cook and stir for 2 minutes or until thickened and bubbly. Stir in Parmesan cheese just until melted.
- Stir in turkey. Drain fettuccine; add to turkey mixture. Heat through. Sprinkle with mozzarella cheese. Broil 4-6 in. from the heat for 2-3 minutes or until the cheese is melted.

YIELD: 6 servings.

NUTRITION FACTS: 1 cup equals 361 calories, 7 g fat (3 g saturated fat), 76 mg cholesterol, 343 mg sodium, 38 g carbohydrate, 2 g fiber, 34 g protein. **DIABETIC EXCHANGES:** 4 very lean meat, 2-1/2 starch, 1/2 fat.

shepherd's pie

Carolyn Wolbers | LOVELAND, OHIO

For a real meat-and-potatoes meal, try this satisfying layered casserole. It's easy to assemble with lean ground beef and mashed potatoes.

- 6 medium potatoes
- 1 pound carrots, cut into 1/4-inch slices
- 1-1/2 pounds lean ground beef
- 1 large onion, chopped

dinners | 351-450 CALORIES

1 jar (12 ounces) fat-free beef gravy

1 teaspoon salt, *divided*

1/2 teaspoon rubbed sage

1/2 teaspoon dried thyme

1/4 teaspoon dried rosemary, crushed

1/4 teaspoon pepper

1/3 cup fat-free milk

1 tablespoon butter

2 tablespoons shredded Parmesan cheese

- Peel and cube potatoes; place in a large saucepan and cover with water. Bring to a boil over medium-high heat; cover and cook for 20 minutes or until tender. Add 1 in. of water to another saucepan; add carrots. Bring to a boil. Reduce heat; cover and simmer until crisp-tender, about 7-9 minutes. Drain.

- In a large nonstick skillet, cook the beef and onion over medium heat until meat is no longer pink; drain. Stir in carrots, gravy, 1/2 teaspoon salt, sage, thyme, rosemary and pepper. Transfer to a shallow 3-qt. baking dish coated with cooking spray.

- Drain potatoes; mash with milk, butter and remaining salt. Spread over meat mixture. Sprinkle with Parmesan cheese. Bake, uncovered, at 375° for 40-45 minutes or until heated through.

YIELD: 6 servings.

NUTRITION FACTS: 1 serving equals 390 calories, 13 g fat (6 g saturated fat), 53 mg cholesterol, 859 mg sodium, 43 g carbohydrate, 6 g fiber, 30 g protein. **DIABETIC EXCHANGES:** 3 lean meat, 2 starch, 2 vegetable, 1/2 fat.

pork soft-shell tacos

Margaret Steele | NORTH VANCOUVER, BRITISH COLUMBIA
It's hard to find recipes that have enough flavor to satisfy my husband without overwhelming our kids. This Southwestern take on pork tenderloin earned a thumbs-up from them all!

1 pork tenderloin (1 pound), cut into 1-inch strips

1 small onion, chopped

1 teaspoon canola oil

SAUCE:

2/3 cup enchilada sauce

1 tablespoon dry roasted peanuts

1 tablespoon semisweet chocolate chips

PORK SOFT-SHELL TACOS

1 tablespoon raisins

1 garlic clove, minced

1 teaspoon ground cumin

1/4 teaspoon crushed red pepper flakes

1/2 cup frozen corn, thawed

8 corn tortillas (6 inches), warmed

1 cup shredded lettuce

1/4 cup reduced-fat sour cream

1/4 cup sliced green onions

- In a large nonstick skillet or wok, stir-fry pork and onion in oil for 3-4 minutes or until pork is no longer pink; drain and keep warm. In same skillet, combine the enchilada sauce, peanuts, chocolate chips, raisins, garlic, cumin and red pepper flakes. Cook and stir over medium heat for 2-3 minutes or until chocolate is melted.

- Pour into a blender; cover and process until smooth. Return to skillet. Stir in corn and pork mixture; cook until heated through.

- Spoon pork mixture down one half of each tortilla; fold remaining side over filling. Serve with lettuce, sour cream and green onions.

YIELD: 4 servings.

NUTRITION FACTS: 2 tacos equals 370 calories, 10 g fat (3 g saturated fat), 67 mg cholesterol, 263 mg sodium, 41 g carbohydrate, 5 g fiber, 30 g protein. **DIABETIC EXCHANGES:** 3 lean meat, 2-1/2 starch.

388 CALORIES

CRANBERRY PORK TENDERLOIN

cranberry pork tenderloin

Betty Helton | MELBOURNE, FLORIDA

I rely on a can of cranberry sauce to create the sweet sauce for this tender pork entree. I add orange juice and ground cloves to the mixture to season it nicely as it simmers in the slow cooker.

    1 pork tenderloin (1 pound)
    1 can (16 ounces) whole-berry cranberry sauce
  1/2 cup orange juice
  1/4 cup sugar
    1 tablespoon brown sugar
    1 teaspoon ground mustard
  1/4 to 1/2 teaspoon ground cloves
    2 tablespoons cornstarch
    3 tablespoons cold water

- Place the tenderloin in a 3-qt. slow cooker. Combine the cranberry sauce, orange juice, sugars, mustard and cloves; pour over pork. Cover and cook on low for 5-6 hours or until a meat thermometer reads 160°.

- Remove pork and keep warm. In a small bowl, combine cornstarch and cold water until smooth; gradually stir into cranberry mixture. Cover and cook on high for 15 minutes longer or until thickened. Serve with pork.

YIELD: 4 servings.

NUTRITION FACTS: 3 ounces cooked pork equals 388 calories, 4 g fat (1 g saturated fat), 63 mg cholesterol, 71 mg sodium, 65 g carbohydrate, 2 g fiber, 23 g protein.

barbecued smoked sausage and lima beans

Myrna Wingate | IRONS, MICHIGAN

There's a slightly sweet flavor to this filling blend of sausage, lima beans and tomatoes. The last time I made this dish, I used homemade sausage from a local store, and it was scrumptious!

    1 cup chopped sweet onion
    1 cup chopped green pepper
    4 garlic cloves, minced
    2 teaspoons olive oil
    1 package (16 ounces) reduced-fat fully cooked smoked Polish sausage, cut into 3/4 slices
    2 cans (14-1/2 ounces *each*) diced tomatoes, undrained
  1/2 cup packed brown sugar
  1/4 cup cider vinegar
1-1/2 teaspoons ground mustard
    1 teaspoon chili powder
  1/2 teaspoon ground ginger
  1/4 teaspoon salt
  1/4 teaspoon pepper
    2 packages (10 ounces *each*) frozen baby lima beans

Hot cooked rice

- In a large nonstick skillet, saute onion, green pepper and garlic in oil for 1 minute. Add sausage; cook and stir 4-5

BARBECUED SMOKED SAUSAGE AND LIMA BEANS

367 CALORIES

minutes longer or until sausage is lightly browned. Stir in tomatoes, brown sugar, vinegar, mustard, chili powder, ginger, salt and pepper. Bring to a boil. Stir in lima beans. Return to a boil. Reduce heat; cover and simmer for 10 minutes or until heated through. Serve over rice.

YIELD: 6 servings.

NUTRITION FACTS: 1-1/3 cups sausage mixture (calculated without rice) equals 367 calories, 9 g fat (4 g saturated fat), 41 mg cholesterol, 1,003 mg sodium, 53 g carbohydrate, 6 g fiber, 21 g protein.

tomato-basil chicken spirals

Sandra Giguere | BREMEN, MAINE

After tasting a comforting pasta dish at an Italian restaurant, I experimented until I came up with this recipe. It's become one of our favorite healthy meals. The riper the tomatoes, the better it is!

- 2 cups finely chopped sweet onions
- 1 cup chopped fresh basil
- 4 garlic cloves, minced
- 1 tablespoon olive oil
- 5 cups chopped seeded tomatoes
- 1 can (6 ounces) tomato paste
- 1/2 teaspoon crushed red pepper flakes
- 1/2 teaspoon salt
- 1/4 teaspoon pepper
- 1 package (16 ounces) spiral pasta
- 3 cups cubed cooked chicken
- 1/2 cup shredded Parmesan cheese

- In a large saucepan or Dutch oven, saute the onion, basil and garlic in oil until onions are tender. Stir in the tomatoes, tomato paste, red pepper flakes, salt and pepper. Bring to a boil. Reduce heat; cover and simmer for 30-45 minutes.

- Meanwhile, cook the pasta according to the package directions. Add chicken to the tomato mixture; heat through. Drain pasta. Top with chicken mixture; sprinkle with Parmesan cheese.

YIELD: 8 servings.

NUTRITION FACTS: 1 cup chicken mixture with 1 cup pasta equals 373 calories, 6 g fat (2 g saturated fat), 44 mg cholesterol, 291 mg sodium, 53 g carbohydrate, 5 g fiber, 27 g protein. **DIABETIC EXCHANGES:** 3 vegetable, 2-1/2 starch, 2 lean meat.

chicken bulgur skillet

Leann Hillmer | SYLVAN GROVE, KANSAS

This recipe was passed on to me by a friend and I've altered it slightly to suit our tastes. We like it with a fresh green salad.

- 1 pound boneless skinless chicken breasts, cut into 1-inch cubes
- 2 teaspoons olive oil
- 2 medium carrots, chopped
- 2/3 cup chopped onion
- 3 tablespoons chopped walnuts
- 1/2 teaspoon caraway seeds
- 1/4 teaspoon ground cumin
- 1-1/2 cups bulgur
- 2 cups reduced-sodium chicken broth
- 2 tablespoons raisins
- 1/4 teaspoon salt
- 1/8 teaspoon ground cinnamon

- In a large nonstick skillet, cook chicken in oil over medium-high heat until meat is no longer pink. Remove and keep warm. In the same skillet, cook and stir the carrots, onion, nuts, caraway seeds and cumin for 3-4 minutes or until onion starts to brown.

- Stir in bulgur. Gradually add broth; bring to a boil over medium heat. Reduce heat; add raisins, salt, cinnamon and chicken. Cover and simmer for 12-15 minutes or until bulgur is tender.

YIELD: 4 servings.

NUTRITION FACTS: 1-1/2 cups equals 412 calories, 8 g fat (1 g saturated fat), 66 mg cholesterol, 561 mg sodium, 51 g carbohydrate, 12 g fiber, 36 g protein. **DIABETIC EXCHANGES:** 3 lean meat, 2-1/2 starch, 2 vegetable.

CHICKEN BULGUR SKILLET

sweet potato ham casserole

Barbara Smith | CANNON FALLS, MINNESOTA

If you like sweet potatoes, here's a great way to serve them. I think of the marshmallows on top as dessert!

- 1 large sweet potato, about (10 ounces)
- 1/4 cup water
- 1 fully cooked reduced-sodium ham slice (1/2 pound and 3/4 inch thick)
- 1 tablespoon reduced-fat butter
- 1/3 cup unsweetened pineapple juice
- 2 tablespoons packed brown sugar
- 1 can (8 ounces) pineapple chunks, drained
- 1/3 cup miniature marshmallows

- Peel the sweet potato and cut into chunks. Place in a microwave-safe dish; add water. Cover and microwave on high for 7-9 minutes or until tender; drain and set aside.

- Cut ham into two pieces. In a skillet, brown ham in butter on both sides. In a bowl, combine pineapple juice and brown sugar; stir until sugar is dissolved. Pour over ham. Bring to a boil. Reduce heat; simmer, uncovered, for 5-7 minutes or until slightly thickened.

- Transfer ham to a greased shallow 1-qt. baking dish. Place the sweet potato and pineapple around edge of dish. Pour brown sugar mixture over the top. Bake, uncovered, at 400° for 12-15 minutes or until heated through. Sprinkle marshmallows around edge. Bake 3-5 minutes longer or until marshmallows are golden brown.

SWEET POTATO HAM CASSEROLE

438 CALORIES

YIELD: 2 servings.

EDITOR'S NOTE: This recipe was tested in a 1,100-watt microwave.

NUTRITION FACTS: 4 ounces cooked ham with 1-1/4 cups potato mixture equals 438 calories, 9 g fat (4 g saturated fat), 70 mg cholesterol, 1,159 mg sodium, 64 g carbohydrate, 3 g fiber, 26 g protein.

389 CALORIES

SEAFOOD 'N' SHELLS CASSEROLE

seafood 'n' shells casserole

Our home economists found that poaching the cod before baking prevents it from watering out this comforting casserole. With pasta and vegetables, the satisfying dish will warm you up.

- 6 cups water
- 1 teaspoon lemon-pepper seasoning
- 1 bay leaf
- 2 pounds cod fillets, cut into 1-inch pieces
- 1 cup uncooked small pasta shells
- 1 *each* medium green and sweet red pepper, chopped
- 1 medium onion, chopped
- 1 tablespoon butter
- 3 tablespoons all-purpose flour
- 2-1/2 cups fat-free evaporated milk
- 3/4 teaspoon salt
- 1/2 teaspoon dried thyme
- 1/4 teaspoon pepper
- 1 cup (4 ounces) shredded Mexican cheese blend

- In a large skillet or Dutch oven, bring the water, lemon-pepper and bay leaf to a boil. Reduce heat; carefully add the cod. Cover and simmer for 5-8 minutes or until the fish flakes easily with a fork; drain and set aside. Discard bay leaf.

- Cook pasta according to package directions. Meanwhile, in a large saucepan, saute peppers and onion in butter over medium heat until tender. Stir in the flour until blended. Gradually stir in the milk. Bring to a boil; cook and stir for 2 minutes or until thickened. Stir in the salt, thyme and pepper. Remove from heat; stir in the cheese until melted.

- Drain pasta. Stir fish and pasta into sauce. Transfer to a 2-qt. baking dish coated with cooking spray. Cover and bake at 350° for 25-30 minutes or until heated through.

YIELD: 6 servings.

NUTRITION FACTS: 1 cup equals 389 calories, 9 g fat (6 g saturated fat), 83 mg cholesterol, 732 mg sodium, 35 g carbohydrate, 2 g fiber, 39 g protein. **DIABETIC EXCHANGES:** 3 very lean meat, 1-1/2 fat, 1 starch, 1 vegetable, 1 fat-free milk.

italian beef

386 CALORIES

Lori Hayes | VENICE, FLORIDA

I make this beef in the slow cooker when I'm having a party so I don't have to spend the whole time in the kitchen. The meat smells so delicious, I can hardly keep my husband from helping himself ahead of time!

- 1 boneless beef top round roast (4 pounds)
- 2 cups water
- 2 tablespoons Italian seasoning
- 1 teaspoon *each* salt, dried oregano, dried basil, garlic powder, dried parsley flakes and pepper
- 1 bay leaf
- 14 French rolls (5 inches long)

- Cut roast in half; place in a 5-qt. slow cooker. Combine the water and seasonings; pour over roast. Cover and cook on low for 10-12 hours or until meat is very tender. Discard bay leaf. Remove meat and shred with a fork. Skim fat from cooking juices; return meat to slow cooker. Serve on rolls.

YIELD: 14 servings.

NUTRITION FACTS: 3 ounces cooked beef and 1/4 cup juice with roll equals 386 calories, 11 g fat (5 g saturated fat), 80 mg cholesterol, 557 mg sodium, 36 g carbohydrate, 2 g fiber, 34 g protein. **DIABETIC EXCHANGES:** 3 lean meat, 2-1/2 starch.

macaroni and cheese

Cora Johnson Schloetzer | TOPEKA, KANSAS

When my husband had heart problems, I searched for recipes that replaced our full-fat standbys. Over the years, I've updated this recipe to take advantage of low-fat products, and my family continues to enjoy it.

- 3 cups uncooked elbow macaroni
- 12 ounces reduced-fat process cheese (Velveeta), sliced
- 1/2 cup finely chopped onion
- 1/3 cup all-purpose flour
- 2 teaspoons ground mustard
- 1/8 teaspoon pepper
- 1 can (12 ounces) fat-free evaporated milk
- 1-1/4 cups fat-free milk
- 1/2 cup dry bread crumbs
- 2 tablespoons butter, melted

- Cook macaroni according to package directions; drain. In a 13-in. x 9-in. baking dish coated with cooking spray, layer a third of the macaroni, half of the cheese and half of the onion. Repeat layers. Top with remaining macaroni.

- In a bowl, combine the flour, mustard, pepper, evaporated milk and milk; pour over layers. Combine bread crumbs and butter; sprinkle over top.

- Cover and bake at 375° for 20 minutes. Uncover; bake 15 minutes longer or until bubbly. Let stand for 10 minutes before serving.

YIELD: 8 servings.

NUTRITION FACTS: 3/4 cup equals 353 calories, 7 g fat (4 g saturated fat), 25 mg cholesterol, 161 mg sodium, 48 g carbohydrate, 2 g fiber, 22 g protein.

MACARONI AND CHEESE

353 CALORIES

363 CALORIES

CORNY CHICKEN WRAPS

corny chicken wraps

Susan Alverson | CHESTER, SOUTH DAKOTA

I'm a clinical dietitian, so I like to prepare foods that are both healthy and lower in calories. This zippy Tex-Mex wrap is a quick alternative to a taco or sandwich for our on-the-go family. To increase the spiciness, use a medium or hot salsa.

1	pound boneless skinless chicken breasts, cut into strips
1/2	cup chopped green pepper
1/4	cup chopped green onions
2	teaspoons canola oil
1-1/2	cups frozen whole kernel corn, thawed
1-1/2	cups salsa
1/4	cup sliced ripe olives
1/2	teaspoon chili powder
6	flour tortillas (8 inches), warmed
1	cup (4 ounces) shredded reduced-fat cheddar cheese

• In a nonstick skillet, saute chicken, green pepper and onions in oil for 3-4 minutes or until chicken juices run clear; drain. Stir in corn, salsa, olives and chili powder.

Cook and stir over medium heat for 3-4 minutes or until heated through.

• Spoon about 1/2 cup chicken mixture over one side of each tortilla. Sprinkle with cheese; roll up and secure with toothpicks.

YIELD: 6 servings.

NUTRITION FACTS: 1 wrap equals 363 calories, 11 g fat (4 g saturated fat), 55 mg cholesterol, 740 mg sodium, 38 g carbohydrate, 4 g fiber, 26 g protein. **DIABETIC EXCHANGES:** 3 lean meat, 2-1/2 starch.

mushroom turkey tetrazzini

Linda Howe | LISLE, ILLINOIS

This creamy, comforting casserole makes a fantastic way to use up leftover turkey. And it's a real family pleaser that won't pack on pounds.

12	ounces uncooked spaghetti, broken into 2-inch pieces
2	teaspoons chicken bouillon granules

MUSHROOM TURKEY TETRAZZINI

362 CALORIES

- 1/2 pound sliced fresh mushrooms
- 2 tablespoons butter
- 2 tablespoons all-purpose flour
- 1/4 cup sherry *or* reduced-sodium chicken broth
- 3/4 teaspoon salt-free lemon-pepper seasoning
- 1/2 teaspoon salt
- 1/8 teaspoon ground nutmeg
- 1 cup fat-free evaporated milk
- 2/3 cup grated Parmesan cheese, *divided*
- 4 cups cubed cooked turkey breast
- 1/4 teaspoon paprika

- Cook spaghetti according to package directions. Drain, reserving 2-1/2 cups cooking liquid. Stir bouillon into cooking liquid and set aside. Place spaghetti in a 13-in. x 9-in. baking dish coated with cooking spray; set aside.

- In a large nonstick skillet, saute the mushrooms in butter until tender. Stir in flour until blended. Gradually stir in sherry or broth and reserved cooking liquid. Add the lemon-pepper, salt and nutmeg. Bring to a boil; cook and stir for 2 minutes or until thickened.

- Reduce heat to low; stir in milk and 1/3 cup Parmesan cheese until blended. Add the turkey; cook and stir until heated through.

- Pour turkey mixture over spaghetti and toss to combine. Sprinkle with paprika and remaining Parmesan cheese. Cover and bake at 375° for 25-30 minutes or until bubbly.

YIELD: 8 servings.

NUTRITION FACTS: 1 cup equals 362 calories, 7 g fat (3 g saturated fat), 75 mg cholesterol, 592 mg sodium, 40 g carbohydrate, 2 g fiber, 33 g protein. **DIABETIC EXCHANGES:** 3 starch, 3 very lean meat, 1/2 fat.

catfish po'boys

Mildred Sherrer | FORT WORTH, TEXAS

When my neighbor prepared these large full-flavored sandwiches, I had to have the recipe. Strips of catfish are treated to a zesty Cajun cornmeal breading, then served on a bun with packaged broccoli coleslaw mix dressed in a homemade sauce.

- 2 tablespoons fat-free mayonnaise
- 1 tablespoon fat-free sour cream
- 1 tablespoon white wine vinegar
- 1 teaspoon sugar
- 2 cups broccoli coleslaw mix
- 1/4 cup cornmeal
- 2 teaspoons Cajun seasoning
- 1/2 teaspoon salt
- 1/8 teaspoon cayenne pepper
- 2 tablespoons fat-free milk
- 1 pound catfish fillets, cut into 2-1/2-inch strips
- 2 teaspoons olive oil
- 4 kaiser rolls, split

- In a small bowl, whisk mayonnaise, sour cream, vinegar and sugar until smooth. Add coleslaw mix; toss to coat. Set aside.

- In a large resealable plastic bag, combine the cornmeal, Cajun seasoning, salt and cayenne. Place the milk in a shallow bowl. Dip a few pieces of fish at a time in milk mixture, then place in bag; seal and shake to coat.

- In a large nonstick skillet, cook catfish over medium heat in oil for 4-5 minutes on each side or until the fish flakes easily with a fork and coating is golden brown. Spoon coleslaw onto rolls; top with catfish.

YIELD: 4 servings.

NUTRITION FACTS: 1 sandwich equals 364 calories, 8 g fat (1 g saturated fat), 53 mg cholesterol, 1,001 mg sodium, 44 g carbohydrate, 4 g fiber, 28 g protein. **DIABETIC EXCHANGES:** 3 starch, 2-1/2 lean meat.

CATFISH PO'BOYS

364 CALORIES

side dishes

Nothing rounds out a meal like a savory side. Mashed potatoes, buttery noodles and more are within reach if you keep calories in mind. Pair any of these recipes with a main course (pages 158-239). No matter which combination you choose, keep complete dinners to about 500 calories.

246   253   251

The first section in this chapter features low-calorie side dishes, making it a breeze to plan menus. Some of the dishes are wonderful main courses, too. Consider Creamy Macaroni 'n' Cheese on page 263 for a meatless entree.

SESAME BROCCOLI

48 CALORIES

sesame broccoli

Janice Cawman | YAKIMA, WASHINGTON

This tasty broccoli dish has become a favorite at our house. It's fast, easy and adds a colorful presentation to any menu. Plus, it inspires my family to eat lots of healthy broccoli.

- 1 pound fresh broccoli, cut into spears
- 1 tablespoon reduced-sodium soy sauce
- 2 teaspoons olive oil
- 2 teaspoons balsamic vinegar
- 1-1/2 teaspoons honey
- 2 teaspoons sesame seeds, toasted

- Place broccoli in a steamer basket; place in a saucepan over 1 in. of water. Bring to a boil; cover and steam for 10-15 minutes or until crisp-tender. Meanwhile, in a small saucepan, combine the soy sauce, oil, vinegar and honey; cook and stir over medium-low heat until heated through.

- Transfer broccoli to a serving bowl; drizzle with soy sauce mixture. Sprinkle with sesame seeds.

YIELD: 6 servings.

NUTRITION FACTS: 3/4 cup equals 48 calories, 2 g fat (trace saturated fat), 0 cholesterol, 127 mg sodium, 6 g carbohydrate, 2 g fiber, 3 g protein. **DIABETIC EXCHANGES:** 1 vegetable, 1/2 fat.

flavorful summer squash

Andrea Yacyk | BRIGANTINE, NEW JERSEY

Sauteed squash with garlic, red onion and herbs is the right combination for garden-fresh goodness. Sprinkled with cheese, it makes a bright side dish that's quick to fix and delicious to eat.

- 3 medium yellow summer squash, sliced
- 2 medium zucchini, sliced
- 1 medium red onion, sliced and separated into rings
- 1 teaspoon minced garlic
- 1 tablespoon olive oil
- 1 teaspoon dried parsley flakes
- 1 teaspoon dried basil
- 1/2 teaspoon dried oregano
- 1/2 teaspoon dried thyme
- 1/4 teaspoon salt
- 1/2 cup shredded part-skim mozzarella cheese

- In a large nonstick skillet, saute the yellow squash, zucchini, onion and garlic in oil until crisp-tender, stirring occasionally.

- Stir in the parsley, basil, oregano, thyme and salt. Remove from the heat. Sprinkle with cheese; cover and let stand until cheese is melted.

YIELD: 6 servings.

NUTRITION FACTS: 2/3 cup equals 83 calories, 4 g fat (1 g saturated fat), 5 mg cholesterol, 147 mg sodium, 9 g carbohydrate, 3 g fiber, 5 g protein. **DIABETIC EXCHANGES:** 2 vegetable, 1/2 fat.

FLAVORFUL SUMMER SQUASH

83 CALORIES

54 CALORIES

PARMESAN TOMATOES

parmesan tomatoes

Marcia Orlando | BOYERTOWN, PENNSYLVANIA

What a great way to use up all those fresh garden tomatoes, and what a simple but scrumptious side dish for entrees of all kinds! This quick and easy recipe is sure to become a summer standard at your house.

- 3 large tomatoes
- 1 tablespoon chicken bouillon granules
- 1/4 cup grated Parmesan cheese
- 1 tablespoon butter

- Remove stems from tomatoes; cut in half widthwise. Place cut side up in an 11-in. x 7-in. baking dish coated with cooking spray.
- Sprinkle with bouillon and Parmesan cheese; dot with butter. Bake, uncovered, at 400° for 20-25 minutes or until heated through.

YIELD: 6 servings.

NUTRITION FACTS: 1 tomato half equals 54 calories, 3 g fat (2 g saturated fat), 8 mg cholesterol, 510 mg sodium, 5 g carbohydrate, 1 g fiber, 2 g protein. **DIABETIC EXCHANGES:** 1 vegetable, 1/2 fat.

68 CALORIES ## roasted italian vegetables

This buttery medley of oven-baked vegetables is ideal with fish or any meat. Zucchini and orange pepper make it colorful, but our home economists suggest trying yellow summer squash or red or green pepper instead.

- 1 medium zucchini, cut into 1/4-inch slices
- 1-1/2 cups sliced baby portobello mushrooms
- 1 medium sweet orange pepper, julienned
- 1 tablespoon olive oil
- 1 tablespoon reduced-fat butter, melted
- 1 teaspoon Italian seasoning
- 1/2 teaspoon salt
- 1/8 teaspoon pepper

- In a large bowl, combine zucchini, mushrooms and orange pepper. Add remaining ingredients and toss to coat.
- Arrange the vegetables in a single layer in a 15-in. x 10-in. x 1-in. baking pan coated with cooking spray. Bake, uncovered, at 450° for 15-20 minutes or until tender, stirring occasionally.

YIELD: 4 servings.

NUTRITION FACTS: 1/2 cup equals 68 calories, 5 g fat (1 g saturated fat), 5 mg cholesterol, 316 mg sodium, 5 g carbohydrate, 2 g fiber, 2 g protein. **DIABETIC EXCHANGES:** 1 vegetable, 1 fat.

66 CALORIES

BAKED SWEET ONION RINGS

baked sweet onion rings

Tonya Vowels | VINE GROVE, KENTUCKY

These are a real family favorite—especially when Vidalias are in season. You can boost the flavor even more with seasoned breadcrumbs or a shake or two of different spices.

1/2 cup egg substitute
2/3 cup dry bread crumbs
1/2 teaspoon salt
1/4 teaspoon pepper
1 sweet onion, sliced and separated into rings

- Place egg substitute in a shallow dish. In another shallow dish, combine the bread crumbs, salt and pepper. Dip onion rings into egg, then roll in crumb mixture.

- Place on a baking sheet coated with cooking spray. Bake at 425° for 15-18 minutes or until golden brown, turning once.

YIELD: 4 servings.

NUTRITION FACTS: 1 serving equals 66 calories, 1 g fat (trace saturated fat), 0 cholesterol, 312 mg sodium, 12 g carbohydrate, 1 g fiber, 3 g protein. **DIABETIC EXCHANGE:** 1 starch.

lemon-pepper vegetables

49 CALORIES

Here's a colorful side dish that's sure to brighten up any dinner table. Our Test Kitchen staff thinks the mild seasoning lets the veggies' delightful flavors shine.

1 pound fresh green beans, trimmed and cut into 2-inch pieces
2 tablespoons water
1 small yellow summer squash, cut into 1/2-inch slices
1 cup halved cherry tomatoes
2 tablespoons reduced-fat butter
3/4 teaspoon lemon-pepper seasoning
1/4 teaspoon Italian seasoning

- In a large microwave-safe bowl, combine green beans and water. Cover and microwave on high for 5-6 minutes or until crisp-tender.

- Stir in the squash. Cover and microwave on high for 2 minutes. Add tomatoes. Cover and cook 30 seconds longer or until heated through; drain. Gently stir in the butter, lemon-pepper and Italian seasoning.

YIELD: 6 servings.

EDITOR'S NOTE: This recipe was tested in a 1,100-watt microwave.

NUTRITION FACTS: 2/3 cup equals 49 calories, 2 g fat (1 g saturated fat), 7 mg cholesterol, 88 mg sodium, 7 g carbohydrate, 3 g fiber, 2 g protein. **DIABETIC EXCHANGES:** 1 vegetable, 1/2 fat.

colorful roasted veggies

Diane Harrison | MECHANICSBURG, PENNSYLVANIA

My mom serves this delicious vegetable dish, which is pleasantly flavored with rosemary. It's my favorite, and it goes with so many main courses.

4 medium carrots, julienned
1-1/2 pounds fresh asparagus, trimmed and halved
1 large green pepper, julienned
1 medium sweet red pepper, julienned
1 medium red onion, sliced and separated into rings
5 cups fresh cauliflowerets
5 cups fresh broccoli florets
1/4 cup olive oil
3 tablespoons lemon juice
3 garlic cloves, minced
1 tablespoon dried rosemary, crushed
1 teaspoon salt
1 teaspoon pepper

- In a large bowl, combine vegetables. In a small bowl, whisk oil, lemon juice, garlic, rosemary, salt and pepper until blended. Drizzle over vegetables and toss to coat.

- Transfer to two greased 15-in. x 10-in. x 1-in. baking pans. Bake, uncovered, at 400° for 20-25 minutes or until tender, stirring occasionally.

YIELD: 12 servings.

NUTRITION FACTS: 3/4 cup equals 88 calories, 5 g fat (1 g saturated fat), 0 cholesterol, 228 mg sodium, 10 g carbohydrate, 4 g fiber, 3 g protein. **DIABETIC EXCHANGES:** 2 vegetable, 1 fat.

COLORFUL ROASTED VEGGIES

88 CALORIES

74 CALORIES

SAVORY ASPARAGUS

savory asparagus

Fresh asparagus dresses up a weeknight meal with aromatic tarragon. This treatment, from our Test Kitchen, also tastes great when broccoli replaces the asparagus. Try it tonight!

  1 pound fresh asparagus, trimmed
  2 tablespoons olive oil
1/4 to 1/2 teaspoon dried tarragon
1/4 teaspoon onion powder
1/8 teaspoon pepper

- In a large skillet, bring 1/2 in. of water to a boil. Add asparagus; cover and cook for 5-7 minutes or until crisp-tender, stirring occasionally.

- Meanwhile, in a small bowl, combine the oil, tarragon, onion powder and pepper until blended. Drain asparagus; drizzle with oil mixture and toss to coat.

YIELD: 4 servings.

NUTRITION FACTS: 1 serving equals 74 calories, 7 g fat (1 g saturated fat), 0 cholesterol, 6 mg sodium, 3 g carbohydrate, 1 g fiber, 1 g protein. DIABETIC EXCHANGES: 1 vegetable, 1 fat.

100 CALORIES

pea pod carrot medley

Josie Smith | WINAMAC, INDIANA

We grow pea pods, and I wanted to use them in something other than stir-fries...this fits the bill! I've taken a bigger batch to church potlucks and received compliments on its pretty orange glaze and fresh taste.

  1 cup sliced carrots
  2 cups fresh sugar snap peas
  1 teaspoon cornstarch
1/3 cup orange juice
  2 teaspoons reduced-sodium soy sauce
1/2 teaspoon grated orange peel
1/4 teaspoon salt

- Place carrots in a small saucepan; cover with water. Bring to a boil. Reduce heat; cover and simmer for 5 minutes. Add the peas. Cover and simmer 2-4 minutes longer or until vegetables are crisp-tender. Drain; set aside and keep warm.

- In the same saucepan, whisk the cornstarch and orange juice until smooth. Bring to a boil; cook and stir for 2 minutes or until thickened. Stir in the soy sauce, orange peel and salt. Pour over vegetables; toss to coat.

YIELD: 2 servings.

NUTRITION FACTS: 1 cup equals 100 calories, trace fat (trace saturated fat), 0 cholesterol, 517 mg sodium, 21 g carbohydrate, 6 g fiber, 4 g protein. DIABETIC EXCHANGES: 2 vegetable, 1/2 fruit.

53 CALORIES

orange broccoli florets

Paula Kenny | NEW HUDSON, MICHIGAN

This light side dish appears regularly on my dinner table. The citrus flavor makes the easy broccoli dish seem extra special.

1-1/2 cups fresh broccoli florets
  2 teaspoons reduced-fat butter
1-1/2 teaspoons all-purpose flour
1/4 cup orange juice
1/2 teaspoon grated orange peel

- Place broccoli and 1 in. of water in a saucepan; bring to a boil. Reduce heat; cover and simmer for 5-8 minutes or until crisp-tender. Meanwhile, in a small saucepan, melt butter. Stir in flour until smooth. Gradually stir in orange juice. Bring to a boil; cook and stir for 1 minute or until thickened. Stir in orange peel. Drain broccoli; add orange juice mixture and toss to coat.

YIELD: 2 servings.

NUTRITION FACTS: 1/2 cup equals 53 calories, 2 g fat (1 g saturated fat), 7 mg cholesterol, 38 mg sodium, 8 g carbohydrate, 2 g fiber, 2 g protein.

pineapple cabbage saute

This dish works well with thinly sliced cabbage, so our home economists think it's best not to use a shredder. Try it with pork for a no-fuss dinner.

- 1 can (8 ounces) crushed pineapple
- 6 cups thinly sliced cabbage
- 1 tablespoon olive oil
- 2 tablespoons honey mustard salad dressing
- 1/8 teaspoon white pepper

- Drain pineapple, reserving 1 tablespoon juice; set aside. In a large skillet, saute cabbage in oil for 5-8 minutes or until crisp-tender. Add the salad dressing, pepper and reserved pineapple and juice. Cook for 1 minute or until heated through.

YIELD: 6 servings.

PINEAPPLE CABBAGE SAUTE

85 CALORIES

NUTRITION FACTS: 3/4 cup equals 85 calories, 4 g fat (1 g saturated fat), 0 cholesterol, 48 mg sodium, 12 g carbohydrate, 2 g fiber, 1 g protein.

ribboned vegetables

67 CALORIES

Julie Gwinn | HERSHEY, PENNSYLVANIA

Make the most of summer produce with this effortless recipe. These colorful veggie strips, sauteed in lemon and horseradish, will add zip to any menu.

- 2 medium carrots
- 2 small zucchini
- 2 small yellow summer squash
- 1 tablespoon butter
- 2 teaspoons lemon juice
- 1 teaspoon prepared horseradish
- 1/2 teaspoon salt
- 1/8 teaspoon pepper

- With a vegetable peeler or metal cheese slicer, cut very thin slices down the length of each carrot, zucchini and yellow squash, making long ribbons.
- In a large skillet, saute vegetables in butter for 2 minutes. Stir in remaining ingredients. Cook 2-4 minutes longer or until vegetables are crisp-tender, stirring occasionally.

YIELD: 4 servings.

NUTRITION FACTS: 3/4 cup equals 67 calories, 3 g fat (2 g saturated fat), 8 mg cholesterol, 342 mg sodium, 9 g carbohydrate, 4 g fiber, 2 g protein. **DIABETIC EXCHANGES:** 2 vegetable, 1/2 fat.

Here are some typical side dishes and the amount of calories in them so you can determine how to stay within your goal of a 500-calorie dinner.

- **1/2 cup cooked long-grain brown rice,** 108 calories
- **1/2 cup cooked long-grain white rice,** 103 calories
- **1 cup cooked egg noodles,** 221 calories

- **1 cup cooked spaghetti,** 182 calories
- **1 cup cooked whole wheat spaghetti,** 176 calories
- **1/2 cup canned corn,** 83 calories

- **1 small baked russet potato,** 138 calories
- **1 small baked sweet potato,** 128 calories
- **1/2 cup canned peas,** 59 calories

For the calorie counts of other side items, see the Free Foods Chart on page 45 and the Smart Snacks List on page 71. For additional calorie calculations, check the Nutrition Facts labels on food packages.

59 CALORIES

SAVORY GREEN BEANS

savory green beans

Carol Ann Hayden | EVERSON, WASHINGTON

Not only are these green beans low in calories and fat, but they go well with just about any main course. This was my mother's favorite way to fix green beans. She always grew savory in her garden and used it to give this dish lots of fresh flavor.

3/4	cup chopped sweet red pepper
1	garlic clove, minced
1	tablespoon canola oil
1-1/2	pounds fresh green beans, trimmed and cut into 2-inch pieces
1/2	cup water
2	tablespoons minced fresh savory *or* 2 teaspoons dried savory
1	tablespoon minced chives
1/2	teaspoon salt

• In a large skillet, saute red pepper and garlic in oil for 2-3 minutes or until tender. Add green beans, water, savory, chives and salt. Bring to a boil. Reduce heat; cover and simmer for 8-10 minutes or until beans are crisp-tender.

YIELD: 6 servings.

NUTRITION FACTS: 3/4 cup equals 59 calories, 3 g fat (trace saturated fat), 0 cholesterol, 203 mg sodium, 9 g carbohydrate, 4 g fiber, 2 g protein. **DIABETIC EXCHANGES:** 2 vegetable, 1/2 fat.

sauteed baby carrot medley

Convenient baby-cut carrots star in this quick-to-fix side dish. It's a colorful, unforgettable vegetable medley from our Test Kitchen.

3	cups fresh baby carrots
2	tablespoons olive oil
1	small yellow summer squash, thinly sliced
1	small sweet red pepper, julienned
1-1/2	cups fresh sugar snap peas
2	garlic cloves, minced
1/2	cup water
2	tablespoons sun-dried tomatoes (not packed in oil), finely chopped
1	tablespoon capers, drained
1/2	teaspoon salt
1/4	teaspoon pepper

• In a large skillet, saute carrots in oil for 1 minute. Add squash; saute 1 minute longer. Stir in the red pepper, peas and garlic; saute 1 minute more.

• Add water. Reduce heat to medium. Cook and stir until liquid is evaporated and vegetables are crisp-tender. Stir in the tomatoes, capers, salt and pepper.

YIELD: 8 servings.

NUTRITION FACTS: 2/3 cup equals 71 calories, 4 g fat (trace saturated fat), 0 cholesterol, 240 mg sodium, 9 g carbohydrate, 2 g fiber, 2 g protein.

SAUTEED BABY CARROT MEDLEY

71 CALORIES

RED POTATOES WITH BEANS

red potatoes with beans

Daria Burcar | ROCHESTER, MICHIGAN

You can serve this homey blend of fresh green beans, potato wedges and chopped red onion hot or cold. Either way, this low-calorie side dish makes a pleasing accompaniment to any meat.

- 1-1/3 **pounds fresh green beans, trimmed**
- 1/3 **cup water**
- 6 **small red potatoes, cut into wedges**
- 1/2 **cup chopped red onion**
- 1/2 **cup fat-free Italian salad dressing**

- Place the beans and water in a 2-qt. microwave-safe dish. Cover; microwave on high for 6-8 minutes or until tender.

- Meanwhile, place the potatoes in a large saucepan and cover with water. Bring to a boil. Reduce heat; cover and cook for 5-7 minutes or until tender. Drain beans and potatoes; place in a bowl. Add onion and dressing; toss to coat.

YIELD: 8 servings.

NUTRITION FACTS: 3/4 cup equals 49 calories, trace fat (trace saturated fat), 1 mg cholesterol, 220 mg sodium, 11 g carbohydrate, 1 g fiber, 2 g protein. **DIABETIC EXCHANGES:** 1 vegetable, 1/2 starch.

garlic green beans

Howard Levine | ARLETA, CALIFORNIA

Here's a simple treatment for fresh green beans that calls for just a handful of ingredients.

- 1 **pound fresh green beans, trimmed**
- 1 **to 2 garlic cloves, minced**
- 1/2 **teaspoon salt**
- 1/8 **teaspoon white pepper**
- 2 **teaspoons olive oil**

- Place beans and enough water to cover in a saucepan; bring to a boil. Cook, uncovered, for 8-10 minutes or until crisp-tender; drain. Toss beans with garlic, salt and pepper. Drizzle with oil. Serve immediately.

YIELD: 4 servings.

NUTRITION FACTS: 3/4 cup equals 61 calories, 3 g fat (trace saturated fat), 0 cholesterol, 298 mg sodium, 9 g carbohydrate, 4 g fiber, 2 g protein. **DIABETIC EXCHANGES:** 1 vegetable, 1/2 fat.

italian mixed vegetables

Dawn Harvey | DANVILLE, PENNSYLVANIA

Bottled salad dressing and herbs dress up frozen vegetables in this eye-catching recipe.

- 1 **package (24 ounces) frozen California-blend vegetables**
- 1/4 **cup water**
- 1/4 **cup reduced-fat Italian salad dressing**
- 1/4 **teaspoon salt**
- 1/4 **teaspoon dried basil**
- 1/8 **teaspoon dried oregano**

- In a large nonstick skillet, bring vegetables and water to a boil. Cover and cook for 10-12 minutes or until the vegetables are crisp-tender. Uncover; cook and stir until liquid is reduced. Add the salad dressing, salt, basil and oregano. Cook and stir until heated through.

YIELD: 6 servings.

NUTRITION FACTS: 3/4 cup equals 51 calories, 1 g fat (trace saturated fat), trace cholesterol, 214 mg sodium, 6 g carbohydrate, 3 g fiber, 3 g protein. **DIABETIC EXCHANGE:** 1 vegetable.

ITALIAN MIXED VEGETABLES

vegetables in dill sauce

Edie Despain | LOGAN, UTAH

This recipe is ideal for using up veggies from your garden. It's a great side dish for a grilled entree. Enjoy!

        4   cups water
    1-1/2   cups pearl onions
        1   medium carrot, sliced
        1   tablespoon butter
      1/2   pound sliced fresh mushrooms
        2   small zucchini, sliced
        2   teaspoons lemon juice
        1   teaspoon dried marjoram
      1/4   teaspoon salt

SAUCE:

        2   tablespoons plus 2 teaspoons fat-free sour cream
        2   tablespoons plus 2 teaspoons reduced-fat mayonnaise
        2   tablespoons fat-free milk
    2-1/4   teaspoons finely chopped onion
      1/2   teaspoon snipped fresh dill

Dash white pepper

- In a large saucepan, bring the water to a boil. Add pearl onions; boil for 3 minutes. Drain onions and rinse in cold water; peel.

- In a large nonstick skillet coated with cooking spray, saute onions and carrot in butter for 1 minute. Add the mushrooms and zucchini; saute 6-8 minutes longer or until vegetables are tender. Stir in the lemon juice, marjoram and salt.

VEGETABLES IN DILL SAUCE

80 CALORIES

- In a small microwave-safe bowl, combine the sauce ingredients. Cover and microwave on high until heated through, stirring once. Serve with vegetables.

YIELD: 6 servings.

NUTRITION FACTS: 1/2 cup vegetables with 1 tablespoon sauce equals 80 calories, 4 g fat (2 g saturated fat), 9 mg cholesterol, 186 mg sodium, 9 g carbohydrate, 2 g fiber, 3 g protein. **DIABETIC EXCHANGES:** 1 vegetable, 1 fat.

68 CALORIES

SESAME STEAMED VEGETABLES

sesame steamed vegetables

Heidi Doudna | FAIRBANKS, ALASKA

Broccoli grows abundantly during the long summer days here in Alaska. I like to harvest it and freeze it along with julienned carrots, so this recipe is always ready to go. The two vegetables are wonderful together.

    1-1/2   cups fresh broccoli florets
        1   small carrot, julienned and cut into 2-inch pieces
      1/4   cup sliced celery
        3   tablespoons sliced water chestnuts
        1   tablespoon water
        1   tablespoon reduced-fat butter
    1-1/2   teaspoons reduced-sodium soy sauce
      3/4   teaspoon sesame seeds, toasted

- In a small saucepan, combine the broccoli, carrot, celery, water chestnuts, water and soy sauce; bring to a boil. Cover and steam for 4-6 minutes or until the vegetables are crisp-tender. Sprinkle with sesame seeds.

YIELD: 2 servings.

NUTRITION FACTS: 2/3 cup equals 68 calories, 4 g fat (2 g saturated fat), 10 mg cholesterol, 229 mg sodium, 8 g carbohydrate, 3 g fiber, 3 g protein. **DIABETIC EXCHANGES:** 2 vegetable, 1/2 fat.

zucchini tomato toss

Kathy Fielder | DALLAS, TEXAS

Fresh-tasting tomatoes, zucchini, green pepper and onion are seasoned with garlic and parsley in this quick side dish that's served warm. This recipe is especially great for the cook that gardens because of all the produce it uses.

- 1/4 **cup chopped green pepper**
- 1 **medium zucchini, cut into 1/4-inch slices**
- 1 **small onion, thinly sliced and separated into rings**
- 1 **garlic clove, minced**
- 1 **teaspoon olive oil**
- 2 **small plum tomatoes, peeled and cut into wedges**
- 1/2 **teaspoon salt**

Dash pepper
- 1 **tablespoon minced fresh parsley**

- In a nonstick skillet, saute green pepper, zucchini, onion and garlic in oil for 3-4 minutes or until crisp-tender. Add the tomatoes, salt and pepper. Reduce heat to low; cover and cook until heated through. Sprinkle with parsley.

YIELD: 2 servings.

NUTRITION FACTS: 3/4 cup equals 59 calories, 3 g fat (trace saturated fat), 0 cholesterol, 597 mg sodium, 9 g carbohydrate, 3 g fiber, 2 g protein. **DIABETIC EXCHANGES:** 1 vegetable, 1/2 fat.

ZUCCHINI TOMATO TOSS

59 CALORIES

74 CALORIES

POTATOES FOR A CROWD

potatoes for a crowd

Merrill Powers | SPEARVILLE, KANSAS

Here's a comforting, creamy potato casserole to make when you need something sure to please a large group, but don't want to stray from your diet. No one guesses it's light.

- 5 **cans (12 ounces *each*) evaporated milk**
- 7-1/2 **cups milk**
- 5 **cans (10-3/4 ounces *each*) condensed cream of chicken soup, undiluted**
- 5 **cans (10-3/4 ounces *each*) condensed cheddar cheese soup, undiluted**
- 1 **pound butter, melted**
- 1 **package (12 ounces) cornflakes, crushed**
- 3 **medium onions, finely chopped**
- 10 **packages (2 pounds *each*) frozen cubed hash brown potatoes, thawed**

- In several large bowls, combine all the ingredients. Transfer to 10 greased 11-in. x 7-in. baking dishes. Bake, uncovered, at 350° for 45-55 minutes or until potatoes are tender.

YIELD: 10 casseroles (about 10 servings each).

NUTRITION FACTS: 3/4 cup equals 74 calories, 5 g fat (3 g saturated fat), 14 mg cholesterol, 122 mg sodium, 7 g carbohydrate, trace fiber, 2 g protein.

90 CALORIES

asparagus with mushrooms

Betty Jean Nichols | EUGENE, OREGON
This side dish is not fussy to make, but it looks special. People say it's delicious!

- 1 **pound fresh asparagus, trimmed and cut into 2-inch pieces**
- 2 **teaspoons ground ginger**
- 2 **tablespoons canola oil**
- 3 **cups sliced fresh mushrooms**
- 1 **teaspoon salt**
- 1/8 **teaspoon sugar**
- 1/8 **teaspoon pepper**

- In a large skillet, saute asparagus and ginger in oil for 2-3 minutes or until asparagus is crisp-tender. Add the mushrooms, salt, sugar and pepper. Cook and stir 2-3 minutes longer or until mushrooms are tender.

YIELD: 4 servings.

NUTRITION FACTS: 3/4 cup equals 90 calories, 7 g fat (1 g saturated fat), 0 cholesterol, 599 mg sodium, 5 g carbohydrate, 2 g fiber, 3 g protein.

stir-fried vegetables

Jane Shapton | TUSTIN, CALIFORNIA
You need less than 30 minutes to prepare this crisp-tender veggie stir-fry. And it tastes just as garden-fresh as it looks.

- 2 **tablespoons cornstarch**
- 1 **teaspoon sugar**

- 1 **teaspoon minced fresh gingerroot**
- 1 **cup reduced-sodium chicken broth** *or* **vegetable broth**
- 1/4 **cup cold water**
- 3 **tablespoons reduced-sodium soy sauce**
- 3 **tablespoons white wine vinegar**
- 2 **medium carrots, julienned**
- 2 **cups fresh broccoli florets**
- 4 **teaspoons canola oil**
- 2 **medium sweet red peppers, julienned**
- 2 **medium green peppers, julienned**
- 1 **cup sliced green onions,** *divided*

- In a small bowl, combine cornstarch, sugar, ginger, broth, water, soy sauce and vinegar until smooth; set aside.

- In a large nonstick skillet or wok, stir-fry the carrots and broccoli in oil for 2 minutes. Add peppers; stir-fry 6-8 minutes longer or until vegetables are crisp-tender.

- Stir cornstarch mixture and add to the skillet. Bring to a boil; cook and stir for 2 minutes or until thickened. Add 3/4 cup onions; cook 2 minutes longer. Garnish with remaining onions.

YIELD: 6 servings.

NUTRITION FACTS: 2/3 cup equals 93 calories, 3 g fat (trace saturated fat), 0 cholesterol, 424 mg sodium, 14 g carbohydrate, 3 g fiber, 3 g protein. **DIABETIC EXCHANGES:** 2 vegetable, 1/2 fat.

93 CALORIES

VEGETABLE SLAW

vegetable slaw

Julie Copenhayer | MORGANTON, NORTH CAROLINA
We've nicknamed this crunchy salad "Christmas slaw" because of its pretty mix of red and green vegetables. But it's tasty any time of year. It's also a great light lunch when stuffed into a whole wheat pita.

    3   cups shredded cabbage
    5   plum tomatoes, seeded and chopped
    1   cup fresh broccoli florets, cut into small pieces
    1   cup cauliflowerets, cut into small pieces
  1/2   cup chopped red onion
  1/2   cup fat-free sour cream
  1/4   cup reduced-fat mayonnaise
    1   tablespoon cider vinegar
  3/4   teaspoon salt
  1/4   teaspoon pepper

• In a bowl, combine the cabbage, tomatoes, broccoli, cauliflower and onion. In a small bowl, combine the sour cream, mayonnaise, vinegar, salt and pepper. Pour over cabbage mixture; toss to coat evenly. Cover and refrigerate until chilled.

YIELD: 6 servings.

NUTRITION FACTS: 3/4 cup equals 84 calories, 5 g fat (1 g saturated fat), 7 mg cholesterol, 402 mg sodium, 10 g carbohydrate, 3 g fiber, 3 g protein. **DIABETIC EXCHANGES:** 2 vegetable, 1 fat.

special cauliflower

Rita Reinke | WAUWATOSA, WISCONSIN
I found this recipe in a local paper and it has become my favorite topping for cauliflower. I like it because the glaze adds color and also enhances the flavor with a little zip. It's hard to believe it's light.

    2   cups fresh cauliflowerets
    1   tablespoon plain yogurt
    1   tablespoon mayonnaise
  1/2   teaspoon Dijon mustard
  1/8   teaspoon dill weed
  1/8   teaspoon salt
  1/8   teaspoon garlic powder
  1/4   cup shredded cheddar cheese

• Place cauliflower in a steamer basket; place in a small saucepan over 1 in. of water. Bring to a boil; cover and steam for 6-8 minutes or until crisp-tender. Meanwhile, in a small bowl, combine yogurt, mayonnaise, mustard, dill, salt and garlic powder.

• Transfer cauliflower to an ungreased 3-cup baking dish; top with yogurt mixture and cheese. Bake, uncovered, at 350° for 5 minutes or until heated through and cheese is melted.

YIELD: 3 servings.

NUTRITION FACTS: 2/3 cup equals 88 calories, 7 g fat (3 g saturated fat), 12 mg cholesterol, 222 mg sodium, 4 g carbohydrate, 2 g fiber, 4 g protein. **DIABETIC EXCHANGES:** 1-1/2 fat, 1 vegetable.

SPECIAL CAULIFLOWER

100-200 calories

113 CALORIES

SUMMER GARDEN MEDLEY

summer garden medley

Elaine Nelson I FRESNO, CALIFORNIA

This colorful side dish brings back sweet memories of the corn-and-tomato dish my mother often prepared in the summer. Farmers in our area supply us with delicious eggplant...so I sometimes substitute them for the zucchini in veggie recipes like this one.

 2 medium zucchini, halved lengthwise and cut into 1/4-inch slices
 1 cup fresh *or* frozen corn, thawed
 3/4 cup diced green pepper
 1 medium leek (white portion only), sliced
 1/2 teaspoon seasoned salt
 1 tablespoon olive oil
 2 medium tomatoes, seeded and diced

- In a large nonstick skillet, saute the zucchini, corn, green pepper, leek and seasoned salt in oil until vegetables are tender. Stir in the tomatoes; heat through.

YIELD: 4 servings.

NUTRITION FACTS: 1 cup equals 113 calories, 4 g fat (1 g saturated fat), 0 cholesterol, 202 mg sodium, 19 g carbohydrate, 3 g fiber, 3 g protein. **DIABETIC EXCHANGES:** 2 vegetable, 1/2 starch, 1/2 fat.

corn potato pancakes

Carolyn Wilson I LYNDON, KANSAS

I love combining different foods to see what I can come up with. For example, I put leftover mashed potatoes to perfect use in these slightly crisp golden-brown cakes.

 2 cups mashed potatoes (with added milk and butter)
 1/4 cup all-purpose flour
 1/4 cup cream-style corn
 1 egg, beaten
 3 tablespoons finely chopped onion
 1 teaspoon minced fresh parsley
 1/2 teaspoon salt
 1/2 teaspoon minced garlic
 1/8 teaspoon pepper
 6 teaspoons vegetable oil, *divided*

- In a large bowl, combine the first nine ingredients. In a large nonstick skillet, heat 2 teaspoons oil; drop four 1/4 cupfuls of batter into skillet. Cook for 1-2 minutes on each side or until golden brown. Repeat with remaining oil and batter.

YIELD: about 1 dozen.

NUTRITION FACTS: 2 pancakes equals 160 calories, 8 g fat (2 g saturated fat), 43 mg cholesterol, 461 mg sodium, 18 g carbohydrate, 1 g fiber, 3 g protein. **DIABETIC EXCHANGES:** 1-1/2 fat, 1 starch.

CORN POTATO PANCAKES

160 CALORIES

VEGETABLE FOCACCIA

vegetable focaccia

Michele Fairchok | GROVE CITY, OHIO

This popular recipe began as herb focaccia but gradually came to include our favorite vegetables. There's no cheese, but some people think it has cheese anyway! What a great side dish to liven up any meal.

2 to 2-1/4 cups bread flour
1 package (1/4 ounce) quick-rise yeast
1 teaspoon salt
1 cup warm water (120° to 130°)
1 tablespoon olive oil

TOPPING:

3 plum tomatoes, chopped
5 medium fresh mushrooms, sliced
1/2 cup chopped green pepper
1/2 cup sliced ripe olives
1/4 cup chopped onion
3 tablespoons olive oil
2 teaspoons red wine vinegar
3/4 teaspoon salt
1/4 teaspoon garlic powder
1/4 teaspoon dried oregano
1/4 teaspoon pepper
2 teaspoons cornmeal

• In a bowl, combine 2 cups flour, yeast and salt. Add water and oil; beat until smooth. Stir in enough remaining flour to form a soft dough. Turn onto a floured surface; knead until smooth and elastic, about 4 minutes. Cover and let rest for 15 minutes. Meanwhile, in a bowl, combine the tomatoes, mushrooms, green pepper, olives, onion, oil, vinegar and seasonings.

• Coat a 15-in. x 10-in. x 1-in. baking pan with cooking spray; sprinkle with cornmeal. Press dough into pan. Prick dough generously with a fork. Bake at 475° for 5 minutes or until lightly browned. Cover with vegetable mixture. Bake 8-10 minutes longer or until edges of crust are golden.

YIELD: 12 servings.

NUTRITION FACTS: 1 piece equals 121 calories, 5 g fat (1 g saturated fat), 0 cholesterol, 376 mg sodium, 17 g carbohydrate, 1 g fiber, 3 g protein. **DIABETIC EXCHANGES:** 1 starch, 1 fat.

spanish rice

Sharon Donat | KALISPELL, MONTANA

This rice recipe has been in our family for years. It's handy when you're in a hurry for a side dish to complement almost any main dish, not just Tex-Mex fare.

1 can (14-1/2 ounces) vegetable broth
1 can (14-1/2 ounces) stewed tomatoes
1 cup uncooked long grain rice
1 teaspoon olive oil
1 teaspoon chili powder
1/4 teaspoon dried oregano
1/4 teaspoon garlic salt

• In a large saucepan, combine all ingredients. Bring to a boil. Reduce heat; cover and simmer for 20-25 minutes or until rice is tender and liquid is absorbed.

YIELD: 6 servings.

NUTRITION FACTS: 2/3 cup equals 156 calories, 1 g fat (trace saturated fat), 0 cholesterol, 350 mg sodium, 32 g carbohydrate, 1 g fiber, 4 g protein. **DIABETIC EXCHANGE:** 2 starch.

SPANISH RICE

antipasto potato bake

Kelley Butler-Ludington | EAST HAVEN, CONNECTICUT
This hearty side dish has a surprising Mediterranean flavor. It's a casserole with lots of color from red peppers and black olives.

2 cans (14-1/2 ounces *each*) sliced potatoes, drained
2 cans (14 ounces *each*) water-packed artichoke hearts, rinsed and drained
2 jars (7 ounces *each*) roasted sweet red peppers, drained
1 can (3.8 ounces) sliced ripe olives, drained
1/4 cup grated Parmesan cheese
1-1/2 teaspoons minced garlic
1/3 cup olive oil
1/2 cup seasoned bread crumbs
1 tablespoon butter, melted

• In a large bowl, combine potatoes, artichokes, peppers, olives, Parmesan cheese and garlic. Drizzle with oil; toss gently to coat. Transfer to a greased 3-qt. baking dish. Toss bread crumbs and butter; sprinkle over the top.

• Bake, uncovered, at 375° for 20-25 minutes or until lightly browned.

YIELD: 10 servings.

NUTRITION FACTS: 3/4 cup equals 152 calories, 10 g fat (2 g saturated fat), 5 mg cholesterol, 484 mg sodium, 12 g carbohydrate, 1 g fiber, 3 g protein.

ANTIPASTO POTATO BAKE

VEGGIE CHEESE CASSEROLE

veggie cheese casserole

Jacque Capurro | ANCHORAGE, ALASKA
This vegetable combination makes a delightful side dish or weekend brunch specialty. It's long been a favorite with my children. I like it because it's so comforting yet easy to put together.

3 cups frozen chopped broccoli, thawed and drained
1/2 cup reduced-fat biscuit/baking mix
1 cup (8 ounces) reduced-fat sour cream
1 cup (8 ounces) fat-free cottage cheese
2 eggs
1/4 cup butter, melted
1/4 teaspoon salt
1 large tomato, thinly sliced and halved
1/4 cup grated Parmesan cheese

• Arrange the broccoli in a greased 8-in. square baking dish; set aside.

• In a large bowl, beat the biscuit mix, sour cream, cottage cheese, eggs, butter and salt; pour over the broccoli. Arrange tomato slices over the top; sprinkle with Parmesan cheese.

• Bake, uncovered, at 350° for 35-40 minutes or until a knife inserted near the center comes out clean. Let stand for 5 minutes before cutting.

YIELD: 9 servings.

NUTRITION FACTS: 1 serving equals 158 calories, 9 g fat (6 g saturated fat), 72 mg cholesterol, 354 mg sodium, 10 g carbohydrate, 1 g fiber, 8 g protein. **DIABETIC EXCHANGES:** 1-1/2 fat, 1 lean meat, 1/2 starch.

cajun buttered corn

Anne-Lise Botting | DULUTH, GEORGIA

I like to spice up veggies with this seasoned butter. Garlic and chili powders make the butter a perfect complement to fresh corn.

- 8 medium ears sweet corn
- 2 tablespoons butter
- 1/4 teaspoon chili powder
- 1/4 teaspoon coarsely ground pepper
- 1/8 teaspoon garlic powder
- 1/8 teaspoon cayenne pepper
- 1 teaspoon cornstarch
- 1/4 cup reduced-sodium chicken *or* vegetable broth

- In a large kettle, bring 3 qts. of water to a boil; add corn. Return to a boil; cook for 3-5 minutes or until tender.

- Meanwhile, in a small saucepan, melt butter. Stir in the chili powder, pepper, garlic powder and cayenne; cook and stir for 1 minute. Combine cornstarch and broth until smooth; gradually whisk into butter mixture. Bring to a boil; cook and stir for 1-2 minutes or until slightly thickened. Drain corn; serve with seasoned butter.

YIELD: 8 servings.

NUTRITION FACTS: 1 ear of corn with 1-1/2 teaspoons seasoned butter equals 105 calories, 4 g fat (2 g saturated fat), 8 mg cholesterol, 63 mg sodium, 18 g carbohydrate, 2 g fiber, 3 g protein. **DIABETIC EXCHANGES:** 1 starch, 1/2 fat.

CAJUN BUTTERED CORN

105 CALORIES

158 CALORIES

STUFFED POTATO SKINS

stuffed potato skins

Hollie Powell | ST. LOUIS, MISSOURI

Fabulous as a side dish, party appetizer, snack or even light meal, these potatoes always make it fun to eat your vegetables.

- 6 medium baking potatoes (6 ounces *each*)
- 1 tablespoon butter, melted
- 1 teaspoon hot pepper sauce, *divided*
- 1 cup thinly sliced green onions
- 1 large sweet red pepper, finely chopped
- 1/2 cup fresh broccoli florets, finely chopped
- 1 cup (4 ounces) shredded reduced-fat cheddar cheese, *divided*

- Scrub and pierce potatoes. Bake at 400° for 40-50 minutes or until tender. Cool slightly; cut each potato in half lengthwise. Scoop out the pulp, leaving a thin shell (save pulp for another use). Place the potato shells on an ungreased baking sheet.

- Combine butter and 1/2 teaspoon hot pepper sauce; brush over shells. Broil 4 in. from the heat for 5 minutes or until edges are crispy and butter is bubbly. Meanwhile, in a bowl, combine the onions, red pepper, broccoli, 3/4 cup cheese and remaining hot pepper sauce; spoon into potato skins. Sprinkle with remaining cheese. Broil 2-3 minutes longer or until cheese is melted.

YIELD: 12 servings.

NUTRITION FACTS: 1 potato skin equals 158 calories, 3 g fat (2 g saturated fat), 9 mg cholesterol, 35 mg sodium, 29 g carbohydrate, 5 g fiber, 5 g protein. **DIABETIC EXCHANGE:** 2 starch.

153 CALORIES

ROSEMARY RED POTATOES

rosemary red potatoes

Sally Ridenour | SALEM, OREGON

The delicious combination of roasted garlic, onion, fresh rosemary and potatoes will make your whole house smell wonderful. Try this dish with grilled steak or roasted chicken.

- 1 large whole garlic bulb
- 2 pounds small red potatoes, quartered
- 1/2 medium onion, cut into chunks
- 4 teaspoons olive oil
- 1/2 teaspoon salt
- 4 to 5 fresh rosemary sprigs
- 3 tablespoons Dijon mustard
- 4-1/2 teaspoons balsamic vinegar

- Remove papery outer skin from garlic; separate into cloves, leaving them unpeeled. In a large bowl, combine potatoes, onion and garlic. Add oil and salt; toss to coat.

- Arrange potato mixture in a single layer in a 15-in. x 10-in. x 1-in. baking pan coated with cooking spray. Top with rosemary sprigs. Bake at 450° for 15-17 minutes or until garlic is tender.

- Remove garlic cloves; cool. Stir potato mixture; bake 5-8 minutes longer or until potatoes are tender, stirring occasionally. Discard rosemary. Squeeze softened garlic into a large bowl; mash with a fork. Add mustard and vinegar. Add potato mixture and stir gently to coat.

YIELD: 6 servings.

NUTRITION FACTS: 3/4 cup equals 153 calories, 4 g fat (trace saturated fat), 0 cholesterol, 397 mg sodium, 27 g carbohydrate, 3 g fiber, 4 g protein. **DIABETIC EXCHANGES:** 2 starch, 1/2 fat.

maple vegetable medley

Lorraine Caland | THUNDER BAY, ONTARIO

This recipe calls for fresh vegetables brushed with a mild maple glaze and then grilled to perfection. They go well with meaty dishes.

- 1/3 cup balsamic vinegar
- 1/3 cup maple syrup
- 1 large red onion
- 1 pound fresh asparagus, trimmed
- 1 pound baby carrots
- 2 medium zucchini, cut lengthwise into thirds and seeded
- 1 medium sweet red pepper, cut into eight pieces
- 1 medium sweet yellow pepper, cut into eight pieces
- 2 tablespoons olive oil
- 1 tablespoon minced fresh thyme *or* 1 teaspoon dried thyme
- 1/2 teaspoon salt
- 1/2 teaspoon pepper

- For glaze, in a saucepan, bring vinegar and syrup to a boil. Reduce heat; cook and stir over medium heat for 6-8 minutes or until thickened. Remove from the heat; set aside.

- Cut onion into eight wedges to 1/2 in. of the bottom. Place the onion, asparagus, carrots, zucchini and peppers in a large bowl. Drizzle with oil and sprinkle with seasonings; toss to coat.

- Coat grill rack with cooking spray before starting the grill. Arrange vegetables on rack. Grill, covered, over medium

MAPLE VEGETABLE MEDLEY

120 CALORIES

heat for 10 minutes on each side. Brush with half of the glaze; grill 5-8 minutes longer or until crisp-tender. Before serving, brush with remaining glaze.

YIELD: 8 servings.

NUTRITION FACTS: 1 serving equals 120 calories, 4 g fat (1 g saturated fat), 0 cholesterol, 201 mg sodium, 21 g carbohydrate, 3 g fiber, 2 g protein. **DIABETIC EXCHANGES:** 2 vegetable, 1/2 starch, 1/2 fat.

186 CALORIES

BAKED CORN PUDDING

baked corn pudding

Peggy West | GEORGETOWN, DELAWARE

Here's a comforting side dish that can turn even ordinary meals into something to celebrate. Guests give it rave reviews.

- 1/2 cup sugar
- 3 tablespoons all-purpose flour
- 3 eggs
- 1 cup milk
- 1/4 cup butter, melted
- 1/2 teaspoon salt
- 1/2 teaspoon pepper
- 1 can (15-1/4 ounces) whole kernel corn, drained
- 1 can (14-3/4 ounces) cream-style corn

- In a large bowl, combine sugar and flour. Whisk in the eggs, milk, butter, salt and pepper. Stir in the whole kernel corn and cream-style corn.

- Pour into a greased 1-1/2-qt. baking dish. Bake, uncovered, at 350° for 45-50 minutes or until a knife inserted near the center comes out clean.

YIELD: 10 servings.

NUTRITION FACTS: 1/2 cup equals 186 calories, 7 g fat (4 g saturated fat), 79 mg cholesterol, 432 mg sodium, 26 g carbohydrate, 1 g fiber, 4 g protein.

southwestern macaroni salad

Nancy Clancy | STANDISH, MAINE

This salad is like having salsa mixed with macaroni—it's yummy! It serves a lot, which makes it a keeper.

- 1 package (16 ounces) uncooked elbow macaroni
- 1 pound cherry tomatoes, quartered
- 1 cup frozen corn, thawed
- 1 medium green pepper, chopped
- 1 small red onion, chopped
- 1 can (2-1/4 ounces) sliced ripe olives, drained
- 1/2 cup lime juice
- 1/4 cup olive oil
- 1 tablespoon red wine vinegar
- 1 tablespoon chili powder
- 1 tablespoon ground cumin
- 1 teaspoon sugar
- 1 teaspoon salt
- 1 teaspoon garlic powder

- Cook pasta according to package directions; drain and rinse in cold water. In a large bowl, combine the pasta, tomatoes, corn, green pepper, red onion and olives.

- In a jar with a tight-fitting lid, combine the lime juice, oil, vinegar and seasonings; shake well. Pour over pasta mixture; toss to coat. Cover and refrigerate for 1 hour or until chilled.

YIELD: 16 servings.

NUTRITION FACTS: 3/4 cup equals 163 calories, 5 g fat (1 g saturated fat), 0 cholesterol, 205 mg sodium, 27 g carbohydrate, 2 g fiber, 4 g protein. **DIABETIC EXCHANGES:** 1-1/2 starch, 1 vegetable, 1/2 fat.

SOUTHWESTERN MACARONI SALAD

163 CALORIES

182 CALORIES

CHILI-SEASONED POTATO WEDGES

chili-seasoned potato wedges

Irene Marshall | NAMPA, IDAHO

When I tried out these roasted potato wedges on my family, it was love at first taste. Since I generally have the onion soup mix and seasonings on hand, the recipe couldn't be easier. Spice amounts can be altered to your liking.

1	tablespoon onion soup mix
1	tablespoon chili powder
1/4	teaspoon salt
1/4	teaspoon garlic powder
1/4	teaspoon pepper
4	large baking potatoes
2	tablespoons vegetable oil

• In a large resealable plastic bag, combine soup mix, chili powder, salt, garlic powder and pepper. Cut each potato into eight wedges; place in bag and shake to coat. Arrange in a single layer in a greased 15-in. x 10-in. x 1-in. baking pan. Drizzle with oil. Bake, uncovered, at 425° for 20 minutes. Turn; bake 15-20 minutes longer or until crisp.

YIELD: 8 servings.

NUTRITION FACTS: 4 pieces equals 182 calories, 4 g fat (1 g saturated fat), 0 cholesterol, 172 mg sodium, 34 g carbohydrate, 3 g fiber, 4 g protein.

stir-fried carrots

Grace Yaskovic | BRANCHVILLE, NEW JERSEY

For a delightful side dish that tastes good, try these fast and fail-proof carrots. It's my husband Tom's favorite way to do carrots, and it just happens to be light, too!

1-1/2	pounds fresh carrots, julienned
1	tablespoon olive oil
1/2	cup chicken broth
1	teaspoon dried rosemary, crushed
1/4	teaspoon pepper

• In a large skillet or wok, stir-fry the carrots in oil until crisp-tender. Stir in the broth, rosemary and pepper. Bring to a boil. Reduce the heat; simmer, uncovered, for 2-3 minutes or until liquid is reduced.

YIELD: 4 servings.

NUTRITION FACTS: 3/4 cup equals 106 calories, 4 g fat (1 g saturated fat), 0 cholesterol, 176 mg sodium, 18 g carbohydrate, 5 g fiber, 2 g protein. **DIABETIC EXCHANGES:** 1 starch, 1/2 fat.

STIR-FRIED CARROTS

106 CALORIES

savory skillet noodles

Lucille Goers | SEMINOLE, FLORIDA

My daughter is a vegetarian, so I created this colorful dish to suit her. She asks for it once a week. Chopped sweet peppers, onion and almonds accent the mild buttery noodles.

8	ounces uncooked yolk-free noodles
1	cup sliced fresh mushrooms
1/4	cup chopped sweet red pepper
1/4	cup chopped green pepper

160 CALORIES

SAVORY SKILLET NOODLES

2 tablespoons chopped onion
2 tablespoons butter
1/3 cup sliced almonds
1 teaspoon chicken bouillon granules *or* 1 vegetable bouillon cube, crushed
2 tablespoons minced fresh parsley

- Cook noodles according to the package directions. Meanwhile, in a large nonstick skillet, saute mushrooms, peppers and onion in butter until tender. Drain noodles; add to skillet. Sprinkle with almonds and bouillon; toss gently to combine. Heat through. Garnish with parsley.

YIELD: 8 servings.

NUTRITION FACTS: 2/3 cup equals 160 calories, 5 g fat (2 g saturated fat), 8 mg cholesterol, 189 mg sodium, 22 g carbohydrate, 2 g fiber, 5 g protein. DIABETIC EXCHANGES: 1-1/2 starch, 1 fat.

117 CALORIES

dilly corn

Bernadette Bennett I WACO, TEXAS

Five items and a few minutes are all you need for this versatile side dish. In this recipe, frozen corn is dressed up with dill weed and a little garlic powder for mild results that complement almost any dish.

1 cup water
1 teaspoon beef bouillon granules
2-1/4 cups frozen corn
3 teaspoons dill weed
1 teaspoon garlic powder

- In a small saucepan, bring water and bouillon to a boil. Stir in corn, dill and garlic powder. Return to a boil. Reduce heat; cover and simmer for 3-4 minutes or until the corn is tender. Drain.

YIELD: 3 servings.

NUTRITION FACTS: 2/3 cup equals 117 calories, 1 g fat (trace saturated fat), trace cholesterol, 204 mg sodium, 27 g carbohydrate, 3 g fiber, 4 g protein. DIABETIC EXCHANGE: 2 starch.

oven french fries

Margaret Taylor I SALEM, MISSOURI

These fries are crisp and offer a flavor you'll enjoy. They're so tasty, you'll never believe they are low in calories and fat.

1 tablespoon cornstarch
2 cups water
1 tablespoon reduced-sodium soy sauce
2 medium potatoes, peeled and cut into strips
2 teaspoons olive oil
1/8 teaspoon salt

- In a large bowl, combine the cornstarch, water and soy sauce until smooth. Add potatoes; cover and refrigerate for 1 hour.

- Drain potatoes and pat dry on paper towels. Toss potatoes with oil and sprinkle with salt. Place on a baking sheet coated with cooking spray.

- Bake at 375° for 15-20 minutes on each side or until tender and golden brown.

YIELD: 2 servings.

NUTRITION FACTS: 3/4 cup equals 167 calories, 5 g fat (1 g saturated fat), 0 cholesterol, 457 mg sodium, 29 g carbohydrate, 2 g fiber, 3 g protein. DIABETIC EXCHANGES: 2 starch, 1 fat.

OVEN FRENCH FRIES

167 CALORIES

supreme potato casserole

Joy Allen | FORSYTH, GEORGIA

Cottage cheese and sour cream give a delicious creamy coating to the tender cubes of potatoes in this side dish. I usually double the recipe when serving it to guests. They never realize it's light.

3	medium potatoes (about 1-1/2 pounds)
1	cup (8 ounces) fat-free cottage cheese
1/2	cup reduced-fat sour cream
1	tablespoon fat-free milk
1	teaspoon sugar
1/2	teaspoon salt
1/8	teaspoon garlic powder
2	tablespoons sliced green onion
1/2	cup shredded reduced-fat cheddar cheese

- Place the potatoes in a large saucepan and cover with water. Cover and bring to a boil. Reduce heat; cook for 10-15 minutes or until tender. Drain. Peel potatoes and cut into cubes.

- In a blender or food processor, combine the cottage cheese, sour cream, milk, sugar, salt and garlic powder; cover and process until smooth. Transfer to a large bowl; stir in the potatoes and onion.

- Pour into a 1-qt. baking dish coated with cooking spray. Bake, uncovered, at 350° for 30 minutes. Sprinkle with cheese. Bake 15 minutes longer or until the cheese is melted.

YIELD: 6 servings.

NUTRITION FACTS: 1/2 cup equals 158 calories, 3 g fat (2 g saturated fat), 15 mg cholesterol, 391 mg sodium, 24 g carbohydrate, 2 g fiber, 12 g protein. **DIABETIC EXCHANGES:** 1-1/2 starch, 1 lean meat.

SUPREME POTATO CASSEROLE

158 CALORIES

131 CALORIES

CREAMED SPINACH

creamed spinach

Susan Geddie | HARKER HEIGHTS, TEXAS

The inspiration for this comforting dish came from a local restaurant. I lightened up the original recipe by using fat-free half-and-half and fat-free cream cheese. Try it tonight.

1/4	cup diced onion
1	garlic clove, minced
1	tablespoon butter
1	tablespoon all-purpose flour
1-1/4	cups fat-free half-and-half
4	ounces fat-free cream cheese, cubed
3/4	teaspoon salt
1/8	teaspoon ground nutmeg
1/8	teaspoon pepper
1	package (16 ounces) frozen leaf spinach, thawed and squeezed dry
1/4	cup plus 1 tablespoon shredded Parmesan cheese, *divided*

- In a large nonstick skillet, saute the onion and garlic in butter until tender. Stir in flour until blended. Gradually whisk in half-and-half until blended. Bring to a boil over medium-low heat; cook and stir for 2 minutes or until slightly thickened.

- Add the cream cheese, salt, nutmeg and pepper, stirring until cream cheese is melted. Stir in spinach and 1/4 cup Parmesan cheese; heat through. Sprinkle with remaining Parmesan cheese. Serve immediately.

YIELD: 5 servings.

NUTRITION FACTS: 1/2 cup equals 131 calories, 4 g fat (3 g saturated fat), 12 mg cholesterol, 704 mg sodium, 13 g carbohydrate, 2 g fiber, 10 g protein.

BARBECUED POTATO WEDGES

barbecued potato wedges

Karen McRowe | AVON, OHIO

So easy to prepare, these toasty, roasted potatoes go well with just about any entree and are a year-round favorite at our house.

- 2 pounds small red potatoes, cut into wedges
- 2 tablespoons butter, melted
- 1 tablespoon honey
- 3 teaspoons chili powder
- 1/2 teaspoon salt
- 1/4 teaspoon garlic powder
- 1/4 teaspoon pepper

- Place the potatoes in a 15-in. x 10-in. x 1-in. baking pan coated with cooking spray. Drizzle with butter and honey. Sprinkle with the chili powder, salt, garlic powder and pepper; toss to coat.

- Bake, uncovered, at 450° for 25-30 minutes or until potatoes are tender and golden brown, stirring once.

YIELD: 6 servings.

NUTRITION FACTS: 1 cup equals 158 calories, 4 g fat (2 g saturated fat), 10 mg cholesterol, 258 mg sodium, 28 g carbohydrate, 3 g fiber, 3 g protein. **DIABETIC EXCHANGE:** 2 starch.

118 CALORIES

seasoned brown rice

Betsy Larimer | SOMERSET, PENNSYLVANIA

The simple seasonings in this recipe dramatically enhance brown rice. It's a zippy yet light side dish I turn to again and again.

- 1-1/3 cups water
- 2/3 cup long grain brown rice
- 1 tablespoon reduced-sodium soy sauce

- 1/2 teaspoon dried basil
- 1/4 to 1/2 teaspoon ground ginger
- 1/8 teaspoon cayenne pepper

- In a small saucepan, bring water and rice to a boil. Reduce heat; cover and simmer for 35-45 minutes or until water is absorbed and rice is tender. Stir in remaining ingredients.

YIELD: 4 servings.

NUTRITION FACTS: 1/2 cup equals 118 calories, 1 g fat (trace saturated fat), 0 cholesterol, 157 mg sodium, 24 g carbohydrate, 2 g fiber, 3 g protein. **DIABETIC EXCHANGE:** 1-1/2 starch.

peas in cheese sauce

June Blomquist | EUGENE, OREGON

Here's a recipe that dresses up convenient frozen peas with a quick-to-fix cheese sauce.

- 4-1/2 teaspoons butter
- 4-1/2 teaspoons all-purpose flour
- 1/4 teaspoon salt
- 1/8 teaspoon white pepper
- 1-1/2 cups milk
- 3/4 cup cubed process cheese (Velveeta)
- 2 packages (10 ounces *each*) frozen peas, thawed

- In a large saucepan, melt butter over low heat. Stir in the flour, salt and pepper until smooth. Gradually add milk. Bring to a boil; cook and stir for 2 minutes or until thickened. Add the cheese; stir until melted. Stir in peas; cook 1-2 minutes longer or until heated through.

YIELD: 8 servings.

NUTRITION FACTS: 2/3 cup equals 114 calories, 6 g fat (4 g saturated fat), 19 mg cholesterol, 284 mg sodium, 9 g carbohydrate, 2 g fiber, 6 g protein.

PEAS IN CHEESE SAUCE

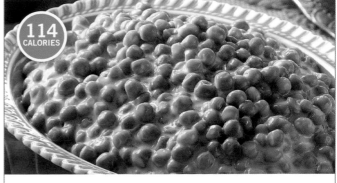

114 CALORIES

200 CALORIES

CARAMELIZED ONION MASHED POTATOES

caramelized onion mashed potatoes

Caramelized onions give a sweet and savory flavor to this side dish. Our Test Kitchen relied on potatoes, reduced-fat cheese and bacon for the heartwarming accompaniment.

      1   tablespoon canola oil
      2   large onions, thinly sliced
      1   teaspoon salt, *divided*
  1-1/2   pounds medium red potatoes, quartered
      3   garlic cloves, peeled and halved
    1/3   cup reduced-fat sour cream
      3   tablespoons fat-free milk
    1/4   teaspoon pepper
      1   tablespoon butter, melted
    1/2   cup shredded reduced-fat cheddar cheese
      2   bacon strips, cooked and crumbled

- Heat oil in a large nonstick skillet over medium heat; add onions and 1/2 teaspoon salt. Cook and stir for 15 minutes or until moisture has evaporated and onions are completely wilted. Reduce the heat to medium-low. Cook and stir for 30-40 minutes or until the onions are caramelized. (If necessary, add water, 1 tablespoon at a time, if onions begin to stick to the pan.)

- Meanwhile, place potatoes and garlic in a large saucepan; cover with water. Bring to a boil. Reduce heat; cover and cook for 18-22 minutes or until tender.

- Drain potatoes; place in a large bowl and mash. Add sour cream, milk, pepper and remaining salt; mash until blended. Stir in caramelized onions. Transfer to a serving bowl. Drizzle with butter; sprinkle with cheese and bacon.

YIELD: 6 servings.

NUTRITION FACTS: 2/3 cup equals 200 calories, 9 g fat (4 g saturated fat), 18 mg cholesterol, 528 mg sodium, 25 g carbohydrate, 3 g fiber, 7 g protein. **DIABETIC EXCHANGES:** 1-1/2 starch, 1-1/2 fat.

201-250 calories

creamy noodles

Brenda Nolen | FOLSOM, LOUISIANA

There's lots of garlic flavor in this filling side dish. I like it with grilled chicken but it works well with beef, too.

      8   ounces uncooked thin spaghetti
      3   garlic cloves, minced
      3   tablespoons butter, *divided*
      6   ounces fat-free cream cheese, cubed
      3   tablespoons reduced-fat sour cream
      3   tablespoons fat-free milk
    3/4   teaspoon salt
    1/2   teaspoon onion powder
    1/4   teaspoon Cajun seasoning
    1/4   teaspoon white pepper
  4-1/2   teaspoons minced fresh parsley

- Cook spaghetti according to package directions. Meanwhile, in a saucepan, saute garlic in 1 tablespoon butter until tender. Add the cream cheese, sour cream, milk, salt, onion powder, Cajun seasoning, pepper and remaining butter. Cook and stir over low heat just until smooth (do not boil). Remove from the heat.

CREAMY NOODLES

234 CALORIES

- Drain spaghetti; toss with cream sauce. Sprinkle with parsley. Serve immediately.

YIELD: 6 servings.

NUTRITION FACTS: 1 cup equals 234 calories, 7 g fat (4 g saturated fat), 20 mg cholesterol, 547 mg sodium, 32 g carbohydrate, 1 g fiber, 10 g protein. **DIABETIC EXCHANGES:** 2 starch, 1 very lean meat, 1 fat.

229 CALORIES

CREAMY MACARONI 'N' CHEESE

creamy macaroni 'n' cheese

Dawn Royer | ALBANY, OREGON

I prepare this cheesy recipe when I'm craving comfort food but trying to eat light. The hint of mustard adds zip to this creamy side dish—and it makes a pleasing meatless entree as well.

- 1/3 **cup finely chopped onion**
- 3-1/2 **cups cooked elbow macaroni**
- 1-3/4 **cups shredded reduced-fat cheddar cheese**
- 2 **tablespoons minced fresh parsley**
- 1/2 **cup fat-free evaporated milk**
- 1-3/4 **cups 2% cottage cheese**
- 1 **teaspoon Dijon mustard**
- 1/2 **teaspoon salt**
- 1/4 **teaspoon pepper**

- In a microwave-safe bowl, cover and microwave onion on high for 1-1/4 minutes or until tender; drain. Add the macaroni, cheddar cheese and parsley.

- In a blender or food processor, combine the milk, cottage cheese, mustard, salt and pepper; cover and process until smooth. Stir into macaroni mixture.

- Pour into a 1-1/2-qt. baking dish coated with cooking spray. Bake, uncovered, at 350° for 20-25 minutes or until lightly browned.

YIELD: 8 servings.

EDITOR'S NOTE: This recipe was tested in a 1,100-watt microwave.

NUTRITION FACTS: 2/3 cup equals 229 calories, 6 g fat (4 g saturated fat), 19 mg cholesterol, 491 mg sodium, 24 g carbohydrate, 1 g fiber, 20 g protein. **DIABETIC EXCHANGES:** 2 lean meat, 1-1/2 starch.

235 CALORIES

cheesy scalloped potatoes

Even with lighter ingredients, this cheesy potato recipe is still satisfying and delicious. It's also versatile so our home economists suggest keeping it on hand.

- 5 **large potatoes, peeled and thinly sliced**
- 3 **tablespoons all-purpose flour**
- 1-1/2 **teaspoons salt**
- 1/4 **teaspoon pepper**
- 1-1/4 **cups shredded reduced-fat cheddar cheese,** *divided*
- 3 **ounces reduced-fat Swiss cheese slices, finely chopped (3/4 cup),** *divided*
- 2 **medium onions, finely chopped**
- 1-1/2 **cups 2% milk**
- 2 **tablespoons minced fresh parsley**

- Place a third of the potatoes in a shallow 3-qt. baking dish coated with cooking spray. In a small bowl, combine the flour, salt and pepper; sprinkle half over potatoes. Sprinkle with 1/4 cup of each cheese and half of the onions. Repeat layers. Top with remaining potatoes. Pour milk over all.

- Cover and bake at 350° for 50-60 minutes or until potatoes are nearly tender. Sprinkle with remaining cheeses. Bake, uncovered, 10 minutes longer or until cheese is melted and potatoes are tender. Sprinkle with parsley.

YIELD: 8 servings.

NUTRITION FACTS: 3/4 cup equals 235 calories, 7 g fat (4 g saturated fat), 22 mg cholesterol, 556 mg sodium, 30 g carbohydrate, 3 g fiber, 15 g protein. **DIABETIC EXCHANGES:** 2 starch, 1 lean meat, 1/2 fat.

spiral pasta salad

Sue Gronholz | BEAVER DAM, WISCONSIN

I love to use home-grown herbs in my recipes. Marjoram, which I think is under-used, gets well-deserved attention in this fresh-tasting salad.

- 1 package (12 ounces) spiral pasta
- 3 plum tomatoes, seeded and chopped
- 1 medium green pepper, chopped
- 1 small onion, thinly sliced
- 1 can (2-1/4 ounces) sliced ripe olives, drained

MARJORAM VINAIGRETTE:

- 3 tablespoons white wine vinegar
- 2 tablespoons honey
- 1 tablespoon minced fresh marjoram *or* 1 teaspoon dried marjoram
- 1-1/2 teaspoons minced fresh basil *or* 1/2 teaspoon dried basil
- 1 teaspoon Dijon mustard
- 3/4 teaspoon salt
- 1/8 teaspoon pepper
- 1/2 cup olive oil

- Cook pasta according to package directions; drain and rinse in cold water. In a large bowl, combine the pasta, tomatoes, green pepper, onion and olives.

- In a small bowl, combine the vinegar, honey, marjoram, basil, mustard, salt and pepper. Gradually whisk in oil. Pour over the pasta mixture and toss to coat. Cover and refrigerate until serving.

YIELD: 12 servings.

NUTRITION FACTS: 1 cup equals 212 calories, 10 g fat (1 g saturated fat), 0 cholesterol, 208 mg sodium, 27 g carbohydrate, 1 g fiber, 4 g protein. **DIABETIC EXCHANGES:** 2 fat, 1-1/2 starch.

SPIRAL PASTA SALAD

212 CALORIES

parmesan potato balls

206 CALORIES

Pat Habiger | SPEARVILLE, KANSAS

Add a dash of fun to weeknight meals with these cute potatoes. The well-seasoned mashed potato bites have a crispy cornmeal coating that young and old find irresistible.

- 2-1/2 pounds potatoes, peeled and cubed (about 3 large potatoes)
- 2 ounces cream cheese, softened
- 2 tablespoons milk
- 1 tablespoon butter, softened
- 1/4 cup grated Parmesan cheese
- 1 tablespoon chopped green onion
- 2-1/2 teaspoons onion soup mix
- 1/2 teaspoon salt
- 1/8 teaspoon hot pepper sauce

Dash pepper

- 1 egg, lightly beaten
- 1-1/2 cups crushed cornflakes

- Place the potatoes in a large saucepan and cover with water. Bring to a boil. Reduce heat; cover and cook for 15-20 minutes or until tender. Drain.

- In a large bowl, mash the potatoes. Beat in the cream cheese, milk and butter until smooth. Stir in the Parmesan cheese, onion, soup mix, salt, hot pepper sauce and pepper. Shape into 1-1/2-in. balls.

- Place the egg and cornflakes in separate shallow bowls. Dip potato balls in egg, then roll in crumbs. Place on ungreased baking sheets.

- Bake at 400° for 15-18 minutes or until crisp and golden brown.

YIELD: 4-1/2 dozen.

NUTRITION FACTS: 4 potato balls equals 206 calories, 5 g fat (3 g saturated fat), 36 mg cholesterol, 382 mg sodium, 36 g carbohydrate, 2 g fiber, 6 g protein.

ham-stuffed tomatoes

245 CALORIES

Delia Kennedy | DEER PARK, WASHINGTON

With a hearty filling and creamy sauce, these baked tomatoes appeal to even picky eaters.

8 large tomatoes

1 teaspoon celery salt

1/8 teaspoon garlic salt

2-1/2 cups soft bread crumbs

1 cup (4 ounces) shredded reduced-fat cheddar cheese

2/3 cup chopped fully cooked lean ham

1/3 cup minced chives

2 tablespoons plus 1/3 cup water, *divided*

2 teaspoons cornstarch

1 cup (8 ounces) reduced-fat sour cream

1/4 cup lemon juice

4 teaspoons sugar

1/2 teaspoon Worcestershire sauce

CRANBERRY CORNMEAL DRESSING

- Cut a thin slice off the top of each tomato; remove core. Scoop out pulp and discard, leaving a 1/2-in. shell. Sprinkle celery salt and garlic salt inside tomatoes; invert onto paper towels to drain for 20 minutes.

- In a bowl, combine bread crumbs, cheese, ham, chives and 2 tablespoons water. Spoon into tomatoes. Place in a 13-in. x 9-in. baking dish coated with cooking spray.

- In a small saucepan, combine cornstarch and sour cream until smooth. Stir in the lemon juice, sugar, Worcestershire sauce and remaining water. Cook and stir over low heat until heated through; drizzle over the tomatoes. Bake, uncovered, at 400° for 15-20 minutes or until heated through.

YIELD: 8 servings.

NUTRITION FACTS: 1 tomato with 2 tablespoons sauce equals 245 calories, 9 g fat (5 g saturated fat), 28 mg cholesterol, 737 mg sodium, 30 g carbohydrate, 3 g fiber, 15 g protein. **DIABETIC EXCHANGES:** 2 vegetable, 1 starch, 1 lean meat, 1 fat.

cranberry cornmeal dressing

Corinne Portteus | ALBUQUERQUE, NEW MEXICO

This moist dressing is perfect when paired with poultry or even pork. The sweet-tart flavor of the dried cranberries really complements the turkey sausage.

3 cups reduced-sodium chicken broth, *divided*

1/2 cup yellow cornmeal

1/2 teaspoon salt

1/2 teaspoon white pepper

1/2 pound Italian turkey sausage links, casings removed

1 large onion, diced

1 large fennel bulb, diced (about 1 cup)

1 garlic clove, minced

1 egg yolk

4 cups soft French *or* Italian bread crumbs

3/4 cup dried cranberries

2 tablespoons minced fresh parsley

1 tablespoon balsamic vinegar

1 teaspoon minced fresh sage

1 teaspoon minced fresh savory

1/4 teaspoon ground nutmeg

- In a small bowl, whisk 1 cup broth, cornmeal, salt and pepper until smooth. In a large saucepan, bring remaining broth to a boil. Add cornmeal mixture, stirring constantly. Return to a boil; cook and stir for 3 minutes or until thickened. Remove from the heat; set aside.

- Crumble the sausage into a large nonstick skillet, add onion, fennel and garlic. Cook over medium heat until sausage is no longer pink; drain. Stir in egg yolk and cornmeal mixture. Add bread crumbs, cranberries, parsley, vinegar, sage, savory and nutmeg.

- Transfer to a 1-1/2-qt. baking dish coated with cooking spray. Cover and bake at 350° for 40-45 minutes or until heated through.

YIELD: 8 servings.

NUTRITION FACTS: 2/3 cup equals 205 calories, 4 g fat (1 g saturated fat), 42 mg cholesterol, 695 mg sodium, 33 g carbohydrate, 3 g fiber, 9 g protein. **DIABETIC EXCHANGES:** 2 starch, 1 lean meat.

desserts

Yes, you can have dessert! Just be sure it fits into your daily calorie allotment. Something sweet and decadent now and then is how you can lose weight without feeling deprived. Simply choose a treat that fits within a 500-calorie supper.

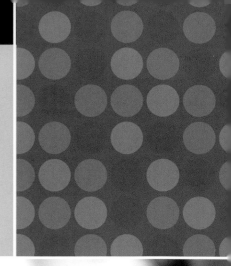

271

290

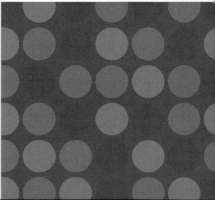

282

See the calorie break-downs below for this chapter. Whether you're looking for a cookie to finish a meal or a dessert you'd be proud to serve to guests, it's all here. See page 269 for a few easy tips that lighten up your own comforting treats.

91 CALORIES

CRANBERRY ALMOND MACAROONS

cranberry almond macaroons

Ramona Cornell | LEVITTOWN, NEW YORK

You'll relish this guilt-free take on a classic cookie, enhanced with cranberries and luscious dark chocolate. My son is diabetic, and he loves these. A co-worker calls them "a piece of coconut heaven."

2	egg whites
1/4	teaspoon almond extract

Sugar substitute equivalent to 2 tablespoons sugar

1	cup flaked coconut
1/4	cup dried cranberries, chopped
1/4	cup chopped almonds
1/4	cup semisweet chocolate chips, melted

• Place egg whites in a small mixing bowl; let stand at room temperature for 30 minutes. Add extract; beat on medium speed until soft peaks form. Gradually beat in sugar substitute on high until stiff glossy peaks form. Fold in the coconut, cranberries and almonds.

• Drop by rounded tablespoonfuls 2 in. apart onto a baking sheet coated with cooking spray. Bake at 325° for 10-15 minutes or until set. Cool for 15 minutes before carefully removing from pan to a wire rack.

• Spread about 1 teaspoon melted chocolate on the bottom of each cookie. Place on waxed paper with chocolate side up; let stand until set.

YIELD: 11 cookies.

EDITOR'S NOTE: This recipe was tested with Splenda No Calorie Sweetener.

NUTRITION FACTS: 1 cookie equals 91 calories, 6 g fat (3 g saturated fat), 0 cholesterol, 33 mg sodium, 10 g carbohydrate, 1 g fiber, 2 g protein. **DIABETIC EXCHANGES:** 1 fat, 1/2 starch.

marshmallow fudge

Holly Mann | AMHERST, NEW HAMPSHIRE

It's nearly impossible to resist this rich chocolate delight. Chock-full of marshmallows and graham crackers, this tantalizing treat is low in fat.

1-1/3	cups semisweet chocolate chips
2/3	cup fat-free sweetened condensed milk
1	teaspoon vanilla extract
1-1/3	cups miniature marshmallows
2	whole reduced-fat graham crackers, broken into bite-size pieces

• Line an 8-in. square pan with foil and coat with cooking spray; set aside. In a heavy saucepan over low heat, melt chocolate chips with milk; stir until smooth. Remove from the heat; cool for 2 minutes. Stir in vanilla. Fold in the marshmallows and graham crackers.

• Pour into prepared pan. Refrigerate for 1 hour or until firm. Lift out the pan and remove foil; cut into 48 pieces.

YIELD: 4 dozen.

NUTRITION FACTS: 1 piece equals 41 calories, 1 g fat (1 g saturated fat), 1 mg cholesterol, 10 mg sodium, 7 g carbohydrate, 1g fiber, 1 g protein. **DIABETIC EXCHANGE:** 1/2 starch.

MARSHMALLOW FUDGE

41 CALORIES

GRANOLA BISCOTTI

75 CALORIES

granola biscotti

Lori Waites | FRANKENMUTH, MICHIGAN

This cranberry-studded treat is low in fat but high in flavor. Because it freezes so well, I always double the recipe!

- 1/4 cup butter, softened
- 3/4 cup sugar
- 1 egg
- 1 egg white
- 1/4 teaspoon almond extract
- 1-1/3 cups all-purpose flour
- 1 teaspoon baking powder
- 1/2 teaspoon baking soda
- 1/4 teaspoon salt
- 3/4 cup reduced-fat granola
- 2/3 cup dried cranberries

- In a small mixing bowl, beat butter and sugar until crumbly, about 2 minutes. Beat in the egg, egg white and extract. Combine the flour, baking powder, baking soda and salt; gradually add to butter mixture. Break apart any large pieces of granola; stir granola and cranberries into dough.

- Divide dough in half. With lightly floured hands, shape each portion into a 12-in. x 1-1/2-in. rectangle; place each on a baking sheet coated with cooking spray.

- Bake at 350° for 20-25 minutes or until golden brown. Carefully remove to wire racks; cool for 5 minutes.

- Transfer to a cutting board; cut with a serrated knife into 3/4-in. slices. Place the cut side down on ungreased baking sheets.

- Bake for 5 minutes. Turn and bake 5-7 minutes longer or until firm. Remove to wire racks to cool. Store in an airtight container.

YIELD: 2-1/2 dozen.

NUTRITION FACTS: 1 cookie equals 75 calories, 2 g fat (1 g saturated fat), 11 mg cholesterol, 80 mg sodium, 14 g carbohydrate, trace fiber, 1 g protein. DIABETIC EXCHANGE: 1 starch.

wonton sundaes

Betty Jo Morris | LITTLE ROCK, ARKANSAS

Served as a dessert or sweet appetizer, these cute little bites always vanish in a flash. I created the recipe by combining two of my favorite treats.

- 24 wonton wrappers
- Refrigerated butter-flavored spray
- 1 tablespoon plus 1/4 cup sugar, *divided*
- 1 teaspoon ground cinnamon
- 1 package (8 ounces) reduced-fat cream cheese
- 1 teaspoon vanilla extract
- 1/4 cup semisweet chocolate chips
- 1/4 cup chopped pecans
- 24 maraschino cherries with stems

- Place wonton wrappers on a work surface; spritz with butter-flavored spray. Combine 1 tablespoon sugar and cinnamon; sprinkle over wontons. Press into miniature muffin cups coated with cooking spray.

- Bake at 350° for 4-5 minutes or until lightly browned. Immediately remove wonton cups to an ungreased baking sheet. Bake 2-3 minutes longer or until bottoms of cups are lightly browned. Remove to a wire rack to cool.

WONTON SUNDAES

83 CALORIES

- In a small mixing bowl, beat the cream cheese, vanilla and remaining sugar until smooth. Stir in chocolate chips and pecans. Spoon into wonton cups. Top each with a cherry.

YIELD: 2 dozen.

EDITOR'S NOTE: This recipe was tested with I Can't Believe It's Not Butter Spray.

NUTRITION FACTS: 1 sundae equals 83 calories, 3 g fat (1 g saturated fat), 6 mg cholesterol, 74 mg sodium, 12 g carbohydrate, trace fiber, 2 g protein. **DIABETIC EXCHANGES:** 1 starch.

banana chocolate chip cookies

Vicki Raatz | WATERLOO, WISCONSIN

These soft cookies have a cake-like texture, chocolate chips and lots of banana flavor. Everyone loves them!

1/3	cup butter, softened
1/2	cup sugar
1	egg
1/2	cup mashed ripe banana
1/2	teaspoon vanilla extract
1	cup all-purpose flour
1	teaspoon baking powder
1/4	teaspoon salt
1/8	teaspoon baking soda
1	cup (6 ounces) semisweet chocolate chips

- In a small mixing bowl, cream butter and sugar until light and fluffy. Beat in the egg, banana and vanilla. Combine the flour, baking powder, salt and baking soda; gradually add to creamed mixture. Stir in chocolate chips.

- Drop by tablespoonfuls 2 in. apart onto baking sheets coated with cooking spray. Bake at 350° for 9-11 minutes or until edges are lightly browned. Remove to wire racks to cool.

YIELD: 3 dozen.

NUTRITION FACTS: 1 cookie equals 66 calories, 3 g fat (2 g saturated fat), 10 mg cholesterol, 51 mg sodium, 9 g carbohydrate, trace fiber, 1 g protein. **DIABETIC EXCHANGES:** 1/2 starch, 1/2 fat.

BANANA CHOCOLATE CHIP COOKIES

66 CALORIES

Try these ideas for making your desserts lighter:

- I turn leftover plain angel food cake into light cookies. I cut the cake into 1/2-inch slices, then cut out shapes with a cookie cutter. I toast these "cookies" in the oven for a few minutes, then serve with fresh fruit or add them to a dessert tray.
  Caron O., DES MOINES, IOWA

- For a lighter moist cake, use any flavor cake mix and beat in a 12-ounce can of diet soda. Try diet lemon-lime soda with white or yellow cake mix and diet cola with a chocolate cake mix. Do not add any other ingredients. Just mix and pour the batter into a pan and

bake as usual. Top each piece with 2 tablespoons of fat-free whipped topping instead of icing.
  Debbie M., OWENSBORO, KENTUCKY

- To lighten up my favorite homemade ice cream recipes, I substitute half-and-half cream or skim milk for the full-fat versions.
  Jennifer P., OMAHA, NEBRASKA

- Here's a smart way to frost an angel food cake or any other cake. Simply thaw a large container of light frozen whipped topping and fold in one package of any flavor sugar-free gelatin powder. This

flavorful frosting mixes up in seconds and tastes great!
  Sandy S., LONDON, ONTARIO

- I'm always trying to find delicious desserts that don't have a lot of sugar and fat. For a sweet treat, I simply spoon a can of light apricot halves (including the syrup) into four parfait glasses. Then I top them with sugar-free instant vanilla pudding prepared with fat-free milk. I chill them until set, and top with a maraschino cherry for a pretty look.
  Evelyn K.
  ELIZABETH CITY, NORTH CAROLINA

marbled chocolate cheesecake bars

Jean Komlos | PLYMOUTH, MICHIGAN

Chocolate and cream cheese are swirled in these yummy bars to create a sensation that's sure to please your sweet tooth...and fool it at the same time! This dessert tastes so rich, it's hard to believe it's low in fat.

- 3/4 cup water
- 1/3 cup butter
- 1-1/2 squares (1-1/2 ounces) unsweetened chocolate
- 2 cups all-purpose flour
- 1-1/2 cups packed brown sugar
- 1 teaspoon baking soda
- 1/2 teaspoon salt
- 1 egg
- 1 egg white
- 1/2 cup reduced-fat sour cream

CREAM CHEESE MIXTURE:

- 1 package (8 ounces) reduced-fat cream cheese
- 1/3 cup sugar
- 1 egg white
- 1 tablespoon vanilla extract
- 1 cup (6 ounces) miniature semisweet chocolate chips

- In a small saucepan, combine the water, butter and chocolate. Cook and stir over low heat until melted; stir until smooth. Cool.

- In a large mixing bowl, combine the flour, brown sugar, baking soda and salt. Beat in the egg, egg white and

MARBLED CHOCOLATE CHEESECAKE BARS

95 CALORIES

sour cream on low speed just until combined. Beat in chocolate mixture until smooth. In another mixing bowl, beat the cream cheese, sugar, egg white and vanilla until smooth; set aside.

- Spread the chocolate batter into a 15-in. x 10-in. x 1-in. baking pan coated with cooking spray. Drop the cream cheese mixture by tablespoonfuls over batter; cut through batter with a knife to swirl. Sprinkle with chocolate chips.

- Bake at 375° for 20-25 minutes or until a toothpick inserted near center comes out clean. Cool on a wire rack.

YIELD: about 4 dozen.

NUTRITION FACTS: 1 bar equals 95 calories, 4 g fat (2 g saturated fat), 10 mg cholesterol, 90 mg sodium, 15 g carbohydrate, trace fiber, 2 g protein. **DIABETIC EXCHANGES:** 1 starch, 1/2 fat.

87 CALORIES

COOKOUT CARAMEL S'MORES

cookout caramel s'mores

Martha Haseman | HINCKLEY, ILLINOIS

Just like the campfire favorites, this lighter version of the classic sweet treat is sure to satisfy.

- 8 large marshmallows
- 2 teaspoons fat-free chocolate syrup
- 4 whole reduced-fat graham crackers, halved
- 2 teaspoons fat-free caramel ice cream topping

- Using a long-handled fork, toast the marshmallows 6 in. from medium-hot heat until golden brown, turning occasionally. Drizzle chocolate syrup over four graham crackers; top each with two toasted marshmallows. Drizzle with caramel topping. Cover with the remaining graham crackers.

YIELD: 4 servings.

NUTRITION FACTS: 1 s'more equals 87 calories, 1 g fat (1 g saturated fat), 1 mg cholesterol, 82 mg sodium, 20 g carbohydrate, 1 g fiber, 1 g protein. **DIABETIC EXCHANGE:** 1 starch.

watermelon berry sorbet

Jill Swavely | GREEN LANE, PENNSYLVANIA

Strawberries, watermelon and three other items are all you need for this freezer treat that's low in calories and virtually free of fat. A friend gave me the recipe, promising it was the ultimate in refreshing, summer desserts. I couldn't agree more.

- 1 cup water
- 1/2 cup sugar
- 2 cups cubed seedless watermelon
- 2 cups fresh strawberries, hulled
- 1 tablespoon minced fresh mint

- In a small heavy saucepan, bring the water and sugar to a boil. Cook and stir until sugar is dissolved. Remove from the heat; cool slightly.

- Place the watermelon and strawberries in a blender; add sugar syrup. Cover and process for 2-3 minutes or until smooth. Strain and discard seeds and pulp. Transfer puree to a 13-in. x 9-in. x 2-in. dish. Freeze for 1 hour or until edges begin to firm.

- Stir in mint. Freeze 2 hours longer or until firm. Just before serving, transfer to a blender; cover and process for 2-3 minutes or until smooth.

YIELD: 6 servings.

NUTRITION FACTS: 1/2 cup equals 95 calories, trace fat (trace saturated fat), 0 cholesterol, 3 mg sodium, 25 g carbohydrate, 2 g fiber, 1 g protein. **DIABETIC EXCHANGES:** 1 starch, 1/2 fruit.

WATERMELON BERRY SORBET

95 CALORIES

65 CALORIES

BANANA-CHIP MINI CUPCAKES

banana-chip mini cupcakes

Beverly Coyde | GASPORT, NEW YORK

These cute little mini cupcakes are packed with banana flavor and chocolate chips, then topped off with creamy frosting. They make a great, fast snack when the kids come home from school. It's nice to enjoy a luscious treat in a small serving.

- 1 package (14 ounces) banana quick bread and muffin mix
- 3/4 cup water
- 1/3 cup sour cream
- 1 egg
- 1 cup miniature semisweet chocolate chips, *divided*
- 1 tablespoon shortening

- In a large bowl, combine the muffin mix, water, sour cream and egg; stir just until moistened. Fold in 1/2 cup chocolate chips.

- Fill greased or paper-lined miniature muffin cups two-thirds full. Bake at 375° for 12-15 minutes or until a toothpick comes out clean. Cool for 5 minutes before removing from pans to wire racks to cool completely.

- For frosting, in a small microwave-safe bowl, melt the shortening and remaining chocolate chips; stir until smooth. Frost cupcakes.

YIELD: 3-1/2 dozen.

NUTRITION FACTS: 1 cupcake equals 65 calories, 2 g fat (1 g saturated fat), 6 mg cholesterol, 57 mg sodium, 10 g carbohydrate, trace fiber, 1 g protein.

76 CALORIES

BAKLAVA TARTLETS

baklava tartlets

Ashley Eagon | KETTERING, OHIO

Want a quick treat that's delicious and easy? These tartlets do the trick. You can serve them right away, but they're better after chilling for about an hour in the refrigerator. A little sprig of mint adds just a lovely touch of color.

>   2   cups finely chopped walnuts
>   3/4 cup honey
>   1/2 cup butter, melted
>   1   teaspoon ground cinnamon
>   1   teaspoon lemon juice
>   1/4 teaspoon ground cloves
>   3   packages (1.9 ounces *each*) frozen miniature phyllo tart shells

- In a small bowl, combine the first six ingredients; spoon 2 teaspoonfuls into each tart shell. Refrigerate tartlets until serving.

YIELD: 45 tartlets.

NUTRITION FACTS: 1 tartlet equals 76 calories, 5 g fat (1 g saturated fat), 5 mg cholesterol, 24 mg sodium, 6 g carbohydrate, trace fiber, 2 g protein.

chocolate gingersnaps

Paula Zsiray | LOGAN, UTAH

When my daughter, Jennifer, was 15 years old, she created this recipe as a way to combine two of her favorite flavors. They're great with a glass of milk.

>   1/2 cup butter, softened
>   1/2 cup packed dark brown sugar

>   1/4   cup molasses
>   1   tablespoon water
>   2   teaspoons minced fresh gingerroot
>   1-1/2 cups all-purpose flour
>   1   tablespoon baking cocoa
>   1-1/4 teaspoons ground ginger
>   1   teaspoon baking soda
>   1   teaspoon ground cinnamon
>   1/4   teaspoon ground nutmeg
>   1/4   teaspoon ground cloves
>   7   squares (1 ounce *each*) semisweet chocolate, chopped
>   1/4   cup sugar

- In a large mixing bowl, cream butter and brown sugar until light and fluffy. Beat in the molasses, water and gingerroot.

- Combine the flour, cocoa, ginger, baking soda, cinnamon, nutmeg and cloves; gradually add to creamed mixture and mix well. Stir in chocolate. Cover and refrigerate for 2 hours or until easy to handle.

- Shape dough into 1-in. balls; roll in sugar. Place 2 in. apart on greased baking sheets.

- Bake at 350° for 10-12 minutes or until tops begin to crack. Cool for 2 minutes before removing to wire racks.

YIELD: 3 dozen.

NUTRITION FACTS: 1 cookie equals 69 calories, 3 g fat (2 g saturated fat), 7 mg cholesterol, 63 mg sodium, 11 g carbohydrate, trace fiber, 1 g protein.

CHOCOLATE GINGERSNAPS

69 CALORIES

70 CALORIES

NUTTY CHOCOLATE FUDGE

cappuccino truffles

Ellen Swenson | NEWPORT CENTER, VERMONT

The dark chocolate, mocha and cinnamon in these truffles create a delectable flavor combination. Smooth and rich, even one or two makes a satisfying dessert. Prepare a lot because they also make great gifts.

- 1 tablespoon boiling water
- 2 teaspoons instant coffee granules
- 2-1/2 teaspoons ground cinnamon, *divided*
- 1/3 cup heavy whipping cream
- 6 squares (1 ounce *each*) bittersweet chocolate, chopped
- 2 tablespoons butter, softened
- 3 tablespoons sugar

- In a small bowl, combine the water, coffee and 1 teaspoon cinnamon; set aside. In a small saucepan, bring cream just to a boil. Remove from the heat; whisk in chocolate and butter until smooth. Stir in coffee mixture. Press plastic wrap onto surface. Refrigerate for 1 hour or until easy to handle.

- In a small bowl, combine sugar and remaining cinnamon. Shape chocolate into 1-in. balls; roll in cinnamon-sugar. Refrigerate for at least 2 hours or until firm.

YIELD: 1-1/2 dozen.

NUTRITION FACTS: 1 truffle equals 43 calories, 4 g fat (2 g saturated fat), 9 mg cholesterol, 15 mg sodium, 3 g carbohydrate, trace fiber, trace protein.

CAPPUCCINO TRUFFLES

nutty chocolate fudge

A.J. Ristow | TUCSON, ARIZONA

I've trimmed down this recipe over the years, and now my family likes it better than ever. They don't even miss all of the sugar that I used to add. Try it with peanut butter or butterscotch chips.

- 1 jar (7 ounces) marshmallow creme
- 2/3 cup fat-free evaporated milk
- 1/2 cup butter, cubed
- 2 teaspoons vanilla extract
- 3 cups (18 ounces) semisweet chocolate chips
- 2 cups chopped pecans *or* walnuts, toasted

- Line a 9-in. square pan with foil and coat foil with cooking spray; set aside.

- In a large saucepan, combine the marshmallow creme, evaporated milk and butter. Cook and stir over medium heat until smooth. Bring to a boil; boil for 5 minutes, stirring constantly. Remove from the heat; add vanilla. Stir in chocolate chips until melted. Add pecans. Pour into prepared pan. Refrigerate for 2 hours or until firm.

- Using foil, remove fudge from pan; carefully remove foil. Cut into 1-in. squares. Store in the refrigerator.

YIELD: 2-2/3 pounds (81 pieces).

NUTRITION FACTS: 1 piece equals 70 calories, 5 g fat (2 g saturated fat), 3 mg cholesterol, 16 mg sodium, 7 g carbohydrate, 1 g fiber, 1 g protein. **DIABETIC EXCHANGES:** 1 fat, 1/2 starch.

43 CALORIES

raspberry-topped cream tarts

Kathy Rairigh | MILFORD, INDIANA

These tarts are as lovely to look at as they are good to eat! Crispy tortilla cups are filled with a cream cheese mixture and topped with fresh raspberries. They're also delicious with sliced strawberries.

- 1 tablespoon brown sugar
- 1/4 teaspoon ground cinnamon
- 1/8 teaspoon ground nutmeg
- 4 flour tortillas (8 inches)

Warm water

- 1 package (8 ounces) reduced-fat cream cheese, softened
- 3 tablespoons sugar
- 1 to 2 tablespoons fat-free milk
- 1/2 teaspoon almond extract
- 1 cup fresh raspberries

- In a bowl, combine brown sugar, cinnamon and nutmeg; set aside. Cut tortillas with a 3-1/2-in. biscuit cutter; discard tortillas scraps. Brush both sides of tortillas rounds with warm water. Spray tops with cooking spray; sprinkle with brown sugar mixture. Press into ungreased muffin cups.

RASPBERRY-TOPPED CREAM TARTS

93 CALORIES

78 CALORIES

CHOCOLATE BISCUIT PUFFS

- Bake at 350° for 12-15 minutes or until lightly browned. Cool in pans on wire racks.

- In a small mixing bowl, combine the cream cheese, sugar, milk and almond extract; mix well. Spoon into the tortillas shells; top with the raspberries. Store leftovers in the refrigerator.

YIELD: 16 servings.

NUTRITION FACTS: 1 tart equals 93 calories, 3 g fat (2 g saturated fat), 8 mg cholesterol, 108 mg sodium, 13 g carbohydrate, 1 g fiber, 3 g protein. **DIABETIC EXCHANGES:** 1 starch, 1/2 fat.

chocolate biscuit puffs

Joy Clark | SEABECK, WASHINGTON

I know my favorite snack is fun for kids to make and eat—I dreamed it up at age 9! These are pretty and yummy whether you make them to have the chocolate peeking out or shaped to hide the chocolate within for a tasty surprise.

- 1 package (7-1/2 ounces) refrigerated flaky buttermilk biscuits
- 1 milk chocolate candy bar (1.55 ounces)
- 2 teaspoons cinnamon-sugar

- Flatten each biscuit into a 3-in. circle. Break candy bar into 10 pieces; place a piece on each biscuit. Bring up edges to enclose candy and pinch to seal.

- Place on an ungreased baking sheet. Sprinkle with the cinnamon-sugar. Bake at 450° for 8-10 minutes or until golden brown.

YIELD: 10 servings.

NUTRITION FACTS: 1 puff equals 78 calories, 2 g fat (1 g saturated fat), 1 mg cholesterol, 185 mg sodium, 14 g carbohydrate, trace fiber, 2 g protein. **DIABETIC EXCHANGE:** 1 starch.

caramel pecan candy

Dick Deacon | LAWRENCEVILLE, GEORGIA

Yummy and chewy, these layered squares are a great sweet treat. I have also made this recipe in a 9-inch pie pan and cut it into small wedges.

- 1/3 cup plus 1/2 cup butter, *divided*
- 20 cream-filled chocolate sandwich cookies, crushed
- 1 package (14 ounces) caramels
- 3 cups chopped pecans, toasted

TOPPING:

- 3/4 cup semisweet chocolate chips
- 3 tablespoons butter
- 3 tablespoons heavy whipping cream
- 3 tablespoons light corn syrup
- 3/4 teaspoon vanilla extract

- In a large saucepan, melt 1/3 cup butter over medium heat; stir in cookie crumbs. Press into an ungreased 9-in. square baking dish. Bake at 325° for 10-12 minutes or until set. Cool on a wire rack. Meanwhile, in a small saucepan, melt caramels and remaining butter over low heat. Stir in the pecans. Pour over crust. Cool.

- For topping, in a small saucepan, combine chocolate chips, butter, cream and corn syrup. Cook and stir over low heat until smooth. Remove from the heat; stir in vanilla. Pour over caramel layer. Cool on a wire rack. Refrigerate until chocolate hardens. Let candy stand at room temperature for 5-10 minutes before cutting into 1-in. squares. Store in the refrigerator.

YIELD: about 6-1/2 dozen.

NUTRITION FACTS: 1 piece equals 94 calories, 7 g fat (3 g saturated fat), 7 mg cholesterol, 55 mg sodium, 8 g carbohydrate, 1 g fiber, 1 g protein.

CARAMEL PECAN CANDY

94 CALORIES

88 CALORIES

CHUNKY PECAN BARS

chunky pecan bars

Hazel Baldner | AUSTIN, MINNESOTA

These gooey bars taste just like chocolate pecan pie. Make a batch and store them in the fridge. Then slowly savor one with coffee for a snack.

- 1-1/2 cups all-purpose flour
- 1/2 cup packed brown sugar
- 1/2 cup cold butter, cubed

FILLING:

- 3 eggs
- 3/4 cup sugar
- 3/4 cup dark corn syrup
- 2 tablespoons butter, melted
- 1 teaspoon vanilla extract
- 1-3/4 cups semisweet chocolate chunks
- 1-1/2 cups coarsely chopped pecans

- In a small bowl, combine the flour and brown sugar; cut in butter until crumbly. Press into a greased 13-in. x 9-in. baking pan. Bake at 350° for 10-15 minutes or until golden brown.

- Meanwhile, in a large bowl, whisk the eggs, sugar, corn syrup, butter and vanilla until blended. Stir in chocolate chunks and pecans. Pour over crust.

- Bake for 20-25 minutes or until set. Cool completely on a wire rack. Cut into bars. Store in an airtight container in the refrigerator.

YIELD: about 6 dozen.

NUTRITION FACTS: 1 bar equals 88 calories, 5 g fat (2 g saturated fat), 13 mg cholesterol, 25 mg sodium, 11 g carbohydrate, 1 g fiber, 1 g protein.

101-150 calories

CHEWY CHOCOLATE BROWNIES

chewy chocolate brownies

Michele Doucette | STEPHENVILLE, NEWFOUNDLAND
Cap off dinner with this scrumptious dessert. These rich and fudgy brownies are so decadent, it's hard to believe they're just 124 calories each!

3	squares (1 ounce *each*) semisweet chocolate, chopped
1	cup packed brown sugar
3	tablespoons unsweetened applesauce
1	egg
1	egg white
2	tablespoons canola oil
4-1/2	teaspoons light corn syrup
2	teaspoons vanilla extract
1	cup all-purpose flour
1/4	cup baking cocoa
1/2	teaspoon baking soda
1/8	teaspoon salt

• In a microwave, melt chocolate; stir until smooth. Cool slightly. Meanwhile, in a large mixing bowl, beat the brown sugar, applesauce, egg, egg white, oil, corn syrup and vanilla. Beat in chocolate until blended. Combine the flour, cocoa, baking soda and salt; beat into brown sugar mixture just until blended.

• Pour into a 13-in. x 9-in. baking pan coated with cooking spray. Bake at 350° for 15-18 minutes or until a toothpick inserted near the center comes out clean. Cool on a wire rack. Cut into bars.

YIELD: 1-1/2 dozen.

NUTRITION FACTS: 1 brownie equals 124 calories, 4 g fat (1 g saturated fat), 12 mg cholesterol, 65 mg sodium, 22 g carbohydrate, 1 g fiber, 2 g protein. **DIABETIC EXCHANGES:** 1-1/2 starch, 1/2 fat.

oatmeal chip cookies

140 CALORIES

Susan Henry | BULLHEAD CITY, ARIZONA
A cookie is a fun way to finish a meal. My mom liked to add different spices to traditional recipes and create unexpected tastes. Molasses and cinnamon make these cookies memorable.

1/2	cup shortening
1	cup sugar
1	tablespoon molasses
1	egg
1	teaspoon vanilla extract
1	cup all-purpose flour
1	cup quick-cooking oats
1	teaspoon baking soda
1	teaspoon ground cinnamon
1/2	teaspoon salt
1	cup (6 ounces) semisweet chocolate chips

• In a large mixing bowl, cream shortening and sugar. Beat in the molasses, egg and vanilla. Combine the flour, oats, baking soda, cinnamon and salt; gradually add to creamed mixture. Stir in chocolate chips.

• Roll into 1-1/2-in. balls. Place 2 in. apart on greased baking sheets. Bake at 350° for 8-10 minutes or until golden brown. Cool for 5 minutes before removing from pans to wire racks.

YIELD: about 1-1/2 dozen.

NUTRITION FACTS: 1 cookie equals 140 calories, 7 g fat (2 g saturated fat), 9 mg cholesterol, 106 mg sodium, 20 g carbohydrate, 1 g fiber, 2 g protein.

PINEAPPLE PUDDING CAKE

131 CALORIES

pineapple pudding cake

Kathleen Worden | NORTH ANDOVER, MASSACHUSETTS

My mother used to love making this easy dessert in the summertime. It's so cool, fluffy and delicious. One piece is quite enough!

- 1 package (9 ounces) yellow cake mix
- 1-1/2 cups cold fat-free milk
- 1 package (1 ounce) sugar-free instant vanilla pudding mix
- 1 package (8 ounces) fat-free cream cheese
- 1 can (20 ounces) unsweetened crushed pineapple, well drained
- 1 carton (8 ounces) frozen fat-free whipped topping, thawed
- 1/4 cup chopped walnuts, toasted
- 20 maraschino cherries, well drained

- Prepare cake mix batter according to package directions; pour into a 13-in. x 9-in. baking pan coated with cooking spray. Bake at 350° for 15-20 minutes or until a toothpick inserted near the center comes out clean. Cool completely on a wire rack.

- In a bowl, whisk milk and pudding mix for 2 minutes. Let stand for 2 minutes or until soft-set. In a small mixing bowl, beat cream cheese until smooth. Beat in pudding mixture until blended. Spread evenly over cake. Sprinkle with pineapple; spread with whipped topping. Sprinkle with walnuts and garnish with cherries. Refrigerate until serving.

YIELD: 20 servings.

NUTRITION FACTS: 1 piece equals 131 calories, 2 g fat (1 g saturated fat), 1 mg cholesterol, 217 mg sodium, 24 g carbohydrate, 1 g fiber, 3 g protein. **DIABETIC EXCHANGE:** 1-1/2 starch.

chippy blond brownies

Anna Jean Allen | WEST LIBERTY, KENTUCKY

If you love chocolate and butterscotch, these are just the brownies to satisfy your cravings. I often include this recipe inside a baking dish as a wedding present. Everyone, young and old, enjoys these goodies.

- 6 tablespoons butter, softened
- 1 cup packed brown sugar
- 2 eggs
- 1 teaspoon vanilla extract
- 1-1/4 cups all-purpose flour
- 1 teaspoon baking powder
- 1/2 teaspoon salt
- 1 cup (6 ounces) semisweet chocolate chips
- 1/2 cup chopped pecans

- In a large mixing bowl, cream butter and brown sugar until light and fluffy. Add the eggs, one at a time, beating well after each addition. Beat in vanilla. Combine the flour, baking powder and salt; gradually add to creamed mixture until blended. Stir in the chocolate chips and pecans.

- Spread into a greased 11-in. x 7-in. baking pan. Bake at 350° for 25-30 minutes or until a toothpick inserted near the center comes out clean. Cool on a wire rack.

YIELD: 2 dozen.

NUTRITION FACTS: 1 brownie equals 141 calories, 7 g fat (3 g saturated fat), 25 mg cholesterol, 104 mg sodium, 19 g carbohydrate, 1 g fiber, 2 g protein.

CHIPPY BLOND BROWNIES

141 CALORIES

chocolate mint crisps

Karen Ann Bland | GOVE, KANSAS

If you like chocolate and mint, you can't help but love these scrumptious, crispy cookies with their creamy icing. We make them for the holidays, and they always get compliments!

- 1-1/2 **cups packed brown sugar**
- 3/4 **cup butter, cubed**
- 2 **tablespoons plus 1-1/2 teaspoons water**
- 2 **cups (12 ounces) semisweet chocolate chips**
- 2 **eggs**
- 2-1/2 **cups all-purpose flour**
- 1-1/4 **teaspoons baking soda**
- 1/2 **teaspoon salt**
- 3 **packages (4.67 ounces** *each***) mint Andes candies**

- In a heavy saucepan, combine the brown sugar, butter and water. Cook and stir over low heat until butter is melted and mixture is smooth. Remove from the heat; stir in chocolate chips until melted.

- Transfer to a mixing bowl. Let stand for 10 minutes. With the mixer on high speed, add eggs one at a time, beating well after each addition. Combine the flour, baking soda and salt; add to chocolate mixture, beating on low until blended. Cover and refrigerate for 8 hours or overnight.

- Roll dough into 1-in. balls. Place 3 in. apart on lightly greased baking sheets. Bake at 350° for 11-13 minutes or until edges are set and tops are puffed and cracked (cookies will become crisp after cooling).

CHOCOLATE MINT CRISPS

149 CALORIES

123 CALORIES

POTATO CHIP COOKIES

- Immediately top each cookie with a mint. Let stand for 1-2 minutes; spread over cookie. Remove to wire racks; let stand until chocolate is set and cookies are cooled.

YIELD: 6-1/2 dozen.

NUTRITION FACTS: 2 cookies equal 149 calories, 7 g fat (4 g saturated fat), 20 mg cholesterol, 114 mg sodium, 22 g carbohydrate, 1 g fiber, 2 g protein.

potato chip cookies

Monna Lu Bauer | LEXINGTON, KENTUCKY

If you like a sweet-and-salty treat, this cookie is perfect! They quickly bake to a crispy golden brown...and they're so much fun to munch!

- 1 **cup butter-flavored shortening**
- 3/4 **cup sugar**
- 3/4 **cup packed brown sugar**
- 2 **eggs**
- 2 **cups all-purpose flour**
- 1 **teaspoon baking soda**
- 2 **cups crushed potato chips**
- 1 **cup butterscotch chips**

- In a large mixing bowl, cream shortening and sugars until light and fluffy. Beat in eggs. Combine flour and baking soda; gradually add to creamed mixture and mix well. Stir in potato chips and butterscotch chips.

- Drop by tablespoonfuls 2 in. apart onto ungreased baking sheets. Bake at 375° for 10-12 minutes or until golden brown. Cool for 1 minute before removing to wire racks.

YIELD: 4 dozen.

NUTRITION FACTS: 1 cookie equals 123 calories, 7 g fat (3 g saturated fat), 9 mg cholesterol, 48 mg sodium, 15 g carbohydrate, trace fiber, 1 g protein.

mother lode pretzels

Carrie Bennett | MADISON, WISCONSIN

I brought these savory-sweet pretzels to a family gathering, and they disappeared from the tray before dessert was even served! My family raves about how awesome they are.

1	package (10 ounces) pretzel rods
1	package (14 ounces) caramels
1	tablespoon evaporated milk
1-1/4	cups miniature semisweet chocolate chips
1	cup plus 2 tablespoons butterscotch chips
2/3	cup milk chocolate toffee bits
1/4	cup chopped walnuts, toasted

- With a sharp knife, cut pretzel rods in half; set aside. In a large saucepan over low heat, melt caramels with milk. In a large shallow bowl, combine the chips, toffee bits and walnuts.

- Pour caramel mixture into a 2-cup glass measuring cup. Dip the cut end of each pretzel piece two-thirds of the way into caramel mixture (reheat in the microwave if mixture becomes too thick for dipping). Allow excess caramel to drip off, then roll the pretzels in the chip mixture. Place on waxed paper until set. Store in an airtight container.

YIELD: 4-1/2 dozen.

NUTRITION FACTS: 1 pretzel equals 114 calories, 5 g fat (3 g saturated fat), 3 mg cholesterol, 104 mg sodium, 17 g carbohydrate, 1 g fiber, 1 g protein. **DIABETIC EXCHANGES:** 1 starch, 1 fat.

MOTHER LODE PRETZELS

114 CALORIES

110 CALORIES

DARK CHOCOLATE BUTTERSCOTCH BROWNIES

dark chocolate butterscotch brownies

Kit Concilus | MEADVILLE, PENNSYLVANIA

I love homemade brownies. I experimented with many recipes and finally came up with this favorite.

4	squares (1 ounce *each*) unsweetened chocolate
3/4	cup butter, cubed
2	cups sugar
3	egg whites
1-1/2	teaspoons vanilla extract
1	cup all-purpose flour
1	cup 60% cocoa bittersweet chocolate baking chips
1	cup butterscotch chips

GLAZE:

1	cup 60% cocoa bittersweet chocolate baking chips
1/4	cup butter, cubed

- In a microwave-safe bowl, melt unsweetened chocolate and butter; stir until smooth. Cool slightly. In a large bowl, combine sugar and chocolate mixture. Stir in egg whites and vanilla. Stir in flour. Stir in chips.

- Spread into a greased 13-in. x 9-in. baking pan. Bake at 350° for 25-30 minutes or until a toothpick inserted near the center comes out clean. Cool on a wire rack.

- For the glaze, melt chips and butter; stir until smooth. Immediately spread over brownies. Cool before cutting.

YIELD: 5 dozen.

EDITOR'S NOTE: This recipe was tested using Ghirardelli 60% cocoa bittersweet chocolate baking chips.

NUTRITION FACTS: 1 brownie equals 110 calories, 6 g fat (4 g saturated fat), 9 mg cholesterol, 39 mg sodium, 14 g carbohydrate, 1 g fiber, 1 g protein.

147 CALORIES

APRICOT DATE SQUARES

apricot date squares

Shannon Koene | BLACKSBURG, VIRGINIA

Memories of my mom's fruity date bars inspired me to create this wonderful recipe. I've had great results replacing the apricot jam with orange marmalade.

1	cup water
1	cup sugar
1	cup chopped dates
1/2	cup 100% apricot spreadable fruit *or* jam
1-3/4	cups old-fashioned oats
1-1/2	cups all-purpose flour
1	cup flaked coconut
1	cup packed brown sugar
1	teaspoon ground cinnamon
1/4	teaspoon salt
3/4	cup cold butter, cubed

- In a small saucepan, combine the water, sugar and dates. Bring to a boil. Reduce heat; simmer, uncovered, for 30-35 minutes or until mixture is reduced to 1-1/3 cups and is slightly thickened, stirring occasionally.

- Remove from the heat. Stir in the spreadable fruit until blended; set aside. In a food processor, combine the oats, flour, coconut, brown sugar, cinnamon and salt. Add the butter; cover and process until the mixture resembles coarse crumbs.

- Press 3 cups crumb mixture into a 13-in. x 9-in. baking dish coated with cooking spray. Spread date mixture to within 1/2 in. of edges. Sprinkle with remaining crumb mixture; press down gently.

- Bake at 350° for 20-25 minutes or until edges are lightly browned. Cool on a wire rack. Cut into squares.

YIELD: 3 dozen.

NUTRITION FACTS: 1 bar equals 147 calories, 5 g fat (3 g saturated fat), 10 mg cholesterol, 65 mg sodium, 25 g carbohydrate, 1 g fiber, 1 g protein. **DIABETIC EXCHANGES:** 1-1/2 starch, 1 fat.

fruity cereal bars

Giovanna Kranenberg | CAMBRIDGE, MINNESOTA

With dried apple and cranberries, these crispy cereal bars are perfect for snacks or brown-bag lunches. Store the extras in plastic containers, that is, if you have any left!

3	tablespoons butter
1	package (10 ounces) large marshmallows
6	cups crisp rice cereal
1/2	cup dried chopped apple
1/2	cup dried cranberries

- In a large saucepan, combine butter and marshmallows. Cook and stir over medium-low heat until melted. Remove from heat; stir in cereal, apples and cranberries.

- Pat into a 13-in. x 9-in. x 2-in. pan coated with cooking spray; cool. Cut into squares.

YIELD: 20 servings.

NUTRITION FACTS: 1 bar equals 105 calories, 2 g fat (1 g saturated fat), 5 mg cholesterol, 102 mg sodium, 22 g carbohydrate, trace fiber, 1 g protein. **DIABETIC EXCHANGES:** 1-1/2 starch, 1/2 fat.

FRUITY CEREAL BARS

105 CALORIES

139 CALORIES

DOUBLE CHOCOLATE CUPCAKES

double chocolate cupcakes

Linda Utter | SIDNEY, MONTANA

You don't have to fudge on chocolate to make a luscious treat. These moist cupcakes are chock-full of sweet flavor but low in calories and saturated fat.

        2   tablespoons butter, softened
      3/4   cup sugar
        1   egg
        1   egg white
      1/2   cup plus 2 tablespoons buttermilk
      1/3   cup water
        1   tablespoon white vinegar
        1   teaspoon vanilla extract
    1-1/2   cups all-purpose flour
      1/4   cup baking cocoa
        1   teaspoon baking soda
      1/2   teaspoon salt
      1/3   cup miniature semisweet chocolate chips

- In a large mixing bowl, cream butter and sugar until light and fluffy. Add egg and egg white, one at a time, beating well after each addition. Beat on high speed until light and fluffy. Stir in the buttermilk, water, vinegar and vanilla. Combine the flour, cocoa, baking soda and salt; add to batter just until moistened. Stir in the chocolate chips.

- Fill muffin cups coated with cooking spray three-fourths full. Bake at 375° for 15-18 minutes or until toothpick comes out clean. Cool for 5 minutes before removing from pans to wire racks.

YIELD: 14 cupcakes.

NUTRITION FACTS: 1 cupcake equals 139 calories, 2 g fat (1 g saturated fat), 1 mg cholesterol, 221 mg sodium, 29 g carbohydrate, 1 g fiber, 3 g protein. **DIABETIC EXCHANGES:** 1-1/2 starch, 1/2 fat.

granola fudge clusters

Loraine Meyer | BEND, OREGON

Short and sweet, this yummy recipe calls for only four ingredients. I always make a double batch because then I have a lot to share.

        1   cup (6 ounces) semisweet chocolate chips
        1   cup butterscotch chips
    1-1/4   cups granola cereal without raisins
        1   cup chopped walnuts

- In a microwave-safe bowl, melt chocolate and butterscotch chips; stir until smooth. Stir in granola and walnuts.

- Drop by tablespoonfuls onto waxed paper-lined baking sheets. Refrigerate for 15 minutes or until firm.

YIELD: about 2-1/2 dozen.

NUTRITION FACTS: 1 fudge cluster equals 114 calories, 7 g fat (3 g saturated fat), trace cholesterol, 9 mg sodium, 12 g carbohydrate, 1 g fiber, 2 g protein.

GRANOLA FUDGE CLUSTERS

114 CALORIES

cappuccino mousse

This rich mousse from our Test Kitchen experts has a hint of coffee and a pleasantly creamy texture. Make it ahead for a delightful finale.

1/2	teaspoon unflavored gelatin
1/4	cup fat-free milk
1-1/2	teaspoons baking cocoa
1/4	teaspoon instant coffee granules
1/3	cup fat-free coffee-flavored yogurt
2	tablespoons sugar
1/2	cup reduced-fat whipped topping

- In a small saucepan, sprinkle gelatin over milk; let stand for 1 minute. Heat over low heat, stirring until gelatin is completely dissolved. Add cocoa and coffee; stir until dissolved. Transfer to a small mixing bowl; refrigerate until mixture begins to thicken.

- Beat until light and fluffy. Combine yogurt and sugar; beat into gelatin mixture. Fold in whipping topping. Divide between two dessert dishes. Refrigerate until firm.

YIELD: 2 servings.

NUTRITION FACTS: 3/4 cup equals 125 calories, 2 g fat (2 g saturated fat), 1 mg cholesterol, 40 mg sodium, 22 g carbohydrate, trace fiber, 3 g protein. **DIABETIC EXCHANGE:** 1-1/2 starch.

CAPPUCCINO MOUSSE

WHITE CHOCOLATE CRANBERRY COOKIES

white chocolate cranberry cookies

Donna Beck | SCOTTDALE, PENNSYLVANIA

These sweet cookies feature white chocolate and cranberries for a scrumptious flavor. And the red and white coloring add a festive feel to any cookie tray.

1/3	cup butter, softened
1/2	cup packed brown sugar
1/3	cup sugar
1	egg
1	teaspoon vanilla extract
1-1/2	cups all-purpose flour
1/2	teaspoon salt
1/2	teaspoon baking soda
3/4	cup dried cranberries
1/2	cup vanilla *or* white chips

- In a large mixing bowl, beat butter and sugars until crumbly, about 2 minutes. Beat in egg and vanilla. Combine the flour, salt and baking soda; gradually add to butter mixture and mix well. Stir in cranberries and chips.

- Drop by heaping tablespoonfuls 2 in. apart onto baking sheets coated with cooking spray. Bake at 375° for 8-10 minutes or until lightly browned. Cool for 1 minute before removing to wire racks.

YIELD: 2 dozen.

NUTRITION FACTS: 1 cookie equals 113 calories, 4 g fat (2 g saturated fat), 16 mg cholesterol, 109 mg sodium, 18 g carbohydrate, trace fiber, 1 g protein. **DIABETIC EXCHANGES:** 1 starch, 1/2 fat.

mixed berry pizza

Gretchen Widner | SUN CITY WEST, ARIZONA

Fresh fruit shines through in this colorful dessert pizza. It's also a tempting appetizer at parties because it's a sweet change of pace from the usual savory dips.

- 1 tube (8 ounces) refrigerated reduced-fat crescent rolls
- 11 ounces reduced-fat cream cheese
- 1/2 cup apricot preserves
- 2 tablespoons confectioners' sugar
- 2 cups sliced fresh strawberries
- 1 cup fresh blueberries
- 1 cup fresh raspberries

- Unroll crescent roll dough and place in a 15-in. x 10-in. x 1-in. baking pan coated with cooking spray. Press onto the bottom and 1 in. up the sides of pan to form a crust; seal seams and perforations. Bake at 375° for 8-10 minutes or until golden. Cool completely.

- In a mixing bowl, beat cream cheese until smooth. Beat in preserves and confectioners' sugar; spread over crust. Cover and refrigerate for 1-2 hours.

- Just before serving, arrange the berries on top. Cut into 20 pieces.

YIELD: 20 servings.

NUTRITION FACTS: 1 piece equals 110 calories, 5 g fat (2 g saturated fat), 9 mg cholesterol, 143 mg sodium, 15 g carbohydrate, 1 g fiber, 3 g protein. **DIABETIC EXCHANGES:** 1 fruit, 1/2 starch.

apple pockets

Sharon Martin | TERRE HILL, PENNSYLVANIA

This is a great way to enjoy the taste of apple pie without the guilt. The cute golden bundles are shaped from a homemade yeast dough, but it's their old-fashioned flavor that is really appealing.

- 2-1/4 cups all-purpose flour, *divided*
- 1 package (1/4 ounce) quick-rise yeast
- 1 tablespoon sugar
- 1/2 teaspoon salt
- 2/3 cup water
- 1/4 cup butter

FILLING:

- 4 cups thinly sliced peeled Rome Beauty *or* other baking apples (2 to 3 medium)

APPLE POCKETS

- 1/3 cup sugar
- 2 tablespoons all-purpose flour
- 1/2 teaspoon ground cinnamon

TOPPING:

- 1/4 cup milk
- 4 teaspoons sugar

- In a large mixing bowl, combine 1 cup flour, yeast, sugar and salt. In a saucepan, heat water and butter to 120°-130°. Add to dry ingredients; beat just until moistened. Stir in enough remaining flour to form a soft dough. Turn onto a floured surface; knead until smooth and elastic, about 6-8 minutes. Cover and let rest for 10 minutes.

- Divide dough into four portions. Roll each portion into an 8-in. square. Cut into four 4-in. squares. Cut apple slices into thirds; toss with sugar, flour and cinnamon. Place 1/4 cup filling on each square; bring up the corners up over filling and pinch to seal. Secure with a toothpick if needed. Place 3 in. apart on baking sheets coated with cooking spray. Cover and let rise in a warm place for 30 minutes.

- Brush with milk; sprinkle with the sugar. Bake at 375° for 12-14 minutes or until golden brown. Remove to wire racks. Discard toothpicks before serving.

YIELD: 16 servings.

NUTRITION FACTS: 1 pocket equals 136 calories, 3 g fat (2 g saturated fat), 8 mg cholesterol, 105 mg sodium, 25 g carbohydrate, 1 g fiber, 2 g protein. **DIABETIC EXCHANGES:** 1 starch, 1/2 fruit, 1/2 fat.

CRANBERRY CHEESECAKE BARS

cranberry cheesecake bars

Rhonda Lund | LARAMIE, WYOMING
I came across this recipe several years ago, and it's become a family favorite.

      2 cups plus 2 tablespoons all-purpose flour, *divided*
      1 cup quick-cooking oats
    3/4 cup packed brown sugar
    1/2 cup butter, melted
      1 package (8 ounces) reduced-fat cream cheese
      1 can (14 ounces) fat-free sweetened condensed milk
      4 egg whites
      1 teaspoon vanilla extract
      1 can (16 ounces) whole-berry cranberry sauce
      2 tablespoons cornstarch

- In a large bowl, combine 2 cups flour, coats, brown sugar and butter; mix until crumbly. Press 2-1/2 cups of the crumb mixture into a greased 13-in. x 9-in. x 2-in. baking dish. Bake at 350° for 10 minutes.

- In a large mixing bowl, beat cream cheese until smooth. Beat in the milk, egg whites, vanilla and remaining flour. Spoon over prepared crust. In a small bowl, combine the cranberry sauce and cornstarch. Spoon over cream cheese mixture. Sprinkle with the remaining crumb mixture. Bake at 350° for 30-35 minutes or until the center is almost set. Cool on a wire rack before cutting.

YIELD: 3 dozen.

NUTRITION FACTS: 1 bar equals 142 calories, 4 g fat (2 g saturated fat), 11 mg cholesterol, 67 mg sodium, 24 g carbohydrate, 1 g fiber, 3 g protein. DIABETIC EXCHANGES: 1-1/2 starch, 1/2 fat.

caramelized pear strudel

139 CALORIES

Leah Beatty | COBOURG, ONTARIO
This easy, stylish dessert is sure to please everyone. Best served warm, it's delicious with a scoop of light vanilla ice cream or reduced-fat whipped topping. No one guesses it's low in calories.

    1/2 cup sugar
      1 tablespoon cornstarch
      3 large pears, peeled and finely chopped
    1/2 cup fresh *or* frozen cranberries, thawed
      2 tablespoons butter
    1/2 cup dried cranberries
      1 teaspoon ground ginger
      1 teaspoon grated orange peel
    1/2 teaspoon ground cinnamon
      6 sheets phyllo dough (14 inches x 9 inches)
      1 teaspoon confectioners' sugar

- In a large bowl, combine sugar and cornstarch. Add pears and cranberries; toss gently to coat. In a large nonstick skillet, melt butter over medium-high heat. Add fruit mixture; cook and stir for 7-8 minutes or until cranberries pop. Stir in the dried cranberries, ginger, orange peel and cinnamon. Cool.

- Line a baking sheet with foil and coat foil with cooking spray; set aside. Place one sheet of phyllo dough on a work surface; coat with cooking spray. (Until ready to use, keep phyllo covered with plastic wrap and a damp towel to prevent drying out.) Repeat five times with remaining phyllo. Spread cranberry mixture over dough to within 1 in. of edges. Fold in sides. Roll up, starting at a long side. Place seam side down on prepared baking sheet.

- Bake at 400° for 20-23 minutes or until golden brown. Remove from pan to a wire rack to cool. Dust with the confectioners' sugar before serving.

YIELD: 10 servings.

NUTRITION FACTS: 1 slice equals 139 calories, 3 g fat (1 g saturated fat), 6 mg cholesterol, 50 mg sodium, 30 g carbohydrate, 2 g fiber, 1 g protein. DIABETIC EXCHANGES: 1 starch, 1 fruit, 1/2 fat.

151-250 calories

177 CALORIES

CARAMEL-CHOCOLATE CRUNCH BARS

caramel-chocolate crunch bars

Agnes Ward | STRATFORD, ONTARIO

These bars are lower in calories and simply scrumptious. The Grape-Nuts and oatmeal give them a nutty crunch. With caramel and chocolate on top, you'd never suspect that these are light.

- 3 tablespoons butter, softened
- 5 tablespoons packed brown sugar
- 1/2 cup quick-cooking oats
- 1/3 cup all-purpose flour
- 1/3 cup Grape-Nuts cereal
- 1/4 cup caramel ice cream topping
- 1/4 cup miniature semisweet chocolate chips

• Line a 9-in. x 5-in. loaf pan with heavy-duty foil. Coat foil with cooking spray and set aside.

• In a small bowl, cream butter and brown sugar. Add the oats, flour and cereal; mix well. Pat into prepared pan. Drizzle caramel topping to within 1/2 in. of edges. Bake at 400° for 10-12 minutes or until golden brown.

• Immediately sprinkle with chocolate chips. Bake 1 minute longer. Cool on a wire rack. Cut into bars.

YIELD: 8 servings.

NUTRITION FACTS: 1 bar equals 177 calories, 6 g fat (4 g saturated fat), 11 mg cholesterol, 100 mg sodium, 30 g carbohydrate, 1 g fiber, 2 g protein. **DIABETIC EXCHANGES:** 2 starch, 1 fat.

mocha pudding cakes

Debora Simmons | EGLON, WEST VIRGINIA

These mouth-watering mini cakes make the perfect treat for a twosome. My mom used to make these when I was a little girl. Now I whip them up for a speedy dessert without a lot of leftovers.

- 1/4 cup all-purpose flour
- 3 tablespoons sugar
- 1-1/2 teaspoons baking cocoa
- 1/2 teaspoon baking powder
- 1/8 teaspoon salt
- 3 tablespoons 2% milk
- 1-1/2 teaspoons butter, melted
- 1/4 teaspoon vanilla extract

TOPPING:

- 2 tablespoons brown sugar
- 1-1/2 teaspoons baking cocoa
- 3 tablespoons hot brewed coffee
- 1 tablespoon hot water

Whipped topping, optional

• In a small bowl, combine the flour, sugar, cocoa, baking powder and salt. Stir in the milk, butter and vanilla until smooth. Spoon into two 4-oz. ramekins or custard cups coated with cooking spray.

• Combine brown sugar and cocoa; sprinkle over batter. Combine coffee and water; pour over topping. Bake at 350° for 15-20 minutes or until a knife inserted near the center comes out clean. Serve warm or at room temperature with whipped topping if desired.

YIELD: 2 servings.

NUTRITION FACTS: 1 serving (calculated without whipped topping) equals 227 calories, 4 g fat (2 g saturated fat), 9 mg cholesterol, 294 mg sodium, 47 g carbohydrate, 1 g fiber, 3 g protein.

MOCHA PUDDING CAKES

227 CALORIES

244 CALORIES

CARAMEL TOFFEE ICE CREAM PIE

caramel toffee ice cream pie

Diane Lombardo | NEW CASTLE, PENNSYLVANIA

This delicious pie is easy to make and so lovely. It comes together in under 30 minutes, and since you can make it in advance, it's ideal for entertaining.

1-1/2 cups chocolate graham cracker crumbs (about 8 whole crackers)
  2 tablespoons sugar
  1 egg white, beaten
  2 tablespoons butter, melted
  4 cups fat-free vanilla frozen yogurt, softened
  2 English toffee candy bars (1.4 ounces *each*), coarsely chopped
1/2 cup caramel ice cream topping

• In a small bowl, combine cracker crumbs and sugar; stir in egg white and butter. Press onto the bottom and up the sides of a 9-in. pie plate coated with cooking spray. Bake at 375° for 6-8 minutes or until set. Cool completely on a wire rack.

• Spread 2-2/3 cups of frozen yogurt into the crust. Sprinkle with half of the toffee bits; drizzle with half of caramel. Repeat with remaining yogurt, toffee and caramel. Cover and freeze for 8 hours or overnight. Remove from the freezer 15 minutes before serving.

YIELD: 10 servings.

NUTRITION FACTS: 1 piece equals 244 calories, 6 g fat (3 g saturated fat), 12 mg cholesterol, 232 mg sodium, 43 g carbohydrate, 1 g fiber, 6 g protein.

strawberry ice cream

153 CALORIES

Leone Mayne | FROSTPROOF, FLORIDA

I've made this ice cream often, and it comes out smooth and creamy every time. I adore strawberries, and this treat showcases their flavor.

      2 eggs
      2 cups milk
1-1/4 cups sugar
      1 cup miniature marshmallows
      2 cups pureed unsweetened strawberries
      1 cup half-and-half cream
  1/2 cup heavy whipping cream
      1 teaspoon vanilla extract

• In a large heavy saucepan, combine eggs and milk; stir in sugar. Cook and stir over medium-low heat until mixture is thick enough to coat a metal spoon and a thermometer reads at least 160°, about 14 minutes. Remove from the heat; stir in the marshmallows until melted.

• Set saucepan in ice and stir the mixture for 5-10 minutes or until cool. Stir in the remaining ingredients. Cover and refrigerate overnight.

• When ready to freeze, pour into the cylinder of an ice cream freezer and freeze according to manufacturer's directions.

YIELD: about 2 quarts.

NUTRITION FACTS: 1/2 cup equals 153 calories, 6 g fat (4 g saturated fat), 48 mg cholesterol, 35 mg sodium, 22 g carbohydrate, 1 g fiber, 3 g protein.

yummy chocolate cake

LaDonna Reed | PONCA CITY, OKLAHOMA

My husband and I are trying to eat lighter, but we still crave sweets. This moist chocolate cake really helps with that. With the rich frosting, it makes a decadent treat!

      1 package (18-1/4 ounces) chocolate cake mix
      1 package (2.1 ounces) sugar-free instant chocolate pudding mix
1-3/4 cups water
      3 egg whites
FROSTING:
1-1/4 cups cold fat-free milk

197 CALORIES

YUMMY CHOCOLATE CAKE

1/4 teaspoon almond extract
1 package (1.4 ounces) sugar-free instant chocolate pudding mix
1 carton (8 ounces) frozen reduced-fat whipped topping, thawed
Chocolate curls, optional

- In a large mixing bowl, combine the cake mix, pudding mix, water and egg whites. Beat on low speed for 1 minute; beat on medium for 2 minutes.

- Pour into a 15-in. x 10-in. x 1-in. baking pan coated with cooking spray. Bake at 350° for 12-18 minutes or until a toothpick inserted near the center comes out clean. Cool on a wire rack.

- For frosting, place milk and extract in a large bowl. Sprinkle with a third of the pudding mix; let stand for 1 minute. Whisk pudding into milk. Repeat twice with remaining pudding mix. Whisk pudding 2 minutes longer. Let stand for 15 minutes. Fold in whipped topping. Frost cake. Garnish with chocolate curls if desired.

YIELD: 16 servings.

NUTRITION FACTS: 1 piece (calculated without chocolate curls) equals 197 calories, 5 g fat (3 g saturated fat), trace cholesterol, 409 mg sodium, 35 g carbohydrate, 1 g fiber, 3 g protein. **DIABETIC EXCHANGES:** 2 starch, 1/2 fat.

tiramisu parfaits

Nancy Granaman | BURLINGTON, IOWA
I whip up this tasty tiramisu and serve it in pretty parfait glasses. These are a long-time favorite dessert. I think they look so pretty with a sprinkle of cocoa on top.

4-1/2 teaspoons instant coffee granules
1/3 cup boiling water

2 cups cold fat-free milk
2 packages (1 ounce *each*) sugar-free instant vanilla pudding mix
4 ounces fat-free cream cheese
1 package (3 ounces) ladyfingers, split and cubed
2 cups fat-free whipped topping
2 tablespoons miniature chocolate chips
1 teaspoon baking cocoa

- Dissolve coffee in boiling water; cool to room temperature. In a large bowl, whisk milk and pudding mixes for 2 minutes. In a large mixing bowl, beat cream cheese until smooth. Gradually fold in pudding.

- Place ladyfinger cubes in a bowl; add coffee and toss to coat evenly. Let stand for 5 minutes. Divide half of the ladyfinger cubes among six parfait glasses or serving dishes. Top with half of the pudding mixture, 1 cup whipped topping and 1 tablespoon chocolate chips. Repeat layers.

- Cover and refrigerate for 8 hours or overnight. Just before serving, dust with cocoa.

YIELD: 6 servings.

NUTRITION FACTS: 1 parfait equals 189 calories, 3 g fat (1 g saturated fat), 55 mg cholesterol, 573 mg sodium, 32 g carbohydrate, 1 g fiber, 7 g protein. **DIABETIC EXCHANGE:** 2 starch.

TIRAMISU PARFAITS

189 CALORIES

raspberry custard tart

This dessert is sure to impress guests at your next gathering. With a yummy raspberry layer and nutty homemade crust, it's hard to believe that a slice isn't an invitation to stray from healthy-eating goals. It's a winner with our home economists.

        3 tablespoons reduced-fat butter
      1/3 cup sugar
      3/4 cup all-purpose flour
      1/4 cup finely chopped pecans, toasted
FILLING:
      1/3 cup sugar
      1/4 cup all-purpose flour
    2-1/4 cups fat-free milk
        1 egg yolk, beaten
      1/4 teaspoon almond extract
        1 jar (12 ounces) seedless raspberry spreadable fruit
    1-1/2 cups fresh raspberries

• In a small mixing bowl, beat butter and sugar for 2 minutes or until crumbly. Beat in flour and nuts. Coat a 9-in. fluted tart pan with removable bottom with cooking spray. Press crumb mixture onto the bottom and up the sides of pan. Bake at 425° for 8-10 minutes or until lightly browned. Cool on a wire rack.

RASPBERRY CUSTARD TART

198 CALORIES

• In a small saucepan, combine sugar and flour. Stir in milk until smooth. Cook and stir over medium-high heat until thickened and bubbly. Reduce heat; cook and stir 2 minutes longer. Remove from the heat. Stir a small amount of hot filling into egg yolk; return all to the pan, stirring constantly. Bring to a gentle boil; cook and stir 2 minutes longer. Remove from the heat; gently stir in extract. Pour over crust. Refrigerate until set.

• In a small bowl, whisk fruit spread until smooth; spread over filling. Garnish with raspberries.

YIELD: 12 servings.

EDITOR'S NOTE: This recipe was tested with Land O'Lakes light stick butter.

NUTRITION FACTS: 1 piece equals 198 calories, 4 g fat (1 g saturated fat), 22 mg cholesterol, 44 mg sodium, 39 g carbohydrate, 2 g fiber, 3 g protein. **DIABETIC EXCHANGES:** 1-1/2 starch, 1 fruit, 1/2 fat.

berry nectarine buckle

Lisa Sjursen-Darling | SCOTTSVILLE, NEW YORK

I found this recipe in a magazine a long time ago and modified it over the years. We enjoy its combination of blueberries, raspberries, blackberries and nectarines, particularly when the cake is served warm with low-fat frozen yogurt.

      1/3 cup all-purpose flour
      1/3 cup packed brown sugar
        1 teaspoon ground cinnamon
        3 tablespoons cold butter
BATTER:
        6 tablespoons butter, softened
      3/4 cup plus 1 tablespoon sugar, *divided*
        2 eggs
    1-1/2 teaspoons vanilla extract
    2-1/4 cups all-purpose flour
    2-1/2 teaspoons baking powder
      1/2 teaspoon salt
      1/2 cup fat-free milk
        1 cup fresh blueberries
        1 pound medium nectarines, peeled, sliced and patted dry *or* 1 package (16 ounces) frozen unsweetened sliced peaches, thawed and patted dry
      1/2 cup fresh raspberries
      1/2 cup fresh blackberries

177 CALORIES

BERRY NECTARINE BUCKLE

1/4 teaspoon ground allspice

5 cups fresh *or* frozen blackberries, thawed

2 tablespoons orange juice

DOUGH:

1 cup all-purpose flour

1/3 cup plus 1 tablespoon sugar, *divided*

1/4 teaspoon baking soda

1/4 teaspoon salt

1/3 cup reduced-fat vanilla yogurt

1/3 cup fat-free milk

3 tablespoons butter, melted

- For topping, in a small bowl, combine flour, brown sugar and cinnamon; cut in butter until crumbly. Set aside.

- In a large mixing bowl, cream the butter and 3/4 cup sugar. Add eggs, one at a time, beating well after each addition. Beat in vanilla. Combine the flour, baking powder and salt; add to creamed mixture alternately with milk. Set aside 3/4 cup batter. Fold blueberries into remaining batter.

- Spoon into a 13-in. x 9-in. baking dish coated with cooking spray. Arrange nectarines on top; sprinkle with remaining sugar. Drop remaining batter by teaspoonfuls over nectarines. Sprinkle with raspberries, blackberries and reserved topping.

- Bake at 350° for 35-40 minutes or until a toothpick inserted near the center comes out clean. Serve warm.

YIELD: 20 servings.

NUTRITION FACTS: 1 piece equals 177 calories, 6 g fat (3 g saturated fat), 35 mg cholesterol, 172 mg sodium, 28 g carbohydrate, 1 g fiber, 3 g protein. **DIABETIC EXCHANGES:** 2 starch, 1 fat.

- In a large bowl, combine sugar, tapioca and allspice. Add blackberries and orange juice; toss to coat. Let stand for 15 minutes. Spoon into a 2-qt. baking dish coated with cooking spray. In a large mixing bowl, combine the flour, 1/3 cup sugar, baking soda and salt. Combine the yogurt, milk and butter; stir into dry ingredients until smooth. Spread over the berry mixture.

- Bake at 350° for 20 minutes. Sprinkle with remaining sugar. Bake 25-30 minutes longer or until golden brown. Serve warm.

YIELD: 10 servings.

NUTRITION FACTS: 1 serving equals 199 calories, 4 g fat (2 g saturated fat), 10 mg cholesterol, 135 mg sodium, 40 g carbohydrate, 4 g fiber, 3 g protein. **DIABETIC EXCHANGES:** 1-1/2 starch, 1 fruit, 1/2 fat.

BLACKBERRY COBBLER

199 CALORIES

blackberry cobbler

Leslie Browning | LEBANON, KENTUCKY

This tasty treat has helped my family stay healthy, lose weight and still be able to enjoy dessert! Other kinds of berries or even fresh peaches are just as delicious in this cobbler.

1/2 cup sugar

4-1/2 teaspoons quick-cooking tapioca

171 CALORIES

LEMON BLUEBERRY CHEESECAKE

lemon blueberry cheesecake

Julia Klee | BONAIRE, GEORGIA

For a light, refreshing alternative to traditional cheesecake, try this no-bake treat. It tastes as luscious as it looks.

  1 package (3 ounces) lemon gelatin
  1 cup boiling water
  1 cup graham cracker crumbs
  2 tablespoons butter, melted
  1 tablespoon canola oil
  3 cups (24 ounces) fat-free cottage cheese
1/4 cup sugar
TOPPING:
  2 tablespoons sugar
1-1/2 teaspoons cornstarch
1/4 cup water
1-1/3 cups fresh *or* frozen blueberries, *divided*
  1 teaspoon lemon juice

• In a large bowl, dissolve gelatin in boiling water. Cool. In a small bowl, combine the crumbs, butter and oil. Press onto the bottom of a 9-in. springform pan. Chill.

• In a blender, cover and process the cottage cheese and sugar until smooth. While processing, slowly add cooled gelatin. Pour into crust; cover and refrigerate overnight.

• For topping, in a small saucepan, combine the sugar and cornstarch; gradually stir in water until smooth. Add 1 cup blueberries. Bring to a boil; cook and stir for 2 minutes or until thickened. Stir in lemon juice; cool slightly. Transfer to a blender; cover and process until smooth. Refrigerate until chilled.

• Carefully run a knife around edge of pan to loosen cheesecake; remove sides of pan. Spread the blueberry mixture over the top. Top with remaining blueberries. Refrigerate leftovers.

YIELD: 12 servings.

NUTRITION FACTS: 1 slice equals 171 calories, 4 g fat (1 g saturated fat), 8 mg cholesterol, 352 mg sodium, 27 g carbohydrate, 1 g fiber, 8 g protein. **DIABETIC EXCHANGES:** 1-1/2 starch, 1/2 fruit, 1/2 fat.

fudgy chocolate dessert

Bonnie Bowen | ADRIAN, MICHIGAN

With a cake-like brownie bottom and layers of chocolate and hot fudge, this scrumptious treat is a chocolate-lover's dream. It's my most-requested recipe.

  1 package (18-1/4 ounces) chocolate cake mix
  1 can (15 ounces) solid-pack pumpkin
  3 cups cold fat-free milk

FUDGY CHOCOLATE DESSERT

200 CALORIES

- 2 packages (1.4 ounces *each*) sugar-free instant chocolate pudding mix
- 1 package (8 ounces) fat-free cream cheese
- 1 carton (8 ounces) frozen reduced-fat whipped topping, thawed
- 1/4 cup fat-free hot fudge ice cream topping
- 1/4 cup fat-free caramel ice cream topping
- 1/4 cup sliced almonds, toasted

• In a large bowl, combine cake mix and pumpkin (mixture will be thick). Spread evenly into a 13-in. x 9-in. baking dish coated with cooking spray.

• Bake at 375° for 20-25 minutes or until a toothpick inserted near the center comes out clean. Cool completely on a wire rack.

• In a large bowl, whisk the milk and pudding mixes for 2 minutes. Let stand for 5 minutes or until soft-set.

• In a small mixing bowl, beat cream cheese until smooth. Add pudding; beat until well blended. Spread over cake. Cover and refrigerate for at least 2 hours.

• Just before serving, spread whipped topping over dessert. Drizzle with fudge and caramel toppings; sprinkle with almonds. Refrigerate leftovers.

YIELD: 20 servings.

NUTRITION FACTS: 1 piece equals 200 calories, 5 g fat (2 g saturated fat), 2 mg cholesterol, 376 mg sodium, 35 g carbohydrate, 2 g fiber, 5 g protein. DIABETIC EXCHANGES: 2 starch, 1/2 fat.

cranberry pecan bars

Sandra Bunte | COVINA, CALIFORNIA

I have been making these bars for over 40 years. I got the recipe from my mother. They are great with vanilla ice cream—low-calorie, of course.

- 3/4 cup all-purpose flour
- 3/4 cup quick-cooking oats
- 1/3 cup packed brown sugar
- 1/3 cup butter, melted

FILLING:
- 1 package (12 ounces) fresh *or* frozen cranberries
- 1/2 cup cranberry juice, *divided*
- 1/2 cup golden raisins
- 1/3 cup honey
- Sugar substitute equivalent to 3 tablespoons sugar
- 1/2 teaspoon ground cinnamon

199 CALORIES

CRANBERRY PECAN BARS

- 1/4 teaspoon ground cloves
- 1/2 teaspoon cornstarch
- 1/4 cup chopped pecans

• In a small bowl, combine the flour, oats and brown sugar. Stir in butter until blended. Set aside 2/3 cup. Pat the remaining mixture onto the bottom of a 9-in. square baking pan coated with cooking spray; set aside.

• In a small saucepan, combine cranberries, 7 tablespoons cranberry juice, raisins, honey, sugar substitute, cinnamon and cloves. Cook and stir over medium heat for 10-12 minutes or until berries pop. Combine the cornstarch and remaining cranberry juice until smooth; stir into berry mixture. Bring to a boil; cook and stir for 1-2 minutes or until thickened.

• Pour filling over crust. Sprinkle with pecans and reserved oat mixture. Bake at 350° for 30-35 minutes or until lightly browned. Cool on a wire rack. Cut into squares. Store in the refrigerator.

YIELD: 1 dozen.

EDITOR'S NOTE: This recipe was tested with Splenda No Calorie Sweetener.

NUTRITION FACTS: 1 bar equals 199 calories, 7 g fat (3 g saturated fat), 14 mg cholesterol, 56 mg sodium, 33 g carbohydrate, 2 g fiber, 2 g protein. DIABETIC EXCHANGES: 1 starch, 1 fruit, 1 fat.

do-it-yourself
MEAL PLANNING
worksheet

date: _____

FOOD	CALORIES	FOOD	CALORIES
planned breakfast		**actual breakfast**	
_____	_____	_____	_____
_____	_____	_____	_____
_____	_____	_____	_____
_____	_____	_____	_____
PLANNED BREAKFAST TOTAL CALORIES:	_____	**ACTUAL BREAKFAST TOTAL CALORIES:**	_____
planned lunch		**actual lunch**	
_____	_____	_____	_____
_____	_____	_____	_____
_____	_____	_____	_____
_____	_____	_____	_____
PLANNED LUNCH TOTAL CALORIES:	_____	**ACTUAL LUNCH TOTAL CALORIES:**	_____
planned dinner		**actual dinner**	
_____	_____	_____	_____
_____	_____	_____	_____
_____	_____	_____	_____
_____	_____	_____	_____
PLANNED DINNER TOTAL CALORIES:	_____	**ACTUAL DINNER TOTAL CALORIES:**	_____
planned snacks		**actual snacks**	
_____	_____	_____	_____
_____	_____	_____	_____
PLANNED SNACKS TOTAL CALORIES:	_____	**ACTUAL SNACKS TOTAL CALORIES:**	_____
PLANNED TOTAL CALORIES:	_____	**ACTUAL TOTAL CALORIES:**	_____

more on the WEB

Log on to www.ComfortFoodDietCookbook.com for additional meal planning worksheets you can print for yourself. Remember to use the code MyDiet.

do-it-yourself
MEAL PLANNING
worksheet

date: _____

FOOD	CALORIES	FOOD	CALORIES

planned breakfast

_____ _____
_____ _____
_____ _____
_____ _____

PLANNED BREAKFAST TOTAL CALORIES: _____

actual breakfast

_____ _____
_____ _____
_____ _____
_____ _____

ACTUAL BREAKFAST TOTAL CALORIES: _____

planned lunch

_____ _____
_____ _____
_____ _____

PLANNED LUNCH TOTAL CALORIES: _____

actual lunch

_____ _____
_____ _____
_____ _____

ACTUAL LUNCH TOTAL CALORIES: _____

planned dinner

_____ _____
_____ _____
_____ _____
_____ _____

PLANNED DINNER TOTAL CALORIES: _____

actual dinner

_____ _____
_____ _____
_____ _____
_____ _____

ACTUAL DINNER TOTAL CALORIES: _____

planned snacks

_____ _____
_____ _____

PLANNED SNACKS TOTAL CALORIES: _____

actual snacks

_____ _____
_____ _____

ACTUAL SNACKS TOTAL CALORIES: _____

PLANNED TOTAL CALORIES: _____

ACTUAL TOTAL CALORIES: _____

exercise _____
_____

do-it-yourself
MEAL PLANNING
worksheet

date: _____

FOOD	CALORIES	FOOD	CALORIES
planned breakfast		**actual breakfast**	
_____	_____	_____	_____
_____	_____	_____	_____
_____	_____	_____	_____
_____	_____	_____	_____
PLANNED BREAKFAST TOTAL CALORIES:	_____	**ACTUAL BREAKFAST TOTAL CALORIES:**	_____
planned lunch		**actual lunch**	
_____	_____	_____	_____
_____	_____	_____	_____
_____	_____	_____	_____
_____	_____	_____	_____
PLANNED LUNCH TOTAL CALORIES:	_____	**ACTUAL LUNCH TOTAL CALORIES:**	_____
planned dinner		**actual dinner**	
_____	_____	_____	_____
_____	_____	_____	_____
_____	_____	_____	_____
_____	_____	_____	_____
PLANNED DINNER TOTAL CALORIES:	_____	**ACTUAL DINNER TOTAL CALORIES:**	_____
planned snacks		**actual snacks**	
_____	_____	_____	_____
_____	_____	_____	_____
PLANNED SNACKS TOTAL CALORIES:	_____	**ACTUAL SNACKS TOTAL CALORIES:**	_____
PLANNED TOTAL CALORIES:	_____	**ACTUAL TOTAL CALORIES:**	_____

exercise _____

_____

do-it-yourself
MEAL PLANNING
worksheet

date: _____

FOOD	CALORIES	FOOD	CALORIES
planned breakfast		**actual breakfast**	
_____	_____	_____	_____
_____	_____	_____	_____
_____	_____	_____	_____
_____	_____	_____	_____
PLANNED BREAKFAST TOTAL CALORIES:	_____	**ACTUAL BREAKFAST TOTAL CALORIES:**	_____
planned lunch		**actual lunch**	
_____	_____	_____	_____
_____	_____	_____	_____
_____	_____	_____	_____
_____	_____	_____	_____
PLANNED LUNCH TOTAL CALORIES:	_____	**ACTUAL LUNCH TOTAL CALORIES:**	_____
planned dinner		**actual dinner**	
_____	_____	_____	_____
_____	_____	_____	_____
_____	_____	_____	_____
_____	_____	_____	_____
PLANNED DINNER TOTAL CALORIES:	_____	**ACTUAL DINNER TOTAL CALORIES:**	_____
planned snacks		**actual snacks**	
_____	_____	_____	_____
PLANNED SNACKS TOTAL CALORIES:	_____	**ACTUAL SNACKS TOTAL CALORIES:**	_____
PLANNED TOTAL CALORIES:	_____	**ACTUAL TOTAL CALORIES:**	_____

exercise _____

_____

index by food category

To help you find the perfect recipe, we've created three distinctively useful indexes.

The first index is divided into food and meal categories as well as major ingredients. This is perfect when looking to use up a bumper crop of tomatoes or finding a great dessert.

In addition, this index often breaks the recipes into subcategories. When looking for beef dishes, for instance, you'll easily see which recipes are lunch items and which make a better fit for dinner. Best of all, every entry offers the recipe's calories per serving making it a snap to plan meals on the Comfort Food Diet.

alphabetical index

When it comes to finding your family's favorite dishes, turn to this no-fuss index. Just like the Index by Food Category, this version offers the calorie count (per serving) of each dish, so planning a heart-smart menu is always a snap.

Can't seem to remember the exact names of all of those comforting dishes you have enjoyed? You could either highlight them here for easy reference or set a blank sticky note on the inside cover.

Then, when your family gives you a thumb's-up rating on a dish, you can simply jot the name of the recipe on the note paper for future reference.

index by calories

To make it as easy as possible to stick to the plan, we've categorized each recipe in this book by type (breakfast, lunch, side dish, etc.). The dishes were then divided into their applicable calorie range.

When looking for a breakfast that's particularly light, see the recipes under "Breakfast—100 Calories or Less." When you can afford a few more calories in the morning, consider any of the 23 recipes found under "Breakfast—201 to 300 Calories."

Refer to this index often, and you'll be amazed at how easy it is to stay on and succeed with the Comfort Food Diet.

STOCK IMAGE CREDITS

stacked fruit
page 9
Julián Rovagnati/Shutterstock.com

mother & daughter preparing food
page 10
Monkey Business Images/Shutterstock.com

fresh basil & tomato wedges
page 11
Magdalena Zurawska/Shutterstock.com

french fries in a bowl
page 14
Janet Hastings/Shutterstock.com

three brown eggs
page 14
sevenke/Shutterstock.com

frozen dinner
page 14
Big Pants Production/Shutterstock.com

asparagus in a bowl
page 15
William Berry/Shutterstock.com

woman eating in kitchen
page 16
style-photographs/Shutterstock.com

spiral pasta background
page 17
Denis & Yulia Pogostins/Shutterstock.com

oatmeal, coffee & fruit
page 19
Ossile/Shutterstock.com

woman drinking bottled water
page 20
MitarArt/Shutterstock.com

glass of milk
page 21
Studio Foxy/Shutterstock.com

water being poured into a wine glass
page 23
Tischenko Irina/Shutterstock.com

salad fixings
page 27
Dan Kaplan/Shutterstock.com

salad on a fork
page 28
Zaneta Baranowska/Shutterstock.com

bowl of tomato soup
page 29
kubrak78/Shutterstock.com

woman deciding what to eat
page 29
Valua Vitaly/Shutterstock.com

fruit tart
page 31
crolique/Shutterstock.com

fruit smoothies
page 33
Ekaterina Vasileva/Shutterstock.com

woman listening to music
page 34
Yuganov Konstantin/Shutterstock.com

bike in motion
page 35
remik44992/Shutterstock.com

shoes
page 35
Elnur/Shutterstock.com

earbuds
page 37
Titov Andriy/Shutterstock.com

woman jogging
page 38
Phase4Photography/Shutterstock.com

woman in swimming pool
page 39
Yuri Arcurs/Shutterstock.com

my favorite recipes

Use this handy chart to jot down all of your favorite dishes and their calories.
As you fill in the chart, you'll find it a snap to whip up the healthy snacks and
put together the low-calorie menus you and your family enjoy most.

RECIPE TITLE	PAGE NUMBER	CALORIES
snacks		
breakfast		
lunch		
main courses		
sides		
desserts		

more on the WEB

Looking for even more low-calorie, family-friendly dishes? Check out the delicious
assortment of free recipes when you visit www.ComfortFoodDietCookbook.com.
Remember to use MyDiet as the private access code.

my favorite recipes

Use this handy chart to jot down all of your favorite dishes and their calories.
As you fill in the chart, you'll find it a snap to whip up the healthy snacks and
put together the low-calorie menus you and your family enjoy most.

RECIPE TITLE	PAGE NUMBER	CALORIES
snacks		
breakfast		
lunch		
main courses		
sides		
desserts		